THE SOHO BIBLIOGRAPHIES
IX

# VIRGINIA WOOLF

# A BIBLIOGRAPHY OF

# VIRGINIA WOOLF

## THIRD EDITION

BY

B. J. KIRKPATRICK

CLARENDON PRESS · OXFORD
1980

*Oxford University Press, Walton Street, Oxford* OX2 6DP

OXFORD LONDON GLASGOW
NEW YORK TORONTO MELBOURNE WELLINGTON
KUALA LUMPUR SINGAPORE JAKARTA HONG KONG TOKYO
DELHI BOMBAY CALCUTTA MADRAS KARACHI
NAIROBI DAR ES SALAAM CAPE TOWN

*Published in the United States by*
*Oxford University Press, New York*



*First Published 1957*
*Second Edition 1967*
*Third Edition 1980*



**British Library Cataloguing in Publication Data**
Kirkpatrick, Brownlee Jean
A bibliography of Virginia Woolf.
– 3rd ed. – (Soho bibliographies; 9).
1. Woolf, Virginia – Bibliography
I. Title II. Series
016.823'9'12 Z8984.2 79-42786

ISBN 0-19-818185-X

*Set by Hope Services, Abingdon*
*and printed in Great Britain*
*by the Fakenham Press Ltd., Fakenham, Norfolk*

*In memory of*
G. J. K.
*and*
W. B. K.

# CONTENTS

# ILLUSTRATIONS

## PLATES



## IN TEXT

# PREFACE

In the twelve years since the publication of the 1967 revision of this bibliography all Virginia Woolf's papers became available following the death of Leonard Woolf in 1969 except for her contributions to the *Hyde Park Gate News*. The most important of these are the series of diaries now in the Henry W. and Albert A. Berg Collection of English and American Literature in the New York Public Library (Astor, Lenox and Tilden Foundations), and the Monk's House Papers in the University of Sussex Library. This material and other papers such as drafts of reviews in the Berg Collection have enabled me to identify a further fifty-eight reviews most of which are unsigned. Even these hitherto unrecorded items do not exhaust the record of Virginia Woolf's work since no doubt some remain embedded in the *Guardian*, the *Speaker*, the *TLS* and possibly the *Outlook*. Additional aids to the identification of unsigned pieces have been the publication of *The Letters of Virginia Woolf* edited by Nigel Nicolson, assisted by Joanne Trautmann (A44, 47, 51, 53-4), and *The Diary* edited by Anne Olivier Bell (A48, 52) due for completion in six and five volumes respectively.

The publication of Quentin Bell's *Virginia Woolf: A Biography* in 1972 (B14–15) stimulated further the already substantial interest in Virginia Woolf which with the publication of her *Letters* and *The Diary* has resulted in other unpublished material appearing in print such as reminiscences, *Moments of Being* (A45), her only play, *Freshwater* (A46), the novel-essay portion of *The Years, The Pargiters* (A50), the transcription of the manuscript of *The Waves* (A16*g–h*), and another volume of uncollected essays, *Books and Portraits* (A49). Publication of further unpublished manuscripts is also envisaged (see p. 241). A new development has been the study of texts and variant editions to which reference has been made in the entry for the work concerned.

Guides to studies of Virginia Woolf's works may be found in 'Criticism of Virginia Woolf: A Selected Checklist with an Index to Studies of Separate Works' by Maurice Beebe, *Modern Fiction Studies*, February 1956, Vol. 2, No. 1, pp. 36-45, in Barbara Weiser's continuation in the same journal, Autumn 1972, Vol. 18, No. 3, pp. 477-86, in 'Recent Criticism of Virginia Woolf January 1970-June 1972: Abstracts of Published Criticism and Unpublished Dissertations' by Jane Novak, *Virginia Woolf Quarterly*, Fall 1972, Vol. 1, No. 1, pp. 141-55 and in *Virginia Woolf: An Annotated Bibliography of Criticism 1915-1974* by Robin Majumdar, New York, Garland, 1976. Information on Leonard and Virginia Woolf's library and its dispersal is given in 'The Monks House Library' by George A. Spater, *American Book Collector*, January 1971, Vol. 21, No. 4, pp. 18-20 (see also the article with the same title in the *Virginia Woolf Quarterly*, Spring 1973, Vol. 1, No. 3, pp. 60-5) and 'The Leonard and Virginia Woolf Library and the Washington State University Woolf Collection' by Diane Filby Gillespie, *Virginia Woolf Miscellany*, Winter 1977, No. 9, p. 4.

Full bibliographical information has been recorded of all first English and American editions; the details of all other editions are briefer. The transcription of title-pages, bindings, and other similar details have been standardized and do not reproduce variations in size and style of type. Endpapers are white or cream unless stated otherwise. Untraced and doubtful items are noted in an appendix to Section C.

The number of copies printed of new editions of books included in the first edition and the revision of 1967 are recorded in this third edition, but not later reprints of editions also noted in the first two editions.

Books which I have not examined personally are marked with an asterisk except where I have been able to transcribe an entry from information sent in the form of xerox copies and other such details.

It is a pleasure to record my debt to the many people

who have helped me with this bibliography and to no one more than the late Leonard Woolf. I am especially grateful for his permission to undertake it, for his unfailing assistance and the ready access he gave me to his collection of Virginia Woolf's works during the first edition and the 1967 revision. I look back in gratitude not only to the pleasure the bibliography has given me but to the many visits I made to Monk's House and the flowers and fruit with which I returned laden to London. I also owe much to the late John Hayward for his generous and incomparable counsel in all things bibliographical.

I have been very fortunate in the help given to me with this revision by Professor and Mrs Quentin Bell who allowed me to see the Monk's House Papers while they were in their care, and for the 'tit bits' sent by Mrs Bell in the form of clues to anonymous contributions; Mr Nigel Nicolson for his permission to read typescripts of letters prior to publication and for his hospitality; and by Mr P. J. Allen; Mr S. N. Clarke; Miss Doris Dormer; Mr John Emery; Mr David V. Erdman; Professor Suzanne Henig; Ms Barbara Kneubuhl; Dr Mary Lyon; Dr Allen McLaurin; Dr C. M. Mayrhofer; Mr Richard Outram; Mr Gordon Phillips (Archivist, *The Times*); Mr Drew Ponder-Greene; Mme Marianne Rodker; Professor Lucio P. Ruotolo; Mr George Spater; Mr George Stern; and Professor J. J. Wilson. I am also grateful to the British Academy for a Research Award towards expenses while I was in New York, to the Trustees of the Henry W. and Albert A. Berg Collection of English and American Literature in the New York Public Library for permission to consult material in the Collection and to Mrs Lola L. Szladits, its Curator, for her kindness while I was working there. Since leaving England in October 1976 I could not have managed without the assistance of the staff of the University of Sussex Library, particularly Mrs Elizabeth Inglis (Assistant Librarian in the Manuscripts Section) who provided photocopies, transcriptions, and other details of new translations and American editions which appeared after my departure; this assistance included the continuance of Leonard Woolf's policy of sending me duplicate copies of such editions. I am extremely grateful for her cheerful and efficient help. I am also much indebted to Mr A. N. Peasgood, Sub-Librarian, who when I discussed the difficulties I would have while in Australia, readily agreed to these arrangements.

I remain indebted to the following who helped me with the first edition and the 1967 revision: Mr F. B. Adams, Jr; Lord Annan; Mr Roy Atterbury; the late Vanessa Bell; Mr Richard Biddle; Mr Benjamin Bromberg; Mr William R. Cagle; Mr Herbert Cahoon; M. Maxime Chastaing; the late Nancy Cunard; Mr Gilbert H. Fabes; Sir Frank Francis; the late Dr John D. Gordan; Sir Rupert Hart-Davis; Miss M. E. Holloway; Mr Edward G. Howard; the late Mrs Alice L. Jones; the late S. S. Koteliansky; Herr Helmut Kröger; Mr G. L. Lazarus; Mr John Lehmann; Mr David Magee; the late Professor J. N. Mavrogordato; the late J. B. Morrell; the late Dr A. N. L. Munby; Mr Gen'ichi Muraoka; the late S. K. Ratcliffe; the late Bertram Rota; the late V. Sackville-West; Mr Simon Nowell-Smith; Mrs Elizabeth Richardson; Mr Robert H. Taylor; Mr Minoru Wada; Mrs M. Whatley; Mr Cecil Woolf; Mr J. T. Yates; and to my late parents for their encouragement, especially my father who drove me to Rodmell on many occasions and in all weathers, snow and ice not withstanding.

In the early 1950s I was able to obtain production details of Virginia Woolf's early publications from a notebook kept by Leonard Woolf at Monk's House and from stock cards at the Hogarth Press which had been maintained by Leonard and Virginia Woolf. Since then I owe information on these details from publishers and printers, especially Messrs R. & R. Clark Ltd. (with the first edition by supplementing the early Hogarth Press records); Penguin Books Ltd. (Mr D. M. Rust); Triad Paperbacks (Ms Linda M. Stearns); and Miss Anne M. Davidson (Hogarth Press) and Miss Margaret Mary McQuillan (Harcourt Brace Jovanovich, Inc.), who have both for the third time provided me with their firms' production details and to whom I am greatly indebted for their patient toleration of tiresome questions over more than twenty years.

Acknowledgements are also made to the following: The Editor of the *Times Literary Supplement* for granting permission for Virginia Woolf's contributions to be identified; The Managing Director and the Editor of the *New Statesman* for allowing me to go through their marked files of the *Athenaeum*, the *New Statesman*, the *Nation & Athenaeum* and the *New Statesman & Nation*; and for permission to reproduce material: Mr F. B. Adams, Jr; the late Vanessa Bell; the late Professor J. N. Mavrogordato; the late Leonard Woolf and The Hogarth Press.

Of the many libraries and other organizations with which I have corresponded I am particularly grateful to the following for help with specific points: British Council, Athens; Fawcett Library, City of London Polytechnic (Ms Amanda Golby); French Institute, London; Harvard University Library; Indiana University, Lilly Library (Ms Saundra Taylor); The Agent, Knole, Sevenoaks, Kent; Lambeth Palace Library; Library of Congress, Rare Books Division; Morley College, London; National Book League, London (Ms Anne Clarke); Royal Academy of Arts (Miss Constance-Anne Parker); St Pancras Library, London Borough of Camden; San Francisco Public Library, Literature Department; Humanities Research Center, University of Texas at Austin (Ms Ellen S. Dunlap); Yale University, Beinecke Rare Book and Manuscript Library (Professor Donald Gallup).

The libraries upon which I relied most and to whose staff I am grateful are the British Library Reference Division (including the Newspaper Library); the University of London Library; and additionally for this revision the London Library recourse to which saved me much time before my departure to Canberra. Lately I have made use of the Australian National University Library and the National Library of Australia.

*Canberra,*
*December 1979*

B. J. KIRKPATRICK

# A.

# BOOKS AND PAMPHLETS

THE VOYAGE OUT 265

try to find out, but can you imagine anything more ludicrous than one person's opinion of another person? ~~One goes along thinking one knows; but one really doesn't know.~~"

As he said this he was leaning on his elbow arranging and rearranging in the grass the stones which had represented Rachel and her aunts at luncheon. He was speaking as much to himself as to Rachel. He was reasoning against the desire, which had returned with intensity, to take her in his arms; to have done with indirectness; to explain exactly what he felt. What he said was against his belief; all the things that were important ~~about her~~ he knew; ~~he felt them in the air around them; but he said nothing; he went on arranging the stones.~~

~~"I like you; d'you like me?" Rachel suddenly observed.~~

"I like you immensely," Hewet replied, speaking with the relief of a person who is unexpectedly given an opportunity of saying what he wants to say. He stopped moving the pebbles.

"Mightn't we call each other Rachel and Terence?" he asked.

"Terence," Rachel repeated. "Terence—that's like the cry of an owl."

She looked up with a sudden rush of delight, and in looking at Terence with eyes widened by pleasure she was struck by the change that had come over the sky behind them. The substantial blue day had faded to a paler and more ethereal blue; the clouds were pink, far away and closely packed together; and the peace of evening had replaced the heat of the southern afternoon, in which they had started on their walk.

"It must be late!" she exclaimed.

It was nearly eight o'clock.

"But eight o'clock doesn't count here, does it?"

At the same time he was extremely anxious to know what Rachel's opinion of him might be. Did she like him? As if she heard him ask the question she said "I like you—" she hesitated. 'D'you like me?' she asked.

First edition of *The Voyage Out*, p. 265, with revision in manuscript by the author, A1*b*

*a. First edition*

THE . . . | VOYAGE OUT | BY | VIRGINIA WOOLF | [*publisher's floral device with motto*] | LONDON | DUCKWORTH & CO. | 3 HENRIETTA STREET | COVENT GARDEN, W.C. | 1915

Crown 8vo. [viii], 464 pp. $7\frac{1}{4} \times 4\frac{3}{4}$ in.

Pp. [i–ii] blank; p. [iii] half-title; p. [iv] blank; p. [v] title; p. [vi] All rights reserved.; p. [vii] dedication: To | L. W.; p. [viii] blank; pp. 1–458 text; p. 458 at foot: Printed by R. & R. Clark, Limited, Edinburgh.; pp. [459–464] publisher's advertisements, integral. 16 pp. of publisher's advertisements inserted.

Bright moss-green cloth boards; lettered in gold on spine: [*double rule across head*] | The | Voyage | Out | Virginia | Woolf | Duckworth | [*double rule across foot*]; lettered in black on upper cover: [*within a double rule:*] The | Voyage | Out | Virginia | Woolf; double rule in blind at head and foot of upper cover; publisher's floral device with motto in blind on lower cover; edges trimmed; end-papers. Grey-green dust-jacket printed in navy-blue.

Published 26 March 1915; 2000 copies printed. 6s.

The publishing rights were sold to the Hogarth Press in February 1929. The second to fourth printing was issued as the Uniform Edition. See A1*e*.

A copy in red cloth, lettered in gold on the spine and on the upper cover, with the floral device and motto in blind on the lower cover, was advertised in Raphael King Ltd.'s catalogue No. 52 (1951) and is now in the library of Mr Robert H. Taylor. It is probably a trial binding.

*b. First American edition. [1920]**

[*within a rule:*] THE | VOYAGE OUT | BY | VIRGINIA WOOLF | NEW [*publisher's monogram*] YORK | GEORGE H. DORAN COMPANY

Crown 8vo. 376 pp. $7\frac{1}{2} \times 5\frac{1}{8}$ in.

P. [1] half-title; p. [2] blank; p. [3] title; p. [4] Copyright, 1920, | By George H. Doran Company | Printed in the United States of America; p. [5] dedication; p. [6] blank; p. [7] fly-title; p. [8] blank; pp. 9–375 text; p. [376] blank.

Green cloth boards; lettered in black on spine: The | Voyage | Out | Virginia | Woolf | Doran; lettered in blind on upper cover: [*within a rule:*] The | Voyage | Out | Virginia | Woolf; edges trimmed; end-papers. White dust-jacket printed in black.

Published 20 May 1920; no record of the number of copies or impressions printed. $2.25.

The publishing rights and plates were sold by George H. Doran Co. to Harcourt, Brace & Co. 20 April 1925. See A1*d*.

The text was revised by the author for the first American edition. A copy of the first English edition in the library of Mr F. B. Adams Jr of New York is clearly the printer's copy for the revised edition. Mr Adams writes that his copy 'has extensive typescript and MS corrections by the author, *and* (in blue pencil) lay-out man's instructions to compositor, altered pagination, etc.' Mr Adams also writes 'On the title-page of my copy only the *date* is circled for alteration. No *new* date is inserted.' As only the date is circled for alteration it is possible that this copy was also used by the printers when providing a cancel-title to be bound up with the sheets supplied by Doran to Duckworth in 1920.

Apart from the American sheets issued by Duckworth in 1920 and in 1927 and by the Hogarth Press in 1929 the revised version has not been published in the United Kingdom. See A1*c*.

See Louise A. DeSalvo's dissertation 'From *Melymbrosia* to *The Voyage Out*: A Description and Interpretation of Virginia Woolf's Revisions', New York University, 1977 for a list of variants between the first English and American editions. See also her 'A Textual Variant in *The Voyage Out*', *Virginia Woolf Miscellany*, Spring 1975, No. 3, pp. 9–10; 'Another Note on Rachel and Beethoven in *The Voyage Out*' by James Hafley, ibid., Fall 1975, No. 4, p. 4; '*The Voyage Out*: Two More Notes on a Textual Variant' by Louise A. DeSalvo, ibid., Spring/Summer 1976, No. 5, p. 3; '*Voyage Out* Variant No. 2' by S. P. Rosenbaum, ibid., ibid., pp. 3–4; and the forthcoming issue of the *Bulletin of Research in the Humanities*, Autumn 1979, Vol. 82, No. 3 for articles on the early and other texts of *The Voyage Out*.

## *c. First American edition – English issue.* [*1920*]

[*within a rule:*] THE | VOYAGE OUT | BY | VIRGINIA WOOLF | LONDON : DUCKWORTH AND COMPANY | 3 HENRIETTA STREET, : : COVENT GARDEN

Crown 8vo. [iv], 380 pp. $7\frac{1}{2} \times 5\frac{1}{8}$ in.

Pp. [i–ii] form paste down end-paper; pp. [iii–iv] blank; p. [1] half-title; p. [2] blank; p. [3] title; p. [4] at centre: Copyright, 1920, | by George H. Doran Company, at foot: Printed in the United States of America; p. [5] dedication; p. [6] blank; p. [7] fly-title; p. [8]

blank; pp. 9–375 text; pp. [376–378] blank; pp. [379–380] form paste down end-paper.

Sage-green cloth boards; lettered in black on spine, double rule across head of spine and across foot; lettered in black on upper cover within a double rule, double rule at head and foot of upper cover; publisher's floral device with motto in blind on lower cover; edges trimmed; no end-papers. No specimen of dust-jacket available.

Issued September 1920; no record of the number of copies bound. 9s. The sheets were supplied by George H. Doran Co.

Harcourt, Brace & Co. supplied a further 1000 sheets to Duckworth on 10 March 1927. They were issued in June 1927 at 5s. in navy-blue cloth boards; lettered in gold on spine; blind rule round upper cover; publisher's device of a swan with monogram in blind on lower cover; edges trimmed; front end-papers.

Five hundred copies were taken over by the Hogarth Press from Duckworth when the publishing rights were purchased by the former in February 1929. The Hogarth Press issued American sheets with a cancel-title as the 'Third Impression' in jade-green cloth boards probably in March or April 1929 at 7s. 6d. It is likely that 100 copies were issued as 400 were pulped on 26 September 1932.

### *d. First American edition – first Harcourt, Brace impression. [1926]*

THE | VOYAGE OUT | BY | VIRGINIA WOOLF | [*publisher's monogram within a rule*] | NEW YORK | HARCOURT, BRACE AND COMPANY

Crown 8vo. [ii], 382 pp. $7\frac{1}{2} \times 5\frac{1}{8}$ in.

P. [i] blank; p. [ii] list of works by the author; p. [1] half-title; p. [2] blank; p. [3] title; p. [4] Copyright, 1920, | by George H. Doran Company, printer's note; p. [5] dedication; p. [6] blank; p. [7] fly-title; p. [8] blank; pp. 9–375 text; pp. [376–382] blank.

Sky-blue cloth boards; mauve paper label printed in black on spine $1\frac{7}{8} \times 1\frac{3}{8}$ in.: [*double rule*] | The | Voyage Out | By | Virginia Woolf | [*rule*] | Harcourt, Brace & Co. | [*double rule*]; top edges trimmed, others partially trimmed; end-papers. Deep cream dust-jacket printed and illustrated in dark blue.

Issued 14 January 1926; 1000 copies printed. $2.50.

There was a re-impression of 2100 copies issued on 29 January 1931 as the Uniform Edition at $1.35. It was bound in pale green cloth boards, lettered in gold on spine; edges trimmed; end-papers; cream dust-jacket printed in blue.

Blue Ribbon Books Inc., New York, distributed a reprint of 5000 copies in June 1937 at 98 cents. It was bound in pale green cloth boards, lettered in gold on spine; top edges green, fore edges untrimmed, bottom trimmed; end-papers; dust-jacket.

*e. First edition – photo-offset reprint* (UNIFORM EDITION). *1929*

THE VOYAGE OUT | VIRGINIA WOOLF | PUBLISHED BY LEONARD & VIRGINIA | WOOLF AT THE HOGARTH PRESS, | TAVISTOCK SQUARE, LONDON, 1929.

Small crown 8vo. [iv], 460 pp. 7 × $4\frac{1}{2}$ in.

P. [i] half-title; p. [ii] list of works in the Uniform Edition; p. [iii] title; p. [iv] publication note; pp. [1]–458 text; p. 458 at foot: printer's imprint; pp. [459–460] blank.

Jade-green cloth boards; lettered in gold on spine; edges trimmed; end-papers. Pale peacock-blue dust-jacket printed in navy-blue.

Issued 26 September 1929; 3200 copies printed. 5s.

A further 3200 copies were printed in February 1933 and a further 5000 in July 1949.

This, the first volume in the Uniform Edition of Virginia Woolf's works, was printed by photo-litho offset by Lowe & Brydone from the text of the first edition, the prelims being re-set. Although the volumes in this Uniform Edition are described in the publication note on the verso of the title as a 'New Edition' they are in fact reprints of the first edition.

The jade-green cloth of the Uniform Edition varies from a dull to a bright jade-green.

*f. First American edition – photo-offset reprint* (HARVEST BOOKS). [*1968*]

VIRGINIA WOOLF | THE VOYAGE OUT | [*double wavy line*] | A HARVEST BOOK | HARCOURT, BRACE & WORLD, INC. | NEW YORK.

Large crown 8vo. 376 pp. 8 × $5\frac{1}{4}$ in.

P. [1] half-title; p. [2] list of works by the author; p. [3] title; p. [4] publication note, printer's note; p. [5] dedication; p. [6] blank; p. [7] fly-title; p. [8] blank; pp. 9–375 text; p. [376] publisher's advertisement.

Stiff white paper wrappers printed in navy-blue, yellow and green; edges trimmed.

Issued 23 October 1968 in *Harvest Books* as Vol. HB151; 6000 copies printed. $2.45.

There were further printings of 2050 copies in March 1973, 5400 in July 1973, 5000 in April 1974, and 5000 in October 1975.

### *g. Second English edition* (PENGUIN BOOKS). [*1970*]

VIRGINIA WOOLF | THE VOYAGE OUT | PENGUIN BOOKS | IN ASSOCIATION WITH THE HOGARTH PRESS

Foolscap 8vo. 384 pp. $7\frac{1}{8} \times 4\frac{3}{8}$ in.

P. [1] half-title; p. [2] blank; p. [3] title; p. [4] publication note, printer's note; pp. 5–[380] text; p. [381] publisher's advertisement; p. [382] blank; pp. [383–384] publisher's advertisements.

Stiff white pictorial paper wrappers printed in blue, brown, black, and grey; edges trimmed.

Published July 1970 in *Penguin Modern Classics*; 20,000 copies printed. 8s.

There were further printings of 10,000 copies in October 1972, 13,000 in April 1974, and 12,000 in May 1975.

### *h. Third English edition* (PANTHER BOOKS). [*1978*]

VIRGINIA WOOLF | THE VOYAGE OUT | A TRIAD PANTHER BOOK | GRANADA PUBLISHING | LONDON TORONTO SYDNEY NEW YORK

Foolscap 8vo. 384 pp. $7\frac{1}{8} \times 4\frac{1}{4}$ in.

P. [1] Biographical note on the author; p. [2] list of works by the author; p. [3] title; p. [4] publication note, copyright note, printer's imprint etc.; pp. 5–382 text; p. [383] blank; p. [384] publisher's advertisement.

Stiff white pictorial paper wrappers printed in black, yellow and sepia; edges trimmed.

Published 23 February 1978; 20,000 copies printed. £1.50.

## A2 THE MARK ON THE WALL 1917

### *a. First edition*

PUBLICATION NO. 1. | [*rule*] | TWO STORIES | WRITTEN AND PRINTED | BY | VIRGINIA WOOLF | AND

| L. S. WOOLF | HOGARTH PRESS | RICHMOND | 1917

Medium 8vo. [ii], 34 pp. 4 woodcuts on pp. [4], 18, [19], 31. $8\frac{7}{8} \times 5\frac{5}{8}$ in.

Pp. [i–ii] blank; p. [1] title; p. [2] blank; p. [3] Contents; p. [4] woodcut; pp. [5]-18 Three Jews by Leonard Woolf; pp. [19]-31 The Mark on the Wall by Virginia Woolf; pp. [32–34] blank.

Japanese paper wrappers; lettered in black on upper cover: Two Stories | [*floral ornament* $\frac{3}{8} \times \frac{1}{2}$ in.] | Hogarth Press | Richmond; edges trimmed; sewn.

Wrappers vary: (1)–(2) Japanese paper, red and white conventional all-over design or dull blue; (3) thin yellow paper wrappers. Some copies lack pp. [i–ii] and [33–34]. Leonard Woolf stated that paper for the wrappers was purchased as wanted from a local stationer. It is therefore possible that the work was issued in other coloured wrappers.

Published July 1971; 150 copies printed. 1s. 6d.

This, the first publication of the Hogarth Press, was printed by the authors on a hand-press. The woodcuts are by Dora Carrington. The short story was not published separately in the United States. It was reprinted (revised) in *Monday or Tuesday* and in *A Haunted House and Other Short Stories*. See A5, A28.

A number of the early publications of the Hogarth Press at Richmond were printed on a hand-press. Of Virginia Woolf's works, these include, in addition to the above, the first edition of *Kew Gardens.* See A3*a*. The Hogarth Press was started in 1917 by Leonard and Virginia Woolf as 'a hobby of printing rather than publishing'.

### *b. First separate edition. 1919*

[*title on upper cover:*] THE MARK ON THE | WALL | BY | VIRGINIA WOOLF | SECOND EDITION | HOGARTH PRESS, RICHMOND | 1919

Small demy 8vo. 12 pp. $8\frac{3}{8} \times 5\frac{1}{2}$ in.

Pp. [1]-10 text; p. 10 at centre: ornament, at foot: Printed at the Pelican Press, 2 Carmelite Street, E.C.; pp. [11–12] blank.

Thin off-white paper wrappers; verso of upper cover: First Published –July 1917 | Second Edition–June 1919; edges trimmed; stapled.

Published June 1919; *c.* 1000 copies printed. 1s. 6d.

### *c. Second (partial) separate edition. [1921]*

[*at head of leaf:*] [*woodcut*] | WOOD IS A PLEASANT THING TO THINK ABOUT. IT COMES FROM A | [*24*

*a*. Woodcut on p. [16]

*Printed by L. and V. Woolf at The Hogarth Press, Richmond*

*b*. Imprint on p. [16] showing cancel-slip

First edition of *Kew Gardens*, A3*a*

*lines*] | SMOKING THEIR CIGARETTES. | [*woodcut*] | FROM THE MARK ON THE WALL BY VIRGINIA WOOLF | BLOCKS BY VANESSA BELL | THE CHELSEA BOOK CLUB BROADSIDE NO. I PTD. AT 43 BELSIZE PARK GARDENS

[1] leaf. 2 illus. 13 × $7\frac{1}{4}$ in.

No wrappers.

Published probably 1921; number of copies printed not ascertained.

Extract from the last paragraph of *The Mark on the Wall* (revised) which was published in *Monday or Tuesday*. The woodcuts by Vanessa Bell did not appear in the latter. See A5*a*. John Rodker, founder of the Ovid Press and the Imago Press, was living at 43 Belsize Park Gardens, Hampstead, from 1920 to 1923 and may have printed the *Broadside*. Mme Marianne Rodker has, however, no recollection of either John Rodker or her mother, Ludmila Savitzky, translator of *The Voyage Out* (D32*a*), mentioning the *Broadside* and there appears to be no reference among the former's files.

## A3 KEW GARDENS 1919

*a. First edition*

KEW GARDENS | BY | VIRGINIA WOOLF | HOGARTH PRESS | RICHMOND | 1919

Demy 8vo. [16] pp. 2 woodcuts on pp. [5], [16]. Size varies from $8\frac{3}{4}$ × $5\frac{5}{8}$ in. to $8\frac{7}{8}$ × $5\frac{3}{4}$ in.

Pp. [1–2] blank; p. [3] title; p. [4] blank; p. [5] woodcut; p. [6] blank; pp. [7–16] text; p. [16] at centre: woodcut, below: Printed by Leonard & Virginia at The Hogarth Press, Richmond, with a cancel-slip 'L. and V. Woolf' pasted over 'Leonard & Virginia' in all copies.

Off-white wall-paper wrappers, hand colour-washed on the outside in royal-blue, chocolate-brown and orange on a black ground; white printed paper label $1\frac{5}{8}$ × $2\frac{7}{8}$ in. on upper cover: Kew Gardens | Virginia Woolf | With woodcuts by Vanessa Bell; edges trimmed; partially uncut; sewn and gummed. Size of wrappers varies from 9 × $5\frac{7}{8}$ in. to $9\frac{3}{8}$ × $5\frac{7}{8}$ in.

Published 12 May 1919; 150 copies printed. 2s.

Leonard Woolf wrote 'we printed about 170 copies' (*Beginning Again*, p. 241; see B12).

The woodcut on p. [16] appears in three states: (1) printed on the page; (2) printed on a separate piece of paper and pasted on to the page; (3) printed on a separate piece of paper and pasted over (1). Leonard Woolf thought that this arose as he and Mrs Woolf probably considered the original woodcut was not clear enough; he could not say which state was the earliest. The wrapper of a copy, at one time in the stock of Bertram Rota Ltd., was backed with plain paper to form paste down end-papers.

It seems certain that the wrappers came from Roger Fry's Omega Workshops. Reference is made to them in a letter from the author to Vanessa Bell dated 4 May 1919 'As the notices are sent out, I want to get the books ready as soon as possible; so that if its likely to take more than 10 days, I think I'd better get ordinary coloured paper, dull though it is. I could send you down white paper from London. But perhaps Roger has done his black & blue; in which case I could cover 80 copies in that, and you might finish off the edition, which is only 150, with yours.' (*The Question of Things Happening*, p. 352, see also pp. 349–350; see A47*a*.) Leonard Woolf thought that wrappers from the Omega Workshops were supplied for the whole edition; no other type of wrapper has been traced.

The short story was reprinted in *Monday or Tuesday* and in *A Haunted House and Other Short Stories*. See A5, A28.

## *b. Second English edition. 1919*

KEW GARDENS | BY VIRGINIA WOOLF | SECOND EDITION | HOGARTH PRESS | RICHMOND 1919

Demy 8vo. 16 pp. 2 woodcuts on pp. [4], [14]. $8\frac{5}{8} \times 5\frac{1}{2}$ in.

P. [1] title; p. [2] First Published, May, 1919. | Second Edition, June, 1919.; p. [3] blank; p. [4] woodcut; pp. [5]-[14] text; p. [14] at centre: woodcut, below: Printed for The Hogarth Press by Richard Madley, Whitfield Street W.1.; pp. [15–16] blank.

Off-white wall-paper wrappers, with floral pattern in pink, green, pale brown and black, painted on the outside in royal-blue, chocolate-brown and orange on a black ground; white printed paper label $1\frac{7}{8} \times 3\frac{1}{8}$ in. on upper cover: Kew Gardens | Virginia Woolf | With Woodcuts by Vanessa Bell; top edges uncut, some fore edges uncut, bottom trimmed; sewn and gummed. Size of wrappers $9\frac{1}{4} \times 6\frac{1}{8}$ in. There is a variation of $\frac{1}{8}$ in. in the size of both the pages and the wrappers.

Published June 1919; 500 copies printed. 2s.

Leonard Woolf thought that these wrappers were not from Roger Fry's Omega Workshops but were copied from the first edition by someone else. He had no recollection of who supplied them and there is no one who handled them now (1957) with the firm of Richard Madley, the printers.

*c. Third English (limited) edition.* [*1927*]

[*in brown: two rows of dots down the left hand margin*] KEW | GARDENS | BY | VIRGINIA | WOOLF | DECORATED BY VANESSA BELL | PUBLISHED BY THE HOGARTH PRESS

Crown 4to. [48] pp. $10\frac{1}{8} \times 7\frac{1}{2}$ in.

P. [1] title; p. [2] blank; p. [3] This edition, published in 1927, | is limited to 500 numbered copies, | of which this is number . . . [*numbered in purple ink*]; p. [4] blank; pp. [5–45] text printed on the recto of the leaf only; pp. [46–47] blank; p. [48] Printed and Engraved by | Herbert Reiach, Limited, | 43 Belvedere Road, S.E.1; each page of the text with illustrations by Vanessa Bell.

White paper boards; decorated upper cover printed in azure-blue, lime-green and milk-chocolate-brown; lettered in milk-chocolate-brown on upper cover, at head: Kew Gardens | By | Virginia Woolf, at foot: Decorations | By | Vanessa Bell | The | Hogarth Press; lettered up the spine: Kew Gardens Virginia Woolf; edges partially trimmed; end-papers. Celophane dust-jacket.

Published November 1927; 500 copies printed. 15s.

The British Museum copy is dated 17 November 1927. Some copies were signed on p. [3] by the author and illustrator.

*d. Third English edition – American photo-offset reprint.* [*1977*] *

[*two rows of dots down the left hand margin*] KEW | GARDENS | BY | VIRGINIA | WOOLF | DECORATED BY VANESSA BELL | PUBLISHED BY THE HOGARTH PRESS

48 pp.

Issued 25 July 1977; 150 copies printed. $20.

Issued by Folcroft Library Editions, Folcroft, Pennsylvania.

## A4 NIGHT AND DAY [1919]

*a. First edition*

NIGHT AND DAY | BY | VIRGINIA WOOLF | AUTHOR OF | "THE VOYAGE OUT" | [*publisher's floral device with motto*] | LONDON: DUCKWORTH AND COMPANY | 3 HENRIETTA STREET, COVENT GARDEN

Crown 8vo. [iv], 540 pp. $7\frac{3}{8} \times 4\frac{7}{8}$ in.

P. [i] half-title; p. [ii] work by the author listed; p. [iii] title; p. [iv] dedication: To | Vanessa Bell | But, Looking for a Phrase, | I Found None to Stand | Beside Your Name, at foot: First published 1919 | All rights reserved; pp. 1–538 text; p. 538 at foot: Printed at the Complete Press | West Norwood, London; pp. [539–540] publisher's advertisements, integral.

Dark grey cloth boards; lettered in pale blue on spine: [*double rule across head*] | Night | and | Day | Virginia | Woolf | Duckworth | [*double rule across foot*]; and on upper cover: Night and Day | Virginia Woolf; double rule in blind at head and foot of upper cover; publisher's floral device with motto in blind on lower cover; edges trimmed; end-papers. White dust-jacket printed in black.

Published 20 October 1919; 2000 copies printed. 9s.

There was a second impression of 1000 copies in 1920 issued at 3s. 6d. Duckworth & Co. write that they were issued in a binding and dust-jacket similar to the first impression with the addition of a paper label, stating the new price (3s. 6d.), pasted on the dust-jacket.

The publishing rights were sold to the Hogarth Press in February 1929. Duckworth sold 1767 copies of the first impression and 566 copies of the second impression; it is therefore likely that 667 copies were taken over by the Hogarth Press. They were issued by the Hogarth Press with a cancel-title as the 'Third Impression' in hyacinth-blue cloth boards in March or April 1929 probably at 7s. 6d. The third to fifth printing was issued as the Uniform Edition. See A4*c*.

## *b. First American edition.* [*1920*] *

[*within a rule:*] NIGHT | AND DAY | BY | VIRGINIA WOOLF | AUTHOR OF "THE VOYAGE OUT," ETC. | NEW | [*publisher's monogram*] | YORK | GEORGE H. DORAN COMPANY

Crown 8vo. 508 pp. $7\frac{1}{2} \times 4\frac{1}{4}$ in.

P. [1] half-title; p. [2] blank; p. [3] title; p. [4] Copyright, 1920, | By George H. Doran Company | Printed in the United States of America; p. [5] dedication; p. [6] blank; p. [7] fly-title; p. [8] blank; pp. 9–508 text.

Bright green cloth boards; lettered in black on spine: Night | and | Day | Virginia | Woolf | Doran, and on upper cover: [*within an ornamental border in blind:*] Night | and | Day | Virginia | Woolf; edges trimmed; end-papers. No specimen of dust-jacket available.

Published 29 September 1920; no record of the number of copies or impressions printed. $2.25.

It is probable that Doran printed only one impression. Sales to 1929 were 1326 copies. It is likely that any balance was taken over by Harcourt, Brace & Co. who purchased the publishing rights and plates on 20 April 1925. See A4*d*.

*c. First edition – photo-offset reprint* (UNIFORM EDITION, *see note to* A1*e*). *1930*

NIGHT AND DAY | VIRGINIA WOOLF | PUBLISHED BY LEONARD AND VIRGINIA WOOLF AT THE | HOGARTH PRESS, 52 TAVISTOCK SQUARE, LONDON, W.C. | 1930

Small crown 8vo. [iv], 540 pp. 7 × 4½ in.

P. [i] half-title; p. [ii] list of works in the Uniform Edition; p. [iii] title; p. [iv] dedication, publication note; pp. 1–538 text; p. 538 at foot: printer's imprint; pp. [539–540] blank.

Jade-green cloth boards; lettered in gold on spine; edges trimmed; end-papers. Pale peacock-blue dust-jacket printed in navy-blue.

Issued 6 November 1930; 3000 copies printed. 5s.

A further 3010 copies were printed in May 1938 and a further 5500 in 1950. The reprints were made by Lowe & Brydone except for that of May 1938 which was by Charles Kimble.

*d. First American edition – first Harcourt, Brace impression* (UNIFORM EDITION). [*1931*]

[*within a rule:*] VIRGINIA WOOLF | [*rule*] | NIGHT | AND DAY | [*rule*] | [*floral design*] | [*rule*] | HARCOURT, BRACE AND COMPANY | NEW YORK

Small crown 8vo. 512 pp. 7⅜ × 4¾ in.

P. [1] half-title; p. [2] list of works by the author; p. [3] title; p. [4] Copyright, 1920, | By George H. Doran Company, printer's note; p. [5] dedication; p. [6] blank; p. [7] fly-title; p. [8] blank; pp. 9–508 text; pp. [509–512] blank.

Cinnamon-brown cloth boards; lettered in gold on spine; edges trimmed; end-papers. Cream dust-jacket printed in blue.

Issued 29 January 1931; 2100 copies printed. $ 1.35.

*e. Second English edition* (PENGUIN BOOKS). [*1969*]

VIRGINIA WOOLF | NIGHT AND DAY | PENGUIN BOOKS | IN ASSOCIATION WITH THE HOGARTH PRESS

Foolscap 8vo. [ii], 478 pp. $7\frac{1}{8} \times 4\frac{3}{8}$ in.

Pp. [i–ii] blank; p. [1] half-title; p. [2] blank; p. [3] title; p. [4] publication note, printer's note; p. [5] dedication; p. [6] blank; pp. 7–[471] text; p. [472] blank; p. [473] publisher's advertisement; p. [474] blank; pp. [475–478] publisher's advertisements.

Stiff white pictorial paper wrappers printed in lemon yellow, brown, pink, blue and grey; edges trimmed.

Published November 1969 in *Penguin Modern Classics*; 22,500 copies printed. 8s.

There were further printings of 12,500 copies in November 1971, 14,000 in January 1974, 12,000 in April 1975, and 10,000 in December 1976.

*f. First American edition – Harcourt, Brace Jovanovich photo-offset reprint* (HARVEST BOOKS). [*1973*]

[*within a rule:*] VIRGINIA WOOLF | NIGHT | AND DAY | [*rule*] | [*floral design*] | [*rule*] | A HARVEST BOOK | HARCOURT BRACE JOVANOVICH, INC., NEW YORK | [*outside rule: publisher's monogram within a rule*]

Large crown 8vo. 512 pp. $8 \times 5\frac{1}{4}$ in.

P. [1] half-title; p. [2] list of works by the author; p. [3] title; p. [4] publication note, printer's note; p. [5] dedication; p. [6] blank; p. [7] fly-title; p. [8] blank; pp. 9–508 text; p. [509] publisher's advertisement; pp. [510–512] blank.

Stiff white pictorial paper wrappers printed in beige, black and bright orange; edges trimmed.

Issued 24 October 1973 in *Harvest Books* as Vol. HB263; 5000 copies printed. $3.95.

There were further printings of 3000 copies each in December 1973 and October 1974, 5000 in April 1975, and 10,158 in October 1976.

*g. Third English edition* (PANTHER BOOKS). [*1978*]

VIRGINIA WOOLF | NIGHT AND DAY | A TRIAD PANTHER BOOK | GRANADA PUBLISHING | LONDON TORONTO SYDNEY NEW YORK

Upper cover of the first edition of *Monday or Tuesday*, A5*a*

Foolscap 8vo. 464 pp. $7 \times 4\frac{3}{8}$ in.

P. [1] Biographical note on the author; p. [2] list of works by the author; p. [3] title; p. [4] publication note, copyright note, printer's note etc.; p. [5] dedication; p. [6] blank; pp. 7-460 text; p. [461] blank; pp. [462-464] publisher's advertisements.

Stiff white pictorial paper wrappers printed in black, brown, pale green and pink; edges trimmed.

Published 18 May 1978; 20,000 copies printed. £1.95.

## A5 MONDAY OR TUESDAY 1921

*a. First edition*

MONDAY | OR TUESDAY | VIRGINIA WOOLF | WITH WOODCUTS BY VANESSA BELL | PUBLISHED BY LEONARD & VIRGINIA WOOLF AT | THE HOGARTH PRESS, HOGARTH HOUSE, RICHMOND. | 1921

Small crown 8vo. 96 pp. 4 woodcuts on pp. [8], [12], [38], [58]. $7\frac{3}{8} \times 4\frac{7}{8}$ in.

Pp. [1-4] blank; p. [5] title; pp. [6-7] blank; p. [8] woodcut; pp. 9-11 text; p. [12] woodcut; pp. 13-37 text; p. [38] woodcut; pp. 39-57 text; p. [58] woodcut; pp. 59-91 text; p. [92] blank; p. [93] publisher's advertisements; pp. [94-96] blank.

White paper boards, brown cloth spine; black woodcut design on upper cover with lettering: Monday or Tuesday | Virginia Woolf | Woodcuts by | Vanessa Bell; edges trimmed; end-papers.

Published 7 or 8 April 1921; 1000 copies printed. 4s. 6d.

Contents: A Haunted House — A Society — Monday or Tuesday — An Unwritten Novel — The String Quartet — Blue and Green — Kew Gardens — The Mark on the Wall (revised, see A2*a*.).

Leonard Woolf stated that this work was printed by F. T. McDermott of the Prompt Press, Richmond, who used to give him advice on printing problems when he and Mrs Woolf first started the Hogarth Press.

*b. First American edition. 1921*

MONDAY OR TUESDAY | BY | VIRGINIA WOOLF | [*publisher's monogram within a rule*] | NEW YORK | HARCOURT, BRACE AND COMPANY | 1921

Crown 8vo. [iv], 116 pp. $7\frac{1}{2} \times 5\frac{1}{8}$ in.

P. [i] title; p. [ii] Copyright, 1921, by | Harcourt, Brace and Company, Inc., at foot: Printed in the U.S.A. by | The Quinn & Boden Company | Rahway, N.J.; p. [iii] Contents; p. [iv] blank; p. [1] fly-title; p. [2] blank; pp. 3–7 text; p. [8] blank; pp. 9–43 text; p. [44] blank; pp. 45–116 text.

Mottled buff paper boards, sage-green cloth spine; white printed paper label on spine $1\frac{3}{4} \times \frac{3}{4}$ in.: [*double rule*] | Monday | or | Tuesday | [*ornament*] | Virginia | Woolf | [*double rule*]; top edges trimmed, others partially trimmed; end-papers. Pale tan dust-jacket printed in dark green.

Published 23 November 1921; 1500 copies printed. $1.50.

## A6 JACOB'S ROOM 1922

*a. First edition*

JACOB'S ROOM | VIRGINIA WOOLF | PUBLISHED BY LEONARD & VIRGINIA WOOLF AT | THE HOGARTH PRESS, HOGARTH HOUSE, RICHMOND | 1922

Crown 8vo. 290, 14 pp. $7\frac{1}{2} \times 5$ in.

P. [1] blank; p. [2] list of works by the author; p. [3] half-title; p. [4] blank; p. [5] title; p. [6] blank; pp. 7–290 text; p. 290 at foot: Printed in Great Britain by R. & R. Clark, Limited, Edinburgh.; 14 pp. of publisher's advertisements, integral.

Crocus-yellow cloth boards; cream printed paper label at head of spine $1\frac{3}{8} \times 1\frac{5}{8}$ in.: [*double rule*] | Jacob's Room | [*short rule*] | Virginia Woolf | [*double rule*]; top edges trimmed, others partially trimmed, some fore edges uncut; end-papers. Cream dust-jacket printed in cinnamon and black, designed by Vanessa Bell.

Published 27 October 1922; *c.*1200 copies printed. 7s. 6d.

There was a second impression of *c.*2000 copies in 1922; Virginia Woolf noted on 1 November 1922 that 1000 copies were printed (*The Question of Things Happening*, p. 579; see A47*a*). The third to fourth printing was issued as the Uniform Edition. See A6*c*.

Some copies were issued with a printed slip $2\frac{1}{2} \times 3\frac{7}{8}$ in. tipped-in on the front free-end-paper: This copy of [*in ink:* Jacob's Room] | is issued to [*in ink:* subscriber's name] | as an A Subscriber to the Hogarth Press and | is therefore signed by the Author: | [*in ink:* Virginia Woolf | Oct. 1922]. The writing in ink is all in the author's hand.

Leonard Woolf had no definite recollection of copies of *Jacob's Room* with the tipped-in slip as recorded above, but stated that in the early days of the Hogarth Press two categories of subscribers were formed, 'A Subscribers' who made a deposit and received all publications of the press, and 'B Subscribers' who were notified of all publications. With the publication of *Jacob's Room* the decision was taken to establish the Hogarth Press as a business concern and in future to publish all Mrs Woolf's works. Mr Woolf thought that in order to acknowledge the support given by the 'A Subscribers' to the early publications of the press each subscriber was sent a signed copy of *Jacob's Room*.

There were forty active 'A Subscribers' in October 1922 and from the records made at the time it is safe to assume that each one received a copy of *Jacob's Room*. It is therefore likely that there are forty copies of the first edition with the tipped-in subscriber's slip.

This copy of Jacob's Room

is issued to J. Mavrogordato Esq.

as an A Subscriber to the Hogarth Press and

is therefore signed by the Author :

Virginia Woolf

Oct. 1922

Tipped-in slip in the 'A Subscribers' ' copies of *Jacob's Room*

*b. First American edition. [1923]* *

JACOB'S ROOM | VIRGINIA WOOLF | [*publisher's monogram*] | NEW YORK | HARCOURT, BRACE AND COMPANY

Crown 8vo. [vi], 314 pp. $7\frac{1}{2} \times 5\frac{1}{2}$ in.

P. [i] blank; p. [ii] list of works by the author; p. [iii] half-title; p. [iv] blank; p. [v] title; p. [vi] Copyright, 1923, By | Harcourt, Brace and Company, Inc. | Printed in the U.S.A. By | The Quinn & Boden Company | Rahway, N.J.; p. [1] fly-title; p. [2] blank; pp. 3–303 text; p. [304] blank; pp. [305–310] publisher's advertisements; pp. [311–314] blank.

Orange cloth boards; cream paper label on spine, $1\frac{3}{8} \times 1\frac{1}{4}$ in. printed in brown: [*double rule*] | Jacob's Room | By | Virginia Woolf | [*rule*] | Harcourt, Brace & Co | [*double rule*]; top edges trimmed, others partially trimmed; end-papers. Cream dust-jacket printed in brown and black, designed by Vanessa Bell.

Published 8 February 1923; 1500 copies printed. $2.

There was a second impression of 1000 copies in March 1923 and a third of 750 in November 1927. The fourth impression of 2100 copies was issued on 29 January 1931 as the Uniform Edition at $1.35; it was bound in maroon cloth boards; lettered in gold on spine; edges trimmed; end-papers; cream dust-jacket printed in blue.

*c. First edition – photo-offset reprint* (UNIFORM EDITION, *see note to* A1*e*). *1929*

JACOB'S ROOM | VIRGINIA WOOLF | PUBLISHED BY LEONARD & VIRGINIA | WOOLF AT THE HOGARTH PRESS, | TAVISTOCK SQUARE, LONDON, 1929.

Small crown 8vo. 288 pp. 7 × $4\frac{1}{2}$ in.

P. [1] half-title; p. [2] list of works in the Uniform Edition; p. [3] title; p. [4] publication note; pp. [5–288, numbered 7–290] text; p. [288 numbered 290] at foot: printer's imprint.

Jade-green cloth boards; lettered in gold on spine; edges trimmed; end-papers. Pale peacock-blue dust-jacket printed in navy-blue.

Issued 26 September 1929; 3200 copies printed. 5s.

A further 2110 copies were printed in May 1935.

*d. Second English edition* (UNIFORM EDITION). *1945**

JACOB'S ROOM | VIRGINIA WOOLF | THE HOGARTH PRESS | 37 MECKLENBURGH SQUARE | LONDON, W.C.1 | 1945

Small crown 8vo. 176 pp. 7 × $4\frac{1}{2}$ in.

P. [1] half-title; p. [2] list of works by the author; p. [3] title; p. [4] publisher's note, printer's imprint; pp. 5–176 text.

Jade-green cloth boards; lettered in gold on spine; edges trimmed; end-papers. Pale green dust-jacket printed in green.

Published April or May 1945; 3100 copies printed. 7s. 6d.

There were second and third impressions of 3000 copies each in 1947 and in April 1949. A further 3500 copies were printed by photo-litho offset in April 1954.

*e. Second American edition* (HARVEST BOOKS). [*1960*]

VIRGINIA WOOLF | JACOB'S ROOM | [*ornamental initials:*] VW | THE WAVES | HARCOURT, BRACE AND COMPANY · NEW YORK | A HARVEST BOOK

Large crown 8vo. 384 pp. 8 × $5\frac{3}{8}$ in.

P. [1] half-title; p. [2] list of works by the author; p. [3] title; p. [4] copyright note, reservation rights, printer's note; p. [5] fly-title; p. [6] blank; pp. 7–176 text of *Jacob's Room*; p. [177] fly-title; p. [178] blank; pp. 179–383 text of *The Waves*; p. [384] list of *Harvest Books.*

Stiff white paper wrappers printed in green, mauve and rust; edges trimmed.

Published 11 April 1960 in *Harvest Books* as Vol. 37; 8177 copies printed. $2.25.

There were further printings totalling 18,000 copies by 30 November 1965.

### *f. Third English edition* (PENGUIN BOOKS). [*1965*]

JACOB'S ROOM | VIRGINIA WOOLF | [*publisher's device of a penguin*] PENGUIN BOOKS | IN ASSOCIATION WITH THE HOGARTH PRESS

Foolscap 8vo. 176 pp. $7\frac{1}{4}$ × $4\frac{1}{2}$ in.

P. [1] half-title; p. [2] blank; p. [3] title; p. [4] publication note, printer's imprint, etc.; pp. 5–[168] text; p. [169] publisher's advertisement; p. [170] blank; pp. [171–176] publisher's advertisements, integral.

Stiff white paper wrappers printed in poppy, black and silver grey; edges trimmed.

Published 25 March 1965 in *Penguin Modern Classics* as Vol. 2259; number of copies printed not available. 3s. 6d.

### *g. Fourth English edition* (PANTHER BOOKS). [*1976*]

VIRGINIA WOOLF | JACOB'S ROOM | TRIAD PANTHER | GRANADA PUBLISHING | LONDON TORONTO SYDNEY NEW YORK

Foolscap 8vo. 176 pp. 7 × $4\frac{1}{4}$ in.

P. [1] Biographical note on the author; p. [2] list of works by the author; p. [3] title; p. [4] publication note, copyright note, printer's imprint etc.; pp. 5–[173] text; p. [174] blank; pp. [175–176] publisher's advertisements.

Stiff white pictorial paper wrappers printed in brown, green and black; edges trimmed.

Published 23 December 1976; 35,000 copies printed. 90p.

*h. Second American edition – photo-offset reprint* (HARVEST/HBJ BOOKS). [*1978*]

VIRGINIA WOOLF | JACOB'S ROOM | [*VW's initials in ornamental open capitals*] | [*publisher's monogram within a rule*] | A HARVEST/HBJ BOOK | HARCOURT BRACE JOVANOVICH | NEW YORK AND LONDON

Crown 8vo. 176 pp. $8 \times 5\frac{1}{4}$ in.

P. [1] half-title; p. [2] list of works by the author; p. [3] title; p. [4] copyright note, reservation rights, printer's note, Library of Congress cataloguing data, etc.; p. [5] fly-title; p. [6] blank; pp. 7–176 text.

Stiff white pictorial paper wrappers printed in black; edges trimmed.

Issued 6 June 1978; 10,125 copies printed. $2.95.

## A7 MR BENNETT AND MRS BROWN 1924

*a. First edition*

MR. BENNETT AND | MRS. BROWN | VIRGINIA WOOLF | PUBLISHED BY LEONARD AND VIRGINIA WOOLF | AT THE HOGARTH PRESS TAVISTOCK SQUARE | LONDON W.C.1 | 1924

Demy 8vo. 24 pp. $8\frac{1}{2} \times 5\frac{1}{2}$ in.

P. [1] title; p. [2] blank; pp. 3–24 text; p. 3 note at foot: A paper read to the Heretics, Cambridge, on May 18, 1924.; p. 24 at foot: Printed in Great Britain by Hazell, Watson & Viney, Ltd., | London and Aylesbury.

Stiff white paper wrappers; printed in black on upper cover, at head: The Hogarth Essays | Mr. Bennett and | Mrs. Brown | Virginia Woolf, at foot: The Hogarth Press; illustration by Vanessa Bell of woman with an open book on upper cover; edges trimmed; end-papers; sewn and gummed.

Published 30 October 1924 in *Hogarth Essays* as Vol. 1; 1000 copies printed. 2s. 6d.

There was a second impression of 1000 copies in 1928.

The essay was reprinted in the *New York Herald Tribune*, 23 and 30 August 1925, in *The Hogarth Essays*, New York, Doubleday, Doran, 1928, 1–29, in *The Captain's Death Bed and Other Essays*, in *Selections from her Essays* and in *Collected Essays*, Vol. 1. It was originally published in the *Criterion*, July 1924 under the title 'Character in Fiction'. See A30, 36–7, C251.

Another essay of the same title was first published in the *Literary Review* of the *New York Evening Post*, 17 November 1923. See C240.

*b. First edition – American photo-offset reprint. [1977]* *

MR. BENNETT AND | MRS. BROWN | VIRGINIA WOOLF | SECOND IMPRESSION | PUBLISHED BY LEONARD AND VIRGINIA WOOLF | AT THE HOGARTH PRESS TAVISTOCK SQUARE | LONDON W.C.1 | 1928

24 pp.

Issued 18 July 1977; 150 copies printed. $8.50.

Issued by Folcroft Library Editions, Folcroft, Pennsylvania.

## A8 THE COMMON READER 1925

*a. First edition*

THE | COMMON READER | VIRGINIA WOOLF | [*quotation in six lines from Johnson's 'Life of Gray' in* The Lives of the Poets *within double quotes*] | [*publisher's device of a wolf's head after a design by Vanessa Bell*] | PUBLISHED BY LEONARD & VIRGINIA WOOLF | AT THE HOGARTH PRESS, 52 TAVISTOCK SQUARE | LONDON, W.C. | 1925

Demy 8vo. 308 pp. $8\frac{5}{8} \times 5\frac{5}{8}$ in.

P. [1] half-title; p. [2] blank; p. [3] title; p. [4] at foot: Printed in Great Britain by R. & R. Clark, Limited, Edinburgh.; p. 5 acknowledgments; p. [6] blank; p. 7 dedication: To | Lytton Strachey; p. [8] blank; pp. 9–10 Contents; pp. 11–305 text; pp. [306–308] blank.

White paper boards, pale grey cloth spine; lettered in black on spine: The | Common | Reader | Virginia | Woolf | The | Hogarth | Press; illustrated upper cover by Vanessa Bell in grass-green and chocolate-brown, lettered at head: The | common | reader, at foot: Virginia Woolf; edges trimmed; end-papers. Cream dust-jacket with upper cover design reproduced in similar colours.

Published 23 April 1925; 1250 copies printed. 12s. 6d.

There is a secondary binding in grey cloth boards. Reference is made to this binding in a letter from the Manager of the Hogarth Press dated 2 November 1934 and published in *Bibliographical Notes and Queries*, Vol. 1, No. 3, 1935. It is there stated that the copies in grey cloth are of the second impression and that the title gives no indication of this. This is not correct, as the second impression issued in grey cloth boards records on the recto of the title: 'Second Edition' and on the verso: 'First published, April 1925. | Second Edition, November 1925.' Leonard Woolf thought that the copies in grey cloth, which lack 'Second Edition' on the recto and verso of the title (i.e. sheets of the first impression), may have been bound in this way for sale to libraries; they were bound in grey cloth probably similar to that of the second impression.

The second impression of 1000 copies was issued in November 1925 at 7s. 6d.; they were bound in pale grey cloth boards; cream paper label on spine printed in dark blue; edges trimmed; end-papers; cream dust-jacket printed in dark blue. The third to eighth printing was issued as the Uniform Edition. See A8*c*.

Contents: The Common Reader – The Pastons and Chaucer – On Not Knowing Greek – The Elizabethan Lumber Room – Notes on an Elizabethan Play – Montaigne – The Duchess of Newcastle – Rambling Round Evelyn – Defoe – Addison – Lives of the Obscure, I. Taylors and Edgeworths; II. Laetitia Pilkington – Jane Austen – Modern Fiction – "Jane Eyre" and "Wuthering Heights" – George Eliot – The Russian Point of View – Outlines, I. Miss Mitford; II. [Dr] Bentley; III. Lady Dorothy Nevill; IV. Archbishop Thomson – The Patron and the Crocus – The Modern Essay – Joseph Conrad – How It Strikes a Contemporary.

The device of the Hogarth Press, after a design by Vanessa Bell, is circular and measures $\frac{3}{4}$ in. There are two exceptions, No. A8*a*, first and second impressions, which are $1\frac{3}{8}$ in. across. In two works, Nos. A17 and A27, the device is after a design by E. McKnight Kauffer.

*a*

*b*

DEVICES OF THE HOGARTH PRESS

*a*. After a design by Vanessa Bell
*b*. After a design by E. McKnight Kauffer

## *b. First American edition. [1925]* *

THE | COMMON READER | BY | VIRGINIA WOOLF | [*quotation in six lines*] | [*publisher's monogram*] | NEW YORK | HARCOURT, BRACE AND COMPANY

Demy 8vo. [ii], 334 pp. $8\frac{3}{4} \times 5\frac{3}{4}$ in.

P. [i] half-title; p. [ii] list of works by the author; p. [1] title; p. [2] Copyright, 1925, By | Harcourt, Brace and Company, Inc. | Printed in the U.S.A. By | The Quinn & Boden Company | Rahway, N.J.; p. [3] dedication; p. [4] blank; p. [5] acknowledgments; p. [6] blank; pp. 7-8 Contents; p. [9] fly-title; p. [10] blank; pp. 11-59 text; p. [60] blank; pp. 61–85 text; p. [86] blank; pp. 87–123 text; p. [124] blank; pp. 125–135 text; p. [136] blank; pp. 137–151 text; p. [152] blank; pp. 153–189 text; p. [190] blank; pp. 191–227 text; p. [228] blank; pp. 229–307 text; p. [308] blank; pp. 309–332 text; pp. [333–334] blank.

Red cloth boards; lettered in gold on spine: [*rule*] | The | Common | Reader | [*ornament*] | Virginia | Woolf | Harcourt, Brace | and Company | [*rule*]; double line border in blind round upper cover; publisher's monogram in blind on upper cover; edges trimmed; end-papers. Cream dust-jacket printed in brown and green, designed by Vanessa Bell.

Published 14 May 1925; 2000 copies printed. $3.50.

There was a second impression of 535 copies in November 1927, a third of 500 in December 1930, a fourth of 1000 in May 1933 and a fifth and sixth of 500 each in January 1942 and July 1944. See also A18*e*.

An additional essay 'Lives of the Obscure, III, Miss Ormerod' is included; it does not appear in the English editions. It was first published in the *Dial*, New York, December 1924. See C257.

### *c. First edition – photo-offset reprint* (UNIFORM EDITION, *see note to* A1*e*). *1929*

THE | COMMON READER | VIRGINIA WOOLF | PUBLISHED BY LEONARD & VIRGINIA | WOOLF AT THE HOGARTH PRESS, | TAVISTOCK SQUARE, LONDON, 1929.

Small crown 8vo. 308 pp. $7 \times 4\frac{1}{2}$ in.

P. [1] half-title; p. [2] list of works in the Uniform Edition; p. [3] title; p. [4] publication note; p. 5 acknowledgments; p. [6] blank; p. 7 dedication; p. [8] blank; pp. 9–10 Contents; pp. 11–305 text; p. 305 at foot: printer's imprint; pp. [306–308] blank.

Jade-green cloth boards; lettered in gold on spine; edges trimmed; end-papers. Pale peacock-blue dust-jacket printed in navy-blue.

Issued 26 September 1929; 3200 copies printed. 5s.

There were further printings of 3200 copies in February 1933, 2400 in July 1942, 3000 in May 1945, 3900 in early 1948 and 4000 in May 1951.

### *d. Second English edition* (PENGUIN BOOKS). [*1938*]

PELICAN BOOKS | THE COMMON READER | BY | VIRGINIA WOOLF | [*publisher's device of a pelican*] |

PUBLISHED BY | PENGUIN BOOKS LIMITED | HARMONDSWORTH MIDDLESEX ENGLAND

Foolscap 8vo. 240, [16] pp. $7\frac{1}{8} \times 4\frac{1}{4}$ in.

P. [1] half-title; p. [2] publisher's note; p. [3] title; p. [4] publication note, printer's imprint; p. [5] acknowledgments; p. [6] blank; p. [7] dedication; p. [8] blank; p. 9 Contents; p. [10] blank; pp. 11-240 text; 16 pp. of publisher's advertisements, integral, pp. [8], [16] blank.

Stiff white paper wrappers printed in bright blue and black; edges trimmed.

Published 8 October 1938 in *Pelican Books* as Vol. A36; 50,000 copies printed. 6d.

*e. Second American edition* (HARVEST BOOKS). [*1955*]

VIRGINIA WOOLF | [*ornament*] | THE COMMON READER | FIRST SERIES | [*ornament*] | [*quotation in seven lines*] | A HARVEST BOOK | HARCOURT, BRACE AND COMPANY | NEW YORK

Foolscap 8vo. x, 246 pp. $7\frac{1}{4} \times 4\frac{1}{4}$ in.

P. [i] half-title; p. [ii] note on the author; p. [iii] title; p. [iv] copyright notice, reservation rights, printer's note; p. [v] dedication; p. [vi] blank; p. [vii] acknowledgments; p. [viii] blank; pp. [ix]-x Contents; pp. [1]-246 text.

Stiff white paper wrappers printed in black, green and mauve; edges trimmed.

Published 4 August 1955 in *Harvest Books* as Vol. 10; 15,000 copies printed. $1.15.

## A9 MRS DALLOWAY 1925

*a. First edition*

MRS. DALLOWAY | VIRGINIA WOOLF | PUBLISHED BY LEONARD & VIRGINIA WOOLF AT THE | HOGARTH PRESS, 52 TAVISTOCK SQUARE, LONDON, W.C. | 1925

Crown 8vo. 296 pp. $7\frac{3}{8} \times 5$ in.

P. [1] blank; p. [2] list of works by the author; p. [3] half-title; p. [4] blank; p. [5] title; p. [6] at foot: Printed in Great Britain by R. & R. Clark, Limited, Edinburgh.; pp. 7-293 text; pp. [294-296] blank.

Deep rust cloth boards; lettered in gold on spine: Mrs. | Dalloway | [*short rule*] | Virginia Woolf | The | Hogarth Press; rule in blind round upper cover; top edges yellow, others partially trimmed; end-papers. Cream dust-jacket printed in black and yellow, designed by Vanessa Bell.

Published 14 May 1925; *c.*2000 copies printed. 7s. 6d.

There was a second impression of 1000 copies in September 1925, called a 'Second Edition'. The third and fourth printings were issued as the Uniform Edition. See A9*d*.

'Royalty Passes', printed in *Senior Scholastic*, New York, High School Teacher Edition, 8 January 1945, 45 : 14, 17–18, is an extract from *Mrs Dalloway*.

### *b. First American edition.* [*1925*] *

MRS. DALLOWAY | BY | VIRGINIA WOOLF | [*publisher's monogram*] | NEW YORK | HARCOURT, BRACE AND COMPANY

Crown 8vo. [vi], 298 pp. $7\frac{1}{2} \times 5\frac{1}{4}$ in.

Pp. [i–ii] blank; p. [iii] half-title; p. [iv] list of works by the author; p. [v] title; p. [vi] Copyright, 1925, By | Harcourt, Brace and Company, Inc. | Printed in the U.S.A.; p. [1] fly-title; p. [2] blank; pp. 3–296 text; pp. [297–298] blank.

Orange cloth boards; white paper label on spine, $1\frac{3}{4} \times 1\frac{1}{4}$ in. printed in brown: [*double rule*] | Mrs. Dalloway | By | Virginia Woolf | [*rule*] | Harcourt, Brace & Co. | [*double rule*]; top edges trimmed, others partially trimmed; end-papers. Cream dust-jacket printed in black and yellow, designed by Vanessa Bell.

Published 14 May 1925; 2100 copies printed. $2.50.

There were second and third impressions of 1500 copies each in May and August 1925, a fourth of 750 in March 1927 and a fifth of 1000 in October 1927. The sixth impression of 2100 copies was issued on 29 January 1931. Most copies of the sixth impression were issued as the Uniform Edition at $1.35; they were bound in azure-blue cloth boards; lettered in gold on spine; edges trimmed; end-papers; cream dust-jacket printed in blue. The remainder were bound in orange cloth boards; cream paper label printed in brown on spine; fore edges untrimmed; end-papers. The seventh impression of 1500 copies was issued on 24 August 1948 at $3; it was bound in dark green cloth boards; lettered in gold on spine; edges trimmed; end-papers; pale grey dust-jacket printed in reddish-brown and green, designed by Vanessa Bell. The eighth to eleventh impression was issued as *Harbrace Modern Classics*. See A9*g*. See also A9*c*.

See 'The American Edition of *Mrs. Dalloway*', by E. F. Shields,

*Studies in Bibliography*, 1974, Vol. 27, pp. 157–75 for a discussion of the textual and other variants.

*c. First American edition – re-impression* (MODERN LIBRARY). [*1928*]

MRS. | DALLOWAY | BY | VIRGINIA WOOLF | INTRODUCTION BY | VIRGINIA WOOLF | THE | MODERN LIBRARY | NEW YORK | [*series device of an Olympic runner facing the last three lines*] | [*rule*]

Small crown 8vo. 304 pp. 7 × 4¾ in.

P. [i] half-title; p. [ii] blank; p. [iii] title; p. [iv] copyright notice . . . Random House is the Publisher of | The Modern Library | . . . printer's imprint etc.; pp. v–ix Introduction by Virginia Woolf; p. [x] blank; pp. [11–304 numbered 3–296] text.

Blue cloth boards; lettered in gold on spine and on upper cover within a double rule on a pale blue panel; edges trimmed, top blue; white end-papers patterned in grey. Pale blue-grey dust-jacket printed in black and dark red.

Issued 24 December 1928 in *The Modern Library of the World's Best Books* as Vol. 96; number of copies of the first impression unknown. 95 cents.

The text was printed from Harcourt, Brace's plates, pp. i–ix being re-set. Sales to November 1948, when the Modern Library's contract with Harcourt, Brace expired, were 61,000 copies. The contract was not renewed and the work was withdrawn from the series.

*d. First edition – photo-offset reprint* (UNIFORM EDITION, *see note to* A1*e*). *1929*

MRS. DALLOWAY | VIRGINIA WOOLF | PUBLISHED BY LEONARD & VIRGINIA | WOOLF AT THE HOGARTH PRESS, | TAVISTOCK SQUARE, LONDON, 1929.

Small crown 8vo. 292 pp. 7 × 4½ in.

P. [1] half-title; p. [2] list of works in the Uniform Edition; p. [3] title; p. [4] publication note; pp. [5–291 numbered 7–293] text; p. [291 numbered 293] at foot: printer's imprint; p. [292] blank.

Jade-green cloth boards; lettered in gold on spine; edges trimmed; end-papers. Pale peacock-blue dust-jacket printed in navy-blue.

Issued 26 September 1929; 3200 copies printed. 5s.

A further 3235 copies were printed in February 1933.

## *e. Second English edition* (UNIFORM EDITION). *1942*

MRS. DALLOWAY | VIRGINIA WOOLF | NEW EDITION | THE HOGARTH PRESS | 37 MECKLENBURGH SQUARE | LONDON, W.C.1 | 1942

Small crown 8vo. [iv], 252 pp. 7 × $4\frac{1}{4}$ in.

Pp. [i–ii] form paste down end-paper; pp. [iii–iv] blank; p. [1] half-title; p. [2] list of works by the author; p. [3] title; p. [4] publication note, at foot: Made and Printed in Great Britain by | The Garden City Press Limited, at | Letchworth, Hertfordshire; pp. 5–248 text; pp. [249–250] blank; pp. [251–252] form paste down end-paper.

Jade-green cloth boards; lettered in gold on spine; edges trimmed; no end-papers. White dust-jacket printed in green.

Published early 1942; 2000 copies printed. 6s.

## *f. Third English edition. 1947*

[*within a rule in pale brown, within two compartments in black and pale brown:*] MRS DALLOWAY | VIRGINIA WOOLF | [*publisher's monogram in pale brown*] | 1947 | THE ZODIAC PRESS | LONDON

Crown 8vo. 216 pp. $7\frac{3}{8}$ × $4\frac{7}{8}$ in.

P. [1] half-title; p. [2] note on the author; p. [3] title; p. [4] Published by | Chatto and Windus | London | . . . at foot: Printed in Great Britain | in complete conformity with | the authorised economy standards | by Hazell, Watson and Viney, Ltd. | London and Aylesbury, reservation rights; pp. 5–213 text; pp. [214–216] blank.

Pale blue-and-white patterned cloth boards; lettered in gold on lime-green panel on spine; top edges blue, fore edges trimmed, bottom edges partially trimmed; end-papers. White dust-jacket printed in lime-green and black.

Published 28 July 1947; 5800 copies printed. 6s.

A second impression of 10,000 copies was printed in July 1949. 2500 were issued as the Uniform Edition in jade-green paper boards in 1950, and 7500 in the New Phoenix Library (by Chatto & Windus in association with the Hogarth Press) in ice-blue cloth boards; lettered in gold on spine on an oval maroon panel edged with gold; deep cream dust-jacket printed in dull red and black, and issued 17 July 1950 at 5s. There was a third impression of 7500 copies in November 1954 issued as the Uniform Edition.

*g. First American edition – eighth impression* (HARBRACE MODERN CLASSICS). *[1949]* *

MRS. DALLOWAY | BY | VIRGINIA WOOLF | *[publisher's monogram]* | NEW YORK | HARCOURT, BRACE AND COMPANY

Crown 8vo. [vi], 298 pp. $7\frac{3}{4} \times 5\frac{1}{4}$ in.

P. [i] blank; p. [ii] list of works by the author; p. [iii] half-title; p. [iv] blank; p. [v] title; p. [vi] Copyright, 1925, by | Harcourt, Brace and Company, Inc., reservation rights, printer's note; p. [1] fly-title; p. [2] blank; pp. 3–296 text; pp. [297–298] blank.

Pale blue cloth boards; lettered on spine and on upper cover; edges trimmed; grey and white end-papers with publisher's monogram. White dust-jacket printed in blue and yellow.

Issued 22 September 1949 in *Harbrace Modern Classics* as Vol. 13; 7500 copies printed. $1.75.

There were re-impressions of 5000 copies each in April 1950, January 1954 and January 1956.

*h. Fourth English edition* (PENGUIN BOOKS). *[1964]*

VIRGINIA WOOLF | MRS DALLOWAY | *[publisher's device of a penguin]* PENGUIN BOOKS | IN ASSOCIATION WITH THE HOGARTH PRESS

Foolscap 8vo. 224 pp. $7\frac{1}{4} \times 4\frac{1}{2}$ in.

P. [1] half-title; p. [2] blank; p. [3] title; p. [4] publication note, printer's imprint etc.; pp. 5–[215] text; p. [216] blank; p. [217] publisher's advertisement; p. [218] blank; pp. [219–224] publisher's advertisements, integral.

Stiff white paper wrappers printed in green, darker green, crimson, silver grey and black, from a portrait of the author by Vanessa Bell; edges trimmed.

Published 24 September 1964 in *Penguin Modern Classics* as Vol. 2159; number of copies printed not available. 4s. 6d.

*i. First American edition – photo-offset reprint* (HARVEST BOOKS). *[1964]*

VIRGINIA WOOLF | MRS. DALLOWAY | HARCOURT, BRACE & WORLD, INC. | NEW YORK | A HARVEST BOOK

Small crown 8vo. [vi], 298 pp. $7\frac{3}{8} \times 4\frac{1}{4}$ in.

Pp. [i–ii] blank; p. [iii] fly-title; p. [iv] list of works by the author; p. [v] title; p. [vi] copyright note, reservation rights, printer's note; p. [1] fly-title; p. [2] blank; pp. 3–296 text; pp. [297–298] blank, integral.

White stiff paper wrappers printed in pale brown, olive green and pink with illustrated upper cover; edges trimmed.

Issued 7 October 1964 in *Harvest Books* as Vol. 81; 15,100 copies printed. $1.45.

There were further printings totalling 10,100 copies by November 1965.

### *j. Third English edition – photo-offset reprint* (QUEEN'S CLASSICS). [*1968*]

MRS. DALLOWAY | BY | VIRGINIA WOOLF | [*series monogram*] | CHATTO AND WINDUS | LONDON

Small crown 8vo. [iv], 220 pp. $7\frac{1}{4} \times 4\frac{3}{4}$ in.

Pp. [i–iv] form upper end-papers; p. [1] half-title; p. [2] list of works in the series; p. [3] title; p. [4] publication note, printer's note; pp. 5–213 text; pp. [214–216] blank; pp. [217–220] form lower end-papers.

Sky-blue paper boards stamped in gilt and orange; edges trimmed; no end-papers. No dust-jacket.

Issued 30 June 1968 as a *Queen's Classic*; 3000 copies printed. 8s.

### *k. Fourth English edition* (PANTHER BOOKS). [*1976*]

VIRGINIA WOOLF | MRS DALLOWAY | TRIAD | PANTHER

Foolscap 8vo. 176 pp. $7 \times 4\frac{3}{8}$ in.

P. [1] Biographical note on the author; p. [2] list of works by the author; p. [3] title; p. [4] publication note, printer's imprint, etc.; pp. 5–172 text; p. [173] blank; pp. [174–176] publisher's advertisements.

Stiff white pictorial paper wrappers printed in red, blue, pink, yellow, brown, green, mauve and black; edges trimmed.

Published 28 October 1976; 40,000 copies printed. 60p.

## A10 TO THE LIGHTHOUSE 1927

### *a. First edition*

TO THE LIGHTHOUSE | VIRGINIA WOOLF | [*publisher's device of a wolf's head*] | PUBLISHED BY LEONARD & VIRGINIA WOOLF AT THE | HOGARTH PRESS, 52 TAVISTOCK SQUARE, LONDON, W.C. | 1927

Crown 8vo. 320 pp. $7\frac{3}{8} \times 4\frac{7}{8}$ in.

Pp. [i–ii] blank; p. [iii] half-title; p. [iv] list of works by the author; p. [v] title; p. [vi] at foot: Printed in Great Britain by R. & R. Clark, Limited, Edinburgh.; p. vii Contents; p. [viii] blank; p. [ix] fly-title; p. [x] blank; pp. 11–191 text; p. [192] blank; p. [193] fly-title; p. [194] blank; pp. 195–221 text; p. [222] blank; p. [223] fly-title; p. [224] blank; pp. 225–[320] text.

Bright blue cloth boards; lettered in gold on spine: To | The Lighthouse | [*ornament*] | Virginia Woolf | Hogarth Press; edges trimmed, top pale yellow; end-papers. Cream dust-jacket printed in pale blue and black, designed by Vanessa Bell.

Published 5 May 1927; 3000 copies printed. 7s. 6d.

There was a second impression of 1000 copies in June 1927 and a third of 1500 in May 1928. 700 copies of the third impression were transferred to the Uniform Edition in April 1943 and called a 'Special Edition'. The fourth to tenth printing was issued as the Uniform Edition. See A10*c*.

A dummy copy bound as the first edition with dust-jacket was presented by the author to V. Sackville-West who wrote 'I should explain that Mrs Woolf gave it to me as a joke. I had been away in Persia for several months and she wrote to me saying that she would have a new book for me to read on my return. I duly found the parcel awaiting me and found that she had written on the fly-leaf "Vita from Virginia (In my opinion the best novel I have ever written.)" I was rather surprised by this as it sounded so unlike her, but when I settled down to read it that night in bed I discovered that all the pages were blank.' It is still in the recipient's study at Sissinghurst Castle.

See 'The First Editions of Virginia Woolf's *To the Lighthouse*', by J. A. Lavin, *Proof*, 1972, Vol. 2, pp. 185–211 for a discussion of the textual and other variants.

### *b. First American edition. [1927]* *

TO | THE LIGHTHOUSE | BY | VIRGINIA WOOLF | [*publisher's monogram*] | NEW YORK | HARCOURT, BRACE & COMPANY

Crown 8vo. 312 pp. $7\frac{1}{2} \times 5\frac{1}{4}$ in.

P. [1] half-title; p. [2] list of works by the author; p. [3] title; p. [4] Copyright, 1927, By | Harcourt, Brace and Company, Inc. | I | Printed in the U.S.A. by | Quinn & Boden Company, Inc. | Rahway, N.J.; p. [5] Contents; p. [6] blank; p. [7] fly-title; p. [8] blank; pp. 9-186 text; p. [187] fly-title; p. [188] blank; pp. 189-214 text; p. [215] fly-title; p. [216] blank; pp. 217-310 text; pp. [311-312] blank.

Pale green cloth boards; lettered in blue on spine: To the | Lighthouse | [*ornament*] | Woolf | Harcourt, Brace | and Company, and on upper cover: To the Lighthouse | [*device of a lighthouse*] | Virginia Woolf; top edges blue-black, front edges untrimmed, bottom trimmed; end-papers. Green dust-jacket printed in black and blue.

Published 5 May 1927; 4000 copies printed. $2.50.

There were second and third impressions of 1500 and 2100 copies in June and August 1927, a fourth of 1500 in June 1930 and a fifth of 1000 in February 1935. 1000 copies, probably of the fourth impression, were issued as the Uniform Edition on 29 January 1931 at $1.35; they were bound in azure-blue cloth boards; lettered in gold on spine; edges trimmed; end-papers; cream dust-jacket. The sixth impression of 1500 copies was issued on 24 August 1948 at $3; it was bound in dark green cloth boards; lettered in gold on spine; edges trimmed; end-papers; pale grey dust-jacket printed in reddish-brown and green. The seventh to eleventh impression was issued as *Harbrace Modern Classics*. See A10*e*.

The Modern Library of the World's Best Books, New York issued a reprint with an introduction by Terence Holliday on 27 September 1937 at 95 cents. It was bound in dull red cloth boards; lettered in gold on spine; device of an Olympic runner in gold on upper cover; blind rules round upper cover; edges trimmed, top dull red; white end-papers patterned in deep buff; white dust-jacket printed in black, grey and blue. In the first reprint 5000 copies were printed; sales to November 1948, when the contract with Harcourt, Brace expired, were 38,000 copies. The Modern Library did not renew the contract and the work was withdrawn from the series.

## *c. First edition – fourth impression* (UNIFORM EDITION). *1930*

TO THE LIGHTHOUSE | VIRGINIA WOOLF | PUBLISHED BY LEONARD & VIRGINIA | WOOLF AT THE HOGARTH PRESS, | TAVISTOCK SQUARE, LONDON. 1930

Small crown 8vo. 320 pp. $7 \times 4\frac{1}{2}$ in.

Pp. [i–ii] blank; p. [iii] half-title; p. [iv] list of works in the Uniform Edition; p. [v] title; p. [vi] publication note, printer's imprint; p. vii Contents; p. [viii] blank; p. [ix] fly-title; p. [x] blank; pp. 11–191 text; p. [192] blank; p. [193] fly-title; p. [194] blank; pp. 195–221 text; p. [222] blank; p. [223] fly-title; p. [224] blank; pp. 225–[320] text; p. [320] at foot: printer's imprint.

Jade-green cloth boards; lettered in gold on spine; edges trimmed; end-papers. Pale peacock-blue dust-jacket printed in navy-blue.

Issued *c.* 19 February 1930; 3000 copies printed. 5s.

This re-impression is incorrectly described as a 'New Edition' in the publication note on the verso of the title. There were further printings by photo-litho offset of 3800 copies in June 1932, 1500 in October 1941, 3000 in March 1946, 3400 in 1949, 3000 in 1951 and 6000 in 1955. They were issued as the Uniform Edition.

*d. Second English edition* (EVERYMAN'S LIBRARY). [*1938*]

TO THE LIGHTHOUSE | [*ornamental series device*] | VIRGINIA WOOLF | LONDON : J. M. DENT & SONS LTD

Foolscap 8vo. xii, 244 pp. $6\frac{3}{4} \times 4\frac{1}{4}$ in.

P. [i] series motto; p. [ii] note on series, London and New York addresses; p. [iii] half-title; p. [iv] note on the author; p. [v] title; p. [vi] reservation rights, printer's imprint, decorator's name, publisher's name, publication note; pp. vii–xii Introduction by D. M. Hoare; p. [1] fly-title; p. [2] blank; pp. 3–242 text; p. [243] blank; p. [244] printer's imprint across device of a flower. 16 pp. of publisher's advertisements inserted.

Cardinal-red cloth boards; lettered in gold on spine; ornamental device in blind on upper cover; edges trimmed, top pale brown; white end-papers patterned in pale pink. White dust-jacket printed in vermilion and black.

Published 27 October 1938 in *Everyman's Library* as Vol. 949; 10,000 copies printed. 3s.

There were further printings of 4000 copies in 1943, 6500 in 1945, 12,000 in 1947, 6000 in 1952 and a further printing in 1955.

*e. First American edition – seventh impression* (HARBRACE MODERN CLASSICS). [*1949*] *

TO | THE LIGHTHOUSE | BY | VIRGINIA WOOLF | [*publisher's monogram*] | NEW YORK | HARCOURT, BRACE & COMPANY

Crown 8vo. 312 pp. $7\frac{3}{4} \times 5\frac{1}{4}$ in.

P. [1] half-title; p. [2] list of works by the author; p. [3] title; p. [4] Copyright, 1927, by | Harcourt, Brace and Company, Inc., reservation rights, printer's note; p. [5] Contents; p. [6] blank; p. [7] fly-title; p. [8] blank; pp. 9–186 text; p. [187] fly-title; p. [188] blank; pp. 189–214 text; p. [215] fly-title; p. [216] blank; pp. 217–310 text; pp. [311–312] blank.

Tan cloth boards; lettered in black on spine and on upper cover; edges trimmed; olive and white end-papers with publisher's monogram. White dust-jacket printed in brown, tan and green.

Issued 22 September 1949 in *Harbrace Modern Classics* as Vol. 14; 7500 copies printed. $1.75.

There was an eighth impression of 5000 copies in April 1950, a ninth of 5000 in January 1954 and a tenth and eleventh of 3000 each in April 1955 and February 1956.

### *f. Third English edition* (PENGUIN BOOKS). [*1964*]

VIRGINIA WOOLF | TO THE LIGHTHOUSE | [*publisher's device of a penguin*] PENGUIN BOOKS | IN ASSOCIATION WITH THE HOGARTH PRESS

Foolscap 8vo. 240 pp. $7\frac{1}{4} \times 4\frac{1}{2}$ in.

P. [1] half-title; p. [2] blank; p. [3] title; p. [4] publication note, printer's imprint etc.; pp. 5–163 text; p. [164] blank; pp. 165–[237] text; p. [238] blank; pp. [239–240] publisher's advertisements, integral.

Stiff white paper wrappers printed in blue, black and silver grey, designed by Duncan Grant; edges trimmed.

Published 24 September 1964 in *Penguin Modern Classics* as Vol. 2165; number of copies printed not available. 4s. 6d.

### *g. First American edition—photo-offset reprint* (HARVEST BOOKS). [*1964*]

VIRGINIA WOOLF | TO THE LIGHTHOUSE | HARCOURT, BRACE & WORLD, INC. | NEW YORK | A HARVEST BOOK

Small crown 8vo. 312 pp. $7\frac{3}{8} \times 4\frac{1}{4}$ in.

P. [1] half-title; p. [2] list of works by the author; p. [3] title; pp. [4] copyright note, reservation rights, printer's note; p. [5] Contents; p. [6] blank; p. [7] section-title; p. [8] blank; pp. 9–186 text; p. [187] section-title; p. [188] blank; pp. 189–214 text; p. [215] section-title; p. [216] blank; pp. 217–310 text; pp. [311–312] blank, integral.

Stiff white paper wrappers printed in sky-blue, sea-blue and pale orange with illustrated upper cover; edges trimmed.

Issued 7 October 1964 in *Harvest Books* as Vol. 82; 15,200 copies printed. $1.45.

There were further printings totalling 13,800 copies by November 1964.

### *h. Fourth English edition* (PANTHER BOOKS). [*1977*]

VIRGINIA WOOLF | TO THE LIGHTHOUSE | TRIAD | PANTHER

Foolscap 8vo. 192 pp. 7 × $4\frac{1}{4}$ in.

P. [1] Biographical note on the author; p. [2] list of works by the author; p. [3] title;p. [4] publication note, copyright note, printer's imprint etc.; p. [5] Conents; p. [6] blank; p. [7] section-title; p. [8] blank; pp. 9–114 text; p. [115] section-title; p. [116] blank; pp. 117–133 text; p. 134 blank; p. [135] section-title; p. [136] blank; pp. 137–[192] text.

Stiff white pictorial paper wrappers printed in black, brown, yellow and gold; edges trimmed.

Published 4 August 1977; 30,000 copies printed. 75p.

## A11 ORLANDO: A BIOGRAPHY 1928

### *a. First (limited) edition*

ORLANDO | A BIOGRAPHY | BY | VIRGINIA WOOLF | [*publisher's device of a ram on a green base*] | NEW YORK: CROSBY GAIGE | 1928

Small royal 8vo. [iv], 336 pp. front., 7 plates facing pp. 48, 106, 112, 144, 224, 240, 288. 9 × $6\frac{1}{8}$ in.

P. [i] half-title; p. [ii] blank, author's signature in purple ink; p. [iii] title; p. [iv] at head: Copyright, 1928, Crosby Gaige, at foot: Made in the printing house of William Edwin Rudge, Inc. | at Mount Vernon, New York, in the United States of America; p. [1] dedication: To | V. Sackville-West; p. [2] blank; pp. [3–5] Preface; p. [6] blank; p. [7] Contents; p. [8] blank; p. [9] list of illustrations; p. [10] blank; p. [11] fly-title; p. [12] blank; pp. 13–329 text; p. [330] blank; pp. 331–333 Index; p. [334] blank; p. [335] Of this Edition of Orlando | 861 copies have been printed on pure rag paper | of which 800 numbered copies, signed by the author, | will be for sale | Distributed in America by Random House | No. [*numbered in red ink*] | Typography by Frederic Warde; p. [336] blank.

Black cloth boards; patterned in gold on spine in six panels, lettered in gold on second panel: Orlando | [*ornament*] | Woolf; pattern on spine protrudes on to upper and lower covers; device of a ram with publisher's monogram in gold on upper cover; top edges gilt, fore edges untrimmed, bottom partially trimmed; end-papers. Plain glassine dust-jacket.

Published 2 October 1928; 861 copies printed. $15. Distributed in the United Kingdom by Dulau & Co.

A further limited number of copies were printed on green paper and bound in marbled paper boards with black morocco spine lettered in gold and with a slip-in case. Mr Crosby Gaige informed Mr D. A. Randall, then of Scribner's, New York, that eleven such copies were printed. One of Crosby Gaige's copies, now in the library of Mr Robert H. Taylor, is signed by the author and dated October 1928. In a copy presented to Austin Keough, Crosby Gaige wrote that it was 'one of an edition of 15 copies printed on *green* paper'; it is in the library of Mr Drew Ponder-Greene. Another is in the Lilly Library, Indiana University.

### *b. First English edition. 1928*

ORLANDO | A BIOGRAPHY | VIRGINIA WOOLF | [*publisher's device of a wolf's head*] | PUBLISHED BY LEONARD AND VIRGINIA WOOLF AT THE | HOGARTH PRESS, 52 TAVISTOCK SQUARE, LONDON, W.C. | 1928

Demy 8vo. 300 pp. front., 7 plates facing pp. 48, 106, 113, 144, 224, 240, 288. $8\frac{5}{8} \times 5\frac{1}{2}$ in.

P. [1] half-title; p. [2] blank; p. [3] title; p. [4] at foot: Printed in Great Britain by R. & R. Clark, Limited, Edinburgh.; p. 5 dedication: To | V. Sackville West; p. [6] blank; pp. 7–9 Preface; p. [10] blank; p. 11 Contents; p. [12] blank; p. 13 list of illustrations; p. [14] blank; pp. 15–295 text; p. [296] blank; pp. 297–299 Index; p. [300] blank.

Orange cloth boards; lettered in gold on spine: Orlando | [*ornament*] | Virginia | Woolf | Hogarth | Press; edges trimmed; end-papers. White dust-jacket printed in black with illustration.

Published 11 October 1928; 5080 copies printed. 9s.

There is a variant of the binding in brown cloth boards. In *Modern First Editions* (1929) by Gilbert H. Fabes it is stated that this is the 'first issue'. Mr Fabes writes 'At the time of compiling my bibliographies I often got into touch with the publishers to check on such details.' It has not been possible to confirm this point now. It is likely that the copies in brown cloth were advance copies.

There was a second impression of 3000 copies in October 1928 and a third of 3000 in January 1929. The fourth to seventh printing was issued as the Uniform Edition. See A11*d*.

A copy bound in niger, lettered in gold on the spine: Orlando | [*within an ornament:*] V S W | 1928, was presented by the author to V. Sackville-West and is still in the latter's study at Sissinghurst Castle. It is inscribed by the author 'Vita from Virginia | Thursday, October the Eleventh, | Nineteenhundred & twenty eight.'

An unpublished passage from *Orlando* was read by V. Sackville-West in a talk on the Third Programme of the B.B.C. and published in 'Virginia Woolf and Orlando', the *Listener*, 27 January 1955, 158. V. Sackville-West read the same passage at a Poetry Platform held by the English Centre of the P.E.N. on 28 April 1954. The context of the passage is Chapter 6. See also F5.

### *c. First American edition – first trade impression.* [*1928*]

ORLANDO | A BIOGRAPHY | BY | VIRGINIA WOOLF | [*publisher's monogram*] | NEW YORK | HARCOURT, BRACE AND COMPANY

Large crown 8vo. 336 pp. front., 7 plates facing pp. 54, 114, 126, 158, 246, 262, 318. $8\frac{1}{8} \times 5\frac{1}{2}$ in.

P. [i] half-title; p. [ii] list of works by the author; p. [iii] title; p. [iv] Copyright, 1928, by Virginia Woolf | First Regular Edition | Typography by Frederic Warde | Composition by | Printing House of William Edwin Rudge, at foot: Printed in the United States of America | by the Quinn and Boden Company | Rahway, N.J.; p. [v] dedication; p. [vi] blank; pp. vii–ix Preface; p. [x] blank; p. [xi] Contents; p. [xii] blank; p. [xiii] list of illustrations; p. [xiv] blank; pp. [15–331 numbered 13–329] text; p. [332] blank; pp. [333–335 numbered 331–333] Index; p. [336] blank.

Dull blue cloth boards; lettered in gold on spine: [*ornament across head*] | Orlando | A Biography | Virginia | Woolf | [*ornament*] | Harcourt, Brace | & Company | [*ornament across foot*]; double rule in blind round upper cover, publisher's monogram within an ornamental design in blind on upper cover; top edges cinnamon, others partially trimmed; end-papers. Cinnamon dust-jacket printed in black and deeper cinnamon.

Published 18 October 1928; 6350 copies printed. $3.

A copy in rough blue cloth boards tinged with reddish-brown is in the collection of Mr George Spater; it is possibly a variant of the Harbrace Edition issued on 29 July 1937.

There were five re-impressions totalling 14,950 copies between November 1928 and February 1933. The seventh impression of 2500 copies was issued as the Harbrace Edition on 29 July 1937 at $1.49; it was bound in sky-blue cloth boards; lettered in gold on spine; top edges yellow, others untrimmed; end-papers; white dust-jacket tinted in blue and brown and printed in black. The eighth impression of 1500 copies was issued on 24 August 1948 at $3; it was bound in dark green cloth boards; lettered in gold on spine; edges trimmed; end-papers; pale grey dust-jacket printed in reddish-brown and green.

## *d. First English edition – photo-offset reprint* (UNIFORM EDITION). *1933*

ORLANDO | A BIOGRAPHY | VIRGINIA WOOLF | NEW EDITION | PUBLISHED BY LEONARD & VIRGINIA | WOOLF AT THE HOGARTH PRESS, | 52 TAVISTOCK SQUARE, LONDON, W.C. | 1933

Small crown 8vo. 298 pp. 7 × $4\frac{5}{8}$ in.

P. [1] half-title; p. [2] list of works in the Uniform Edition; p. [3] title; p. [4] publication note; p. [5] dedication; p. [6] blank; pp. 7–9 Preface; p. [10] blank; p. 11 Contents; p. [12] blank; pp. [13–293 numbered 15–295] text; p. [294] blank; pp. [295–297 numbered 297–299] Index; p. [297 numbered 299] at foot: printer's imprint; p. [298] blank.

Jade-green cloth boards; lettered in gold on spine; edges trimmed; end-papers. Pale peacock-blue dust-jacket printed in navy-blue.

Issued 5 October 1933; 4270 copies printed. 5s.

This reprint is incorrectly described as a 'New Edition' on the recto and verso of the title. There were further printings of 2000 copies in May 1942, 4000 in 1949 and 3000 in 1954.

## *e. Second English edition* (PENGUIN BOOKS). [*1942*]

ORLANDO | A BIOGRAPHY | BY | VIRGINIA WOOLF | [*publisher's device of a penguin*] | PENGUIN BOOKS | HARMONDSWORTH MIDDLESEX ENGLAND | 41 EAST 28TH STREET NEW YORK U.S.A.

Foolscap 8vo. 192 pp. $7\frac{1}{8}$ × $4\frac{1}{2}$ in.

P. [1] half-title; p. [2] portrait of the author with caption; p. [3] title; p. [4] publication note, dedication, printer's imprint; pp. 5–6 Preface; p. 7 Contents; p. [8] blank; pp. 9–189 text; p. [190] blank; pp. 191–192 Index.

Stiff white paper wrappers printed in orange and black; edges trimmed; stapled.

Published probably July 1942 in *Penguin Books* as Vol. 381; 75,000 copies printed. 9d.

Owing to wartime difficulties the date of publication is uncertain. It is given as April 1942 in the publication note on the verso of the title and the British Library copy is dated 17 July 1942. The publisher's think that the date was probably 21 July 1942.

*f. Second American edition* (PENGUIN BOOKS INC.). [*1946*]

ORLANDO | A BIOGRAPHY | BY VIRGINIA WOOLF | [*publisher's device of a penguin*] | PENGUIN BOOKS, INC · NEW YORK

Foolscap 8vo. [viii], 216 pp. $7\frac{1}{8} \times 4\frac{1}{4}$ in.

P. [i] note on the book; p. [ii] list of works by the author; p. [iii] title; p. [iv] copyright notice, publication note, dedication, publisher's name etc., printer's note; p. [v] Contents; p. [vi] blank; pp. [vii–viii] Preface; pp. 1–214 text; pp. 215–216 Index.

Glazed stiff coloured paper wrappers with illustrated upper cover; edges pink; end-papers.

Published 29 April 1946 in *Penguin Books* as Vol. 590; 203,175 copies printed. 25 cents.

*g. Third American edition* (SIGNET CLASSICS). [*1960*] *

VIRGINIA WOOLF | ORLANDO | A BIOGRAPHY | WITH AN AFTERWORD BY | ELIZABETH BOWEN | [*publisher's monogram*] A SIGNET CLASSIC | PUBLISHED BY | THE NEW AMERICAN LIBRARY

Small crown 8vo. 224 pp. 2 plates between pp. 112–113. $7\frac{1}{4} \times 4\frac{1}{4}$ in.

P. [1] note on the author; p. [2] blank; p. [3] title; p. [4] quotation, dedication, copyright note etc.; pp. [5–6] Preface; pp. 7–215 text; pp. 216–222 Afterword by Elizabeth Bowen; pp. [223–224] Index.

Stiff white paper wrappers printed in grey, pink, red, yellow, blue and black with illustrated upper cover; edges trimmed.

Published February 1960 in *Signet Classics* as Vol. CP 156; 61,903 copies printed. 60 cents.

There were further printings of 16,181 copies in March 1963 and 15,885 in March 1965.

*h. Third English edition* (PENGUIN BOOKS). [*1963*]

VIRGINIA WOOLF | [*swelled rule*] | ORLANDO | A BIOGRAPHY | PENGUIN BOOKS

Foolscap 8vo. 240 pp. $7\frac{1}{8} \times 4\frac{3}{8}$ in.

P. [1] half-title; p. [2] blank; p. [3] title; p. [4] publication note, printer's imprint; p. [5] dedication; p. [6] blank; pp. 7–[8] Preface; pp. 9–[232] text; pp. [233–234] Index; p. [235] publisher's advertisement; p. [236] blank; pp. [237–240] publisher's advertisements, integral.

Stiff white paper wrappers printed in orange and black; edges trimmed.

Published 28 March 1963 in *Penguin Books* as Vol. 381; number of copies printed not available. 3s. 6d.

*i. First English edition – photo-offset reprint* (QUEEN'S CLASSICS). [*1964*]

ORLANDO | BY | VIRGINIA WOOLF | [*series monogram*] | CHATTO AND WINDUS | LONDON

Crown 8vo. [vi], 11–300 pp. $7\frac{3}{8} \times 4\frac{7}{8}$ in.

P. [i] half-title; p. [ii] list of works in the series; p. [iii] title; p. [iv] publisher's note, publication note, printer's note; p. [v] dedication; p. [vi] blank; pp. 11–13 preface; p. [14] blank; pp. 15–295 text; p. [296] blank; pp. 297–299 index; p. [300] blank.

Sky-blue paper boards stamped in gilt and orange; edges trimmed; end-papers. No dust-jacket.

Issued 14 December 1964 as a *Queen's Classic*; 5000 copies printed. 7s.

*j. First American edition – photo-offset reprint* (HARVEST BOOKS). [*1973*]

ORLANDO | A BIOGRAPHY | BY | VIRGINIA WOOLF | A HARVEST BOOK | [*publisher's monogram within a rule*] | HARCOURT BRACE JOVANOVICH, INC. | NEW YORK

Large crown 8vo. [iv], 334 pp. $8 \times 5\frac{3}{8}$ in. 8 illus. front. i.e. p. [iv] and facing pp. 54, 114, 126, 158, 246, 262, 318.

P. [i] half-title; p. [ii] list of works by the author; p. [iii] blank; p. [iv] illus., i.e. front.; p. [1] title; p. [2] publication note, printer's note; p. [3] dedication; p. [4] blank; pp. [5–7 numbered vii–ix]

Preface; p. [8] blank; p. [9] Contents; p. [10] blank; p. [11] Illustrations; p. [12] blank; pp. 13–329 text; p. [330] blank; pp. 331–333 Index; p. [334] publisher's advertisement.

Stiff white pictorial paper wrappers printed in orange, black and red; edges trimmed.

Issued 24 October 1973 in *Harvest Books* as Vol. HB266; 6000 copies printed. $2.95.

There were further printings of 2000 copies in December 1973, 5000 each in August 1974 and April 1975, 10,000 in October 1975, and 15,237 in December 1976.

### *k. Fourth English edition* (PANTHER BOOKS). [*1977*]

VIRGINIA WOOLF | ORLANDO | A BIOGRAPHY | TRIAD | PANTHER

Foolscap 8vo. 208 pp. 7 × 4⅜ in.

P. [1] Biographical note on the author; p. [2] list of works by the author; p. [3] title; p. [4] publication note, copyright note, printer's imprint etc.; p. [5] dedication; p. [6] blank; pp. 7–8 Preface; pp. 9–205 text; pp. 206–208 Index.

Stiff white pictorial paper wrappers printed in black, red, brown and cream; edges trimmed.

Published 17 February 1977; 35,000 copies printed. 85p.

## A12 A ROOM OF ONE'S OWN 1929

### *a. First (limited) edition*

A ROOM OF | ONE'S OWN | [*rule*] | [*ornament*] | [*rule*] | VIRGINIA WOOLF | NEW YORK · THE FOUNTAIN PRESS | LONDON · THE HOGARTH PRESS | 1929

Small royal 8vo. [viii], 162 pp. 9⅝ × 5⅝ in.

Pp. [i–ii] blank; p. [iii] half-title, author's signature in purple ink; p. [iv] blank; p. [v] title; p. [vi] at head: Copyright, 1929, | By Harcourt, Brace and Company, at foot: Printed in U.S.A.; p. [vii] note on the origin of the essay; p. [viii] blank; p. [1] fly-title; p. [2] blank; pp. 3–159 text; p. [160] blank; p. [161] Of this book four hundred ninety-two copies, of | which four hundred fifty are for sale, have been | printed by Robert S. Josephy, in October, 1929. | Distributed in America by Random House, and | in Great Britain by Leonard and Virginia Woolf | at The Hogarth Press, London. Each copy signed | by the author. Numbers one to one hundred | inclusive are reserved for Great Britain. | This is number [*numbered in ink*]; p. [162] blank.

Maroon cloth boards; lettered in gold on spine: [*ornament*] | [*double rule*] | A | Room | of | One's | Own | [*rule*] | Virginia | Woolf | [*rule*]; top edges uncut, others partially trimmed; end-papers. No specimen of dust-jacket available.

Published 21 October 1929 in the U.S.A. and in the United Kingdom on 24 October 1929 simultaneously with the first English edition; 492 copies printed. £2. 2s.

### *b. First English edition. 1929*

A ROOM OF ONE'S OWN | VIRGINIA WOOLF | [*publisher's device of a wolf's head*] | PUBLISHED BY LEONARD AND VIRGINIA WOOLF AT THE | HOGARTH PRESS, 52 TAVISTOCK SQUARE, LONDON, W.C. | 1929

Small crown 8vo. 172 pp. $7 \times 4\frac{1}{2}$ in.

P. [1] half-title; p. [2] list of works by the author; p. [3] title; p. [4] at foot; Printed in Great Britain by R. & R. Clark, Limited, Edinburgh.; pp. 5–172 text.

Cinnamon cloth boards; lettered in gold on spine: A | Room | of | One's | Own | Virginia | Woolf | The | Hogarth | Press; edges trimmed; end-papers. Pale pink dust-jacket printed in navy-blue, designed by Vanessa Bell.

Published 24 October 1929; 3040 copies printed. 5s.

There was a second impression of 3030 copies in November 1929, a third and fourth of 3030 and 3050 copies in December 1929, and a fifth of 2500 in March 1930. The sixth to twelfth printing was issued as the Uniform Edition. See A12*d*.

### *c. First American trade edition. [1929]* *

A ROOM | OF ONE'S OWN | [*rule*] | VIRGINIA WOOLF | [*publisher's monogram*] | HARCOURT, BRACE AND COMPANY | NEW YORK

Crown 8vo. [vi], 202 pp. $7\frac{1}{2} \times 5\frac{1}{8}$ in.

P. [i] half-title; p. [ii] list of works by the author; p. [iii] title; p. [iv] Copyright, 1929, by | Harcourt, Brace and Company, Inc. Printed in the United States of America | by Quinn & Boden Company, Inc., Rahway, N.J. Typography by Robert S. Josephy.; p. [v]

note on the work; p. [vi] blank; p. [1] fly-title; p. [2] blank; pp. [3]-199 text; pp. [200-202] blank.

Dark blue cloth boards; lettered in gold on spine: [*double rule*] | Virginia Woolf | [*rule*] | A Room | of | One's | Own | [*double rule*] | Harcourt, Brace | & Company; top edges yellow, fore edges untrimmed, bottom trimmed; end-papers. Slate dust-jacket printed in black and blue.

Published 24 October 1929; 4000 copies printed. $2.

There were thirteen re-impressions totalling 18,640 copies between November 1929 and February 1953.

### *d. First edition – sixth impression* (UNIFORM EDITION). *1931* [*i.e. 1930*]

A ROOM OF ONE'S OWN | VIRGINIA WOOLF | PUBLISHED BY LEONARD & VIRGINIA | WOOLF AT THE HOGARTH PRESS, | TAVISTOCK SQUARE, LONDON. 1931

Small crown 8vo. 172 pp. $7 \times 4\frac{1}{2}$ in.

P. [1] half-title; p. [2] list of works in the Uniform Edition; p. [3] title; p. [4] publication note, printer's imprint; pp. 5–172 text.

Jade-green cloth boards; lettered in gold on spine; edges trimmed; end-papers. Pale peacock-blue dust-jacket printed in navy-blue.

Issued 6 November 1930; 3268 copies printed. 5s.

This re-impression is incorrectly described as a 'New Edition' in the publication note on the verso of the title. There were further printings by photo-litho offset of 3250 copies in November 1931, 3375 in May 1935, 2530 in April 1942, 3000 in February 1946, 3000 in April 1949 and 3000 in January 1954. They were issued as the Uniform Edition.

### *e. Second English edition* (PENGUIN BOOKS). [*1945*]

VIRGINIA WOOLF | [*rule*] | A ROOM OF | ONE'S OWN | [*publisher's device of a penguin*] | PENGUIN BOOKS | HARMONDSWORTH MIDDLESEX ENGLAND | 245 FIFTH AVENUE NEW YORK U.S.A.

Foolscap 8vo. 96 pp. $7\frac{1}{8} \times 4\frac{3}{8}$ in.

P. [1] half-title; p. [2] blank; p. [3] title; p. [4] publication note, printer's imprint; pp. 5–94 text; pp. [95–96] publisher's advertisements, integral.

Stiff white paper wrappers printed in mauve and black; edges trimmed.

Published *c.* 13 July 1945 in *Penguin Books* as Vol. 481; 100,000 copies printed. 9d.

### *f. Third English edition* (PENGUIN BOOKS). [*1963*]

VIRGINIA WOOLF | A ROOM OF ONE'S OWN | [*swelled rule*] | PENGUIN BOOKS

Foolscap 8vo. 112 pp. $7\frac{1}{4} \times 4\frac{1}{2}$ in.

P. [1] half-title; p. [2] blank; p. [3] title; p. [4] publication note, printer's imprint etc.; pp. 5–[112] text.

Stiff white paper wrappers printed in black, silver grey and orange; edges trimmed.

Published 28 March 1963 in *Penguin Modern Classics* as Vol. 481; number of copies printed not available. 3s. 6d.

### *g. Second American edition* (HARBINGER BOOK). [*1963*]

VIRGINIA WOOLF | [*rule*] | A ROOM | OF ONE'S OWN | A HARBINGER BOOK [*publisher's monogram*] | HARCOURT, BRACE & WORLD, INC. | [*rule*] NEW YORK AND BURLINGAME

Large crown 8vo. [vi], 122 pp. $8\frac{1}{8} \times 5\frac{1}{2}$ in.

P. [i] half-title; p. [ii] list of works by the author; p. [iii] title; p. [iv] copyright note, etc., printer's note; p. [v] note on the work; p. [vi] blank; p. [1] fly-title; p. [2] blank; pp. 3–41 text; p. [42] blank; pp. 43–59 text; p. [60] blank; pp. 61–81 text; p. [82] blank; pp. 83–[118] text; pp. [119–122] blank, integral.

Stiff white paper wrappers printed in turquoise, black and blue with illustrated upper cover; edges trimmed.

Published 1 May 1963 in *Harbinger Books* as Vol. 020; 7744 copies printed. $1.65.

### *h. Fourth English edition* (PANTHER BOOKS). [*1977*]

VIRGINIA WOOLF | A ROOM OF ONE'S OWN | TRIAD | PANTHER

Foolscap 8vo. 112 pp. $7 \times 4\frac{3}{8}$ in.

P. [1] Biographical note on the author; p. [2] list of works by the author; p. [3] title; p. [4] publication note, copyright note, printer's imprint etc.; pp. 5–[108] text; p. [109] blank; pp. [110–112] publisher's advertisements.

Stiff white pictorial paper wrappers printed in black, pale yellow and brown; edges trimmed.

Published 14 April 1977; 25,000 copies printed. 60p.

## A13 STREET HAUNTING 1930

*First edition*

STREET HAUNTING | BY VIRGINIA WOOLF | [*publisher's device of a bird in flight*] | THE WESTGATE PRESS | SAN FRANCISCO [*ornament*] 1930

Crown 8vo. [xii], 44 pp. $7\frac{7}{8} \times 5$ in.

Pp. [i–ii] form paste down end-paper; pp. [iii–viii] blank; p. [ix] [*in blue: initial occupying three lines*] T [*in black:*] HIS EDITION, limited | to five hundred copies, has | been printed by The Grab- | horn Press of San Francisco in May, | 1930. The type used is Weiss Anti- | qua, hand-set. Each copy is signed | by the author, | [*author's signature in purple ink*] | Copy No. [*numbered in purple ink*]; p. [x] blank; p. [xi] title; p. [xii] at foot: Copyright 1930 by Virginia Woolf | Printed in the United States of America; pp. [1]–[36] text; pp. [37–42] blank; pp. [43–44] form paste down end-paper.

Grey paper boards patterned in gold and blue, blue leather spine; lettered in gold up the spine: [*ornament*] Street Haunting [*ornament*]; raised bands at head and foot of spine; top and fore edges partially trimmed, bottom trimmed; no end-papers. Grey slip-in case.

Published May 1930; 500 copies printed. $7.50. Distributed in the United Kingdom by Simpkin Marshall in February 1931. £1. 11s. 6d.

There is at least one variant of the binding in sage-green paper boards patterned in gold and darker green with emerald-green leather spine and a green slip-in case. Mr David Magee, joint compiler of a *Bibliography of the Grabhorn Press, 1914–1940*, San Francisco (1940) wrote 'I have seen copies with green leather backstrip, but the majority of the edition was bound in blue . . . It has been my experience—and I've had many copies of this book—that the ratio is 10–1 in favor of blue.' Mr Magee had seen one copy with a purple leather spine; it is probably a trial binding. Mr Magee also noted some variation in the number of blank preliminary and final pages. Mr George Spater, however, believes that the majority of copies were bound with a green leather spine; of 20 copies examined personally, he has only seen one blue leather spine.

The essay was not published separately in the United Kingdom. It was reprinted in *The Death of the Moth and Other Essays* and in *Collected Essays*, Vol. 4. It was first published in the *Yale Review*, October 1927. See A27, 39, C291.

## A14 ON BEING ILL 1930

*First separate edition*

ON BEING ILL | BY VIRGINIA WOOLF | PRINTED AND PUBLISHED BY LEONARD & | VIRGINIA WOOLF AT THE HOGARTH PRESS | 1930

Large crown 8vo. 36 pp. $8 \times 5\frac{1}{8}$ in.

Pp. [1–2] blank; p. [3] half-title; p. [4] blank; p. [5] This edition is limited to 250 numbered copies, | signed by the author, for sale. The type has been | set by the author. This is No. [*numbered in purple ink*] | [*author's signature in purple ink*]; p. [6] blank; p. [7] title; p. [8] blank; pp. [9]–34 text; p. [35] illustration of two birds and flowers in a basket; p. [36] blank.

Pale blue-green cloth boards, vellum spine; lettered in gold up the spine: On Being Ill—Virginia Woolf; top edges uncut, other untrimmed; marbled end-papers, mainly in shades of grey. White pictorial dust-jacket printed in grey, black and yellow.

Published early November 1930; 250 copies printed. £1. 1s.

There is a preliminary state in which p. [5] is printed: 'This edition is limited to ~~125~~ 250 numbered copies, . . .' and in place of the number in purple ink 'out of series' is recorded in purple ink by Leonard Woolf. Leonard Woolf stated that this limited edition was heavily over-subscribed, and that probably after printing the free copies, it was decided to double the number of copies printed. The copies, already printed, were altered as above, and the printed number 125 then changed to 250. The preliminary state probably comprises 25 copies which were distributed free, probably without a dust-jacket. J. Howard Woolmer refers to copy No. 250 which he has seen and notes in his *A Checklist of the Hogarth Press 1917–1938*, London, The Hogarth Press, 1976, Item 245; it carries the altered limitation and has a dust-jacket. It is possible, therefore, that the limitation of more than 25 copies was altered as above.

The essay was not published separately in the United States. It was first published in the *New Criterion*, January 1926, reprinted in *Forum*, April 1926, under the title of 'Illness: An Unexplored Mine', reprinted in *The Moment and other Essays* as 'On Being Ill' and in *Collected Essays*, Vol. 4. See A29, 39, C270. In this limited edition, in *The Moment and Other Essays* and in *Collected Essays* the text is slightly revised.

## A15 BEAU BRUMMELL 1930

*a. First separate edition*

BEAU BRUMMELL | VIRGINIA WOOLF | [*rule*] | 1930 | RIMINGTON & HOOPER | NEW YORK

Royal 4to. [x], 18 pp. $12\frac{5}{8} \times 9\frac{1}{4}$ in.

Pp. [i–iv] blank; p. [v] half-title; p. [vi] blank, [*signed by the author in purple ink*]; p. [vii] title; p. [viii] Copyright, 1930 | by Rimington & Hooper, at foot: Manufactured in the | United States of America; p. [ix] illustration; p. [x] blank; pp. [1]-8 text; pp. [9-10] blank; p. [11] illustration; p. [12] blank; p. [13] [*device of an archer kneeling in red*] | An edition of 550 copies | signed by the author and published by | Rimington & Hooper | at 21 East 54th Street | New York | of which edition 500 copies are for sale: | 250 copies for distribution in England by | Douglas Cleverdon | at 18 Charlotte Street | Bristol | Designed and embellished by | W. A. Dwiggins | Printed and bound by | The Printing House of | William Edwin Rudge | N° [*numbered in red ink*]; pp. [14–18] blank.

Putty coloured paper boards, red cloth spine; lettered in gold up the spine: [*ornament*] Beau Brummell Virginia Woolf; pale pink paper label on upper cover with illustration in white; top edges gilt, others partially trimmed; buff end-papers. Green mottled slip-in case.

Published 22 November 1930; 550 copies printed. $10. Distributed in the United Kingdom December 1930. £2. 2s.

The essay was first published in the *Nation & Athenaeum*, 28 September 1929. It was reprinted in the *New York Herald Tribune*, 29 September 1929, in *The Common Reader: Second Series* and in *Collected Essays*, Vol. 3. See A18, 39, C315. Another essay of the same title was published in the *Listener*, 27 November 1929. See C321.

*b. First edition – photo-offset reprint.* [*1977*] *

BEAU BRUMMELL | VIRGINIA WOOLF | [*rule*] | 1930 | RIMINGTON & HOOPER | NEW YORK

[x], 18 pp.

Issued 8 July 1977; 150 copies printed. $12.50.

Issued by Folcroft Library Editions, Folcroft, Pennsylvania.

## A16 THE WAVES 1931

*a. First Edition*

THE WAVES | VIRGINIA WOOLF | [*publisher's device of a wolf's head*] | PUBLISHED BY LEONARD AND VIRGINIA WOOLF AT | THE HOGARTH PRESS, TAVISTOCK SQUARE, LONDON | 1931

Crown 8vo. 328 pp. $7\frac{1}{4} \times 4\frac{7}{8}$ in.

P. [1] half-title; p. [2] list of works by the author; p. [3] title; p. [4] at head: First published in 1931, at centre: Copyright, at foot: Printed in Great Britain by R. & R. Clark, Limited, Edinburgh.; pp. 5–[325] text; pp. [326–328] blank.

Purple cloth boards; lettered in gold on spine: The Waves | [*ornament*] | Virginia Woolf | The | Hogarth Press; edges trimmed; end-papers. Cream dust-jacket printed in lime-green and brown, designed by Vanessa Bell.

Published 8 October 1931; 7113 copies printed. 7s. 6d.

There was a second impression of 4940 copies in October 1931. The third impression was issued as the Uniform Edition. See A16*c*.

*The Dictionary of National Biography: The Concise Dictionary*, Part II, 1901–1950, Oxford University Press, 1961, p. 478, records that Virginia Woolf's works include *The Weaver* (1931); *The Waves* is intended.

### *b. First American edition. [1931]*

[*within a compartment:*] VIRGINIA WOOLF | THE | WAVES | [*publisher's monogram*] | HARCOURT, BRACE AND COMPANY | NEW YORK

Crown 8vo. [ii], 302 pp. $7\frac{3}{8} \times 5$ in.

Pp. [i–ii] blank; p. [1] half-title; p. [2] list of works by the author; p. [3] title; p. [4] Copyright, 1931, by | Harcourt, Brace and Company, Inc., reservation rights, first edition, at foot: Typography by Robert S. Josephy | Printed in the United States of America | by Quinn & Boden Company, Inc., Rahway, N.J.; p. [5] fly-title; p. [6] blank; pp. 7–297 text; pp. [298–302] blank.

Dull blue cloth boards; lettered in gold on spine: [*within a compartment, within a rule:*] Virginia | Woolf | [*double rule*] | The | Waves, at foot: Harcourt, Brace | & Company; edges trimmed, top mauve; end-papers. Pale buff dust-jacket printed in lime-green and brown, designed by Vanessa Bell.

Published 22 October 1931; 10,000 copies printed. $2.50.

There was a second impression of 2000 copies in November 1931. The third impression of 1500 copies was issued on 24 August 1948 at $3; it was bound in dark green cloth boards; lettered in gold on spine; edges trimmed; end-papers; pale grey dust-jacket printed in reddish-brown and green, designed by Vanessa Bell. There was a fourth impression of 1000 copies in September 1952 and a fifth of 1500 in February 1956.

*c. First English edition – third impression* (UNIFORM EDITION). *1933*

THE WAVES | VIRGINIA WOOLF | PUBLISHED BY LEONARD & VIRGINIA | WOOLF AT THE HOGARTH PRESS, | TAVISTOCK SQUARE, LONDON. 1933

Small crown 8vo. 328 pp. 7 × $4\frac{1}{2}$ in.

P. [1] half-title; p. [2] list of works in the Uniform Edition; p. [3] title; p. [4] publication note, printer's imprint; pp. 5–[325] text; pp. [326–328] blank.

Jade-green cloth boards; lettered in gold on spine; edges trimmed; end-papers. Pale peacock-blue dust-jacket printed in navy-blue.

Issued 5 October 1933; 4130 copies printed. 5s.

This re-impression is incorrectly described as a 'New Edition' in the publication note on the verso of the title.

*d. Second English edition* (UNIFORM EDITION). *1943*

THE WAVES | VIRGINIA WOOLF | NEW EDITION | THE HOGARTH PRESS | 37 MECKLENBURGH SQUARE | LONDON, W.C.1 | 1943

Small crown 8vo. 212 pp. 7 × $4\frac{1}{2}$ in.

P. [1] half-title; p. [2] list of works by the author; p. [3] title; p. [4] publication note, war-time economy note, at foot: Made and Printed in Great Britain by The | Garden City Press Ltd., Letchworth, Herts; pp. [5]–211 text; p. [212] blank.

Pale jade-green cloth boards; lettered in gold on spine; edges trimmed; end-papers. Pale green dust-jacket printed in green.

Published probably June 1943; 3000 copies printed. 7s. 6d.

There were further printings by photo-litho offset of 3000 copies in 1950, 2550 in 1953, and 5000 in 1955.

*e. Third English edition* (PENGUIN BOOKS). [*1951*]

[*within a border, within a double rule:*] THE | WAVES | [*ornament*] | VIRGINIA WOOLF | PENGUIN BOOKS | HARMONDSWORTH | MIDDLESEX

Foolscap 8vo. 256 pp. $7\frac{1}{8}$ × $4\frac{3}{8}$ in.

P. [1] half-title; p. [2] blank; p. [3] title; p. [4] publication note, at foot: printer's imprint; pp. 5–[256] text.

Stiff white paper wrappers printed in orange and black; edges trimmed.

Published March 1951 in *Penguin Books* as Vol. 808; 40,000 copies printed. 1s. 6d. The further printing of September 1964 was issued as *Penguin Modern Classics.*

## *f. Second American edition* (HARVEST BOOKS). [*1960*] see A6*e*

## *g. First Canadian edition – manuscript.* [*1976*]

[*within a double oval, thick, thin,* $3\frac{1}{8} \times 4\frac{1}{2}$ *in. : in script:*] VIRGINIA WOOLF | [*looped curving line*] THE WAVES [*looped curving line*] | THE TWO HOLOGRAPH DRAFTS | TRANSCRIBED AND EDITED | BY J. W. GRAHAM | [*below oval:*] UNIVERSITY OF TORONTO PRESS | IN ASSOCIATION WITH | THE UNIVERSITY OF WESTERN ONTARIO

Royal 8vo. [896]: 62 [*i.e.* 60], [824], [63 *i.e.* 61]-[74 *i.e.* 72] pp. 4 facsimiles. $9\frac{3}{4} \times 6\frac{5}{8}$ in.

P. [1] half-title; p. [2] blank; p. [3] title; p. [4] towards head: The two holograph drafts of *The Waves* and | extracts from the Monk's House Papers | © Quentin Bell and Angelica Garnett 1976 | Introduction, Table of the text and drafts, | notes, and appendices B, C, and D | © University of Toronto Press 1976 | Toronto and Buffalo | Printed in USA, towards foot: [*long rule*] | Library of Congress [*cataloguing data in eight lines, including:*] ISBN 0-8020-1628-6 | [*long rule*]; p. [5] dedication: [*in script:*] For Leonard Woolf; p. [6] blank; p. [7] Contents; p. [8] Acknowledgments; p. [9] fly-title; p. [10] blank; pp. 13-48 [*i.e.* 11-46] Introduction; pp. [49]-52 [*i.e.* 47-50] Table of the text and drafts; p. [51] blank; pp. 54-55 [*i.e.* 52-53] Signs and abbreviations; p. [54] blank; p. [55] section-title: [*within a double oval, thick, thin: in script:*] The Waves | draft one; p. [56] blank; p. [57] holograph facsimile; p. [58] blank; p. [59] holograph facsimile; p. [60] blank; pp. [1-434] Annotated transcription numbered: 1, 1 verso, 2-14, 14 verso, 15-20, 20 verso, 21, 21 verso, 22-58, 58 verso, 59-67, 67 verso, 68-87, 87 verso, 88-90, 90 verso, 91-105, 105 verso, 106-111, 111 verso, 112, 112 verso, 113, 113 verso, 114-115, 115 verso, 116-117, 117 verso, 118-119, 119 verso, 120-127, 127 verso, 128-187, 187 verso, 188-192, 192 verso, 193-198, 198 verso, 199-203, 203 verso, 204-206, 206 verso, 207-209, 209 verso, 210-212, 212 verso, 213-215, 215 verso, 216-221, 221 verso, 222-231, 231 verso, 232-242, 242 verso, 243–250, 250 verso, 251–278, 278 verso, 279–312, 312 verso, 313–320, 320 verso, 321–325, 325 verso, 326–363, 363 verso, 364–380, 380 verso, 381–398, 398 verso, 399; p. [400 *i.e.* 435] section-title: [*within a double oval, thick, thin: in script:*] The Waves | draft two; p. [436] blank; p. [437] holograph facsimile; p. [438] blank; p. [439] holograph facsimile; p. [440] blank; pp. [441–823] Annotated transcription, numbered: 400–476, 476 verso, 477–549, 549 verso, 550, 550 verso, 551–582, 582 verso, 583–585, 585 verso, 586–599, 599 verso, 600–608, 608 verso, 609–645, 645 verso, 646, 646 verso, 647–649, 649 verso, 650–671, 671 verso, 672–745, 745 verso, 746–752, 752 verso, 753–769; p. [770 *i.e.* 824] blank; Appendices: pp. [63 *i.e.* 61]–64 [*i.e.* 62] A: Extracts from the Monk's House Papers; pp. 65–66 [*i.e.* 63–64] B: Description of the manuscript; pp. 67–68 [*i.e.* 65–66] C: Index of speakers; pp. 69–70 [*i.e.* 67–68] D: A Collation of dates; pp. 71–72 [*i.e.* 69–70] Collation: Draft II; p. [71] blank; p. [72] This book | was designed by | Laurie Lewis | under the direction of | Allan Fleming | The text was set in | IBM Press Roman by | Becky Painter | and the book was manufactured by | Edward Brothers | for | University of | Toronto | Press | 1976.

Grey buckram boards with an overall pattern in darker shades of grey; lettered in black on spine: [*in script:*] Virginia Woolf | [*ornament*] | The Waves | [*ornament*] | transcribed and | edited by | J. W. Graham | University of | Toronto Press; and in black on upper cover: [*within a double oval, thick, thin,* $3\frac{1}{8} \times 4\frac{1}{2}$ *in.: in script as title-page*]; edges trimmed; orange end-papers.

Published 19 October 1976; 1250 copies printed. $29.50.

Five hundred copies in sheets were sent to the Hogarth Press. See A16*h*.

### *h. First Canadian edition – manuscript – English issue. 1976*

[*within a double oval, thick, thin,* $3\frac{1}{8} \times 4\frac{1}{2}$ *in.: in script:*] [*as g. above*] | [*below oval:*] 1976 | THE HOGARTH PRESS | LONDON

Royal 8vo. [896] pp. 4 facsimiles. $9\frac{3}{4} \times 6\frac{5}{8}$ in.

P. [1] half-title; p. [2] blank; p. [3] title; p. [4] towards head: Published by | The Hogarth Press Ltd | 42 William IV Street | London WC2N 4DG | [*reservation rights in six lines*] | ISBN 0 7012 0406 0 | The two holograph drafts of *The Waves* and | extracts from the Monk's House Papers | © Quentin Bell and Angelica Garnett 1976 | Introduction, Table of the texts and drafts, | notes, and appendices B, C, and D | © University of Toronto Press 1976 | Printed in the United States of America; pp. [5–60, 1–824; 61–71 as *g.* above];

p. [72] at head: This book | was designed by | Laurie Lewis | under the direction of | Allan Fleming.

Grey buckram boards as *g.* above; lettered in black on spine: [*as g. above, lines* 1–7, *then:*] The Hogarth Press; and in black on upper cover: [*as g. above*]; edges trimmed; orange end-papers.

Issued 2 December 1976; 500 copies bound. £20. The sheets with a cancel title were supplied by the University of Toronto Press.

## *i. Fourth English edition* (PANTHER BOOKS). [*1977*]

VIRGINIA WOOLF | THE WAVES | TRIAD PANTHER | GRANADA PUBLISHING | LONDON TORONTO SYD-NEY NEW YORK

Foolscap 8vo. 200 pp. 7 × $4\frac{3}{8}$ in.

P. [1] Biographical note on the author; p. [2] list of works by the author; p. [3] title; p. [4] publication note, copyright note, printer's imprint, etc.; pp. 5–200 text.

Stiff white pictorial paper wrappers printed in yellow, brown, green, blue and black; edges trimmed.

Published 13 October 1977; 25,000 copies printed. 80p.

## *j. First American edition—photo-offset reprint* (HARVEST /HBJ BOOKS). [*1978*]

[*within a compartment:*] VIRGINIA WOOLF | [*following two lines in open capitals:*] THE | WAVES | [*publisher's monogram within a rule*] | A HARVEST/HBJ BOOK | HARCOURT BRACE JOVANOVICH | NEW YORK AND LONDON

Large crown 8vo. 304 pp. 8 × $5\frac{1}{4}$ in.

P. [1] half-title; p. [2] list of works by the author; p. [3] title; p. [4] copyright note, reservation rights, printer's note, Library of Congress cataloguing data, etc.; p. [5] fly-title; p. [6] blank; pp. 7–297 text; p. [298] blank; p. [299] list of works by the author; pp. [300–304] blank.

Stiff white pictorial paper wrappers printed in blue, pink and yellow; edges trimmed.

Issued 5 June 1978; 10,187 copies printed. $3.95.

## A17 A LETTER TO A YOUNG POET 1932

*a. First separate edition*

A LETTER TO | A YOUNG POET | VIRGINIA WOOLF | [*publisher's device of a wolf's head after a design by E. McKnight Kauffer*] | PUBLISHED BY LEONARD & VIRGINIA WOOLF AT THE | HOGARTH PRESS, 52 TAVISTOCK SQUARE, LONDON, W.C.1 | 1932

Small crown 8vo. [ii], 30 pp. $7\frac{1}{4} \times 4\frac{7}{8}$ in.

P. [i–ii] blank; p. [1] half-title; p. [2] list of works in the Hogarth Letters series; p. [3] title; p. [4] at head: First Published 1932, at foot: Made and Printed in Great Britain by | The Garden City Press Ltd., Letchworth, Herts.; pp. 5–28 text; pp. [29–30] blank.

Stiff cream paper wrappers; printed in black on upper cover: A Letter to a | Young Poet | by | Virginia Woolf, at foot: The Hogarth Letters No. 8; illustration designed by John Banting in black and grass-green of writing pad with a hand holding a pencil on upper cover; edges trimmed; sewn.

Published 1 July 1932 in *Hogarth Letters* as Vol. 8; 6000 copies printed. 1s.

Five hundred copies of the above were bound up in the collection entitled *The Hogarth Letters* with ten other volumes in the series. They were issued in 1933 in buff paper boards; brown cloth spine; lettered in black on spine; illustrated upper cover printed in black and brown.

The essay was first published in the *Yale Review*, June 1932 and reprinted in *The Death of the Moth and Other Essays* and in *Collected Essays*, Vol. 2. See A27, 37, C334.

The letter was addressed to John Lehmann.

*b. First separate edition – American photo-offset reprint. [1975]* *

A LETTER TO | A YOUNG POET | VIRGINIA WOOLF | [*publisher's device*] | PUBLISHED BY LEONARD & VIRGINIA WOOLF AT THE | HOGARTH PRESS, 52 TAVISTOCK SQUARE, LONDON, W.C.1 | 1932

[ii], 30 pp.

Issued 19 December 1975; 150 copies printed. $5.

Issued by Folcroft Library Editions, Folcroft, Pennsylvania.

## A18 THE COMMON READER: SECOND SERIES 1932

### *a. First edition*

THE | COMMON READER | SECOND SERIES | VIRGINIA WOOLF | [*quotation from Johnson's 'Life of Gray' in* The Lives of the Poets *within double quotes*] | [*publisher's device of a wolf's head*] | PUBLISHED BY LEONARD & VIRGINIA WOOLF | AT THE HOGARTH PRESS, 52 TAVISTOCK SQUARE | LONDON, W.C. | 1932

Demy 8vo. 272 pp. $8\frac{1}{2} \times 5\frac{5}{8}$ in.

P. [1] half-title; p. [2] list of works by the author; p. [3] title; p. [4] at foot: Printed in Great Britain by R. & R. Clark, Limited, Edinburgh.; p. 5 acknowledgments; p. [6] blank; pp. 7-8 Contents; pp. 9-270 text; pp. [271-272] blank.

Bright jade-green cloth boards; lettered in gold on spine: The | Common | Reader | Second | Series | Virginia | Woolf | The Hogarth | Press; edges trimmed; end-papers. White dust-jacket printed in vermilion and azure, designed by Vanessa Bell.

Published 13 October 1932; 3200 copies printed. 10s. 6d.

There was a second impression of 1515 copies in November 1932. The third to sixth printing was issued as the Uniform Edition. See A18*c*.

Contents: The Strange Elizabethans – Donne After Three Centuries – "The Countess of Pembroke's Arcadia" – "Robinson Crusoe" – Dorothy Osborne's "Letters" – Swift's "Journal to Stella" – The "Sentimental Journey" – Lord Chesterfield's Letters to His Son – Two Parsons, I. James Woodforde; II. [The Rev.] John Skinner – Dr Burney's Evening Party – Jack Mytton – De Quincey's Autobiography – Four Figures, I. Cowper and Lady Austen; II. Beau Brummell; III. Mary Wollstonecraft; IV. Dorothy Wordsworth – William Hazlitt – Geraldine and Jane – "Aurora Leigh" – The Niece of an Earl – George Gissing – The Novels of George Meredith – "I Am Christina Rossetti" – The Novels of Thomas Hardy – How Should One Read a Book?

### *b. First American edition. [1932]*

THE SECOND | COMMON READER | BY | VIRGINIA WOOLF | [*double rule*] | [*quotation in six lines*] | [*rule*] | HARCOURT, BRACE AND COMPANY | NEW YORK

Demy 8vo. viii, 296 pp. $8\frac{5}{8} \times 5\frac{7}{8}$ in.

P. [i] half-title; p. [ii] list of works by the author; p. [iii] title; p. [iv] Copyright, 1932, by | Harcourt, Brace and Company, Inc., reservation rights, first printing, at foot: Printed in the United States of America | by Quinn & Boden Company, Inc., Rahway, N.J. | Typography by Robert S. Josephy; p. [v] acknowledgments; p. [vi] blank; pp. vii–viii Contents; p. [1] fly-title; p. [2] blank; pp. 3–295 text; p. [296] blank.

Dark blue cloth boards; lettered in gold on spine: [*double rule across head*] | The | Second | Common | Reader | [*ornament*] | Virginia | Woolf | Harcourt, Brace | and Company | [*rule across foot*]; double rule in blind round upper cover, publisher's monogram within a rule in blind on upper cover; top edges trimmed, others partially trimmed, some fore edges uncut; end-papers. Cream dust-jacket printed in crimson and bright blue, designed by Vanessa Bell.

Published 27 October 1932; 2000 copies printed. $2.50.

There were second and third impressions of 1500 copies each in November and December 1932. The fourth impression of 2000 copies was issued as the Harbrace Edition on 2 February 1939 at $1.49; it was bound in azure-blue cloth boards; lettered in gold on spine; edges trimmed; end-papers; white dust-jacket printed in blue, green and black. See also A18*e*.

### *c. First edition – photo-offset reprint* (UNIFORM EDITION). *1935*

THE | COMMON READER | SECOND SERIES | VIRGINIA WOOLF | [*quotation in six lines within double quotes*] | NEW EDITION | PUBLISHED BY LEONARD & VIRGINIA | WOOLF AT THE HOGARTH PRESS, | 52 TAVISTOCK SQUARE, LONDON, W.C. | 1935

Small crown 8vo. 272 pp. $7\frac{1}{8} \times 4\frac{1}{2}$ in.

P. [1] half-title; p. [2] list of works in the Uniform Edition; p. [3] title; p. [4] publication note, printer's imprint; p. 5 acknowledgments; p. [6] blank; pp. 7–8 Contents; pp. 9–270 text; pp. [271–272] blank.

Jade-green cloth boards; lettered in gold on spine; edges trimmed; end-papers. Pale peacock-blue dust-jacket printed in navy-blue.

Issued 25 October 1935; 5124 copies printed. 5s.

This reprint is incorrectly described as a 'New Edition' on the recto and verso of the title.

There were further printings of 3000 copies in May 1945, 3750 in March 1948, and 3000 in December 1952.

*d. Second English edition* (PENGUIN BOOKS). [*1944*]

PELICAN BOOKS | THE SECOND | COMMON READER | BY | VIRGINIA WOOLF | [*quotation in six lines*] | [*publisher's device of a pelican*] | PUBLISHED BY | PENGUIN BOOKS LIMITED | HARMONDSWORTH MIDDLESEX ENGLAND | 245 FIFTH AVENUE NEW YORK U.S.A.

Foolscap 8vo. 208 pp. front. (port). 7 × $4\frac{3}{8}$ in.

P. [1] half-title; p. [2] portrait of the author, with caption; p. [3] title; p. [4] publication note, printer's imprint; p. [5] Contents; p. [6] acknowledgments; pp. [7]-206 text; pp. [207-208] advertisements, integral.

Stiff white paper wrappers printed in blue and black; edges trimmed.

Published July 1944 in *Pelican Books* as Vol. A132; 50,000 copies printed. 9d.

*e. First American edition. First Series – seventh impression. Second Series – fifth impression.* [*1948*]

VIRGINIA WOOLF | [*rule*] | THE | COMMON READER | FIRST AND SECOND SERIES | COMBINED IN ONE VOLUME | [*double rule*] | [*quotation in six lines*] | [*rule*] | HARCOURT, BRACE AND COMPANY | NEW YORK

Large crown 8vo. 338, 300 pp. 8 × $5\frac{3}{8}$ in.

Pp. [i–ii] blank; p. [iii] half-title; p. [iv] list of works by the author; p. [v] title; p. [vi] copyright notice, reservation rights, printer's note; pp. [vii–ix numbered v–vii] Contents; p. [x] blank; p. [xi] dedication; p. [xii] blank; p. [xiii] acknowledgments; p. [xiv] blank; p. [xv] fly-title; p. [xvi] blank; pp. [17–65 numbered 11–59] text; p. [66] blank; pp. [67–91 numbered 61–85] text; p. [92] blank; pp. [93–129 numbered 87–123] text; p. [130] blank; pp. [131–141 numbered 125–135] text; p. [142] blank; pp. [143–157 numbered 137–151] text; p. [158] blank; pp. [159–195 numbered 153–189] text; p. [196] blank; pp. [197–233 numbered 191–227] text; p. [234] blank; pp. [235–313 numbered 229–307] text; p. [314] blank; pp. [315–338 numbered 309–332] text; p. [i] divisional title: The Second | Common Reader; p. [ii] blank; p. [1] acknowledgments; p. [2] blank; pp. 3–295 text; pp. [296–300] blank.

Dark blue cloth boards; lettered in gold on spine: [*double rule across head:*] | The | Common | Reader | [*ornament*] | Virginia | Woolf | Harcourt, Brace | and Company | [*rule across foot*]; edges trimmed;

end-papers. Grey-blue dust-jacket printed in brown and pale navy-blue, with design as on dust-jacket to *The Common Reader First Series*. See A8*a*.

Issued 22 March 1948; 2500 copies printed. $4.

There were re-impressions of 2500 and 1000 copies in June 1948 and January 1954. See also A8*b*, A18*b*. An additional essay 'Lives of the Obscure, III, Miss Ormerod' pp. 175–189 is included in the *First Series*; it does not appear in the English editions of *The Common Reader First Series*. It was first published in the *Dial*, N.Y., December 1924. See C257.

*f. Second American edition* (HARVEST BOOKS). [*1956*]

VIRGINIA WOOLF | [*ornament*] | THE SECOND | COMMON READER | [*ornament*] | [*quotation in seven lines*] | A HARVEST BOOK | HARCOURT, BRACE AND COMPANY | NEW YORK

Foolscap 8vo. viii, 248 pp. $7\frac{1}{4} \times 4\frac{3}{8}$ in.

P. [i] half-title; p. [ii] note on the author; p. [iii] title; p. [iv] copyright notice, reservation rights, printer's note; p. [v] author's note; p. [vi] blank; pp. [vii]–viii Contents; p. [1] fly-title; p. [2] blank; pp. [3]–245 text; pp. [246–248] blank.

Stiff white paper wrappers printed in leaf-green, maroon and black; edges trimmed.

Published 14 September 1956 in *Harvest Books* as Vol. 24; 12,000 copies printed. $1.15.

## A19 FLUSH: A BIOGRAPHY 1933

*a. First edition*

FLUSH | A BIOGRAPHY | VIRGINIA WOOLF | [*publisher's device of a wolf's head*] | PUBLISHED BY LEONARD AND VIRGINIA WOOLF AT THE | HOGARTH PRESS, 52 TAVISTOCK SQUARE, LONDON, W.C. | 1933

Demy 8vo. 164 pp. front., 9 plates facing pp. 14, 20, 32, 48, 80, (and 4 line drawings by Vanessa Bell) 16, 28, 112, 145. $8\frac{1}{2} \times 5\frac{1}{2}$ in.

P. [i] half-title; p. [ii] list of works by the author; p. [iii] title; p. [iv] at head: First published, October 1933, at foot: Printed in Great Britain by R. & R. Clark, Limited, Edinburgh.; p. v Contents, list of illustrations; p. [vi] blank; pp. 7-150 text; p. 151 Authorities; pp. 152-163 Notes; p. [164] blank.

Pale buff cloth boards; lettered in gold on spine: Flush | A | Biography | Virginia | Woolf | The | Hogarth | Press; edges trimmed; end-papers. Cream dust-jacket printed in brown with illustration of dog.

Published 5 October 1933; 12,680 copies printed. 7s. 6d.

The dust-jacket records this as the 'Large Paper Edition'. There was a second impression of 3000 copies in October 1933. The third to fifth printing was issued as the Uniform Edition. See A19*c*.

## *b. First American edition. [1933]*

FLUSH | A BIOGRAPHY | BY | VIRGINIA WOOLF | [*double rule*] | [*publisher's monogram within a compartment*] | HARCOURT, BRACE AND COMPANY | NEW YORK

Large crown 8vo. [ii], 190 pp. front., 2 plates facing pp. 24, 128. $8 \times 5\frac{3}{8}$ in.

Pp. [i-ii] blank; p. [1] half-title; p. [2] list of works by the author; p. [3] title; p. [4] Copyright, 1933, by | Harcourt, Brace and Company, Inc. | Copyright, 1933, by | The Atlantic Monthly Company, reservation rights, first edition, at foot: Designed by Robert Josephy | Printed in the United States of America | by Quinn & Boden Company, Inc., Rahway, N.J.; p. [5] Contents; p. [6] blank; p. [7] list of illustrations; p. [8] blank; p. [9] fly-title; p. [10] blank; pp. 11-31 text; p. [32] blank; p. [33] fly-title; p. [34] blank; pp. 33-51 text; p. [52] blank; p. [53] fly-title; p. [54] blank; pp. 55-82 text; p. [83] fly-title; p. [84] blank; pp. 85-114 text; p. [115] fly-title; p. [116] blank; pp. 117-151 text; p. [152] blank; p. [153] fly-title; p. [154] blank; pp. 155-169 text; p. [170] blank; p. 171 Authorities; p. [172] blank; pp. 173-185 Notes; pp. [186-190] blank.

Pinkish-brown cloth boards; lettered in silver on spine: Flush | A | Biography | [*double rule*] | Virginia | Woolf | Harcourt, | Brace & Co.; edges trimmed; white end-papers with a brown line drawing by Vanessa Bell printed on each. White dust-jacket printed in chrome-yellow and black with illustration of dog.

Published 5 October 1933; 7500 copies printed. $2.

There were twelve re-impressions totalling 23,782 copies between October 1933 and January 1956.

The Book of the Month Club Inc., New York, distributed copies of the regular edition to their members as an alternative selection in October 1933. See also C338.

*c. First English edition – third impression* (UNIFORM EDITION). *1933*

FLUSH | A BIOGRAPHY | VIRGINIA WOOLF | [*publisher's device of a wolf's head*] | PUBLISHED BY LEONARD AND VIRGINIA WOOLF AT THE | HOGARTH PRESS, 52 TAVISTOCK SQUARE, LONDON, W.C. | 1933

Small crown 8vo. 164 pp. front., 2 plates facing pp. 16, 80. 7 × $4\frac{5}{8}$ in.

P. [i] half-title; p. [ii] list of works by the author; p. [iii] title; p. [iv] publication note, printer's imprint; p. v Contents, list of illustrations; p. [vi] blank; pp. 7–150 text; p. 7 errata slip tipped-in; p. 151 Authorities; pp. 152–163 Notes; p. [164] blank.

Jade-green cloth boards; lettered in gold on spine; edges trimmed; white end-papers with a brown line drawing by Vanessa Bell printed on each. Pale peacock-blue dust-jacket printed in navy-blue.

Issued 16 November 1933; 11,762 copies printed. 5s.

This re-impression is incorrectly described as a 'New Edition' in the publication note on the verso of the title. There were further printings by photo-litho offset of 3400 copies in January 1947 and 3000 in 1952. They were issued as the Uniform Edition. The errata were corrected in the 1947 printing.

*d. Second English edition.* [*1956*]

[*across two pages:*] KINGSLEY AMIS [*two illustrations*] | LUCKY JIM | VIRGINIA WOOLF FLUSH LOUISE DE VILMORIN MADAME DE | [*on a brown panel with illustration at each end:*] THE | RUSSELL READER | EDITED BY LEONARD RUSSELL AND PUBLISHED BY CASSELL [*end of panel*] | MARY NORTON THE BORROWERS ROY FULLER THE SECOND CURTAIN | [*two illustrations*] EVELYN WAUGH | SCOTT-KING'S | MODERN EUROPE

Small royal 8vo. 584 pp. $9\frac{1}{8}$ × 6 in.

P. [1] half-title; pp. [2–3] title; p. [4] publisher's note, publication note, reservation rights, printer's imprint; p. 5 Contents; pp. 6–8 Introduction; p. [9] fly-title: Flush | A Biography | [*double rule*] | Drawings by Leonard Rosoman | [*illustration*] | Virginia Woolf; pp. 10–11 Editor's note; p. [12] illustration; pp. 13–77 text of *Flush*; pp. 78–83 Author's notes; p. [84] blank; pp. [85]–584 text of other works including editor's notes, fly-titles and illustrations.

Red cloth boards; lettered on spine on a gold panel: [*ornament*] | The | Russell | Reader | [*ornament*], at foot in gold: Cassell; edges trimmed; end-papers. White dust-jacket printed in blue, black, yellow, dull red, brown and green.

Published 20 September 1956; 15,000 copies printed. £1. 5s.

## *e. Third English edition* (VENTURE LIBRARY). [*1960*]

FLUSH | A BIOGRAPHY | [*double rule*] | VIRGINIA WOOLF | WITH DRAWINGS BY | VANESSA BELL | LONDON | METHUEN & CO LTD | 36 ESSEX STREET · WC2

Small crown 8vo. 136 pp. front., 4 illus. $6\frac{7}{8} \times 4\frac{3}{8}$ in.

P. [1] note on the book; p. [2] frontispiece; p. [3] title; p. [4] publication note, printer's imprint, catalogue number; p. [5] Contents; p. [6] illustrations; pp. 7–114 text; pp. 115–123 Notes; p. 124 Authorities; pp. 125–128 To Flush, my Dog, by Elizabeth Barrett Browning; pp. 129–136 Elizabeth Barrett Browning: A Note on her Life, by Caroline Scott.

White paper covered boards printed in pale brown, deep red and black; edges trimmed; end-papers. No dust-jacket.

Published 14 January 1960 in the *Venture Library*; 7500 copies printed. 5s.

## *f. Second American edition.* [*1966*]

VIRGINIA WOOLF | FLUSH | A BIOGRAPHY | [*ornaments*] | [*publisher's monogram*] | HARBRACE PAPERBACK LIBRARY | HARCOURT, BRACE & WORLD, INC. | NEW YORK

Foolscap 8vo. [vi], 122 pp. $7\frac{1}{8} \times 4\frac{1}{8}$ in.

P. [i] half-title; p. [ii] list of works by the author; p. [iii] title; p. [iv] publication note, printer's note; p. [v] Contents; p. [vi] blank; p. [1] fly-title; p. [2] blank; pp. 3–108 text; p. 109 Authorities; p. [110] blank; pp. 111–120 Notes; pp. [121–122] blank.

Stiff white pictorial paper wrappers printed in powder-blue, black, brown, pink and bright blue; edges trimmed.

Published 28 September 1966 in *Harbrace Paperback Library* as Vol. HPL12; 35,880 copies printed. 45 cents.

*g. Fourth English edition* (PENGUIN BOOKS). [*1977*]

FLUSH | A BIOGRAPHY | VIRGINIA WOOLF | PENGUIN BOOKS

Foolscap 8vo. 112 pp. $7\frac{1}{8} \times 4\frac{3}{8}$ in.

P. [1] note on the author; p. [2] blank; p. [3] title; p. [4] publication note, copyright note, printer's note etc.; p. [5] Contents; p. [6] blank; pp. 7–[102] text; p. 103 Authorities; pp. 104–[111] Notes; p. [112] blank.

Stiff white pictorial paper wrappers printed in brown, greenish-yellow, black and orange; edges trimmed.

Published November 1977; 20,000 copies printed. 65p.

There was a further printing of 20,000 copies in February 1978.

## A20 WALTER SICKERT: A CONVERSATION 1934

*a. First separate edition*

WALTER SICKERT | A CONVERSATION | VIRGINIA WOOLF | [*publisher's device of a wolf's head*] | PUBLISHED BY LEONARD AND VIRGINIA WOOLF AT THE | HOGARTH PRESS, 52 TAVISTOCK SQUARE, LONDON, W.C.1 | 1934

Crown 8vo. 32 pp. $7\frac{1}{4} \times 4\frac{7}{8}$ in.

P. [1] half-title; p. [2] blank; p. [3] title; p. [4] at head: First published 1934, at foot: Made and printed in Great Britain by the | Garden City Press Ltd., Letchworth, Herts; pp. 5–28 text; pp. [29–32] blank.

Stiff pale duck-egg-blue paper wrappers; lettered in black on upper cover, at head: Walter Sickert: | a conversation. By | Virginia Woolf., at foot: the Hogarth Press one shilling & sixpence net; illustration of a dinner table on upper cover by Vanessa Bell; edges trimmed; sewn.

Published 25 October 1934; 3800 copies printed. 1s. 6d.

The essay was first published in the *Yale Review*, September 1934 as 'A Conversation About Art' and reprinted in *The Captain's Death Bed and Other Essays* and in *Collected Essays*, Vol. 2. See A30, 37, C344. In this separate edition, in *The Captain's Death Bed and Other Essays* and in *Collected Essays* the text is slightly revised.

*b. Second separate edition. 1960*

SICKERT | CENTENARY EXHIBITION | OF PICTURES FROM PRIVATE | COLLECTIONS | IN AID OF | THE

WORLD REFUGEE YEAR | ALL PROCEEDS FROM THIS EXHIBITION WILL BE DEVOTED TO THE CLEARANCE OF CAMP SANKT MARTIN | IN UPPER AUSTRIA | [*rule*] | ILLUSTRATED CATALOGUE PRICE FIVE SHILLINGS | [*rule*] | THOS. AGNEW & SONS, LTD. | 43 OLD BOND STREET | AND 3 ALBEMARLE STREET, LONDON, W.1 | MARCH 15–APRIL 14, 1960

Foolscap 4to. 64 pp. 12 plates between pp. 24-25 (2), 28-29 (2), 32-33 (4), 36 (2), 40 (2). 9 × 7 in.

P. [1] title; p. [2] blank; p. [3] acknowledgments; p. [4] blank; pp. 5-[18] Walter Sickert: A Conversation, by Virginia Woolf; pp. 19-64 catalogue.

Stiff white paper wrappers, printed in black and red; edges trimmed; stapled.

Published 14 March 1960; 3000 copies printed. 5s.

The text follows that of the first separate edition. See A20*a*.

*c. First separate edition – American photo-offset reprint.* [*1977*] *

WALTER SICKERT | A CONVERSATION | VIRGINIA WOOLF | [*publisher's device*] | PUBLISHED BY LEONARD AND VIRGINIA WOOLF AT THE | HOGARTH PRESS, 52 TAVISTOCK SQUARE, LONDON, W.C.1 | 1934

32 pp.

Issued 14 July 1977; 150 copies printed. $8.50.

Issued by Folcroft Library Editions, Folcroft, Pennsylvania.

## A21 THE ROGER FRY MEMORIAL EXHIBITION: AN ADDRESS 1935

*First edition*

[*title on upper cover:*] THE ROGER FRY | MEMORIAL EXHIBITION | AN ADDRESS GIVEN BY VIRGINIA | WOOLF AT THE OPENING OF THE | ROGER FRY MEMORIAL EXHIBI- | TION AT THE BRISTOL MUSEUM

| AND ART GALLERY ON FRIDAY, | JULY 12TH, 1935

Crown 8vo. 12 pp. 7⅜ × 5 in.

P. [1] title; p. [2] blank; pp. 3-11 text; p. [12] at foot: The Garden City Press Ltd., Letchworth, Herts—E. 1972.

White paper wrappers; edges trimmed; stapled.

Published 18 September 1935; 125 copies printed. The pamphlet was not for sale.

The pamphlet was not available at the time of the address.

The essay was not published separately in the United States. It was reprinted as 'Roger Fry' in *The Moment and Other Essays*, and in *Collected Essays*, Vol. 4. See A29, 39.

## A22 THE YEARS 1937

*a. First edition*

THE YEARS | VIRGINIA WOOLF | [*publisher's device of a wolf's head*] | PUBLISHED BY LEONARD AND VIRGINIA WOOLF AT | THE HOGARTH PRESS, TAVISTOCK SQUARE, LONDON | 1937

Crown 8vo. [iv], 472 pp. 7⅛ × 4¾ in.

P. [i] half-title; p. [ii] list of works by the author; p. [iii] title; p. [iv] at head: First published in 1937, at centre: Copyright, at foot: Made in Great Britain | Printed by R. & R. Clark, Ltd., Edinburgh; pp. 1-469 text; pp. [470-472] blank.

Pale jade-green cloth boards; lettered in gold on spine: The | Years | [*ornament*] | Virginia Woolf | The | Hogarth Press; edges trimmed; end-papers. Cream dust-jacket printed in black and brown, designed by Vanessa Bell.

Published 15 March 1937; 18,142 copies printed. 8s. 6d.

3400 copies were issued as the Uniform Edition. See A22*c*.

*b. First American edition. [1937]*

VIRGINIA WOOLF | THE YEARS | HARCOURT, BRACE AND COMPANY | NEW YORK

Large crown 8vo. [iv], 436 pp. 8 × 5½ in.

P. [i] half-title; p. [ii] list of works by the author; p. [iii] title; p. [iv] Copyright, 1937, by | Harcourt, Brace and Company, Inc., reservation rights, first American edition, at foot: Typography by Robert Josephy | Printed in the United States of America | by Quinn

& Boden Company, Inc., Rahway, N.J.; p. [1] fly-title; p. [2] blank; pp. 3–435 text; p. [436] blank.

Royal-blue cloth boards; lettered in gold on spine on a brown panel, $1\frac{7}{8} \times 1\frac{3}{8}$ in.: The | Years | Virginia | Woolf, at foot: Harcourt, Brace | and Company; top and bottom edges trimmed, top chocolate-brown, fore edges partially trimmed; end-papers. White dust-jacket printed in dark brown and royal-blue with coloured illustration.

Published 8 April 1937; 10,000 copies printed. $2.50.

There were twelve re-impressions totalling 37,900 copies between April and October 1937.

### *c. First edition – second issue* (UNIFORM EDITION). *1940*

THE YEARS | VIRGINIA WOOLF | PUBLISHED BY LEONARD & VIRGINIA | WOOLF AT THE HOGARTH PRESS, | MECKLENBURGH SQUARE, LONDON. | 1940

Crown 8vo. [iv], 472 pp. $7 \times 4\frac{1}{2}$ in.

P. [i] half-title; p. [ii] list of works in the Uniform Edition; p. [iii] title; p. [iv] publication note, printer's imprint; pp. 1–469 text; pp. [470–472] blank.

Jade-green cloth boards; lettered in gold on spine; edges trimmed; end-papers. Pale primrose-yellow dust-jacket printed in green.

Issued November 1940; 3400 copies bound. 5s.

This second issue of the first impression is incorrectly described as a 'New Edition' in the publication note on the verso of the title. A further 5000 copies were printed by photo-litho offset in 1951. They were issued as the Uniform Edition.

### *d. Second American edition (Armed Services edition). [1945]* *

THE YEARS | BY | VIRGINIA WOOLF | EDITIONS FOR THE ARMED SERVICES, INC. | A NON-PROFIT ORGANIZATION ESTABLISHED BY | THE COUNCIL ON BOOKS IN WARTIME, NEW YORK

Foolscap 8vo. 416 pp. $4\frac{1}{2} \times 6\frac{1}{2}$ in.

P. [1] note on publishing arrangement with Harcourt, Brace and Co., copyright notice, title; p. [2] Manufactured in the United States of America; pp. 3–[416] text.

Stiff white paper wrappers printed in blue, yellow, black and red; edges trimmed.

Published 1945 in *Armed Services Editions* as Vol. 772; 156,700 copies printed. 1 cent.

Each page is printed in two columns comprising two pages printed side by side. The edition was 'intended for exclusive distribution to members of the American Armed Forces'.

### *e. Second English edition* (PAN BOOKS). [*1948*]

THE YEARS | VIRGINIA WOOLF | A NOVEL | [*publisher's device of Pan*] | PAN BOOKS LTD : LONDON

Foolscap 8vo. 328 pp. $7\frac{1}{8} \times 4\frac{3}{8}$ in.

P. [1] half-title; p. [2] list of Pan Books; p. [3] title; p. [4] publication note; pp. 5–[328] text; p. [328] at foot: Made and printed in France. | 7341-4-48.—Imp. Crété, Corbeil.—C.O.L. 31-1631.

Stiff white paper wrappers printed in deep buff, black and blue with illustrated upper cover; edges trimmed.

Published 20 May 1948 in *Great Pan Double-Volumes* as Vol. 5; 40,000 copies printed. 2s. 6d.

### *f. Third English edition* (PENGUIN BOOKS). [*1968*]

VIRGINIA WOOLF | [*broken swelled rule*] | THE YEARS | [*publisher's device*] | PENGUIN BOOKS | IN ASSOCIATION WITH THE HOGARTH PRESS

Foolscap 8vo. 352 pp. $7 \times 4\frac{3}{8}$ in.

P. [1] half-title; p. [2] blank; p. [3] title; p. [4] publication note, printer's imprint; pp. 5–[349] text; p. [350] blank; pp. [351-352] publisher's advertisements.

Stiff white pictorial paper wrappers printed in brown, pink, grey and black; edges trimmed.

Published July 1968 in *Penguin Modern Classics*; 25,000 copies printed. 7s. 6d.

There were further printings of 15,000 copies in March 1971, 12,000 in July 1973, and 15,000 in August 1974.

### *g. First American edition—photo-offset reprint* (HARVEST BOOKS). [*1969*]

VIRGINIA WOOLF | THE YEARS | A HARVEST BOOK | HARCOURT, BRACE & WORLD, INC. | NEW YORK

Large crown 8vo. [viii], 440 pp. 8 × $5\frac{3}{8}$ in.

Pp. [i–ii] blank; p. [iii] half-title; p. [iv] blank; p. [v] list of works by the author; p. [vi] blank; p. [vii] title; p. [viii] publisher's monogram, publication note, printer's note; p. [1] fly-title; p. [2] blank; pp. 3–435 text; p. [436] blank; p. [437] publisher's advertisement; pp. [438–440] blank.

Stiff white pictorial paper wrappers printed in brown, black and yellow; edges trimmed.

Issued 22 October 1969 in *Harvest Books* as Vol. HB166; 7000 copies printed. $2.85.

There were further printings of 3000 copies each in June and October 1973, 5000 in September 1974, and 5085 in November 1975.

### *h. Fourth English edition* (PANTHER BOOKS). [*1977*]

VIRGINIA WOOLF | THE YEARS | TRIAD | PANTHER

Foolscap 8vo. 336 pp. 7 × $4\frac{3}{8}$ in.

P. [1] Biographical note on the author; p. [2] list of works by the author; p. [3] title; p. [4] publication note, copyright note, printer's imprint etc.; pp. 5–331 text; p. [332] blank; pp. [333–336] publisher's advertisements.

Stiff white pictorial paper wrappers printed in black, pale yellow and brownish-grey; edges trimmed.

Published 9 June 1977; 30,000 copies printed. £1.25.

## A23 THREE GUINEAS 1938

### *a. First edition*

THREE GUINEAS | VIRGINIA WOOLF | [*publisher's device of a wolf's head*] | THE HOGARTH PRESS, | 52 TAVISTOCK SQUARE, | LONDON, W.C.1 | 1938

Small crown 8vo. 336 pp. 5 plates facing pp. 37, 39, 43, 113, 220. $7\frac{1}{4}$ × $4\frac{3}{4}$ in.

P. [1] half-title; p. [2] list of works by the author; p. [3] title; p. [4] at head: First published 1938, at foot: Made and Printed in Great Britain by the Garden | City Press Ltd., at Letchworth, Hertfordshire; p. [5] list of illustrations; p. [6] blank; pp. 7–261 text; p. [262] blank; pp. 263–329 Notes and references; pp. [330–334] blank; pp. [335–336] form paste down end-paper.

Lemon-yellow cloth boards; lettered in gold on spine: Three | Guineas | [*ornament*] | Virginia Woolf | The | Hogarth Press; edges trimmed; front end-papers. Cream dust-jacket printed in mauve and blue, designed by Vanessa Bell.

Published 2 June 1938; 16,250 copies printed. 7s. 6d.

It is probable that more than 8000 copies were bound in lemon-yellow cloth boards. The rest were issued as the Uniform Edition. See A23*c*.

A summary 'Women Must Weep' was published in the *Atlantic Monthly*, May and June 1938. See C357.

*Three Guineas* was written as a sequel to *A Room of One's Own.*

## *b. First American edition.* [*1938*]

[*within a rule:*] VIRGINIA WOOLF | THREE GUINEAS | [*publisher's monogram*] | HARCOURT, BRACE AND COMPANY | NEW YORK

Large crown 8vo. [vi], 286 pp. 5 plates facing pp. 30, 32, 34, 94, 184. 8 × $5\frac{3}{8}$ in.

P. [i] half-title; p. [ii] list of works by the author; p. [iii] title; p. [iv] Copyright, 1938, by | Harcourt, Brace and Company, Inc., reservation rights, first American edition, at foot: Typography by Robert Josephy | Printed in the United States of America; p. [v] list of illustrations; p. [vi] blank; p. [1] fly-title; p. [2] blank; pp. 3–220 text; pp. 221–285 Notes and references; p. [286] blank.

Deep pink cloth boards; lettered in gold on spine: [*rule across head*] | Three | Guineas | Virginia | Woolf | [*rule*] | Harcourt, Brace | and Company; edges trimmed, top blue-grey; end-papers. Cream dust-jacket printed in mauve and darkish blue, designed by Vanessa Bell.

Published 25 August 1938; 7500 copies printed. $2.50.

## *c. First edition – second issue* (UNIFORM EDITION). *1943*

THREE GUINEAS | VIRGINIA WOOLF | NEW EDITION | THE HOGARTH PRESS | 37 MECKLENBURGH SQUARE | LONDON, W.C.1 | 1943

Small crown 8vo. 332 pp. 5 plates facing pp. 37, 39, 43, 113, 220. 7 × $4\frac{1}{2}$ in.

P. [1] half-title; p. [2] list of works in the Uniform Edition; p. [3] title; p. [4] publication note, printer's imprint; p. [5] list of illustrations; p. [6] blank; pp. 7–261 text; p. [262] blank; pp. 263–329 Notes and references; pp. [330–332] blank.

Jade-green cloth boards; lettered in gold on spine; edges trimmed; end-papers. Dust-jacket, probably pale green printed in green.

Issued November 1943; 1000 copies bound. 7s. 6d.

The rest of the first impression, a maximum of 7250 copies, was bound as the Uniform Edition. A further 2000 copies were printed by photo-litho offset in 1952. They were issued as the Uniform Edition.

## *d. Second American edition* (HARBINGER BOOK). [*1963*]

THREE GUINEAS | [*rule*] | VIRGINIA WOOLF | A HARBINGER BOOK [*publisher's monogram*] | NEW YORK · BURLINGAME | HARCOURT, BRACE & WORLD, INC.

Large crown 8vo. [iv], 188 pp. $8\frac{1}{8} \times 5\frac{1}{2}$ in.

P. [i] half-title; p. [ii] list of works by the author; p. [iii] title; p. [iv] copyright note, etc., printer's note; p. [1] fly-title; p. [2] blank; pp. 3–144 text; pp. 145–188 Notes and references.

Stiff white paper wrappers printed in maroon, yellow and black with illustrated upper cover; edges trimmed.

Published 1 May 1963 in *Harbinger Books* as Vol. 021; 7500 copies printed. $1.95.

## *e. Second English edition* (PENGUIN BOOKS). [*1977*]

VIRGINIA WOOLF | THREE GUINEAS | PENGUIN BOOKS

Foolscap 8vo. 208 pp. $7\frac{1}{8} \times 4\frac{3}{8}$ in.

P. [1] note on the author; p. [2] blank; p. [3] title; p. [4] publication note, copyright note, printer's note, etc.; pp. 5–[164] text; pp. 165–[178] Notes and references: One; pp. 179–190 Notes and references: Two; pp. 191–[206] Notes and references: Three; p. [207] publisher's advertisement; p. [208] blank.

Stiff white pictorial paper wrappers printed in brown, pink, blue, black and orange; edges trimmed.

Published November 1977; 20,000 copies printed. 80p.

There was a further printing of 11,000 copies in June 1978.

## A24 REVIEWING 1939

*a. First edition*

REVIEWING | VIRGINIA WOOLF | WITH A NOTE BY LEONARD WOOLF | [*publisher's device of a wolf's head*] | THE HOGARTH PRESS | 37 MECKLENBURGH SQUARE, | LONDON, W.C.1 | 1939

Small crown 8vo. 32 pp. $7\frac{1}{4} \times 4\frac{7}{8}$ in.

P. [1] half-title; p. [2] blank; p. [3] title; p. [4] at head: First published 1939, at foot: Printed in Great Britain by the Garden City Press Ltd. | at Letchworth, Hertfordshire.; pp. 5-26 text; pp. 27-31 Note by Leonard Woolf; p. [32] blank.

Stiff pale blue paper wrappers; printed in mauve on upper cover: Virginia Woolf | Reviewing | With a Note by Leonard Woolf | Hogarth Sixpenny Pamphlets | Number Four; edges trimmed; sewn.

Published 2 November 1939 in *Hogarth Sixpenny Pamphlets* as Vol. 4; 5140 copies printed. 6d.

The essay was reprinted in *The Captain's Death Bed and Other Essays* and in *Collected Essays*, Vol. 2. See A30, 37.

*b. First edition – American photo-offset reprint. [1977]* *

REVIEWING | VIRGINIA WOOLF | WITH A NOTE BY LEONARD WOOLF | [*publisher's device*] | THE HOGARTH PRESS | 37 MECKLENBURGH SQUARE, | LONDON, W.C.1 | 1939

32 pp.

Issued 16 June 1977; 150 copies printed. $10.

Issued by Folcroft Library Editions, Folcroft, Pennsylvania.

## A25 ROGER FRY: A BIOGRAPHY 1940

*a. First edition*

ROGER FRY | A BIOGRAPHY | VIRGINIA WOOLF | [*publisher's device of a wolf's head*] | THE HOGARTH PRESS | 37 MECKLENBURGH SQUARE, | LONDON, W.C.1 | 1940

Demy 8vo. 308 pp. front., 15 plates facing pp. 22 (2 ports.), 26 (2 ports.), 82, 124, 162, 164, 222, 236, 254, 266, 268, 270, 272, 276, 278. $8\frac{1}{2} \times 5\frac{1}{2}$ in.

P. [1] half-title; p. [2] blank; p. [3] title; p. [4] at head: First published 1940, at foot: Made in Great Britain | Printed by R. & R. Clark, Ltd., Edinburgh; p. 5 Foreword by Margery Fry; p. [6] blank; p. 7 Contents; p. [8] blank; p. 9 list of illustrations; p. [10] blank; pp. 11–298 text; pp. 299–301 Appendix; p. [302] blank; pp. 303–307 Index; p. [308] blank.

Pale jade-green cloth boards; lettered in gold on spine: Roger | Fry | A Biography | [*ornament*] | Virginia Woolf | The | Hogarth Press; edges trimmed; end-papers. Cream dust-jacket printed in black, with portrait of Roger Fry by Vanessa Bell.

Published 25 July 1940; 2530 copies printed. 12s. 6d.

There was a second impression of 1130 copies in August 1940 and a third of 1010 in November 1940.

*b. First edition – American photo-offset reprint.* [*1940*]

[*within a rule:*] ROGER FRY | A BIOGRAPHY | VIRGINIA WOOLF | [*publisher's monogram*] | HARCOURT, BRACE AND COMPANY | NEW YORK

Demy 8vo. 312 pp. front., 15 plates facing pp. 22 (2 ports.), 26 (2 ports.), 82, 124, 162, 164, 222, 236, 254, 266, 268, 270, 272, 276, 278. $8\frac{1}{2} \times 5\frac{5}{8}$ in.

P. [1] half-title; p. [2] blank; p. [3] title; p. [4] Copyright, 1940, by | Harcourt, Brace and Company, Inc., reservation rights, first American edition, at foot: Printed in the United States of America; p. [5] Foreword by Margery Fry; p. [6] blank; p. 7 Contents; p. [8] blank; p. 9 list of illustrations; p. [10] blank; pp. 11–298 text; pp. 299–301 Appendix; p. [302] blank; pp. 303–307 Index; pp. [308–312] blank.

Pale jade-green cloth boards; lettered in gold on spine: Virginia Woolf | [*within a rule:*] Roger | Fry | A | Biography, at foot: Harcourt, Brace | and Company; edges trimmed; end-papers. Primrose-yellow dust-jacket printed in brown.

Issued 24 October 1940; 2500 copies printed. $3.50.

*c. First edition – American photo-offset reprint* (HARVEST BOOKS). [*1976*]

VIRGINIA WOOLF | ROGER FRY | A BIOGRAPHY | A HARVEST BOOK | [*publisher's monogram within a rule*] | HARCOURT BRACE JOVANOVICH | NEW YORK AND LONDON

Large crown 8vo. 304 pp. 18 illus. front. [i.e. p. 4], between pp. 22-23, 86-87, 164-165, 222-223, 256-257, 268-269, 274-275, and facing p. 278. 8 × $5\frac{3}{8}$ in.

P. [1] half-title; p. [2] blank; p. [3] list of works by the author; p. [4] frontispiece; p. [5] title; p. [6] copyright note etc., printer's note, Library of Congress cataloguing data etc.; p. [7] Contents; p. [8] blank; p. [9] list of illustrations; p. [10] blank; pp. 11-298 text; pp. 299-303 Index; p. [304] list of works by the author in paperback.

Stiff white pictorial paper wrappers printed in mauve, brown and black; edges trimmed.

Issued 15 March 1976 in *Harvest Books* as Vol. HB338; 7223 copies printed. $4.50.

The Appendix was omitted.

## A26 BETWEEN THE ACTS 1941

*a. First edition*

BETWEEN THE ACTS | VIRGINIA WOOLF | THE HOGARTH PRESS | 37 MECKLENBURGH SQUARE, | LONDON, W.C.1 | 1941

Small crown 8vo. 256 pp. $7\frac{1}{8}$ × $4\frac{3}{4}$ in.

P. [1] half-title; p. [2] list of works by the author; p. [3] title; p. [4] at head: First published 1941 | Distributed in Canada by our exclusive agent, The Macmillan | Company of Canada Limited, 70 Bond Street, Toronto, at foot: Made and Printed in Great Britain by the | Garden City Press Ltd., at Letchworth, | Hertfordshire; p. [5] Note by Leonard Woolf; p. [6] blank; pp. 7-256 text.

Bright blue cloth boards; lettered in gold on spine: Between | the | Acts | [*ornament*] | Virginia Woolf | The | Hogarth Press; edges trimmed; end-papers. White dust-jacket printed in black, designed by Vanessa Bell.

Published 17 July 1941; 6358 copies printed. 7s. 6d.

There was a second impression of 4600 copies in July 1941 and a third of 2000 in November 1941. A further 3000 copies were printed by photo-litho offset in January 1947; they were bound in rust cloth boards; lettered in gold on spine; edges trimmed, top rust; buff dust-jacket printed in black. The fifth printing was issued as the Uniform Edition. See A26*c*.

*b. First American edition.* [*1941*]

[*within a rule:*] VIRGINIA WOOLF | [*rule*] | BETWEEN | THE ACTS | [*rule*] | [*publisher's monogram*] | NEW YORK | HARCOURT, BRACE AND COMPANY

Large crown 8vo. [iv], 220 pp. 8 × $5\frac{5}{8}$ in.

P. [i] half-title; p. [ii] list of works by the author; p. [iii] title; p. [iv] Copyright, 1941, by | Harcourt, Brace and Company, Inc., reservation rights, first American edition, at foot: Printed in the United States of America | by Quinn & Boden Company, Inc., Rahway, N.J.; p. [1] Note by Leonard Woolf; p. [2] blank; pp. 3-219 text; p. [220] blank.

Bright blue cloth boards; lettered in gold on spine: [*rule*] | [*within a rule:*] Virginia | Woolf | [*rule*] | Between | the Acts | [*rule*] | Harcourt, | Brace and | Company | [*rule*]; edges trimmed, top canary-yellow; end-papers. Buff dust-jacket printed in bright blue and brown, designed by Vanessa Bell.

Published 2 October 1941; 12,500 copies printed. $2.50.

*c. First edition – photo-offset reprint* (UNIFORM EDITION). *1953*

BETWEEN THE ACTS | VIRGINIA WOOLF | FIFTH IMPRESSION | LONDON | THE HOGARTH PRESS | 1953

Small crown 8vo. 256 pp. $7\frac{1}{4}$ × $4\frac{7}{8}$ in.

P. [1] half-title; p. [2] list of works by the author; p. [3] title; p. [4] publisher's note, publication note, printer's note, reservation rights; p. [5] Note by Leonard Woolf; p. [6] blank; pp. 7–256 text.

Jade-green cloth boards; lettered in gold on spine; edges trimmed; end-papers. Bright yellow dust-jacket printed in green.

Issued 9 April 1953; 3000 copies printed. 8s. 6d.

*d. Second English edition* (PENGUIN BOOKS). [*1953*]

BETWEEN THE ACTS | [*rule*] | VIRGINIA WOOLF | PENGUIN BOOKS | MELBOURNE · LONDON · BALTIMORE

Foolscap 8vo. 160 pp. $7\frac{1}{8}$ × $4\frac{3}{8}$ in.

P. [1] half-title; p. [2] blank; p. [3] title; p. [4] publication note, Published in Penguin Books 1953, printer's imprint; p. [5] Note by

Leonard Woolf; p. [6] blank; pp. 7–[152] text; p. [153] publisher's advertisement; p. [154] blank; pp. [155–160] publisher's advertisements, integral.

Stiff white paper wrappers printed in orange and black; edges trimmed.

Published 18 September 1953 in *Penguin Books* as Vol. 896; 35,000 copies printed. 2s.

### *e. Third English edition* (ACE BOOKS). [*1961*]

BETWEEN THE | ACTS | VIRGINIA WOOLF | ACE BOOKS LIMITED | 44 BEDFORD ROW, LONDON, W.C.1

Small crown 8vo. 144 pp. $7\frac{1}{8} \times 4\frac{1}{2}$ in.

P. [1] half-title; p. [2] list of works by the author; p. [3] title; p. [4] publisher's note, Note by Leonard Woolf, printer's imprint; pp. 5–140 text; pp. [141–144] publisher's advertisements, integral.

Stiff white paper wrappers printed in dull red, yellow and black; edges trimmed.

Published 20 January 1961 in *Ace Books* as Vol. H419; number of copies printed not available. 2s. 6d.

### *f. First American edition—photo-offset reprint* (HARVEST BOOKS). [*1970*]

[*within a rule:*] VIRGINIA WOOLF | [*rule*] | BETWEEN | THE ACTS | [*rule*] | A HARVEST BOOK | HARCOURT BRACE JOVANOVICH, INC. | NEW YORK

Large crown 8vo. [iv], 220 pp. $8 \times 5\frac{3}{8}$ in.

P. [i] half-title; p. [ii] list of works by the author; p. [iii] title; p. [iv] publication note, printer's note; p. [1] Note by Leonard Woolf; p. [2] blank; pp. 3–219 text; p. [220] publisher's advertisement.

Stiff white pictorial paper wrappers printed in purple and emerald green; edges trimmed.

Issued 21 October 1970 in *Harvest Books* as Vol. HB189; 6000 copies printed. $2.45.

There were further printings of 3000 copies in January 1973, 6000 in July 1973, 7500 in September 1974, and 7773 in April 1977.

*g. Fourth English edition. 1974.*

VIRGINIA WOOLF | BETWEEN THE ACTS | INTRODUCTION BY | QUENTIN BELL | LITHOGRAPHS BY | GILLIAN BARLOW | LONDON | THE FOLIO SOCIETY | 1974

Demy 8vo. 164 pp. front., 7 illus. facing pp. 33, 48, 64, 81, 97, 137, 158. $8\frac{3}{4} \times 5\frac{5}{8}$ in.

P. [1] title; p. [2] at head: © Copyright the Executors of the Estate of | Leonard Woolf 1941 | The text of this Edition is used by | kind permission of The Hogarth Press Limited, London, at foot: Printed and Bound in Great Britain | by W & J Mackay Limited, Chatham; pp. 3–9 Introduction by Quentin Bell; p. [10] blank; p. [11] Illustrations; p. [12] blank; p. [13] Note by Leonard Woolf; p. [14] blank; pp. 15–160 text; p. [161] towards head: Set in 12-point Walbaum type | leaded 1 point. | Letterpress text and lithographic | illustrations printed by | W & J Mackay Limited, Chatham | on Mellotex Matt Cartridge paper. | Bound by W & J Mackay Limited | using Red Bridge Chelsea cloth and | printed paper sides designed by | Fiona Campbell.; pp. [162–164] blank.

White patterned paper boards printed in greenish-grey and brown; ruby cloth spine, lettered in gold up the spine: Virginia Woolf • Between the Acts; edges trimmed, top ruby; ruby end-papers. Greenish-grey slip-case.

Published April 1974; number of copies printed not disclosed. £2.75 to Folio Society Members only.

*h. Fifth English edition* (PANTHER BOOKS). [*1978*]

VIRGINIA WOOLF | BETWEEN THE ACTS | A TRIAD PANTHER BOOK | GRANADA PUBLISHING | LONDON TORONTO SYDNEY NEW YORK

Foolscap 8vo. 160 pp. $7 \times 4\frac{1}{4}$ in.

P. [1] Biographical note on the author; p. [2] list of works by the author; p. [3] title; p. [4] publication note, copyright note, printer's imprint, etc.; p. [5] Note by Leonard Woolf; p. [6] blank; pp. 7–[159] text; p. [160] blank.

Stiff white pictorial paper wrappers printed in red, brown, pink, yellow, grey, green and black; edges trimmed.

Published 2 February 1978; 20,000 copies printed. 95p.

## A27 THE DEATH OF THE MOTH AND OTHER ESSAYS 1942

*a. First edition*

THE DEATH OF THE MOTH | AND OTHER ESSAYS | VIRGINIA WOOLF | [*publisher's device of a wolf's head after a design by E. McKnight Kauffer*] | THE HOGARTH PRESS | 37 MECKLENBURGH SQUARE | LONDON, W.C.1 | 1942

Small demy 8vo. 160 pp. $8\frac{1}{2} \times 5\frac{3}{8}$ in.

P. [1] half-title; p. [2] list of works by the author; p. [3] title; p. [4] at head: First Published in 1942 | Distributed in Canada by our exclusive agent, The Macmillan | Company of Canada Limited, 70 Bond Street, Toronto, at foot: The typography and binding of this book conform to the | authorized economy standard | Made and Printed in Great Britain by | The Garden City Press Limited, at | Letchworth, Hertfordshire; p. 5 Contents; p. [6] blank; pp. 7–8 Editorial note by Leonard Woolf; pp. 9–157 text; pp. [158–160] blank.

Bright blue cloth boards; lettered in gold on spine: The | Death of | the Moth | [*ornament*] | Virginia | Woolf | The | Hogarth Press; edges trimmed; end-papers. White dust-jacket printed in black, designed by Vanessa Bell.

Published 9 June 1942; 4500 copies printed. 9s.

There was a second impression of 4600 copies in June 1942, a third of 2000 in July 1942 and a fourth of 1200 in March 1945. A further 3000 copies were printed by photo-litho offset in March 1947.

The Readers Union distributed a reprint of 6000 copies on 4 December 1943 to members as an additional (optional) choice at 3s. 6d. It was bound in grey paper boards, probably with a glassine dust-jacket; portrait of the author as frontispiece.

Contents: The Death of the Moth – Evening Over Sussex: Reflections in a Motor Car – Three Pictures – Old Mrs Grey – Street Haunting: A London Adventure – Jones and Wilkinson – "Twelfth Night" at the Old Vic – Madame de Sévigné – The Humane Art – Two Antiquaries: Walpole and Cole – The Rev. William Cole: A Letter – The Historian and "The Gibbon" – Reflections at Sheffield Place – The Man at the Gate – Sarah Coleridge – "Not One of Us" – Henry James: I, *Within the Rim*; II, The Old Order; III, The Letters of Henry James – George Moore – The Novels of E. M. Forster – Middlebrow – The Art of Biography – Craftsmanship – A Letter to a Young Poet – Why? – Professions for Women – Thoughts on Peace in an Air Raid.

*b. First American edition. [1942]*

[*within a triple rule:*] THE DEATH OF | THE MOTH | AND OTHER ESSAYS | BY | VIRGINIA WOOLF | HARCOURT, BRACE AND COMPANY | NEW YORK

Demy 8vo. viii, 248 pp. $8\frac{1}{2} \times 5\frac{3}{4}$ in.

P. [i] half-title; p. [ii] list of works by the author; p. [iii] title; p. [iv] Copyright, 1942, by | Harcourt, Brace and Company, Inc., reservation rights, first American edition, at foot: Printed in the United States of America; pp. v–vi Contents; pp. vii–viii Editorial note by Leonard Woolf; p. [1] fly-title; p. [2] blank; pp. 3–248 text.

Dark green cloth boards; lettered in cream on spine: [*double rule across head*] | The | Death | of the | Moth | [*ornament*] | Virginia | Woolf | Harcourt, Brace | and Company | [*rule across foot*]; top edges trimmed, others partially trimmed; end-papers. Cream dust-jacket printed in green and brown, designed by Vanessa Bell.

Published 24 September 1942; 3475 copies printed. $3.

There was a second impression of 1500 copies in December 1942.

*c. Second English edition* (PENGUIN BOOKS). *[1961]*

VIRGINIA WOOLF | THE DEATH OF THE MOTH AND OTHER ESSAYS | PENGUIN BOOKS

Foolscap 8vo. 216 pp. $7\frac{1}{4} \times 4\frac{1}{2}$ in.

P. [1] half-title; p. [2] blank; p. [3] title; p. [4] publication note, printer's imprint etc.; pp. [5–6] Contents; pp. 7–[8] Editorial note by Leonard Woolf; pp. 9–[212] text; p. [213] publisher's advertisement; p. [214] blank; pp. [215–216] publisher's advertisements, integral.

Stiff white paper wrappers printed in silver grey, black and orange, designed by Vanessa Bell; edges trimmed.

Published 27 July 1961 in *Penguin Modern Classics* as Vol. 1644; number of copies printed not available. 3s. 6d.

*d. First American edition—photo-offset reprint* (HARVEST BOOKS). *[1974]* *

THE DEATH OF THE MOTH AND OTHER ESSAYS. HARCOURT BRACE JOVANOVICH, INC., NEW YORK

Large crown 8vo. viii, 248 pp. $8 \times 5\frac{1}{4}$ in.

Issued 23 October 1974 in *Harvest Books* as Vol. HB294; 6000 copies printed. $2.95.

There was a further printing of 6000 copies in December 1974.

## A28 A HAUNTED HOUSE AND OTHER SHORT STORIES 1943 [*i.e.* 1944]

*a. First edition*

A HAUNTED HOUSE | AND OTHER SHORT STORIES | VIRGINIA WOOLF | THE HOGARTH PRESS | 37 MECKLENBURGH SQUARE | LONDON, W.C.1 | 1943

Small crown 8vo. 128 pp. $7\frac{1}{4} \times 4\frac{7}{8}$ in.

P. [1] half-title; p. [2] list of works by the author; p. [3] title; p. [4] at head: First published 1943 | Distributed in Canada by our exclusive agent, The Macmillan | Company of Canada Limited, 70 Bond Street, Toronto, towards foot: This book is produced in complete conformity | with the authorized economy standards, at foot: Made and Printed in Great Britain by The Garden City Press Ltd. | at Letchworth, Hertfordshire; p. 5 Contents; p. [6] blank; pp. 7–8 Foreword by Leonard Woolf; pp. 9–124 text; pp. [125–126] blank; pp. [127–128] form paste down end-paper.

Dull crimson cloth boards; lettered in gold down the spine: A Haunted House [*ornament*] Virginia Woolf, across foot: H.P.; edges trimmed; front end-papers. White dust-jacket printed in black, designed by Vanessa Bell.

Published 31 January 1944; 6000 copies printed. 7s. 6d.

There was a second impression of 3000 copies in February 1944 and a third of 6000 in June 1944. A further 2800 copies were printed by photo-litho offset in May 1947; they were bound in powder-blue cloth boards; lettered in gold on spine; edges trimmed, top blue; front end-papers; blue dust-jacket printed in black.

A copy (dated 1943), probably a trial one, formerly in Leonard Woolf's collection (1957) has pp. [127–128] removed and front and back end-papers.

Contents: A Haunted House – Monday or Tuesday – An Unwritten Novel – The String Quartet – Kew Gardens – The Mark on the Wall – The New Dress – The Shooting Party – Lappin and Lapinova – Solid Objects – The Lady in the Looking-Glass – The Duchess and the Jeweller – Moments of Being: "Slater's Pins Have No Points" – The Man Who Loved his Kind – The Searchlight – The Legacy – Together and Apart – A Summing Up.

*b. First American edition.* [*1944*]

A HAUNTED HOUSE | AND OTHER | SHORT STORIES | BY | VIRGINIA WOOLF | HARCOURT, BRACE AND COMPANY | NEW YORK

Large crown 8vo. [2], viii, 150 pp. 8 × $5\frac{3}{8}$ in.

Pp. [1–2] blank; p. [i] half-title; p. [ii] list of works by the author; p. [iii] title; p. [iv] Copyright, 1944, by | Harcourt, Brace and Company, Inc. | Copyright, 1921, by | Harcourt, Brace and Company, Inc. . . . reservation rights, first American edition | [*device of an eagle in flight with legend*] | A Wartime Book, war-time economy note, Printed in the United States of America; pp. v–vi Foreword by Leonard Woolf; p. vii Contents; p. [viii] blank; p. [1] fly-title; p. [2] blank; pp. 3–148 text; pp. [149–150] blank.

Navy-blue cloth boards; lettered in white down the spine: Virginia Woolf A Haunted House [*in two lines:*] Harcourt, Brace | and Company; edges trimmed; end-papers. Pale buff dust-jacket printed in bright blue, designed by Vanessa Bell.

Published 13 April 1944; 4000 copies printed. $2.

There were second and third impressions of 3500 copies each in April and May 1944.

### *c. Second English edition* (UNIFORM EDITION). *1953* [*i.e. 1954*]

A HAUNTED HOUSE | AND OTHER SHORT STORIES | VIRGINIA WOOLF | [*publisher's device of a wolf's head*] | FIFTH IMPRESSION | LONDON | THE HOGARTH PRESS | 1953

Small crown 8vo. 144 pp. $7\frac{1}{4}$ × $4\frac{3}{4}$ in.

P. [1] half-title; p. [2] list of works by the author; p. [3] title; p. [4] at head: Published by | The Hogarth Press Ltd. | London | [*ornament*] | Clark, Irwin & Co., Ltd. | Toronto, at foot: publication note, reservation rights; p. [5] Contents; p. [6] blank; pp. 7–8 Foreword by Leonard Woolf; pp. 9–[141] text; p. [142] Printed in Great Britain at | The Blackmore Press, Gillingham, Dorset | by T. H. Brickell & Son Ltd; pp. [143–144] blank.

Bright jade-green paper boards; lettered in gold on spine; edges trimmed; end-papers. Bright yellow dust-jacket printed in green.

Published 25 January 1954; 3000 copies printed. 8s. 6d.

This second English edition is incorrectly described on the recto of the title as the 'Fifth Impression'; the publication note on the verso reads 'Fifth Impression (Reset)'.

### *d. First American edition—photo-offset reprint* (HARVEST BOOKS). [*1966*]

VIRGINIA WOOLF | [*ornament*] | A HAUNTED HOUSE

| AND OTHER SHORT STORIES | [*ornament*] | A HARVEST BOOK | HARCOURT, BRACE & WORLD, INC. | NEW YORK

Foolscap 8vo. [2], viii, 150 pp. $7\frac{1}{8} \times 4\frac{1}{4}$ in.

Pp. [1–2] blank; p. [i] half-title; p. [ii] list of works by the author; p. [iii] title; p. [iv] publication note, printer's note; pp. v–vi Foreword by Leonard Woolf; p. [vii] Contents; p. [viii] blank; p. [1] fly-title; p. [2] blank; pp. 3–148 text; pp. [149–150] blank.

Stiff white pictorial paper wrappers printed in mauve, pink and olive green; edges trimmed.

Issued 23 March 1966 in *Harvest Books* as Vol. HB105; 6000 copies printed. $1.35.

There were nine further printings totalling 42,375 copies between March 1967 and April 1977.

*e. Third English edition* (PENGUIN BOOKS). [*1973*]

VIRGINIA WOOLF | A HAUNTED HOUSE | AND OTHER STORIES | PENGUIN BOOKS

Foolscap 8vo. 160 pp. $7\frac{1}{8} \times 4\frac{3}{8}$ in.

P. [1] half-title; p. [2] blank; p. [3] title; p. [4] publication note etc., printer's imprint; p. [5] Contents; p. [6] blank; pp. [7]–8 Foreword by Leonard Woolf; pp. 9–154 text; p. [155] publisher's advertisement; p. [156] blank; pp. [157–160] publisher's advertisements.

Stiff white pictorial paper wrappers printed in brown, yellow, grey and black; edges trimmed.

Published May 1973 in *Penguin Modern Classics*; 18,000 copies printed. 30p.

There were further printings of 15,000 copies in December 1973, 10,000 in January 1975, and 12,000 in January 1976.

## A29 THE MOMENT AND OTHER ESSAYS 1947

*a. First edition*

THE MOMENT | AND OTHER ESSAYS | VIRGINIA WOOLF | [*publisher's device of a wolf's head*] | LONDON | THE HOGARTH PRESS | 1947

Large crown 8vo. 192 pp. $8 \times 5$ in.

P. [1] half-title; p. [2] list of works by the author; p. [3] title; p. [4] at head: Published by | The Hogarth Press Ltd | London |

[*ornament*] | Oxford University Press | Toronto, at foot: Printed in Great Britain | in complete conformity with | the authorized economy standards | All rights reserved; pp. 5–6 Contents; pp. 7–8 Editorial note by Leonard Woolf; pp. 9–191 text; p. [192] at centre: Printed in Great Britain | by R. & R. Clark, Limited | Edinburgh.

Pale ruby-red cloth boards; lettered in gold on spine: [*ornaments in six lines*] | The | Moment | [*ornament*] | Virginia | Woolf | [*ornaments in six lines*] | The | Hogarth | Press; top and fore edges trimmed, bottom partially untrimmed; end-papers. Pink dust-jacket printed in black, designed by Vanessa Bell.

Published 5 December 1947; 10,000 copies printed. 10s. 6d.

A copy in brilliant crimson cloth, with bottom edges untrimmed, is in the collection of Mr P. J. Allen; it is probably a trial binding.

There was a second impression of 3000 copies in November 1948. 1250 copies of the second impression were issued as the Uniform Edition. See A29*c*.

Contents: The Moment: Summer's Night – On Being Ill – *The Faery Queen* – Congreve's Comedies – Sterne's Ghost – Mrs Thrale – Sir Walter Scott, I. Gas at Abbotsford; II. *The Antiquary* – Lockhart's Criticism – *David Copperfield* – Lewis Carroll – Edmund Gosse – Notes on D. H. Lawrence – Roger Fry – The Art of Fiction – American Fiction – The Leaning Tower – On Re-Reading Novels – Personalities – Pictures – Harriette Wilson – Genius: R. B. Haydon – The Enchanted Organ: Anne Thackeray – Two Women: Emily Davies and Lady Augusta Stanley – Ellen Terry – To Spain – Fishing – The Artist and Politics – Royalty – Royalty.

Leonard Woolf wrote in the Editorial Note: 'I have included two essays with the same title, *Royalty*; the first was commissioned, but, for obvious reasons, not published by *Picture Post*; the second was published in *Time and Tide*'.

## *b. First American edition.* [*1948*]

[*within a triple rule:*] THE MOMENT | AND OTHER ESSAYS | VIRGINIA WOOLF | HARCOURT, BRACE AND COMPANY | NEW YORK

Large crown 8vo. viii, 240 pp. $8 \times 5\frac{1}{4}$ in.

P. [i] half-title; p. [ii] list of works by the author; p. [iii] title; p. [iv] Copyright, 1948, by | Harcourt, Brace and Company, Inc., reservation rights . . . at foot: Printed in the United States of America; pp. v–vi Contents; pp. vii–viii Editorial note by Leonard Woolf; p. [1] fly-title; p. [2] blank; pp. 3–240 text.

Maroon cloth boards; lettered in gold on spine: [*double rule across head*] | The | Moment | and Other | Essays | [*ornament*] | Virginia | Woolf | Harcourt, Brace | and Company | [*double rule*]; edges trimmed; end-papers. Pink dust-jacket printed in black, designed by Vanessa Bell.

Published 22 March 1948; 3500 copies printed. $3.

There was a second impression of 2500 copies in April 1948.

*c. First edition – second impression – second issue* (UNIFORM EDITION). *1952*

THE MOMENT | AND OTHER ESSAYS | VIRGINIA WOOLF | [*publisher's device of a wolf's head*] | LONDON | THE HOGARTH PRESS | 1952

Small crown 8vo. 192 pp. $7\frac{3}{8} \times 4\frac{7}{8}$ in.

P. [1] half-title; p. [2] list of works by the author; p. [3] title; p. [4] publisher's note, publication note, printer's note, reservation rights; pp. 5-6 Contents; pp. 7-8 Editorial note by Leonard Woolf; pp. 9-191 text; p. [192] printer's imprint.

Bright jade-green cloth boards; lettered in gold on spine; edges trimmed; end-papers. Bright yellow dust-jacket printed in green.

Issued February 1952; 750 copies bound. 7s. 6d.

A further 500 copies of the second impression were issued as the Uniform Edition in June 1954 (dated 1952). They were bound in bright jade-green paper boards; top edges green; bright yellow dust-jacket.

*d. First American edition—photo-offset reprint* (HARVEST BOOKS). [*1974*]

THE | MOMENT | AND OTHER ESSAYS | [*ornament*] | VIRGINIA WOOLF | A HARVEST BOOK | HARCOURT BRACE JOVANOVICH | NEW YORK AND LONDON | [*publisher's monogram within a rule*]

Large crown 8vo. [2], viii, 246 pp. $8 \times 5\frac{1}{4}$ in.

Pp. [1-2] blank; p. [i] half-title; p. [ii] list of works by the author; p. [iii] title; p. [iv] publication note, printer's note; pp. [v-vi] Contents; pp. vii-viii Editorial Note by Leonard Woolf; p. [1] fly-title; p. [2] blank; pp. 3-240 text; p. [241] publisher's advertisement; pp. [242-246] blank.

Stiff white pictorial paper wrappers printed in blue, black and green; edges trimmed.

Issued 23 October 1974 in *Harvest Books* as Vol. HB295; 6000 copies printed. $2.95.

There was a further printing of 6000 copies in December 1974.

## A30 THE CAPTAIN'S DEATH BED AND OTHER ESSAYS [1950]

*a. First edition*

[*within a triple rule:*] THE CAPTAIN'S | DEATH BED | AND OTHER ESSAYS | BY | VIRGINIA WOOLF | HARCOURT, BRACE AND COMPANY | NEW YORK

Large crown 8vo. viii, 248 pp. 8 × $5\frac{3}{8}$ in.

P. [i] half-title; p. [ii] list of works by the author; p. [iii] title; p. [iv] at head: Copyright, 1950, by | Harcourt, Brace and Company, Inc. | All rights reserved, including | the right to reproduce this book | or portions thereof in any form. | first American edition, at foot: Printed in the United States of America; pp. v–vi Contents; pp. vii–viii Editorial note by Leonard Woolf; p. [1] fly-title; p. [2] blank; pp. 3-248 text.

Slate blue cloth boards; lettered in gold on spine: [*double rule across head*] | The | Captain's | Death | Bed | and Other | Essays | [*ornament*] | Virginia | Woolf | Harcourt, Brace | and Company | [*double rule*]; edges trimmed; end-papers. Blue-grey dust-jacket printed in brown, designed by Vanessa Bell.

Published 4 May 1950; 5000 copies printed. $3.00.

Contents: Oliver Goldsmith – White's Selborne – Life Itself – Crabbe – Selina Trimmer – The Captain's Death Bed – Ruskin – The Novels of Turgenev – Half of Thomas Hardy – Leslie Stephen – Mr Conrad: A Conversation – The Cosmos – Walter Raleigh – Mr Bennett and Mrs Brown – All About Books – Reviewing, note by Leonard Woolf – Modern Letters – Reading – The Cinema – Walter Sickert – Flying Over London – The Sun and the Fish – Gas – Thunder at Wembley – Memories of a Working Women's Guild.

*b. First English edition. 1950*

THE | CAPTAIN'S DEATH BED | AND OTHER ESSAYS | VIRGINIA WOOLF | [*publisher's device of a wolf's head*] | LONDON | THE HOGARTH PRESS | 1950

Crown 8vo. 224 pp. $7\frac{7}{8}$ × 5 in.

P. [1] half-title; p. [2] list of works by the author; p. [3] title; p. [4] at head: Published by | The Hogarth Press Ltd. | London | [*ornament*] | Clarke, Irwin & Co. Ltd. | Toronto, at foot: Printed in Great Britain | All rights reserved; pp. 5–[6] Contents; p. 7 Editorial note by Leonard Woolf; p. [8] blank; pp. 9–[224] text; p. [224] at foot: Made and printed in Great Britain | by Ebenezer Baylis and Son, Ltd., The | Trinity Press, Worcester, and London.

Cedar-brown cloth boards; lettered in gold on spine: The | Captain's | Death | Bed | [*ornament*] | Virginia | Woolf | The | Hogarth | Press; edges trimmed, top dark brown; end-papers. White dust-jacket printed in lemon-yellow and black, designed by Vanessa Bell.

Published 11 May 1950; 10,000 copies printed. 10s. 6d.

1000 copies of the first impression were issued as the Uniform Edition. See A30*c*.

*c. First English edition – second issue* (UNIFORM EDITION). *1950* [*i.e. 1955*]

THE | CAPTAIN'S DEATH BED | AND OTHER ESSAYS | VIRGINIA WOOLF | [*publisher's device of a wolf's head*] | LONDON | THE HOGARTH PRESS | 1950

Crown 8vo. 224 pp. $7\frac{1}{4} \times 4\frac{7}{8}$ in.

P. [1] half-title; p. [2] list of works by the author; p. [3] title; p. [4] publisher's note, printer's note, reservation rights; pp. 5-[6] Contents; p. 7 Editorial note by Leonard Woolf; p. [8] blank; pp. 9-[224] text; p. [224] at foot: printer's imprint.

Bright jade-green paper boards; lettered in gold on spine; edges trimmed; end-papers. Bright yellow dust-jacket printed in green.

Issued January 1955; 1000 copies bound. 7s. 6d.

*d. First American edition–photo-offset reprint* (HARVEST BOOKS). [*1973*]

[*within a triple rule:*] THE CAPTAIN'S | DEATH BED | AND OTHER ESSAYS | BY | VIRGINIA WOOLF | [*publisher's monogram within a rule*] | A HARVEST BOOK | HARCOURT BRACE JOVANOVICH, INC. | NEW YORK

Large crown 8vo. viii, 248 pp. $8 \times 5\frac{3}{8}$ in.

P. [i] half-title; p. [ii] list of works by the author; p. [iii] title; p. [iv] publication note, printer's note; pp. v–vi Contents; pp. vii–viii Editorial Note; p. [1] fly-title; p. [2] blank; pp. 3–248 text.

Stiff white pictorial paper wrappers printed in bright yellow, pink and green; edges trimmed.

Issued 21 March 1973 in *Harvest Books* as Vol. HB253; 5000 copies printed. $2.45.

There were further printings of 4000 copies in February 1974, and 3675 in April 1977.

## A31 A WRITER'S DIARY 1953

*a. First edition*

A | WRITER'S DIARY | BEING EXTRACTS FROM THE DIARY OF | VIRGINIA WOOLF | EDITED BY | LEONARD WOOLF | [*publisher's device of a wolf's head*] | 1953 | THE HOGARTH PRESS | LONDON

Demy 8vo. x, 374 pp. $8\frac{3}{4} \times 5\frac{1}{2}$ in.

P. [i] half-title; p. [ii] list of works by the author; p. [iii] title; p. [iv] Published by | The Hogarth Press Ltd. | London | [*ornament*] | Clarke, Irwin & Co. Ltd. | Toronto, at foot: Printed in Great Britain | All rights reserved; p. v Contents; p. vi Glossary of names used in the diary; pp. vii–x Preface by Leonard Woolf; pp. 1–365 text; p. [366] blank; p. 367 Chronological bibliography of the books of Virginia Woolf; p. [368] blank; pp. 369–370 Index of books &c by Virginia Woolf; pp. 371–372 General index; p. [373] blank; p. [374] Printed in Great Britain | by Butler & Tanner Ltd., | Frome and London.

Orange cloth boards; lettered in gold on spine: A | Writer's | Diary | [*ornament*] | Virginia | Woolf | The | Hogarth | Press; edges trimmed, top orange; end-papers. White dust-jacket printed in orange and black, designed by Vanessa Bell.

Published 2 November 1953; 9000 copies printed. 18s.

There was a second impression of 5250 copies in December 1953.

Extracts appeared in *Encounter*, London, October 1953, I:I, 5–11.

*b. First American edition. [1954]*

A WRITER'S DIARY | [*rule*] | BEING EXTRACTS FROM THE DIARY OF | VIRGINIA WOOLF | [*rule*] | EDITED BY LEONARD WOOLF | HARCOURT, BRACE AND COMPANY | NEW YORK

Demy 8vo. xii, 356 pp. $8\frac{3}{8} \times 5\frac{5}{8}$ in.

P. [i] half-title; p. [ii] blank; p. [iii] title; p. [iv] Copyright, 1953, 1954, by Leonard Woolf | All rights reserved, including | the right to reproduce this book | or portions thereof in any form. | first American edition | Library of Congress Catalog Card Number: 54-5257 | Printed in the United States of America; p. [v] Contents; p. [vi] blank; pp. vii–x Preface by Leonard Woolf; p. [xi] Glossary of names used in the diary; p. [xii] blank; pp. 1–351 text; p. 352 Chronological bibliography of the books of Virginia Woolf; p. 353 Index of books &c by Virginia Woolf; p. [354] blank; pp. 355–356 General index.

Pink cloth boards; lettered in silver on spine: [*double rule*] | A | Writer's | Diary | [*ornament*] | Virginia | Woolf | Harcourt, Brace | and Company | [*double rule*]; edges trimmed; end-papers. White dust-jacket printed in black and orange, designed by Vanessa Bell.

Published 18 February 1954; 7000 copies printed. $5.

There was a second impression of 5125 copies in March 1954 and a third of 3000 in January 1956.

The Readers Subscription Inc., New York, issued a reprint of 5000 copies to their members in July 1955 at $3.95. A further 1000 copies were distributed to members in April 1956.

### *c. First American edition—photo-offset reprint* (HARVEST BOOKS). [*1973*]

A WRITER'S DIARY | [*swelled rule*] | BEING EXTRACTS FROM THE DIARY OF | VIRGINIA WOOLF | [*swelled rule*] | EDITED BY LEONARD WOOLF | A HARVEST BOOK | HARCOURT BRACE JOVANOVICH, INC. | NEW YORK | [*publisher's monogram within a rule*]

Large crown 8vo. xii, 356 pp. $8 \times 5\frac{3}{8}$ in.

P. [i] half-title; p. [ii] list of works by the author; p. [iii] title; p. [iv] publication note, printer's note; p. [v] Contents; p. [vi] blank; pp. vii–x Preface by Leonard Woolf; p. xi Glossary of Names used in the Diary; p. [xii] blank; pp. 1–351 text; p. [352] blank; pp. 353–354 General Index; p. 355 Index of books by Virginia Woolf; p. [356] publisher's advertisements.

Stiff white pictorial paper wrappers printed in mauve, pale brown and black; edges trimmed.

Issued 24 October 1973 in *Harvest Books* as Vol. HB264; 6000 copies printed. $2.95.

There were further printings of 5000 copies each in December 1973 and May 1974, 8000 in October 1974, and 10,242 in December 1976.

### *d. Second English edition* (PANTHER BOOKS). [*1978*]

A WRITER'S DIARY | BEING EXTRACTS FROM THE | DIARY OF VIRGINIA WOOLF | EDITED BY LEONARD WOOLF | TRIAD PANTHER

Foolscap 8vo. 352 pp. $7 \times 4\frac{3}{8}$ in.

P. [1] Biographical note on the author; p. [2] list of works by the author; p. [3] title; p. [4] publication note, copyright note, printer's imprint, etc.; p. [5] Contents; p. [6] Glossary of names used in the diary; p. [7]-10 Preface by Leonard Woolf; pp. [11]-345 text; p. [346] Chronological bibliography of the books of Virginia Woolf; pp. [347]-348 General index; pp. [349]-350 Index of books, etc. by Virginia Woolf; p. [351] blank; p. [352] publisher's advertisements.

Stiff white pictorial paper wrappers printed in cream, grey, pale and dark brown; edges trimmed.

Published 8 June 1978; 15,000 copies printed. £1.95.

## A32 VIRGINIA WOOLF & LYTTON STRACHEY: LETTERS [1956]

*a. First edition*

VIRGINIA WOOLF | & | LYTTON STRACHEY | [*ornament*] | LETTERS | EDITED BY | LEONARD WOOLF & JAMES STRACHEY | THE HOGARTH PRESS | [*ornament*] | CHATTO AND WINDUS

Demy 8vo. 124 pp. front. $8\frac{1}{2} \times 5\frac{1}{2}$ in.

Pp. [1-2] blank; p. [3] half-title; p. [4] list of works by the authors; p. [5] title; p. [6] at head: Published by | The Hogarth Press Ltd | & | Chatto & Windus Ltd | London | [*ornament*] | Clarke, Irwin & Co Ltd | Toronto, at foot: 1956 | Printed in Great Britain by | R. & R. Clark Ltd. Edinburgh | All Rights Reserved; pp. 7-8 Preface by Leonard Woolf and James Strachey; pp. 9-118 text; p. [119] blank; p. [120] at centre: Printed by R. & R. Clark, Ltd., Edinburgh; pp. [121-124] blank.

Pale tan cloth boards; lettered in gold on spine: Let- | ters | [*ornament*] | Virginia | Woolf | & | Lytton | Strachey | The | Hogarth | Press | [*ornament*] | Chatto | & | Windus; edges trimmed; end-papers. Cream dust-jacket printed in black and tan, designed by Vanessa Bell.

Published 14 November 1956; 4000 copies printed. 18s.

A copy in black cloth boards is in the collection of Mr P. J. Allen; it is probably one of a secondary issue.

See 'Silences in the Text: *Virginia Woolf & Lytton Strachey: Letters*' by Michael Holzman, *Virginia Woolf Quarterly*, Winter/Spring 1977, Vol. 3, Nos. 1/2, pp. 33-7 for Leonard Woolf's editorial omissions.

*b. First American edition. [1956]*

VIRGINIA | WOOLF | & | LYTTON | STRACHEY | LETTERS | EDITED BY LEONARD WOOLF & JAMES

STRACHEY | HARCOURT, BRACE AND COMPANY • NEW YORK [*publisher's monogram*]

Large crown 8vo. x, 166 pp. 8 × 5 in.

P. [i] half-title; p. [ii] blank; p. [iii] title; p. [iv] at head: © 1956 By | Leonard Woolf and James Strachey | All rights reserved, including | the right to reproduce this book | or portions thereof in any form. | first American edition, towards centre: Library of Congress Catalog Card Number: 56-11962, towards foot: Printed in the United States of America; pp. v–vii Preface; p. [viii] Chronological bibliography of the books of Virginia Woolf; p. [ix] Chronological bibliography of the books of Lytton Strachey; p. [x] Glossary of names; p. [1] fly-title; p. [2] blank; pp. 3–166 text.

Pale duck-egg blue paper boards; half bound, darker duck-egg blue cloth spine; lettered in silver down the spine: Virginia Woolf & Lytton Strachey: Letters [*across the spine within an oval ring: publisher's monogram*] and on upper cover in silver on the cloth of the spine: LS | [*rule*] | VW; edges trimmed; end-papers. White dust-jacket printed in rust, olive-green and brown.

Published 27 December 1956; 4000 copies printed. $4.50.

## A33 HOURS IN A LIBRARY 1958

*First separate edition*

HOURS | IN | A LIBRARY | BY VIRGINIA WOOLF | HARCOURT, BRACE AND COMPANY | NEW YORK | [*publisher's monogram*]

Crown 8vo. 24 pp. front. (port., p. [4]). $7\frac{5}{8} \times 4\frac{7}{8}$ in.

P. [1] half-title; p. [2] Note by the publisher on the essay; p. [3] blank; p. [4] portrait of the author; p. [5] title; p. [6] note on frontispiece, copyright note, reservation rights, printer's note; pp. 7–9 Note by Leonard Woolf; p. [10] blank; p. [11] fly-title; p. [12] blank; pp. 13–24 text.

Black cloth boards, royal-blue cloth spine; lettered in gold on upper cover: Hours | in a | Library | By | Virginia | Woolf | [*publisher's monogram*], and in blind: VW; edges trimmed; royal-blue end-papers. Wax-paper dust-jacket.

Published 1 January 1958; 1800 copies printed. Unpriced.

The essay was privately printed for the friends of the publishers as a New Year's greeting. It was first published in the *TLS*, 30 November 1916, and reprinted in *Granite and Rainbow* and in *Collected Essays*, Vol. 2. See A34, 37, C59.

## A34 GRANITE AND RAINBOW 1958

### *a. First edition*

GRANITE | AND RAINBOW | ESSAYS BY | VIRGINIA WOOLF | [*publisher's device of a wolf's head*] | 1958 | THE HOGARTH PRESS | LONDON

Small demy 8vo. 240 pp. $8\frac{5}{8} \times 5\frac{1}{2}$ in.

P. [1] half-title; p. [2] list of works by the author; p. [3] title; p. [4] Published by | The Hogarth Press Ltd | [*ornament*] | Clarke, Irwin & Co Ltd | Toronto, at foot: © Leonard Woolf 1958 | Printed in Great Britain by | R. & R. Clark Ltd. Edinburgh | All rights reserved; pp. [5]-6 Contents; pp. [7-8] Editorial note by Leonard Woolf; p. [9] fly-title; p. [10] blank; pp. 11-145 text; p. [146] blank; p. [147] fly-title; p. [148] blank; pp. 149-[240] text.

Sky-blue cloth boards; lettered in gold on spine: Granite | and | Rainbow | [*ornament*] | Virginia | Woolf | The | Hogarth | Press; edges trimmed; end-papers. White dust-jacket printed in black and sky-blue, designed by Vanessa Bell.

Published 16 June 1958; 6000 copies printed. 18s.

There was a second impression of 2000 copies.

Contents: The Narrow Bridge of Art – Hours in a Library – Impassioned Prose – Life and the Novelist – On Rereading Meredith – The Anatomy of Fiction – Gothic Romance – The Supernatural in Fiction – Henry James's Ghost Stories – A Terribly Sensitive Mind – Women and Fiction – An Essay in Criticism – Phases of Fiction – The New Biography – A Talk about Memoirs – Sir Walter Raleigh – Sterne – Eliza and Sterne – Horace Walpole – A Friend of Johnson – Fanny Burney's Half-Sister – Money and Love – The Dream – The Fleeting Portrait, I. Waxworks at the Abbey; II. The Royal Academy – Poe's Helen – Visits to Walt Whitman – Oliver Wendell Holmes.

### *b. First edition – American photo-offset reprint.* [*1958*]

GRANITE | AND RAINBOW | [*rule*] | ESSAYS BY | VIRGINIA WOOLF | HARCOURT, BRACE | AND COMPANY | NEW YORK

Large crown 8vo. 240 pp. $8\frac{1}{8} \times 5\frac{3}{8}$ in.

P. [1] half-title; p. [2] list of works by the author; p. [3] title; p. [4] copyright note, reservation rights, first American edition, at foot: Library of Congress Catalog Card Number: 58-10898 | Printed in the United States of America; pp. [5]-[240] as *a* above.

Dull blue cloth boards; lettered in silver on spine: Virginia | Woolf |

[*down the spine:*] Granite and Rainbow | [*across the spine:*] [*publisher's monogram*] | Harcourt, | Brace | and | Company; device in silver on upper and lower covers; edges trimmed; end-papers. Pale blue dust-jacket printed in blue and black, designed by Vanessa Bell.

Issued 10 September 1958; 4100 copies printed. $3.75.

There was a second reprint of 500 copies in January 1965.

*c. First edition—American photo-offset reprint* (HARVEST BOOKS). [*1975*] *

GRANITE AND RAINBOW: ESSAYS. HARCOURT BRACE JOVANOVICH, INC., NEW YORK

Large crown 8vo. 240 pp. 8 × $5\frac{1}{4}$ in.

Issued 15 October 1975 in *Harvest Books* as Vol. HB318; 7000 copies printed. $5.75.

There was a further printing of 5385 copies in January 1976.

## A35 CONTEMPORARY WRITERS 1965

*a. First edition*

CONTEMPORARY | WRITERS | BY | VIRGINIA WOOLF | WITH A PREFACE BY | JEAN GUIGUET | [*publisher's device of a wolf's head*] | 1965 | THE HOGARTH PRESS | LONDON

Crown 8vo. 160 pp. $7\frac{7}{8}$ × $5\frac{1}{8}$ in.

P. [1] half-title; p. [2] list of works by the author; p. [3] title; p. [4] at head: Published by | The Hogarth Press Ltd | 42 William IV Street | London WC2 | [*ornament*] | Clarke, Irwin & Co. Ltd | Toronto, at foot: © Leonard Woolf 1965 | Printed in Great Britain by | T. & A. Constable Ltd | Hopetoun Street, Edinburgh; pp. [5]-6 Contents; pp. [7]-12 Preface by Jean Guiguet; p. [13] fly-title; p. [14] blank; pp. [15]-35 text; p. [36] blank; p. [37] fly-title; p. [38] blank; pp. [39]-160 text.

Dark brown paper boards; lettered in gold on spine: [*across head:*] Virginia | Woolf | [*down the spine:*] Contemporary Writers [*across foot:*] The | Hogarth | Press; edges trimmed; end-papers. Cream dust-jacket printed in dark green and poppy.

Published 11 November 1965; 3500 copies printed. £1. 1s.

Contents: The Claim of the Living — Caution and Criticism — In a Library — Women Novelists — A Man with a View — *The Way of All Flesh* — Journeys in Spain — *The Sentimental Traveller* — The

*Inward Light* – *One Immortality* – *A Room with a View* – *The Park Wall* – *Before Midnight* – *South Wind* – *Books and Persons* – Mr Galsworthy's Novel – Philosophy in Fiction – *The Green Mirror* – Moments of Vision – Mr Merrick's Novels – The "Movie" Novel – *Sylvia and Michael* – War in the Village – The Rights of Youth – Mr Hudson's Childhood – Honest Fiction – *September* – *The Three Black Pennys* – *Java Head* – *Gold and Iron* – The Pursuit of Beauty – Pleasant Stories – *Mummery* – *The Tunnel* – Romance and the Heart – *The Obstinate Lady* – Mr Norris's Method – Mr Norris's Standard – A Real American – *Sonia Married* – Winged Phrases – A Born Writer – Cleverness and Youth – Freudian Fiction – *Revolution* – Postscript or Prelude?

*b. First American edition. [1966]*

CONTEMPORARY | WRITERS | BY VIRGINIA WOOLF | WITH A PREFACE BY JEAN GUIGUET | [*ornamental rule*] | [*publisher's monogram within a rule*] | HAR-COURT, BRACE & WORLD, INC. | NEW YORK

Large crown 8vo. 160 pp. 8 × $5\frac{3}{8}$ in.

P. [1] half-title; p. [2] list of works by the author; p. [3] title; p. [4] copyright note, reservation rights, at foot: First American edition 1966 | Library of Congress Catalog Card Number: 66–19489 | Printed in the United States of America; pp. 5–6 Contents; pp. [7]–12 Preface by Jean Guiguet; p. [13] section-title; p. [14] blank; pp. [15]–35 text; p. [36] blank; p. [37] section-title; p. [38] blank; pp. [39]–160 text.

Ash-grey cloth boards; lettered in gold down the spine: Virginia Woolf [*ornament*] Contemporary Writers [*ornament*] Harcourt, Brace & World [*publisher's monogram within a rule*]; edges trimmed; blue end-papers. White pictorial dust-jacket printed in grey, blue and pink.

Published 14 September 1966; 3000 copies printed. $3.95.

## A36 SELECTIONS FROM HER ESSAYS [1966]

*First edition*

VIRGINIA WOOLF | SELECTIONS FROM HER ESSAYS | EDITED WITH AN INTRODUCTION | BY | WALTER JAMES | [*series device*] | CHATTO AND WINDUS | LONDON

Small crown 8vo. 206 pp. $7\frac{1}{4} \times 4\frac{3}{4}$ in.

P. [1] half-title; p. [2] list of works in the series; p. [3] title; p. [4] at head: Published by | Chatto & Windus (Educational) Ltd | 42 William IV Street | London W.C.2 | [*ornament*] | Clarke, Irwin & Co. Ltd | Toronto, at foot: Introduction and Selection | © Walter James | Printed in Great Britain | by T. & A. Constable Ltd | Hopetoun Street, Edinburgh; pp. [5-6] Contents; pp. 7-20 Introduction; p. 21 Biographical Table; p. 22 List of Major Works; pp. 23-202 text; pp. 203-205 Notes; p. [206] blank.

Turquoise paper boards; lettered in gold on spine: [*triple rule across head*] | Virginia | Woolf | Selections | from her | Essays | [*ornament*] | [*triple rule*] | [*series device*]; edges trimmed; end-papers.

Published 30 June 1966 as a *Queen's Classic Certificate Edition*; 6000 copies printed. 9s.

Contents: *Political Writings: A Room of One's Own* (3 extracts) – *Three Guineas* (2 extracts) – Thoughts on Peace in an Air Raid – Memories of a Working Women's Guild – *Literary and Other Critical Essays*: The Niece of an Earl – *A Room of One's Own* (2 extracts) – Professions for Women – The Patron and the Crocus – Mr Bennett and Mrs Brown – Modern Fiction – The Modern Essay – The Leaning Tower (extract) – Middlebrow – Walter Raleigh – Why? – All About Books – The Cinema – The "Sentimental Journey" – The New Biography – *Biography*: The Rev. William Cole – Outlines III, Lady Dorothy Nevill.

## A37 COLLECTED ESSAYS VOLUMES 1-2 1966

*a. First edition*

COLLECTED | ESSAYS | BY | VIRGINIA WOOLF | VOLUME ONE [VOLUME TWO] | [*publisher's device of a wolf's head*] | 1966 | THE HOGARTH PRESS | LONDON

Large crown 8vo. Vol. 1: [viii], 364 pp. Vol. 2: [xii], 308 pp. $7\frac{3}{4} \times 5$ in.

Vol. 1: P. [i] half-title; p. [ii] list of works by the author; p. [iii] title; p. [iv] at head: Published by | The Hogarth Press Ltd | [*ornament*] | Clarke, Irwin & Co. Ltd | Toronto, at foot: © 1925, 1932, 1942, 1947, 1950, 1958, Leonard Woolf 1966 | Printed by lithography in Great Britain by | Filmset Limited, Crawley; p. [v] Editorial Note, by Leonard Woolf; p. [vi] Key to Abbreviations of Virginia Woolf's Works in Contents List; pp. [vii-viii] Contents; pp. 1-361 text; pp. [362-364] blank. Vol. 2: Pp. [i-iv] form upper end-papers; p. [v] half-title; p. [vi] list of works by the author; p. [vii] title; p. [viii] six lines as p. [iv] above, at foot: Filmset and

Printed in Great Britain by | Bookprint Limited, London and Crawley; p. [ix] as p. [vi] above; p. [x] blank; pp. [xi–xii] Contents; pp. 1–304 text; pp. [304–308] form lower end-papers.

Dark brown rexine boards; lettered in gold on spine: Virginia | Woolf | [*within an oval blue panel edged with gold:*] Collected | Essays | I [II] | [*below panel: ornament*] | The | Hogarth Press; edges trimmed; end-papers. White dust-jacket printed in blue and black on Vol. 1, and printed in yellow and black on Vol. 2.

Published 20 October 1966; 5500 copies printed of each volume. £1. 15s. and £1. 10s. respectively.

There was a further printing of 3000 copies of Vol. 1 in January 1968 of which 200 copies were issued in paperback. Two thousand, five hundred copies of Vol. 2 were issued in paperback; there was a further printing of 2000 copies in July 1972 of which 1250 were were issued in paperback.

Contents: Vol. 1: On Not Knowing Greek – *The Faery Queen* – The Countess of Pembroke's Arcadia – *Twelfth Night* at the Old Vic – Donne after Three Centuries – The Elizabethan Lumber Room – Notes on an Elizabethan Play – Defoe – *Robinson Crusoe* – Congreve's Comedies – Addison – The Sentimental Journey – The Humane Art – Oliver Goldsmith – The Historian and 'The Gibbon' – Reflections at Sheffield Place – Gothic Romance – Sir Walter Scott, I. Gas at Abbotsford; II. *The Antiquary* – Jane Austen – William Hazlitt – Impassioned Prose – The Captain's Death Bed – Lockhart's Criticism – *Jane Eyre* and *Wuthering Heights* – *David Copperfield* – George Eliot – Ruskin – *Aurora Leigh* – The Niece of an Earl – The Novels of George Meredith – On Re-reading Meredith – The Russian Point of View – The Novels of Turgenev – Lewis Carroll – The Novels of Thomas Hardy – Henry James, I. *Within the Rim*; II. *The Old Order*; III. *The Letters of Henry James* – Henry James's Ghost Stories – The Supernatural in Fiction – George Gissing – Joseph Conrad – Mr Conrad: A Conversation – Walter Raleigh – Mr Bennett and Mrs Brown – George Moore – The Novels of E. M. Forster – Notes on D. H. Lawrence – A Terribly Sensitive Mind – The Death of the Moth. Vol. 2: How Should One Read a Book? – Reading – Hours in a Library – The Modern Essay – The Art of Fiction – Phases of Fiction – Modern Fiction – American Fiction – On Re-Reading Novels – Life and the Novelist – The Anatomy of Fiction – Women and Fiction – The Patron and the Crocus – How It Strikes a Contemporary – The Leaning Tower – A Letter to a Young Poet – Middlebrow – Reviewing – The Narrow Bridge of Art – The Artist and Politics – Walter Sickert – Craftsmanship – An Essay in Criticism – Modern Letters – All About Books – The Cinema – Personalities – Why? – Professions for Women – Evening over Sussex: Reflections in a Motor Car – The Moment: Summer's Night – Gas – Fishing.

*b. First edition – American photo-offset reprint. [1967]*

[*first line in open capitals:*] VOLUME I [VOLUME II] | COLLECTED | ESSAYS | [*ornament*] | VIRGINIA WOOLF | HARCOURT, BRACE & WORLD, INC., NEW YORK

Large crown 8vo. Vol. 1: [xvi], 368 pp. Vol. 2: [xiv], 306 pp. 8 × 5¼ in.

Vol. 1: Pp. [i–ii] blank; p. [iii] half-title; p. [iv] blank; p. [v] list of works by the author; p. [vi] blank; p. [vii] title; p. [viii] Copyright © 1925, 1932, 1942, 1947, 1950 | by Harcourt, Brace & World, Inc. | Copyright © 1953, 1958, 1960, 1966 by Leonard Woolf, reservation rights, First American edition 1967 | Library of Congress Catalog Card Number: 67-20327 | Printed in the United States of America | [*publisher's monogram within a rule*]; p. [ix] Editorial Note by Leonard Woolf; p. [x] blank; p. [xi] Key to Abbreviations of Virginia Woolf's Works in Contents List; p. [xii] blank; pp. [xiii–xiv] Contents; p. [xv] fly-title; p. [xvi] blank; pp. 1–361 text; pp. [362–368] blank. Vol. 2: Pp. [i–ii] blank; p. [iii] half-title; p. [iv] blank; p. [v] list of works by the author; p. [vi] blank; p. [vii] title; p. [viii] as p. [viii] above; p. [ix] as p. [xi] above; p. [x] blank; pp. [xi–xii] Contents; p. [xiii] fly-title; p. [xiv] blank; pp. 1–304 text; pp. [305–306] blank.

Vol. 1: Brown cloth boards; lettered in gold down the spine: Virginia Woolf [*black rule*] Collected Essays [*in black: above rule, in open number:*] I [II] | [*at foot:*] [*publisher's monogram within a rule*] | Harcourt, | Brace | & World, ornament in blind on upper cover; edges trimmed, top yellow; yellow end-papers. White dust-jacket printed in tan, yellow and black. Vol. 2: Bright blue cloth boards; then as above. White dust-jacket printed in bright blue, yellow and black.

Issued 25 October 1967; 4000 copies printed. $5.95.

## A38 NURSE LUGTON'S GOLDEN THIMBLE 1966

*First separate edition*

NURSE LUGTON'S | GOLDEN THIMBLE | BY | VIRGINIA WOOLF | WITH PICTURES BY | DUNCAN GRANT | [*publisher's device of a wolf's head*] | 1966 | THE HOGARTH PRESS | LONDON

12mo. [iv], 20 pp. front., 5 illus. on pp. [6, 9–10, 13–14]. 7¾ × 6 in.

Pp. [i–iv] form upper end-papers; p. [1] half-title; p. [2] frontispiece; p. [3] title; p. [4] Foreword by Leonard Woolf; p. 5 text; p. [6] illus.; pp. 7–8 text; pp. [9–10] illus.; pp. 11–12 text; pp. [13–14] illus.; p. 15 text; p. [16] at head: Published by | The Hogarth

Press | 42 William IV Street | London W.C.2. | [*ornament*] | Clarke Irwin & Co. Ltd. | Toronto, at foot: Text © Leonard Woolf 1965 | Pictures by © Duncan Grant 1966 | Printed in Great Britain by | T. H. Brickell and Son Ltd | The Blackmore Press, Gillingham, Dorset; pp. [17–20] form lower end-papers.

Violet paper boards; lettered in gold on upper cover: Nurse Lugton's | Golden Thimble | By | Virginia Woolf | With pictures by | Duncan Grant | [*illus. of a thimble*] | The Hogarth Press, and on lower cover at foot: 6s. | net.

Printed on lavender paper.

Published 8 December 1966; 4000 copies printed. 6s.

The short story was first published as 'The . . .' in *TLS*, 17 June 1965. See C376.

## A39 COLLECTED ESSAYS VOLUMES 3–4 1967

*a. First edition*

COLLECTED | ESSAYS | BY | VIRGINIA WOOLF | VOLUME THREE [VOLUME FOUR] | [*publisher's device of a wolf's head*] | 1967 | THE HOGARTH PRESS | LONDON

Large crown 8vo. Vol. 3: viii, 232 pp. Vol. 4: [viii], 240 pp. $7\frac{3}{4} \times 5$ in.

Vol. 3: P. [i] half-title; p. [ii] list of works by the author; p. [iii] title; p. [iv] at head: Published by | The Hogarth Press Ltd | [*ornament*] | Clarke, Irwin & Co. Ltd | Toronto, at foot: © 1925, 1932, 1942, 1947, 1950, 1958, Leonard Woolf 1967 | Printed by lithography in Great Britain by | Filmset Limited, Crawley; p. [v] Key to Abbreviations of Virginia Woolf's Works in Contents List; p. [vi] blank; pp. vii–viii Contents; pp. 1–231 text; p. [232] blank. Vol. 4: Pp. [i–viii] as above; pp. 1–235 text; p. [236] blank; pp. [237–240] form lower end-papers.

Dark brown rexine boards; lettered in gold on spine: Virginia | Woolf | [*within an oval blue panel edged with gold:*] Collected | Essays | III [IV] | [*below panel: ornament*] | The | Hogarth Press; edges trimmed; end-papers in Vol. 3, upper end-papers in Vol. 4. White dust-jacket printed in brownish-red and brown on Vol. 3, and printed in turquoise and black on Vol. 4.

Published February 1967; 5500 copies printed of each volume. £1. 5s. each.

Two thousand, five hundred copies of each volume were issued in paperback.

Contents: Vol. 3: The Pastons and Chaucer – Montaigne – Sir Walter Raleigh – The Strange Elizabethans – Rambling Round Evelyn – The Duchess of Newcastle – Dorothy Osborne's *Letters* – Madame de Sévigné – Swift's *Journal to Stella* – Lord Chesterfield's Letters to His Son – Sterne – Sterne's Ghost – Eliza and Sterne – Horace Walpole – Two Antiquaries: Walpole and Cole – The Rev. William Cole: A Letter – White's Selborne – A Friend of Johnson – Dr. Burney's Evening Party – Fanny Burney's Half-Sister – Mrs. Thrale – Two Parsons, I. James Woodforde; II. The Rev. John Skinner – Money and Love – Four Figures, I. Cowper and Lady Austen; II. Beau Brummell; III. Mary Wollstonecraft; IV. Dorothy Wordsworth – Jones and Wilkinson – Selina Trimmer – The Man at the Gate – Sara Coleridge – Harriette Wilson. Vol. 4: De Quincey's Autobiography – Genius: R. B. Haydon – Jack Mytton – Crabbe – 'Not One of Us' – Geraldine and Jane – Poe's Helen – Oliver Wendell Holmes – Visits to Walt Whitman – 'I am Christina Rossetti' – Two Women: Emily Davies and Lady Augusta Stanley – Ellen Terry – The Enchanted Organ: Anne Thackeray – Leslie Stephen – Edmund Gosse – Roger Fry – The Cosmos – The Dream – Outlines, I. Miss Mitford; II. Dr. Bentley; III. Lady Dorothy Nevill; IV. Archbishop Thomson – Lives of the Obscure, I. Taylors and Edgeworths; II. Laetitia Pilkington – Memories of a Working Women's Guild – Old Mrs Grey – Three Pictures – Street Haunting: A London Adventure – Flying Over London – Thoughts on Peace in an Air Raid – The Sun and the Fish – Thunder at Wembley – To Spain – On Being Ill – The Fleeting Portrait, I. Waxworks at the Abbey; II. The Royal Academy – Royalty – A Talk about Memoirs – The Art of Biography – The New Biography.

*b. First Edition – American photo-offset reprint.* [*1967*]

[*first line in open capitals:*] VOLUME III [VOLUME IV] | COLLECTED | ESSAYS | [*ornament*] | VIRGINIA WOOLF | HARCOURT, BRACE & WORLD INC., NEW YORK

Large crown 8vo. Vol. 3: [xiv], 234 pp. Vol. 4: [xiv], 242 pp. 8 × $5\frac{1}{4}$ in.

Vol. 3: Pp. [i–ii] blank; p. [iii] half-title; p. [iv] blank; p. [v] list of works by the author; p. [vi] blank; p. [vii] title; p. [viii] Copyright © 1925, 1932, 1942, 1947, 1950 | by Harcourt, Brace & World, Inc. | Copyright © 1953, 1958, 1960, 1967 by Leonard Woolf, reservation rights, First American edition | Library of Congress Catalog Card Number: 67-20327 | Printed in the United States of America | [*publisher's monogram within a rule*]; p. [ix] Key to Abbreviations of Virginia Woolf's Works in Contents List; p. [x] blank; pp. [xi–xii]

Contents; p. [xiii] fly-title; p. [xiv] blank; pp. 1–231 text; pp. [232–234] blank. Vol. 4: Pp. [i–ii] blank; p. [iii] half-title; p. [iv] blank; p. [v] list of works by the author; p. [vi] blank; p. [vii] title; p. [viii] as p. [viii] above; p. [ix] as p. [ix] above; p. [x] blank; pp. [xi–xii] Contents; p. [xiii] fly-title; p. [xiv] blank; pp. 1–235 text; pp. [236–242] blank.

Vol. 3: Bright orange cloth boards; lettered in gold down the spine: Virginia Woolf [*black rule*] Collected Essays [*in black: above rule:*] III [IV] | [*at foot:*] [*publisher's monogram within a rule*] | Harcourt, | Brace | & World, ornament in blind on upper cover; edges trimmed, top yellow; yellow end-papers. White dust-jacket printed in orange, yellow and black. Vol. 4: Pale olive green cloth boards; then as above. White dust-jacket printed in green, yellow and black.

Issued 25 October 1967; 4000 copies printed. $5.95.

## A40 STEPHEN VERSUS GLADSTONE 1967

*First edition*

VIRGINIA WOOLF | STEPHEN | VERSUS | GLADSTONE | HEADINGTON QUARRY | 1967

Royal 8vo. [8] pp. $9\frac{3}{4} \times 6\frac{1}{8}$ in.

Pp. [1–2] blank; p. [3] title; p. [4] extract from a letter from Leslie Stephen to C. E. Norton dated 7 December 1892 on his election as President of the London Library printed in *The Life and Letters of Leslie Stephen*, by Frederic W. Maitland, at foot: The paragraph opposite is taken from a manuscript news- | paper conducted sporadically by the Stephen children. It is | printed by kind permission of Mr. Leonard Woolf.; p. [5] paragraph signed: Virginia Stephen | (aged 10), at head: From *The Hyde Park Gate News*, vol. ii, no. 45, Monday, 21 November 1892.; p. [6] at centre: Fifty copies printed by | Will and Sebastian Carter at | The Rampant Lions Press, Cambridge | No. [*numbered in ink*]; pp. [7–8] blank.

Reddish-brown paper wrappers, printed on upper wrapper: Virginia Woolf | [*ornament*] | Stephen | versus | Gladstone | [*ornament*] | Headington Quarry | 1967; oval water mark, $2\frac{7}{8} \times 3\frac{3}{4}$ in., of Romulus and Remus and the wolf on lower wrapper; edges trimmed; wrapper top and fore edges trimmed, bottom untrimmed; sewn.

Published 10 August 1967; 50 copies printed. Not for sale.

Written in 1892 when the author was 10.

## A41 A COCKNEY'S FARMING EXPERIENCES 1972 [*i.e.* 1973]

*First edition*

VIRGINIA WOOLF | A | COCKNEY'S FARMING | EXPERIENCES | WITH | INTRODUCTION | BY | SUZANNE HENIG | SAN DIEGO STATE UNIVERSITY PRESS | 1972

[6], viii, 14 pp. $8\frac{1}{2} \times 6$ in.

P. [1] blank; p. [2] at centre: Two thousand copies of which this is copy number [*numbered in ink over short rule*].; p. [3] title; p. [4] at centre: Copyright © 1972 by San Diego State University Press; p. [5] Preface; p. [6] blank; pp. [i]–viii Introduction; pp. [1]–4 text of A Cockney's Farming Experiences; pp. 5–11 The Experiences of a Pater-Familias; pp. [12–14] blank.

Navy-blue cloth boards; lettered in gold on upper cover: Virginia Woolf | A Cockney's Farming Experience [*sic*] | and | The Experiences of a Pater-familias; edges trimmed; pale blue paste-down end-papers.

Printed on pale blue paper.

Published early 1973; 2000 copies printed. Included free in the subscription to the *Virginia Woolf Quarterly* with Vol. 1, No. 2, Winter 1973.

Written in 1892 when the author was 10.

## A42 MRS DALLOWAYS' PARTY 1973

*a. First edition*

[*within a frame:*] MRS DALLOWAY'S PARTY | A SHORT STORY SEQUENCE | BY | VIRGINIA WOOLF | EDITED WITH AN INTRODUCTION BY | STELLA McNICHOL | 1973 | THE HOGARTH PRESS | LONDON

Crown 8vo. 72 pp. $7\frac{3}{4} \times 5$ in.

P. [1] half-title; p. [2] blank; p. [3] title; p. [4] at head: Published by | The Hogarth Press Ltd | 42 William IV Street | London W.C. 2 | [*ornament*] | Clarke Irwin & Co. Ltd | Toronto, reservation rights, at foot: ISBN 0 7012 03781 | © Quentin Bell and Angelica Garnett 1923, | 1943 and 1973 | Introduction © Stella McNichol 1973 | Printed in Great Britain by | T. & A. Constable Ltd, Edinburgh; p. [5] Contents; p. [6] Acknowledgments; p. [7] fly-title; p. [8] blank; pp. 9–17 Introduction; p. [18] blank; pp. 19–[70] text; pp. [71–72] blank.

Navy-blue cloth boards; lettered in gold down the spine: Virginia Woolf [*ornament*] Mrs Dalloway's Party The Hogarth Press; edges trimmed; end-papers. White pictorial dust-jacket printed in pale blue, navy-blue and pink.

Published 3 May 1973; 4000 copies printed. £1.25.

Contents: Mrs Dalloway in Bond Street – The Man Who Loved His Kind – The Introduction – Ancestors – Together and Apart – The New Dress – A Summing Up.

The Introduction and Ancestors are published for the first time.

*b. First edition – American photo-offset reprint* (HARVEST BOOKS). [*1975*]

[*within a frame:*] MRS DALLOWAY'S PARTY | A SHORT STORY SEQUENCE | BY | VIRGINIA WOOLF | EDITED, WITH AN INTRODUCTION, BY | STELLA McNICHOL | [*publisher's monogram within a rule*] | AN ORIGINAL HARVEST BOOK | HARCOURT BRACE JOVANOVICH | NEW YORK AND LONDON

Large crown 8vo. [vi], 74 pp. 8 × $5\frac{5}{8}$ in.

Pp. [i–ii] blank; p. [iii] half-title; p. [iv] blank; p. [v] list of works by the author; p. [vi] blank; p. [1] title; p. [2] publication note, etc., printer's note; p. [3] Contents; p. [4] blank; p. [5] Acknowledgments; p. [6] blank; p. [7] fly-title; p. [8] blank; pp. 9–17 Introduction; p. [18] blank; pp. 19–70 text; p. [71] list of works by the author in paperback; pp. [72–74] blank.

Stiff white pictorial paper wrappers printed in pink, yellow, orange, brown and black; edges trimmed.

Issued 12 March 1975 in *Harvest Books* as Vol. HB279; 10,000 copies printed. $1.95.

There was a further printing of 5314 copies in June 1976.

## A43 THE LONDON SCENE [1975]

*First separate edition*

THE LONDON SCENE | [*ornament in red*] FIVE ESSAYS BY | VIRGINIA WOOLF | NEW YORK: FRANK HALLMAN

Small royal 8vo. 48 pp. $9\frac{1}{4}$ × 6 in.

Pp. [1–2] blank; p. [3] title; p. [4] at head: First published in 1975 by | Frank Hallman | Box 246, Cooper Station | New York, New

York 1003, at foot: Copyright © 1975 Angelica Garnett and Quentin Bell. | All rights reserved. | Library of Congress Catalog Card Number: 74-5248.; p. [5] Contents; p. [6] blank; pp. 7-44 text; p. [45] at head: 750 copies designed by Ronald Gordon | & printed at The Stinehour Press.; pp. [46-48] blank.

Dull stone cloth boards; lettered in gold down the spine: The London Scene; edges trimmed; cream end-papers. Pale blue dust-jacket printed in black.

Published 15 April 1975; 750 copies printed. $15.

This series of essays was first published in *Good Housekeeping*, December 1931, January, March, May and October 1932. A sixth essay 'Portrait of a Londoner' was published in December 1932. *See* C332.1-2, 333.1-2, 334.1, 335.1.

Contents: The Docks of London – Oxford Street Tide – Great Men's Houses – Abbeys and Cathedrals – "This is the House of Commons".

## A44 THE FLIGHT OF THE MIND 1975

*a. First edition*

[*first two lines in open capitals:*] THE FLIGHT | OF THE MIND | THE LETTERS OF | VIRGINIA WOOLF | VOLUME I: 1888-1912 | (VIRGINIA STEPHEN) | EDITOR: NIGEL NICOLSON | ASSISTANT EDITOR: JOANNE TRAUTMANN | 1975 | THE HOGARTH PRESS | LONDON

Small royal 8vo. xxiv, 532 pp. front. (port.), 2 illus. on pp. 5, 225; 10 plates between pp. 20-21, 28-29, 200-201, 232-233, 424-425. $9\frac{1}{4} \times 6$ in.

P. [i] half-title; p. [ii] blank; p. [iii] title; p. [iv] at head: Published by | The Hogarth Press Ltd | 42 William IV Street | London WC2N 4DF | [*ornament*] | Clarke, Irwin & Co. Ltd | Toronto | [*reservation rights in seven lines*] | Editorial Note and Introduction | © Nigel Nicolson 1975 | Letters © Quentin Bell and | Angelica Garnett 1975 | ISBN 0 7012 0403 6 | Printed in Great Britain by | T. & A. Constable Ltd | Hopetoun Street, Edinburgh; p. [v] Contents; p. [vi] blank; p. [vii] list of illustrations; p. [viii] blank; pp. ix-xii Editorial Note; pp. xiii-xxi Introduction; pp. [xxii-xxiii] Family Tree; p. [xxiv] list of abbreviations; pp. 1-47 text; p. [48] blank; pp. 49-127 text; p. [128] blank; pp. 129-237 text; p. [238] blank; pp. 239-401 text; p. [402] blank; pp. 403-419 text; p. [420] blank; pp. 421-481 text; p. [482] blank; pp. 483-508 text; pp. 509-510 Appendix: Nicknames used in Volume I; pp. 511-531 Index; p. [532] blank.

Peacock-blue cloth boards; lettered in gold on spine: The | Flight | of the | Mind | [*short rule, ornament, short rule*] | The | Letters | of | Virginia | Woolf | Volume 1 | 1888–1912 | The | Hogarth | Press; edges trimmed; end-papers. White pictorial dust-jacket printed in pale terra cotta, black, grey and orange, designed by Angelica Garnett.

Published 18 September 1975; 10,000 copies printed. £7.75.

Brief extracts were published in the *Sunday Times Weekly Review*, 17 August 1975, pp. 21–22 and 24 August, pp. 21–22.

*b. First edition – American photo-offset reprint. [1975]* *

THE LETTERS OF | VIRGINIA WOOLF | VOLUME I: 1888–1912 | (VIRGINIA STEPHEN) | [*swelled rule*] | EDITOR: NIGEL NICOLSON | ASSISTANT EDITOR: JOANNE TRAUTMANN | [*publisher's monogram within a rule*] | HARCOURT BRACE JOVANOVICH | NEW YORK AND LONDON

Small royal 8vo. xxiv, 536 pp. front., 2 illus., plates. $9\frac{1}{4} \times 6$ in.

P. [i] half-title; p. [ii] blank; p. [iii] title; p. [iv] copyright notes, reservation rights, towards centre: Printed in the United States of America | First American edition 1975 | BCDE | Library of Congress Cataloging in Publication Data | [*seven lines*] | ISBN 0-15-150924-7; pp. [v]–[xxiv], 1–531 as *a* above; pp. [532–536] blank.

Cream paper boards, wine cloth spine; lettered in gold on spine; edges trimmed; end-papers. Cream pictorial dust-jacket printed in wine, gold and black.

Issued 17 November 1975; 8000 copies printed. $14.95.

There were further printings of 2500 copies each in March and April 1976.

*c. First edition – American photo-offset reprint* (HARVEST BOOKS). [*1977*]

THE LETTERS OF | VIRGINIA WOOLF | VOLUME I: 1888–1912 | (VIRGINIA STEPHEN) | [*swelled rule*] | EDITOR: NIGEL NICOLSON | ASSISTANT EDITOR: JOANNE TRAUTMANN | [*monogram*] | A HARVEST BOOK | HARCOURT BRACE JOVANOVICH | NEW YORK AND LONDON | ORIGINALLY PUBLISHED IN ENGLAND AS THE FLIGHT OF THE MIND

Large crown 8vo. xxvi, 540 pp. front. (p. [ii] port.), 2 illus., plates. 8 × $5\frac{3}{8}$ in.

P. [i] half-title; p. [ii] portrait; p. [iii] title; p. [iv] copyright notes, reservation rights, printer's note etc.; pp. [v]-[xxiv], 1-531 as *a* above; p. [532] blank; p. [533] list of works by the author in paperback; pp. [534-540] blank.

Stiff white pictorial paper wrappers printed in cream, brown, black and grey; edges trimmed.

Issued 4 May 1977 in *Harvest Books* as Vol. HB358; 15,229 copies printed. $5.95.

## A45 MOMENTS OF BEING 1976

*a. First edition*

[*first line in open capitals:*] VIRGINIA WOOLF | MOMENTS OF BEING | UNPUBLISHED AUTOBIOGRAPHICAL | WRITINGS | [*ornaments*] | EDITED | WITH AN INTRODUCTION AND NOTES | BY | JEANNE SCHULKIND | 1976 | THE UNIVERSITY PRESS | SUSSEX

Small demy 8vo. 208 pp. $8\frac{1}{2}$ × $5\frac{3}{8}$ in.

P. [1] half-title; p. [2] blank; p. [3] title; p. [4] at head: Published for | Sussex University Press | by | Chatto & Windus Ltd | 40 William IV Street | London WC2N 4DF | [*ornament*] | Clarke, Irwin & Co, Ltd | Toronto | [*reservation rights in seven lines*] | ISBN 0 85621 050 1 | Text © Quentin Bell and Angelica Garnett 1976 | Introduction and Editorial Matter © Jeanne Schulkind 1976 | Printed in Great Britain by | Ebenezer Baylis and Son Limited | The Trinity Press, Worcester, and London; p. [5] Contents; p. [6] Acknowledgements; pp. 7-10 Editor's Note; pp. 11-24 Introduction; pp. 25-27 Editor's Note; pp. 28-59 text; p. [60] blank; pp. 61-63 Editor's Note; pp. 64-137 text; p. [138] blank; pp. 139-141 Editor's Note; pp. 142-155 text; p. [156] blank; pp. 157-158 Editor's Note; pp. 159-179 text; p. [180] blank; p. 181 Editor's Note; pp. 182-198 text; p. 199 Appendix; p. [200] blank; pp. 201-207 Index; p. [208] blank.

Sapphire blue rexine boards; lettered in gold on spine: Moments | of | Being | [*ornament*] | Virginia | Woolf | Edited | by | Jeanne | Schulkind | Sussex | University | Press; end-papers; edges trimmed. White pictorial dust-jacket printed in pale brown and black, designed by Philippa Bramson.

Published 3 June 1976; 4000 copies printed. £4.80.

There was a further printing of 2000 copies in August 1976.

Contents: Reminiscences – A Sketch of the Past – The Memoir Club Contributions: 22 Hyde Park Gate – Old Bloomsbury – Am I a Snob?

### *b. First edition – American photo-offset reprint.* [*1977*]

[*first line in open capitals:*] VIRGINIA WOOLF | MOMENTS OF BEING | UNPUBLISHED AUTOBIOGRAPHICAL | WRITINGS | [*ornaments*] | EDITED AND | WITH AN INTRODUCTION AND NOTES | BY | JEANNE SCHULKIND | [*publisher's monogram within a rule*] | HARCOURT BRACE JOVANOVICH | NEW YORK AND LONDON

Small demy 8vo. 208 pp. $8\frac{3}{8} \times 5\frac{1}{4}$ in.

P. [1] half-title; p. [2] list of works by the author; p. [3] title; p. [4] copyright note, reservation rights, towards centre: Printed in the United States of America | Library of Congress Catalog Card Number 76-27410 | ISBN 0-15-162034-2, at foot: First American edition | BCDE; pp. [5]-[208] as *a* above.

Grey paper boards, black cloth spine; lettered in silver down the spine: Virginia Woolf Moments of Being [*publisher's monogram in black on a silver ground*] Harcourt Brace Jovanovich, and on lower cover: 0-15-162034-2; edges trimmed; grey end-papers. White pictorial dust-jacket printed in cream, black and pink.

Issued 14 January 1977; 15,000 copies printed. $8.95.

There was a further printing of 3500 copies in January 1977.

### *c. Second English edition* (PANTHER BOOKS). [*1978*]

VIRGINIA WOOLF | MOMENTS OF BEING | UNPUBLISHED AUTOBIOGRAPHICAL | WRITINGS | EDITED | WITH AN INTRODUCTION AND NOTES | BY | JEANNE SCHULKIND | TRIAD PANTHER

Foolscap 8vo. 240 pp. $7 \times 4\frac{3}{8}$ in.

P. [1] Biographical note on the author; p. [2] list of works by the author; p. [3] title; p. [4] publication note, copyright note, printer's imprint, etc.; p. [5] Contents; p. [6] Acknowledgements; pp. [7]-11 Editor's Note; p. [12] blank; pp. [13]-28 Introduction; pp. [29]-31 Editor's Note; pp. [32]-69 text; p. [70] blank; pp. [71]-73 Editor's Note; pp. 74-159 text; p. [160] blank; pp. [161]-164 Editor's Note; pp. [165]-180 text; pp. [181]-182 Editor's Note;

pp. [183]-207 text; p. [208] blank; pp. [209]-210 Editor's Note; pp. [211]-230 text; p. [231] Appendix; p. [232] blank; pp. [233]-239 Index; p. [240] publisher's advertisements.

Stiff white pictorial paper wrappers printed in stone, grey, pink and brown; edges trimmed.

Published 21 September 1978; 20,000 copies printed. £1.35.

## A46 FRESHWATER [1976]

*a. First edition*

[*first two lines in open capitals:*] VIRGINIA | WOOLF | [*rule*] | FRESHWATER | · A COMEDY · | [*illustration of photographer with camera*] | [*double rule*] | EDITED AND WITH A PREFACE | BY LUCIO P. RUOTOLO | ILLUSTRATED BY LORETTA TREZZO | [*publisher's monogram*] | HARCOURT BRACE JOVANOVICH · NEW YORK AND LONDON

Small demy 8vo. [2], xii, 82 pp. front., 5 illus. on pp. [i, 1, 5, 19, 31]. $8\frac{3}{8} \times 5\frac{3}{8}$ in.

Pp. [1-2] blank; p. [i] illustration; p. [ii] blank; p. [iii] list of works by the author; p. [iv] blank; p. [v] title; p. [vi] copyright note, reservation rights, at centre: Printed in the United States of America, Library of Congress cataloguing data, below centre: ISBN 0-15-133487-0 | First edition | BCDE; pp. vii-xi Editor's Preface; p. [xii] blank; p. [1] illustration; p. [2] blank; p. [3] facsimile of the author's casting for the play; p. [4] blank; p. [5] illustration; p. [6] blank; pp. 7-18 text; p. [19] illustration; p. [20] blank; pp. 21-30 text; p. [31] illustration; p. [32] blank; pp. 33-44 text; pp. 45-52 Notes, 1935 Version; p. [53] section-title; p. [54] blank; pp. 55-74 text; pp. 75-76 Notes, 1923 Version; pp. [77-82] blank, integral.

White cloth boards; lettered down the spine: [*in bronze:*] Virginia Woolf [*in green:*] Freshwater [*in maroon:*] [*across the spine: publisher's monogram*] [*down the spine:*] Harcourt Brace Jovanovich, and on lower cover: [*in maroon:*] 0-15-133487-0; illustration of photographer with camera stamped in green on upper cover; edges trimmed; olive yellow end-papers. White pictorial dust-jacket printed in olive green, black, orange, yellow and pink.

Published 28 June 1976; 10,000 copies printed. $6.95.

Two thousand, one hundred and forty copies were sent to the Hogarth Press.

*b. First edition – English issue. 1976*

[*first two lines in open capitals:*] VIRGINIA | WOOLF | [*rule*] | FRESHWATER | · COMEDY · | [*illustration of photographer with camera*] | [*double rule*] | EDITED AND WITH A PREFACE | BY LUCIO P. RUOTOLO | ILLUSTRATED BY LORETTA TREZZO | THE HOGARTH PRESS · LONDON · 1976

Small demy 8vo. [2], xii, 82 pp. front., 5 illus. $8\frac{3}{8} \times 5\frac{3}{8}$ in.

Pp. [1-2] blank; p. [i] illustration; p. [ii] blank; p. [iii] list of works by the author; p. [iv] blank; p. [v] title; p. [vi] towards centre: Published by | The Hogarth Press Ltd. | London | [*ornament*] | Clarke, Irwin & Co. Ltd. | Toronto | [*reservation rights in seven lines*] | ISBN 0 7012 0421 4 | Copyright © 1976 Quentin Bell and Angelica Garnett | Preface copyright © 1976 by Lucio P. Ruotolo | Printed in United States of America; pp. vii–[xii], [1]–[82] as *a* above.

Olive-brown rexine boards; lettered in gold down the spine: Virginia Woolf · Freshwater · A Comedy [*across foot: publisher's monogram*]; edges trimmed; olive-yellow end-papers. White pictorial dust-jacket printed in olive green, black, orange, yellow and pink.

Issued 7 October 1976; 2140 copies bound. £3. Copies with a cancel title were supplied by Harcourt Brace Jovanovich.

## A47 THE QUESTION OF THINGS HAPPENING 1976

*a. First edition*

[*first three lines in open capitals:*] THE QUESTION | OF THINGS | HAPPENING | THE LETTERS OF | VIRGINIA WOOLF | VOLUME II : 1912–1922 | EDITOR: NIGEL NICOLSON | ASSISTANT EDITOR: JOANNE TRAUTMANN | 1976 | THE HOGARTH PRESS | LONDON

Small royal 8vo. xxviii, 628 pp. illus. on p. 153; 8 plates between pp. 4–5, 36–37, 452–453, 484–485. $9\frac{1}{4} \times 6$ in.

P. [i] half-title; p. [ii] blank; p. [iii] title; p. [iv] at head: Published by | The Hogarth Press Ltd | 42 William IV Street | London WC2N 4DF | [*ornament*] | Clarke, Irwin & Co. Ltd | Toronto | [*reservation rights in seven lines*] | Editorial Note and Introduction | © Nigel Nicolson 1976 | Letters © Quentin Bell and | Angelica Garnett 1976 | ISBN 7012 0420 6 | Printed in Great Britain by | T. & A. Constable Ltd | Hopetoun Street, Edinburgh; p. [v] quotation from letter to Janet Case; p. [vi] blank; p. [vii] Contents; p. [viii] blank; p. [ix] Illustrations; p. [x] blank; pp. xi–xii Editorial Note; pp. xiii–xxiv Introduction; p. [xxv] blank; pp. [xxvi–xxvii] Family Tree; p. [xxviii] list of abbreviations; pp. 1–152 text; p. 153 illustration; pp. 154–602 text; pp. 603–627 Index; p. [628] blank.

Peacock-blue cloth boards; lettered in gold on spine: The | Question | of Things | Happening | [*short rule, ornament, short rule*] | The | Letters | of | Virginia | Woolf | Volume 2 | 1912–1922 | The | Hogarth | Press; edges trimmed; end-papers. White pictorial dust-jacket printed in lilac, black, brown and grey, designed by Angelica Garnett.

Published 25 September 1976; 11,500 copies printed. £9.50.

See also 'Virginia Woolf's Letters, Volume II, A Note' by S. P. Rosenbaum, *Virginia Woolf Miscellany*, Spring 1977, No. 7, p. 8; and ibid., Special Summer Issue 1977, No. 8, p. [2] for passages omitted from Letters 905, 1020, 1126, 1127, 1179 and 1261, and p. [1] for note by Nigel Nicolson on the omissions.

### *b. First edition – American photo-offset reprint. [1976]* *

THE LETTERS OF | VIRGINIA WOOLF | VOLUME II: 1912–1922 | [*swelled rule*] | EDITOR: NIGEL NICOLSON | ASSISTANT EDITOR: JOANNE TRAUTMANN | [*publisher's monogram within a rule*] | HARCOURT BRACE JOVANOVICH | NEW YORK AND LONDON | ORIGINALLY PUBLISHED IN ENGLAND AS THE QUESTION OF THINGS HAPPENING

Small royal 8vo. xxviii, 628 pp. illus., plates. $9\frac{1}{4} \times 6$ in.

P. [i] half-title; p. [ii] blank; p. [iii] title; p. [iv] copyright notes, reservation rights, towards centre: Printed in the United States of America | First American edition 1976 | BCDE | Library of Congress Cataloging in Publication Data | [*eight lines*] | ISBN 0-15-150925-5; pp. [v–xxiv] as *a* above; p. [xxv] list of abbreviations; pp. [xxvi–xxvii] Family Tree; p. [xxviii] blank; pp. 1–[628] as *a* above.

Cream paper boards, lilac cloth spine; lettered in gold on spine; edges trimmed; end-papers. Cream pictorial dust-jacket printed in lilac.

Issued 19 November 1976; 15,000 copies printed. $14.95.

There was a further printing of 2500 copies in February 1977.

*c. First edition – American photo-offset reprint* (HARVEST/HBJ BOOKS). [*1978*] *

THE LETTERS OF VIRGINIA WOOLF, VOLUME II: 1912–1922, EDITOR: NIGEL NICOLSON, ASSISTANT EDITOR: JOANNE TRAUTMANN, HARCOURT BRACE JOVANOVICH, NEW YORK AND LONDON

Large crown 8vo. xxviii, 628 pp. illus., plates. 8 × $5\frac{3}{8}$ in.
Issued 13 April 1978; 19,826 copies printed. $5.95.

## A48 THE DIARY OF VIRGINIA WOOLF VOLUME I 1977

*a. First edition*

THE DIARY OF | VIRGINIA WOOLF | VOLUME I: 1915–1919 | INTRODUCED BY | QUENTIN BELL | EDITED BY | ANNE OLIVIER BELL | [*publisher's device of a wolf's head*] | 1977 | THE HOGARTH PRESS | LONDON

Small royal 8vo. xxviii, 356 pp. $9\frac{1}{8}$ × 6 in.

P. [i] half-title; p. [ii] blank; p. [iii] title; p. [iv] at head: Published by | The Hogarth Press Ltd | 40 William IV Street | London WC2N 4DG | [*ornament*] | Clarke, Irwin & Co. Ltd | Toronto | [*reservation rights in seven lines*] | British Library Cataloguing | in Publication Data | [*four lines*] | ISBN 0-7012-0424-9 | [*three lines*] | Preface and Editorial Notes © Anne Olivier Bell 1977 | Introduction © Quentin Bell 1977 | Diary © Quentin Bell and Angelica Garnett 1977 | Printed in Great Britain by | T. & A. Constable Ltd | Hopetoun Street, Edinburgh; p. [v] Contents; p. [vi] blank; pp. vii–xii Editor's Preface; pp. xiii–xxviii Introduction; p. [1] section-title; p. [2] blank; pp. 3–35 text; p. [36] blank; p. [37] section-title; p. [38] blank; pp. 39–95 text; p. [96] blank; p. [97] section-title; p. [98] blank; pp. 99–229 text; p. [230] blank; p. [231] section-title; p. [232] blank; pp. 233–318 text; p. [319] section-title; p. [320] blank; pp. 321–324 Appendix 1: The Diaries of Virginia Woolf; pp. 325–327 Appendix 2: First version of Diary entries for 20, 22 and 24 January 1919; p. 328 Abbreviations; p. [329] section-title; pp. 330–331 Family Tree; p. [332] blank; p. 333 note on the Index; pp. 334–356 Index.

Dark ruby rexine boards; lettered in gold on spine: The | Diary | of | Virginia | Woolf | [*ornament*] | Volume | One | [*ornament*] | 1915–1919 | The | Hogarth | Press; edges trimmed; end-papers. White pictorial dust-jacket printed in turquoise, pale blue, mauve and black, designed by Duncan Grant.

Published 26 May 1977; 7500 copies printed. £8.50.

See *Virginia Woolf Miscellany*, Spring/Summer 1978, No. 10, p. 7 for 'Corrections and Additions to Volume I of *The Diary*' by Anne Olivier Bell. See also the issue for Winter 1977, No. 9, p. 10 for 'Postscript to *The Diary of Virginia Woolf*, Vol. I: "Effie's Story" and *Night and Day*' by Elizabeth Heine.

*b. First edition – American photo-offset reprint.* [*1977*]

THE DIARY | [*spanning first and second line:*] OF [*line two:*] VIRGINIA | WOOLF | EDITED BY | ANNE OLIVIER BELL | INTRODUCTION BY QUENTIN BELL | VOLUME ONE | 1915–1919 | [*ornament*] | HARCOURT BRACE JOVANOVICH | NEW YORK AND LONDON | [*publisher's monogram within a rule*]

Royal 8vo. xxviii, 356 pp. $9\frac{1}{4} \times 6\frac{1}{4}$ in.

P. [i] half-title; p. [ii] blank; p. [iii] title; p. [iv] Preface and Editorial Notes copyright © 1977 by Anne Olivier Bell | Introduction copyright © 1977 by Quentin Bell | Diary copyright © 1977 by Quentin Bell and Angelica Garnett | [*reservation rights in five lines*] | Printed in the United States of America | [*Library of Congress cataloguing data in eight lines*] | ISBN 0-15-125597-0 | First American edition | BCDE; p. [v] Contents; p. [vi] blank; pp. vii–xii Editor's Preface; pp. xiii–xxviii Introduction; pp. [1]–356 as *a* above.

Black cloth boards; lettered in gold on spine: The | Diary | of | Virginia | Woolf | Volume | One | 1915–1919 | [*ornament*] | Edited by | Anne | Olivier | Bell | Harcourt | Brace | Jovanovich | [*publisher's monogram within a rule*]; gold ornament on upper cover; edges trimmed; end-papers. White dust-jacket printed in dark green with portrait of the author.

Issued 31 August 1977; 15,000 copies printed. $12.95.

*c. First edition – American photo-offset reprint* (HARVEST/HBJ BOOKS). [*1979*]*

THE DIARY OF VIRGINIA WOOLF, EDITED BY ANNE OLIVIER BELL, VOLUME ONE, 1915–1919, HARCOURT BRACE JOVANOVICH, NEW YORK AND LONDON

Large crown 8vo. xxviii, 356 pp. 8 × 5¼ in.
Issued 15 May 1979; 15,203 copies printed. $3.95.

## A49 BOOKS AND PORTRAITS 1977

*a. First edition*

BOOKS | AND PORTRAITS | SOME FURTHER SELECTIONS FROM THE | LITERARY AND BIOGRAPHICAL WRITINGS OF | VIRGINIA WOOLF | EDITED BY | MARY LYON | 1977 | THE HOGARTH PRESS | LONDON

Demy 8vo. x, 222 pp. 8½ × 5⅜ in.

P. [i] half-title; p. [ii] list of works by the author; p. [iii] title; p. [iv] at head: Published by | The Hogarth Press Ltd. | 42 William IV Street | London WC2n 4df | [*ornament*] | Clarke, Irwin & Co. Ltd. | Toronto | [*reservation rights in seven lines*] | British Library Cataloguing | in Publication Data | [*six lines*] | ISBN 0-7012-0405-2 | Text © Quentin Bell and Angelica | Garnett 1904, 1905, 1908, 1909, 1910, | 1916, 1917, 1918, 1919, 1920, 1921, | 1922, 1923, 1924, 1926, 1927, 1928 | Selection and Preface © Mary Lyon 1977 | Printed in Great Britain by | T. and A. Constable Limited | Edinburgh; pp. v–vi Contents; pp. vii–x Preface, and Acknowledgements; p. [1] section-title; p. [2] blank; pp. 3-169 text; p. [170] blank; p. [171] section-title; p. [172] blank; pp. 173-221 text; p. [222] blank.

Pale coral red rexine boards; lettered in gold on spine: Books | and | Por- | traits | • | Literary | & | Biographical | Writings | • |Virginia | Woolf | The | Hogarth | Press; edges trimmed; end-papers. White pictorial dust-jacket printed in mustard yellow and black, designed by Angelica Garnett.

Published 25 August 1977; 5600 copies printed. £5.50.

Contents: Part I, Of Writing and Writers: In the Orchard – A Woman's College from Outside – On a Faithful Friend – English Prose – Impressions at Bayreuth – Modes and Manners of the Nineteenth Century – Men and Woman – Coleridge as Critic – Patmore's Criticism – Papers on Pepys – Sheridan – Thomas Hood – Praeterita – Mr Kipling's Notebook – Emerson's Journals – Thoreau – Herman Melville – Rupert Brooke – The Intellectual Imagination – These are the Plans – Mr Sassoon's Poems – A Russian Schoolboy – A Glance at Turgenev – A Giant with Very Small Thumbs – Dostoevsky the Father – More Dostoevsky – Dostoevsky in Cranford – The Russian Background – A Scribbling Dame – Maria Edgeworth and Her Circle – Jane Austen and the Geese – Mrs Gaskell – The Compromise – Wilcoxiana – The Genius of Boswell – Shelley and Elizabeth Hitchener – Literary Geography – Flumina Amem Silvasque – Haworth, November 1904 – Part II, Mainly Portraits: The Girlhood of Queen Elizabeth – The Diary of a Lady in Waiting – Queen Adelaide – Elizabeth Lady Holland – Lady Hester Stanhope – The Memoirs of Sarah Bernhardt – Lady Strachey – John Delane – Body and Brain.

*b. First edition – American photo-offset reprint.* [*1978*]

BOOKS | AND PORTRAITS | SOME FURTHER SELECTIONS FROM THE | LITERARY AND BIOGRAPHICAL WRITINGS OF | VIRGINIA WOOLF | EDITED AND WITH A PREFACE BY | MARY LYON | [*publisher's monogram within a rule*] | HARCOURT BRACE JOVANOVICH | NEW YORK AND LONDON

Small demy 8vo. x, 230 pp. $8\frac{1}{4} \times 5\frac{3}{8}$ in.

P. [i] half-title; p. [ii] list of works by the author; p. [iii] title; p. [iv] copyright note, reservation rights, towards centre: Printed in the United States of America | Library of Congress Cataloging in Publication Data | [*four lines*] | ISBN 0-15-113478-2 | First American edition 1978 | BCDE; pp. v–x, [1]–[222] as *a* above; p. [223] list of works by the author; pp. [224–230] blank.

Lilac paper boards, black cloth spine; lettered in silver on spine; edges trimmed; lilac end-papers. White pictorial dust-jacket printed in black, lilac and grey.

Issued 20 February 1978; 10,000 copies printed. $10.

*c. Second English edition* (PANTHER BOOKS). [*1979*]

SOME FURTHER SELECTIONS FROM THE | LITERARY AND BIOGRAPHICAL WRITINGS OF | VIRGINIA WOOLF | BOOKS AND PORTRAITS | EDITED BY MARY LYON | TRIAD PANTHER

Foolscap 8vo. 256 pp. $7 \times 4\frac{3}{8}$ in.

P. [1] Biographical note on the author; p. [2] list of works by the author; p. [3] title; p. [4] publication note, copyright note, printer's imprint, etc.; pp. [5–6] Contents; pp. [7]–11 Preface; p. [12] Acknowledgments; p. [13] section-title; p. [14] blank; pp. [15]–197 text; p. [198] blank; p. [199] section-title; p. [200] blank; pp. [201]–253 text; p. [254] blank; pp. [255–256] publisher's advertisements.

Stiff white pictorial paper wrappers printed in pale brown, grey and black; edges trimmed.

Published 11 October 1979; 15,000 copies printed. £1.50.

## A50 THE PARGITERS 1977

*a. First edition*

THE PARGITERS | BY VIRGINIA WOOLF | THE NOVEL-ESSAY PORTION OF THE YEARS | EDITED WITH AN INTRODUCTION BY | MITCHELL A. LEASKA | NEW YORK | THE NEW YORK PUBLIC LIBRARY | ASTOR, LENOX AND TILDEN FOUNDATIONS | & READEX BOOKS | A DIVISION OF READEX MICROPRINT CORPORATION | 1977

Royal 8vo. xxxxiv, 168 pp. plate facing p. [4]. $9\frac{1}{2} \times 6\frac{1}{2}$ in.

P. [i] half-title; p. [ii] blank; p. [iii] title; p. [iv] at head: This volume has been produced with the assistance of the | Judge and Mrs Samuel D. Levy Memorial Publication Fund. | First edition | Text of *The Pargiters* copyright © 1977 Quentin Bell and Angelica Garnett. | Introductory and editorial matter copyright © 1977 Mitchell A. Leaska. | The first impression of two thousand copies, set in Caledonia type, with Centaur and | Arrighi display types, was printed on Curtis Rag paper at the Printing Office of | The New York Public Library. It was designed by Marilan Lund., Library of Congress cataloguing data, including: ISBN 0-87104-268-1 | Distributed in the United States by Readex Books; p. [v] Contents; p. vi Acknowledgments; pp. vii–xxii Introduction; pp. xxiii–xxiv Explanation of Editorial Symbols and Procedures; p. [xxv] section-title; p. [xxvi] blank; pp. xxvii–xxxxiv Speech before the London/National Society for Women's Service, January 21 1931; p. [1] fly-title; p. [2] Genealogical tree; p. [3] section-title; p. [4] blank; pp. 5–159 text; p. [160] blank; p. [161] section-title; p. [162] blank; pp. 163-167 Appendix – Speech; p. [168] blank.

Magenta cloth boards; lettered in gold in two lines in three sections down the spine with ornaments separating the sections: The Pargiters | by Virginia Woolf | [*ornament*] | Edited by | Mitchell A. Leaska | [*ornament*] | The New York | Public Library; in blind on upper cover: The | Pargiters; edges trimmed; end-papers. White pictorial dust-jacket printed in magenta, navy-blue and yellow, designed by Marilan Lund.

Published 15 September 1977; 2000 copies printed. $16.

Errata slip inserted inside upper cover.

*b. First edition – English photo-offset reprint. 1978*

THE PARGITERS | BY VIRGINIA WOOLF | THE NOVEL-ESSAY PORTION OF THE YEARS | EDITED

WITH AN INTRODUCTION BY | MITCHELL A. LEASKA | 1978 | THE HOGARTH PRESS | LONDON

Small demy 8vo. xliv, 168 pp. $8\frac{3}{8} \times 5\frac{3}{8}$ in.

P. [i] half-title; p. [ii] blank; p. [iii] title; p. [iv] lines 1–5 as *a* above, then: [*two lines*] | British Library Cataloguing in Publication Data | [*four lines*] | ISBN 0-7012-0435-4 | [*at centre:*] Printed and bound in Great Britain by Redwood Burn Limited, Trowbridge & Esher; pp. [v]–xliv, [1–3] as *a* above; p. [4] holograph facsimile of the First page of the Novel-Essay; pp. 5–[168] as *a* above.

Rose-red rexine boards; lettered in gold on spine: The | Pargiters | [*ornament*] | Virginia | Woolf | The | Hogarth | Press; edges trimmed; end-papers. White pictorial dust-jacket printed in pink and black, designed by Angelica Garnett.

Issued 5 January 1978; 2500 copies printed. £6.50.

The errata were corrected in this reprint except for those on pp. 23 and 28.

*c. First edition – second photo-offset reprint* (HARVEST/ HBJ BOOKS). [*1978*] *

THE PARGITERS, THE NOVEL-ESSAY PORTION OF THE YEARS, EDITED WITH AN INTRODUCTION BY MITCHELL A. LEASKA, HARCOURT BRACE JOVANOVICH, NEW YORK AND LONDON

xxxxiv, 168 pp.

Issued 20 February 1978; 9831 copies printed. $4.95.

## A51 A CHANGE OF PERSPECTIVE 1977

*a. First edition*

[*first two lines in open capitals:*] A CHANGE OF | PERSPECTIVE | THE LETTERS OF | VIRGINIA WOOLF | VOLUME III: 1923–1928 | EDITOR: NIGEL NICOLSON | ASSISTANT EDITOR: JOANNE TRAUTMANN | 1977 | THE HOGARTH PRESS | LONDON

Small royal 8vo. xxiv, 600 pp. 3 illus. on pp. 87, 203, 461; 8 plates between pp. 136–137, 168–169, 328–329, 360–361. $9\frac{1}{4} \times 6$ in.

P. [i] half-title; p. [ii] list of the volumes of *The Letters*; p. [iii]

title; p. [iv] Published by | The Hogarth Press Ltd | 42 William IV Street | London WC2N 4DF | [*ornament*] | Clarke, Irwin & Co. Ltd | Toronto | [*reservation rights in seven lines*] | British Library Cataloguing | in Publication Data | [*six lines*] | ISBN 0-7012-0443-5 | [*towards foot:*] Editorial Note and Introduction | © Nigel Nicolson 1977 | Letters © Quentin Bell and | Angelica Garnett 1977 | Printed in Great Britain by | T & A Constable Ltd | Hopetoun Street, Edinburgh; p. [v] quotation from letter to Vita Sackville-West; p. [vi] blank; p. [vii] Contents; p. [viii] blank; p. [ix] Illustrations; p. [x] blank; pp. xi–xiii Editorial Note; p. [xiv] blank; pp. xv–xxii Introduction; p. [xxiii] blank; p. [xxiv] Abbreviations at foot of letters; pp. 1-521 text; p. 522 Family Tree of the Woolfs; pp. 523–571 text; pp. 572–575 Appendix; p. [576] blank; pp. 577–600 Index.

Peacock-blue cloth boards; lettered in gold on spine: A | Change of | Perspec- | tive | [*short rule, ornament, short rule*] | The | Letters | of | Virginia | Woolf | Volume 3 | 1923–1928 | The | Hogarth | Press; edges trimmed; end-papers. White pictorial dust-jacket printed in pale brown, black, grey, and orange-brown, designed by Angelica Garnett.

Published 22 September 1977; 11,500 copies printed. £12.50.

### *b. First edition – American photo-offset reprint. [1978]* *

THE LETTERS OF | VIRGINIA WOOLF | VOLUME III: 1923–1928 | [*swelled rule*] | EDITED BY NIGEL NICOLSON | AND JOANNE TRAUTMANN | [*publisher's monogram within a rule*] | HARCOURT BRACE JOVANOVICH | NEW YORK AND LONDON | ORIGINALLY PUBLISHED IN ENGLAND AS A CHANGE OF PERSPECTIVE

Small royal 8vo. xxiv, 600 pp. illus., plates. $9\frac{1}{4} \times 6$ in.

P. [i] half-title; p. [ii] blank; p. [iii] title; p. [iv] copyright notes, reservation rights, towards centre: Printed in the United States of America | First American edition 1978 | BCDE | Library of Congress Cataloging in Publication Data | [*eleven lines*] | ISBN 0-15-150926-3; pp. [v]–xxii as *a* above; p. [xxiii] fly-title; pp. [xxiv], 1–600 as *a* above.

Cream paper boards, green cloth spine; lettered in gold on spine; edges trimmed; end-papers. Cream pictorial dust-jacket printed in green.

Issued 12 April 1978; 15,000 copies printed. $14.95.

## A52 THE DIARY OF VIRGINIA WOOLF VOLUME II 1978

*a. First edition*

THE DIARY OF | VIRGINIA WOOLF | VOLUME II: 1920-1924 | EDITED BY | ANNE OLIVIER BELL | ASSISTED BY | ANDREW McNEILLIE | [*publisher's device of a wolf's head*] | 1978 | THE HOGARTH PRESS | LONDON

Small royal 8vo. xii, 372 pp. $9\frac{1}{4} \times 6\frac{1}{8}$ in.

P. [i] half-title; p. [ii] blank; p. [iii] title; p. [iv] at head: Published by | The Hogarth Press Ltd | 40 William IV Street | London WC2N 4DG | [*ornament*] | Clarke, Irwin & Co. Ltd | Toronto | [*reservation rights in seven lines*] | British Library Cataloguing | in Publication Data | [*seven lines*] | ISBN 0-7012-0557-8 | [*towards foot:*] Preface and Editorial Notes © Anne Olivier Bell 1978 | Diary © Quentin Bell and Angelica Garnett 1978 | Printed in Great Britain by | T. & A. Constable Ltd | Hopetoun Street, Edinburgh; p. [v] Contents; p. [vi] blank; pp. vii-xii Editor's Preface; p. [1] section-title; p. [2] blank; pp. 3-82 text; p. [83] section-title; p. [84] blank; pp. 85-152 text; p. [153] section-title; p. [154] blank; pp. 155-217 text; p. [218] blank; p. [219] section-title; p. [220] blank; pp. 221-278 text; p. [279] section-title; p. [280] blank; pp. 281-327 text; p. [328] blank; p. [329] section-title; p. [330] blank; pp. 331-332 Abbreviations; pp. 333-336 Appendix I: Biographical Outlines of Persons Most Frequently Mentioned; pp. 337-338 Appendix II: *From* The Woman's Leader, 23 July 1920, 'The Plumage Bill'; pp. 339-342 Appendix III: 'The Intellectual Status of Women'; p. [343] section-title; pp. 344-371 Index; p. [372] blank.

Dark ruby rexine boards; lettered in gold on spine: The | Diary | of | Virginia | Woolf | [*ornament*] | Volume | Two | [*ornament*] | 1920-1924 | The | Hogarth | Press; edges trimmed; end-paper maps by J. Bell. White pictorial dust-jacket printed in pale green, orange and black, designed by Duncan Grant.

Published 24 August 1978; 8500 copies printed. £9.50.

*b. First edition – American photo-offset reprint. [1978]*

THE DIARY | [*spanning first and second line:*] OF [*line two:*] VIRGINIA | WOOLF | EDITED BY | ANNE OLIVIER BELL | ASSISTED BY ANDREW McNEILLIE | VOLUME TWO | 1920-1924 | [*ornament*] | HARCOURT

BRACE JOVANOVICH | NEW YORK AND LONDON | [*publisher's monogram within a rule*]

Royal 8vo. xii, 372 pp. $9\frac{1}{4} \times 6\frac{1}{4}$ in.

P. [i] half-title; p. [ii] blank; p. [iii] title; p. iv Preface and Editorial Notes copyright © 1978 by Anne Olivier Bell | Diary copyright © 1978 by Quentin Bell and Angelica Garnett | [*reservation rights and permission requests in nine lines*] | Printed in the United States of America | [*Library of Congress cataloging data in eight lines*] | ISBN 0-15-125598-9 | First American edition | BCDE; pp. [v]-xii, [1]-[372] as *a* above.

Black cloth boards; lettered in gold on spine: The | Diary | of | Virginia | Woolf | Volume | Two | 1920-1924 | [*ornament*] | Edited by | Anne | Olivier | Bell | Harcourt | Brace | Jovanovich | [*publisher's device within a rule*]; gold ornament on upper cover; edges trimmed; violet end-papers. White dust-jacket printed in dark purple and olive green with portrait of the author.

Issued 7 November 1978; 15,000 copies printed. $12.95.

This reprint lacks the end-paper maps by J. Bell.

## A53 A REFLECTION OF THE OTHER PERSON 1978

*a. First edition*

[*first three lines in open capitals:*] A REFLECTION | OF THE OTHER | PERSON | THE LETTERS OF | VIRGINIA WOOLF | VOLUME IV: 1929-1931 | EDITOR: NIGEL NICOLSON | ASSISTANT EDITOR: JOANNE TRAUTMANN | 1978 | THE HOGARTH PRESS | LONDON

Small royal 8vo. xxii, 442 pp. 8 plates between pp. 106-107, 138-139, 362-363, 394-395. $9\frac{1}{4} \times 6$ in.

P. [i] half-title; p. [ii] list of the volumes of *The Letters*; p. [iii] title; p. [iv] Published by | The Hogarth Press Ltd | 42 William IV Street | London WC2N 4DF | [*ornament*] | Clarke, Irwin & Co. Ltd | Toronto | [*reservation rights in seven lines*] | British Library Cataloguing | in Publication Data | [*eight lines*] | ISBN 0-7012-0448-6 | Editorial Note and Introduction | © Nigel Nicolson 1978 | Letters © Quentin Belland [*sic*] | Angelica Garnett 1978 | Printed in Great Britain by | T & A Constable Ltd | Hopetoun Street, Edinburgh; p. [v] quotation from letter to Gerald Brenan; p. [vi] blank; p. [vii] Contents; p. [viii] blank; p. [ix] Illustrations; p. [x] blank; pp. xi-xii Editorial Note; pp. xiii-xxi Introduction; p. [xxii] Abbreviations at foot of letters; pp. 1-425 text; p. [426] blank; pp. 427-442 Index.

Peacock-blue cloth boards; lettered in gold on spine: A | Reflection | of | the Other | Person | [*short rule, ornament, short rule*] | The | Letters | of | Virginia | Woolf | Volume 4 | 1929–1931 | The | Hogarth | Press; edges trimmed; end-papers. White pictorial dust-jacket printed in pale grey, brown, black, darker grey and pink, designed by Angelica Garnett.

Published 19 October 1978; 8500 copies printed. £11.95.

*b. First edition – American photo-offset reprint.* [*1979*] *

THE LETTERS OF | VIRGINIA WOOLF | VOLUME IV: 1929–1931 | [*swelled rule*] | EDITED BY NIGEL NICOLSON | AND JOANNE TRAUTMANN | [*publisher's monogram within a rule*] | HARCOURT BRACE JOVANOVICH | NEW YORK AND LONDON | ORIGINALLY PUBLISHED IN ENGLAND AS A REFLECTION OF THE OTHER PERSON

Small royal 8vo. xii, 442 pp. plates. $9\frac{1}{4} \times 6$ in.

P. [i] half-title; p. [ii] blank; p. [iii] title; p. [iv] copyright notes, reservation rights, towards centre, Printed in the United States of America | First American edition 1979 | BCDE | Library of Congress Cataloging in Publication Data | [*thirteen lines*] | ISBN 0-15-150927-1; pp. [v]–xxii, 1–442 as *a* above.

Cream paper boards, blue cloth spine; lettered in gold on spine; blue end-papers. Cream dust-jacket printed in blue.

Issued 30 March 1979; 10,000 copies printed. $14.95.

## A54 THE SICKLE SIDE OF THE MOON 1979

*A. First edition*

[*first two lines in open capitals:*] THE SICKLE SIDE | OF THE MOON | THE LETTERS OF | VIRGINIA WOOLF | VOLUME V: 1932–1935 | EDITOR: NIGEL NICOLSON | ASSISTANT EDITOR: JOANNE TRAUTMANN | 1979 | THE HOGARTH PRESS | LONDON

Small royal 8vo. xx, 476 pp. front. (port.). $9\frac{1}{4} \times 6$ in.

P. [i] half-title; p. [ii] list of volumes of *The Letters*; p. [iii] title; p. [iv] Published by | The Hogarth Press Ltd | 42 William IV Street | London WC2N 4DF | [*ornament*] | Clarke, Irwin & Co. Ltd |

Toronto | [*reservation rights in seven lines*] | British Library Cataloguing | in Publication Data | [*eight lines*] | ISBN 0-7012-0469-9 | Editorial Note and Introduction | © Nigel Nicolson 1979 | Letters © Quentin Bell and | Angelica Garnett 1979 | Printed in Great Britain by | T & A Constable Ltd | Hopetoun Street, Edinburgh; p. [v] quotation from letter to Ethel Smyth; p. [vi] blank; p. [vii] Contents; p. [viii] blank; pp. ix–x Editorial Note; pp. xi–xviii Introduction; p. [xix] blank; p. xx Abbreviations at foot of letters; pp. 1–456 text; pp. 457–476 Index.

Peacock-blue cloth boards; lettered in gold on spine: The | Sickle | Side of | the | Moon | [*short rule, ornament, short rule*] | The | Letters | of | Virginia | Woolf | Volume 5 | 1932–1935 | The | Hogarth | Press; edges trimmed; end-papers. White pictorial dust-jacket printed in brownish-orange, grey and black, designed by Angelica Garnett.

Published 20 September 1979; 8500 copies printed. £12.50.

### *b. First edition – American photo-offset reprint. [1979]* *

THE LETTERS OF | VIRGINIA WOOLF | VOLUME V: 1932–1935 | [*swelled rule*] | EDITED BY NIGEL NICOLSON | AND JOANNE TRAUTMANN | [*publisher's monogram within a rule*] | HARCOURT BRACE JOVANOVICH | NEW YORK AND LONDON | ORIGINALLY PUBLISHED IN ENGLAND AS THE SICKLE SIDE OF THE MOON

Small royal 8vo. xx, 476 pp. front. $9\frac{1}{4} \times 6$ in.

P. [i] half-title; p. [ii] blank; p. [iii] title; p. [iv] copyright notes, reservation rights, towards centre: Printed in the United States of America | First American edition | BCDE | Library of Congress Cataloging in Publication Data | [*fourteen lines*] | ISBN 0-15-150928-X; pp. [v]–xx, 1–476 as *a* above.

Cream paper boards, vermilion cloth spine; lettered in gold on spine; vermilion end-papers. Cream dust-jacket printed in vermilion.

Issued 25 September 1979; 8000 copies printed. $14.95.

# B.

# CONTRIBUTIONS TO BOOKS AND BOOKS TRANSLATED BY VIRGINIA WOOLF (EXCLUDING SELECTIONS REPRINTED IN ANTHOLOGIES)

## B1 THE LIFE AND LETTERS OF LESLIE STEPHEN 1906

*a. First edition*

[*in black:*] THE LIFE AND LETTERS OF | [*in red:*] LESLIE STEPHEN | [*in black:*] BY FREDERIC WILLIAM MAITLAND | [*publisher's floral device with motto*] | LONDON: DUCKWORTH & CO. | HENRIETTA STREET, COVENT GARDEN | MCMVI

Small royal 8vo. [2], x, 412 pp. front. (port), 4 plates. $8\frac{7}{8} \times 6\frac{3}{8}$ in.

Navy-blue cloth boards; lettered in gold on spine; publisher's floral device with motto in blind on lower cover; top edges gilt, others partially trimmed; end-papers. No specimen of dust-jacket available.

Published *c.* 8 November 1906; no record of the number of copies printed. 18s.

There was a second impression in 1907. Copies were also issued in 1910 in Duckworth's Crown Library at 5s. They were probably sheets of the second impression and were bound in olive-green cloth boards; lettered in gold on spine; quadruple rule in blind round upper cover; publisher's floral device with motto in blind on lower cover; edges trimmed, top gilt; end-papers; pale blue dust-jacket printed in navy-blue.

Pp. 474–476 impressions of Sir Leslie Stephen by 'one of his daughters', *i.e.* Virginia Stephen.

*b. First edition – American issue. 1906**

[*in black:*] THE LIFE AND LETTERS OF | [*in red:*] LESLIE STEPHEN | [*in black:*] BY FREDERIC WILLIAM MAITLAND | NEW YORK: G. P. PUTNAM'S SONS | LONDON: DUCKWORTH AND CO. | MCMVI

Small royal 8vo. [2], x, 512 pp. front. (port.), 4 plates. $9\frac{1}{8} \times 6\frac{1}{2}$ in.

Green cloth boards; lettered in gold on spine; top edges gilt, others untrimmed; end-papers. No specimen of dust-jacket available.

Issued 8 December 1906; no record of the number of copies bound. $4.50. The sheets were supplied by Duckworth & Co.

## B2 STAVROGIN'S CONFESSION 1922

*a. First edition*

F. M. DOSTOEVSKY | [*rule*] | STAVROGIN'S CONFESSION | AND | THE PLAN OF | THE LIFE OF A GREAT SINNER | WITH INTRODUCTORY AND EXPLANATORY NOTES | TRANSLATED BY | S. S. KOTELIANSKY AND VIRGINIA WOOLF | PUBLISHED BY LEONARD & VIRGINIA WOOLF AT | THE HOGARTH PRESS, PARADISE ROAD, RICHMOND | 1922

Crown 8vo. 170, 6 pp. $7\frac{1}{2} \times 5$ in.

White paper boards printed in ice-blue conventional design, with ice-blue cloth spine; white printed paper labels on upper cover $2\frac{1}{8} \times 3\frac{7}{8}$ in. and on spine $5\frac{7}{8} \times \frac{5}{8}$ in.; top edges trimmed, others partially trimmed, some fore edges uncut; end-papers. Wax paper dust-jacket.

Published 4 October 1922; *c.* 1000 copies printed. 6s.

There is a secondary binding in ice-blue cloth with white paper label on spine. See note to B3.

Pp. 5–6 Translators' note.

*The Life of a Great Sinner* was first published in the *Criterion*, October, 1922, pp. 16–33.

Leonard Woolf wrote 'Mrs. Woolf did not know Russian. We taught ourselves a little Russian in order to be able to understand Koteliansky's problems in translating. The procedure was that Koteliansky translated the Russian book into very bad English in double-spaced lines, that Mrs. Woolf went through the text with him, sentence by sentence, and then put the translation into good English.'

*b. First edition – American photo-offset reprint. 1947*

F. M. DOSTOEVSKY | STAVROGIN'S CONFESSION | TRANSLATED BY | VIRGINIA WOOLF AND S. S. KOTELIANSKY | WITH A PSYCHOANALYTIC STUDY OF THE AUTHOR BY | SIGMUND FREUD | [*publisher's device of a lion*] | LEAR PUBLISHERS NEW YORK 1947

Large crown 8vo. 136 pp. $8\frac{1}{2} \times 5\frac{3}{8}$ in.

Black cloth boards; lettered in gold down the spine and on upper cover; edges trimmed; end-papers. No specimen of dust-jacket available.

Published 15 October 1947; number of copies printed not ascertained. $2.75.

Pp. 9–83, [117]–136 were printed by photo-litho offset from pp. 9–83, 125–144 of the first edition.

The publisher did not obtain permission from either Leonard Woolf or S. S. Koteliansky to reprint this translation.

*c. Fawcett World Library edition.* [*1966*]

THE POSSESSED | FYODOR DOSTOYEVSKY | TRANSLATED BY CONSTANCE GARNETT | "AT TIKHON'S" TRANSLATED BY VIRGINIA WOOLF AND | S. S. KOTELIANSKY. | INTRODUCTION BY PHILIP RAHV | A FAWCETT PREMIER BOOK | FAWCETT PUBLICATIONS, INC., GREENWICH, CONN. | MEMBER OF AMERICAN BOOK PUBLISHERS COUNCIL

Foolscap 8vo. 672 pp. $7\frac{1}{8} \times 4\frac{1}{4}$ in.

Stiff white pictorial paper wrappers printed in black, yellow and red; edges trimmed.

Published 1 February 1966; 30,000 copies printed. 95 cents.

## B3 TOLSTOI'S LOVE LETTERS 1923

*First edition*

TOLSTOI'S | LOVE LETTERS | WITH A STUDY | ON THE AUTOBIOGRAPHICAL ELEMENTS | IN TOLSTOI'S WORK | BY | PAUL BIRYUKOV | TRANSLATED FROM THE RUSSIAN BY | S. S. KOTELIANSKY AND VIRGINIA WOOLF | PUBLISHED BY LEONARD & VIRGINIA WOOLF AT | THE HOGARTH PRESS, PARADISE ROAD, RICHMOND | 1923

Crown 8vo. 134, 6 pp. $7\frac{1}{2} \times 5$ in.

White paper boards printed in red and green with conventional design, grass-green cloth spine; white printed paper label on spine $1\frac{1}{4} \times \frac{3}{4}$ in.; top edges trimmed, others partially trimmed, some fore edges uncut; end-papers. Wax paper dust-jacket.

Published May 1923; *c.* 1000 copies printed. 5s.

There is a secondary binding in grass-green cloth with white paper label on spine similar to that noted above. Leonard Woolf did not recall the reason for this, but thought that the paper, of Czechoslovak origin, may have run out and that the later copies were bound in the grass-green cloth which was used originally for the spine only.

## B4 TALKS WITH TOLSTOI 1923

*First edition*

TALKS | WITH TOLSTOI | BY | A. B. GOLDENVEIZER | TRANSLATED BY | S. S. KOTELIANSKY AND VIRGINIA WOOLF | PUBLISHED BY LEONARD & VIRGINIA WOOLF AT | THE HOGARTH PRESS, PARADISE ROAD, RICHMOND | 1923

Crown 8vo. 182, 6 pp. $7\frac{3}{8} \times 5$ in.

Mauve and pink marbled paper boards, buff cloth spine; white printed paper label on spine $1\frac{7}{8} \times 1$ in.; top edges trimmed, others partially trimmed, some fore edges uncut; end-papers. Wax paper dust-jacket.

Published *c.* 13 June 1923; *c.* 1000 copies printed. 5s.

P. v Translators' note.

Extracts were first published in *Cassell's Weekly*, 18 and 25 April 1923. See C232.1.

## B5 VICTORIAN PHOTOGRAPHS OF FAMOUS MEN & FAIR WOMEN 1926

*a. First edition*

VICTORIAN PHOTOGRAPHS OF | FAMOUS MEN & FAIR WOMEN | BY JULIA MARGARET CAMERON | WITH INTRODUCTIONS BY | VIRGINIA WOOLF | AND ROGER FRY | PUBLISHED BY LEONARD & VIRGINIA WOOLF | AT THE HOGARTH PRESS, LONDON, 1926

Royal 4to. [viii], 18 pp. front. (port.) 24 plates. $12\frac{1}{2} \times 10$ in.

Pale pink paper boards, vellum spine; lettered in gold on spine; top and bottom edges trimmed, fore edges partially trimmed; pale pink end-papers. Pale pink dust-jacket similar to covers.

Published 28 October 1926; 710 copies printed. £2. 2s.

Two hundred and sixty copies with a cancel title were sent to Harcourt, Brace & Company. See B5*b*.

Pp. 1–8 'Julia Margaret Cameron' by Virginia Woolf.

*b. First edition – American issue. [1927]* *

NEW YORK, HARCOURT, BRACE & COMPANY

Royal 4to. [viii], 18 pp. front. (port.) 24 plates. $12\frac{1}{2} \times 10$ in.

Blue paper boards, buff buckram spine; buff label on spine printed in black; buff label on upper cover printed in black and red; edges trimmed; end-papers. Slip case with two labels; one similar to upper cover, and the other printed: Edition limited to 250 numbered copies | price 10 dollars.

Issued 13 January 1927; 260 copies bound. $10.

Copies with a cancel title were supplied by the Hogarth Press. The issue was limited to 250 numbered copies; it is possible that the 10 additional copies were for review purposes.

### *c. Second edition. 1973*

VICTORIAN PHOTOGRAPHS OF | FAMOUS MEN & FAIR WOMEN | BY JULIA MARGARET CAMERON | WITH INTRODUCTIONS BY | VIRGINIA WOOLF & ROGER FRY | EXPANDED AND REVISED EDITION EDITED BY | TRISTRAM POWELL | 1973 | THE HOGARTH PRESS | LONDON

Royal 4to. [ii, 126] pp. 44 illus. $12\frac{1}{2} \times 10$ in.

Chocolate-brown cloth boards; lettered in gold down the spine; edges trimmed; pale maroon end-papers.

Published 29 November 1973; 7500 copies printed. £4.95.

Pp. 13–19 'Julia Margaret Cameron' by Virginia Woolf.

## B6 ATALANTA'S GARLAND 1926

### *First edition*

[*in pale blue:*] ATALANTA'S GARLAND | [*in black:*] BEING THE BOOK OF THE | EDINBURGH UNIVERSITY | WOMEN'S UNION | 1926 | EDINBURGH | PRINTED AT THE UNIVERSITY PRESS | BY T. AND A. CONSTABLE LTD.

Medium 8vo. [2], xiv, 192 pp. front. (col.), 11 plates. $8\frac{3}{4} \times 5\frac{1}{2}$ in.

White paper boards, printed in a tan design; white cloth spine; white printed paper label on upper cover $2\frac{1}{4} \times 3\frac{1}{4}$ in.; top and fore edges trimmed, bottom partially trimmed; end-papers. Cream dust-jacket printed in brown, designed by Otto Schlapp.

Published *c.* 1 November 1926; 2000 copies printed. 6s.

There are at least three variants of the binding: (1) black paper boards patterned in yellow, white and red, with a white cloth spine;

(2) cream paper boards patterned in olive-green, with a white cloth spine and frontispiece trimmed and mounted on a stiff grey leaf; (3) 50 numbered copies in black paper boards patterned in gold and red, with a vellum spine, top edges gilt, cream dust-jacket printed in brown.

Of the 2000 copies printed 950 were bound with white cloth spines and 50 numbered copies with vellum spines. These 1000 copies were bound by November 1926; a further 250 copies were bound in 1927. The remaining 750 copies were pulped in June 1956. It is possible that the copies with cream paper boards patterned in olive-green and frontispiece mounted on a stiff grey leaf, described as variant (2) above, comprised the 250 copies bound in 1927 and therefore constitute a secondary binding rather than a variant.

Pp. 11–16 'A Woman's College from Outside' by Virginia Woolf.

This essay was reprinted in *Books and Portraits*. See A49.

## B7 A SENTIMENTAL JOURNEY THROUGH FRANCE AND ITALY [1928]

*The World's Classics edition*

A SENTIMENTAL JOURNEY | THROUGH | FRANCE AND ITALY | BY | LAURENCE STERNE | WITII AN INTRODUCTION | BY | VIRGINIA WOOLF | [*series device of a globe with* 'The World's Classics' *on a scroll at foot*] | OXFORD UNIVERSITY PRESS | LONDON: HUMPHREY MILFORD

Demy 16mo. [ii], xviii, 236 pp. $5\frac{7}{8} \times 3\frac{5}{8}$ in.

Olive-green cloth boards; lettered in gold on spine; quadruple rule in blind round upper and lower covers; ornament in blind on spine; edges trimmed; end-papers. White pictorial dust-jacket printed in blue.

Published 1 November 1928 in *The World's Classics* as Vol. 333; 5000 copies printed. 3s. 6d.

There were further printings of 3000 copies in 1935, 1500 in 1942, 3000 in 1949 and 5000 in 1951.

Pp. [v]–xvii Introduction by Virginia Woolf.

The introduction was first published in the *New York Herald Tribune*, 23 September 1928. It was reprinted (slightly revised) in *The Common Reader: Second Series, Selections from Her Essays*, and in *Collected Essays*, Vol. 1. See A18, 36–7, C303.

## B8 MRS DALLOWAY [1928]

*The Modern Library impression* see A9*c*

## B9 SELECTIONS AUTOBIOGRAPHICAL AND IMAGINATIVE [1929]

*First edition*

SELECTIONS | AUTOBIOGRAPHICAL AND | IMAGINATIVE | FROM THE | WORKS OF GEORGE GISSING | WITH BIOGRAPHICAL | AND CRITICAL NOTES BY HIS SON | [*publisher's device of a bowl of fruit with publisher's monogram*] | WITH AN INTRODUCTION BY | VIRGINIA WOOLF | JONATHAN CAPE | THIRTY BEDFORD SQUARE | LONDON

Large crown 8vo. 320 pp. 8 × $5\frac{3}{8}$ in.

Coffee-brown cloth boards; lettered in gold on spine; publisher's device of a bowl of fruit with monogram in blind on lower cover; top and fore edges trimmed, bottom partially trimmed; end-papers. Saxe-blue dust-jacket printed in yellow.

Published 11 February 1929; number of copies printed not disclosed. 7s. 6d.

Pp. 9–16 Introduction by Virginia Woolf.

The introduction was first published in the *Nation & Athenaeum*, 26 February 1927. It was reprinted in the *New Republic*, 2 March 1927, and reprinted (revised) in *The Common Reader: Second Series*, as the introduction to *By the Ionian Sea*, by George Gissing published in the Travellers' Library by Cape in 1933, and in *Collected Essays*, Vol. 1. See A18, 37, C280, 336.

## B10 RECENT PAINTINGS BY VANESSA BELL 1930

*First edition*

[*title on upper cover:*] THE LONDON | ARTISTS' ASSOCIATION | GUARANTORS: | SAMUEL COURTAULD ESQ. J. MAYNARD KEYNES ESQ. C. B. | L. H. MYERS ESQ. F. HINDLEY SMITH ESQ. | [*four ornaments*] | RECENT PAINTINGS BY | VANESSA BELL | WITH A

FOREWORD BY | VIRGINIA WOOLF | FEBRUARY 4TH TO MARCH 8TH 1930 | [*four ornaments*] | 92 NEW BOND STREET | TELEPHONE: MAYFAIR 5224 SECRETARY: ANGUS DAVIDSON

Crown 8vo. [8] pp. $7\frac{1}{2} \times 4\frac{7}{8}$ in.

Thin white paper wrappers; edges trimmed; stapled.

Published 4 February 1930; *c.* 500 copies printed. It is probable that the catalogue was distributed free.

Pp. [2–5] Foreword by Virginia Woolf.

## B11 LIFE AS WE HAVE KNOWN IT 1931

*a. First edition*

LIFE AS WE HAVE | KNOWN IT | BY | CO-OPERATIVE WORKING WOMEN | EDITED BY | MARGARET LLEWELYN DAVIES | WITH AN INTRODUCTORY LETTER BY | VIRGINIA WOOLF | PUBLISHED BY LEONARD AND VIRGINIA WOOLF AT THE | HOGARTH PRESS, 52 TAVISTOCK SQUARE, LONDON, W.C. | 1931

Small crown 8vo. xl, 144 pp. front., 7 plates. $7\frac{1}{4} \times 4\frac{7}{8}$ in.

Crocus-yellow cloth boards; lettered in black on spine; edges trimmed; end-papers. White pictorial dust-jacket printed in black.

Published 5 March 1931; *c.* 1500 copies printed. 5s.

Copies in stiff cream paper were issued to Guildswomen at 2s. 6d.; a duplicated letter in Mr P. J. Allen's copy indicates that a limited number were thus bound.

Pp. xv–xxxix Introductory Letter to Margaret Llewelyn Davies by Virginia Woolf.

The Introductory Letter is a revised version of 'Memories of a Working Women's Guild' first published in the *Yale Review*, September 1930. The original version was reprinted in *The Captain's Death Bed and Other Essays*, in *Selections from Her Essays* and in *Collected Essays*, Vol. 4. See A30, 36, 39, C326.

*b. First edition – photo-offset reprint. 1977*

LIFE | AS WE HAVE | KNOWN IT | BY | CO-OPERATIVE | WORKING WOMEN | EDITED BY | MARGARET LLEWELYN DAVIES | WITH AN INTRODUCTORY

LETTER BY | VIRGINIA WOOLF | NEW INTRODUCTION BY | ANNA DAVIN | VIRAGO

Large crown 8vo. xxxxii, 142 pp. $7\frac{3}{4} \times 5\frac{1}{8}$ in.

Stiff white pictorial wrappers printed in dark brown and pale yellow; edges trimmed.

Issued 24 March 1977; 10,000 copies printed. £1.50.

## B11.1 CATALOGUE OF RECENT PAINTINGS BY VANESSA BELL 1934

*First edition*

[*title on upper wrapper: in blue:*] CATALOGUE | OF | RECENT PAINTINGS | BY | [*in red:*] VANESSA BELL | [*in blue:*] MARCH 1934 | WITH A FOREWORD BY | [*in red:*] VIRGINIA WOOLF | [*in blue:*] ALEX. REID & LEFEVRE, LTD. | (THE LEFEVRE GALLERIES) | 1a, KING STREET, ST. JAMES'S, | LONDON, S.W.1

[4] pp. $8\frac{1}{4} \times 5\frac{5}{8}$ in.

Pale blue paper wrappers; printed in darker blue and red; top and bottom edges trimmed, front edges rough trimmed; stapled.

Published *c.* 7 March 1934; no record of the number of copies printed. Not for sale.

P. [1] Foreword by Virginia Woolf.

## B12 BEGINNING AGAIN 1964

*a. First edition*

BEGINNING | AGAIN | AN AUTOBIOGRAPHY | OF THE YEARS 1911–1918 | BY | LEONARD WOOLF | [*publisher's device of a wolf's head*] | 1964 | THE HOGARTH PRESS | LONDON

Small demy 8vo. 260 pp. front. 5 plates. $8\frac{1}{2} \times 5\frac{1}{2}$ in.

Sky-blue cloth boards; lettered in gold on spine; edges trimmed; endpapers. Pale turquoise dust-jacket printed in green and orange.

Published 7 May 1964; 4550 copies printed. £1. 10s.

There were further printings of 1600 copies in August 1964, 1500 copies in August 1965 and in April 1968, 1250 copies in September 1972 and 500 copies in March 1978.

Pp. 117–118, 140–141, 205–207 and 246–247 unpublished extracts from Virginia Woolf's diary.

*b. First edition – American photo-offset reprint. 1964**

BEGINNING AGAIN, HARCOURT BRACE JOVANOVICH, NEW YORK AND LONDON

260 pp. plates.

Issued 9 September 1964; 3200 copies printed. $6.95.

There were further printings of 1500 copies in October 1964, 2200 copies in January 1965 and 1000 copies in August 1971. Issued 15 March 1972 in *Harvest Books* of which 5966 copies were printed; there was a further printing of 10,271 copies in October 1975 of which 5000 copies were transferred to the boxed set of 5 volumes of *The Autobiography of Leonard Woolf.*

## B13 JOURNEY TO THE FRONTIER [1966]

*a. First edition*

JOURNEY TO THE FRONTIER | JULIAN BELL & JOHN CORNFORD : THEIR LIVES AND THE 1930S | PETER STANSKY & | WILLIAM ABRAHAMS | CONSTABLE LONDON

Demy 8vo. xviii, 430 pp. 8 plates. $8\frac{5}{8} \times 5\frac{1}{2}$ in.

Black cloth boards; lettered in silver on spine; edges trimmed; endpapers. White dust-jacket printed in black, crimson, yellow and mauve.

Published 2 May 1966; 3500 copies printed. £2. 10s.

Pp. 16, 18, 279 and 399 extracts from Virginia Woolf's unpublished 'Reminiscences of Julian'. See also p. 392.

*b. First edition – American photo-offset reprint. [1966]*

JOURNEY TO THE FRONTIER | TWO ROADS TO THE SPANISH CIVIL WAR | PETER STANSKY AND WILLIAM ABRAHAMS | WITH PHOTOGRAPHS | [*publisher's device*] | AN ATLANTIC MONTHLY PRESS BOOK | LITTLE, BROWN AND COMPANY · BOSTON · TORONTO

Small demy 8vo. xviii, 430 pp. 8 plates. $8\frac{3}{8} \times 5\frac{1}{2}$ in.

Red cloth boards; lettered in gold on spine; publisher's device in blind on upper cover; edges trimmed; yellow end-papers. White dust-jacket printed in black, crimson, yellow and mauve.

Issued 13 September 1966; 4000 copies printed. $7.50.

## B14 DOWNHILL ALL THE WAY 1967

*a. First edition*

DOWNHILL | ALL THE WAY | AN AUTOBIOGRAPHY | OF THE YEARS 1919–1939 | BY | LEONARD WOOLF | [*publisher's device of a wolf's head*] | 1967 | THE HOGARTH PRESS | LONDON

Small demy 8vo. 260 pp. 5 plates. $8\frac{1}{8} \times 5\frac{1}{2}$ in.

Sky-blue cloth boards; lettered in gold on spine; edges trimmed; end-papers. White pictorial dust-jacket printed in sky-blue and black.

Published 27 April 1967; 5000 copies printed. £1. 15s.

There were further printings of 1750 copies in May 1967, 1500 copies each in February 1968 and July 1970 and 1250 in May 1975.

Pp. 49–50, 81, 90, 99, 108, 111, 115–117, 150 unpublished extracts from Virginia Woolf's diary.

*b. First edition – American photo-offset reprint. 1967**

DOWNHILL ALL THE WAY, HARCOURT BRACE JOVANOVICH, NEW YORK AND LONDON

260 pp. plates.

Issued 25 October 1967; 5100 copies printed. $5.95.

There was a further printing of 2000 copies in August 1968. Issued 22 October 1975 in *Harvest Books* of which 10,000 copies were printed; 5000 copies were transferred to the boxed set of 5 volumes of *The Autobiography of Leonard Woolf.*

## B15 THE JOURNEY NOT THE ARRIVAL MATTERS 1969

*a. First edition*

THE JOURNEY | NOT THE ARRIVAL | MATTERS | AN AUTOBIOGRAPHY | OF THE YEARS 1939–1969 |

BY | LEONARD WOOLF | [*publisher's device of a wolf's head*] | 1969 | THE HOGARTH PRESS | LONDON

Small demy 8vo. 218 pp. 8 plates. $8\frac{1}{2} \times 5\frac{3}{8}$ in.

Sky-blue cloth boards; lettered in gold on spine; edges trimmed; end-papers. White pictorial dust-jacket printed in madder red and black.

Published 16 October 1969; 5500 copies printed. £1.75.

There were further printings of 1500 copies each in November 1969 and June 1970, and 1250 in September 1973.

Pp. 70, 74, 77, 86–90, 93–94 unpublished extracts from Virginia Woolf's diary and letters.

*b. First edition – American photo-offset reprint. 1970**

THE JOURNEY NOT THE ARRIVAL MATTERS, HARCOURT BRACE JOVANOVICH, NEW YORK AND LONDON

218 pp. plates.

Issued 25 March 1970; 5100 copies printed. $5.95.

There was a further printing of 2000 copies in July 1970. Issued 22 October 1977 in *Harvest Books* of which 10,000 copies were printed; 2750 copics were transferred to the boxed set of 5 volumes of *The Autobiography of Leonard Woolf.*

## B16 VIRGINIA WOOLF A BIOGRAPHY VOLUME ONE 1972

*First edition*

VIRGINIA WOOLF | A BIOGRAPHY | [*ornament*] | VOLUME ONE | VIRGINIA STEPHEN | 1882–1912 | [*ornament*] | QUENTIN BELL | 1972 | THE HOGARTH PRESS | LONDON

Small royal 8vo. xvi, 232 pp. front. (port.), 2 illus., 7 plates and end-paper maps. $9\frac{1}{4} \times 6$ in.

Pale grey rexine boards; lettered in gold on spine; edges trimmed; white end-paper maps printed in grey and black. White pictorial dust-jacket printed in brownish-orange, grey and black.

Published 15 June 1972; 5000 copies printed. £3.

There were further printings of 2500 and 4500 copies in June 1972 of which 800 copies of the second printing were accidentally destroyed, 8000 copies in July 1972 and 3000 copies each in

December 1972, February, May and September 1973. Issued 15 April 1976 in *Paladin* paperbacks of which 40,000 copies were printed.

Pp. 25, 28-29 quotations from letters, *Hyde Park Gate News*, etc. *et passim*; pp. 202-204 Report on Teaching at Morley College, July 1905; pp. 205-206 Virginia Woolf and the Authors of *Euphrosyne*, *i.e.* commentary by V.W. on *Euphrosyne*; pp. 207, 210-212 Clive Bell and the Writing of *The Voyage Out*, *i.e.* letters between Virginia Stephen and Clive Bell.

Translations of both volumes were published in French by Stock, Paris, 1973-4, in German by Insel Verlag, Frankfurt, 1977, in Italian by Garzanti, Milan, 1974, in Japanese by Misuzu Shobo, Tokyo, 1976-7 and in Spanish by Editorial Lumen, Barcelona, 1979.

## B17 VIRGINIA WOOLF A BIOGRAPHY VOLUME TWO 1972

*a. First edition*

VIRGINIA WOOLF | A BIOGRAPHY | [*ornament*] | VOLUME TWO | MRS WOOLF | 1912-1941 | [*ornament*] | QUENTIN BELL | 1972 | THE HOGARTH PRESS | LONDON

Small royal 8vo. xii, 300 pp. front. (port.), 1 illus., 7 plates, and end-paper maps. $9\frac{1}{4} \times 6$ in.

Pale grey rexine boards; lettered in gold on spine; edges trimmed; white end-paper maps printed in grey and black. White pictorial dust-jacket printed in blue, grey and black.

Published 19 October 1972; 7500 copies printed. £3.

There were further printings of 5000 and 7500 copies in November and December 1972, 5390 copies in February, 3100 copies in April and 4100 copies in September 1973. Issued 2 September 1976 in *Paladin* paperbacks of which 30,000 copies were printed.

Pp. [xi] holograph facsimile of part of the manuscript 'A Dinner Party at 46'; pp. 1-2, 5-7 *et passim* quotations from letters; pp. 253-254 quotation from her diary, and text of 'Fantasy upon a Gentleman Who Converted his Impressions of a Private House into Cash'; pp. 255-259 Virginia Woolf and Julian Bell, a memoir of Julian Bell.

*b. First edition – American photo-offset reprint.* [*1972*]

VIRGINIA WOOLF | A BIOGRAPHY | [*swelled rule*] | QUENTIN BELL | [*publisher's monogram*] | HARCOURT BRACE JOVANOVICH, INC., NEW YORK

Small royal 8vo. 2 vols. (in one): xx, 230, 320 pp. 3 illus. and 16 plates. $9\frac{1}{4} \times 6\frac{1}{2}$ in.

Dark grey cloth boards; lettered in silver on spine; edges trimmed; bright blue end-papers. White pictorial dust-jacket printed in dark grey and blue.

Issued 15 November 1972; 6300 copies printed. $12.50.

There were further printings of 3775 copies in November, two of 10,200 and 11,725 in December 1972, 5300 in April and 5000 in June 1973. Issued 20 March 1974 in *Harvest Books* as Vol. HB269 of which 20,000 copies were printed. There were further printings of 20,000 copies each in June 1974 and January 1975.

# C.

# CONTRIBUTIONS TO PERIODICALS AND NEWSPAPERS

All contributions are signed 'Virginia Stephen' or 'Virginia Woolf' unless stated otherwise except those published in *The Times Literary Supplement* which are anonymous.

The following abbreviations are used:

*TLS, The Times Literary Supplement*, London
N.S. New Series.

The numbers of volumes and parts of volumes are printed in bold type.

Points are used for the insertion of new entries in this and other sections.

## 1904

C01 REVIEW OF *The Son of Royal Langbrith*, by W. D. Howells. *Guardian*, 14 December 1904, 2120. Unsigned.

C02 HAWORTH, NOVEMBER, 1904. *Guardian*, 21 December 1904, 2159. Unsigned.

Reprinted in: *Books and Portraits*, 1977.

## 1905

C03 REVIEW OF *Next-Door Neighbours*, by W. Pett Ridge. *Guardian*, 4 January 1905, 36. Unsigned.

C04 ON A FAITHFUL FRIEND. *Guardian*, 18 January 1905, 126–7. Unsigned. On 'Shag', a dog.

Reprinted in: *Books and Portraits*, 1977.

C05 A BELLE OF THE FIFTIES. *Guardian*, 8 February 1905, 247. Review of *A Belle of the Fifties: Memoirs of Mrs. Clay, of Alabama.* Unsigned.

C06 MR. HENRY JAMES'S LATEST NOVEL. *Guardian*, 22 February 1905, 339. Review of *The Golden Bowl*, by Henry James. Unsigned.

C07 THE DECAY OF ESSAY-WRITING. *Academy and Literature*, 25 February 1905, 165–6.

C1 LITERARY GEOGRAPHY. *TLS*, 10 March 1905, 81. Review of *The Thackeray Country*, by Lewis Melville and *The Dickens Country*, by F. G. Kitton.

Reprinted in: *Books and Portraits*, 1977.

C1 "BARHAM OF BELTANA". *TLS*, 17 March 1905, 90.
.1 Review of *Barham of Beltana*, by W. E. Norris.

C1 THE FORTUNES OF FARTHINGS. *TLS*, 31 March 1905,
.2 106. Review of *The Fortunes of Farthings*, by A. J. Dawson.

C1 REVIEW OF *A Dark Lantern*, by Elizabeth Robins. *Guardian*,
.3 24 May 1905, 899. Unsigned.

C2 JOURNEYS IN SPAIN. *TLS*, 26 May 1905, 167. Review of *Letters from Catalonia*, by Rowland Thirlmere and *The Land of the Blessed Virgin*, by W. S. Maugham.

Reprinted in: *Contemporary Writers*, 1965.

C2 REVIEW OF *Rose of Lone Farm*, by Eleanor G. Hayden.
.01 *Guardian*, 19 July 1905, 1224. Unsigned.

C2 AN ANDALUSIAN INN. *Guardian*, 19 July 1905, 1224–
.02 5. Unsigned.

C2.03 A PRIORY CHURCH. *Guardian*, 26 July 1905, 1261. On the church at Christchurch, near the New Forest. Unsigned.

C2.1 THE LETTERS OF JANE WELSH CARLYLE. *Guardian*, 2 August 1905, 1295. Unsigned.

C2.2 THE VALUE OF LAUGHTER. *Guardian*, 16 August 1905, 1367. Unsigned.

C2.3 THEIR PASSING HOUR. *Academy*, 26 August 1905, 871–2. Review of *Some Famous Women of Wit and Beauty*, by John Fyvie. Unsigned.

C2.4 REVIEW OF *The Letter Killeth*, by A. C. Inchbold. *TLS*, 27 October 1905, 359.

C2.5 REVIEW OF *Lone Marie*, by W. E. Norris. *Guardian*, 1 November 1905, 1851. Unsigned.

C2.6 REVIEW OF *The Devil's Due*, by G. B. Burgin. *Guardian*, 1 November 1905, 1851. Unsigned.

C2.7 REVIEW OF *The House of Mirth*, by Edith Wharton. *Guardian*, 15 November 1905, 1940. Unsigned.

C2.8 REVIEW OF *The Debtor*, by Mary E. Wilkins. *TLS*, 17 November 1905, 396.

C2.9 REVIEW OF *A Flood Tide*, by Mary Debenham. *TLS*, 17 November 1905, 397.

C2.10 REVIEW OF *The Making of Michael*, by Mrs Fred Reynolds. *TLS*, 17 November 1905, 397.

C2.11 A DESCRIPTION OF THE DESERT. *Guardian*, 6 December 1905, 2085. Review of *The Voice of the South*, by Gilbert Watson. Unsigned.

C2.12 REVIEW OF *The Brown House and Cordelia*, by Margaret Booth. *Guardian*, 6 December 1905, 2085–6. Unsigned.

C2.13 "DELTA". *Guardian*, 13 December 1905, 2131. Review of *The Life of Mansie Wauch*, by D. M. Moir. Unsigned.

C2.14 TWO IRISH NOVELS. *TLS*, 15 December 1905, 445. Review of *Dan the Dollar*, by Shan F. Bullock and *The Red Haired Woman: Her Autobiography*, by Louise Kenny.

C2.15 REVIEW OF *The Tower of Siloam*, by Mrs Henry Graham. *Guardian*, 20 December 1905, 2172. Unsigned.

C3 STREET MUSIC. *National Review*, London, 1905, 45, 144–8.

## 1906

C3.1 A NINETEENTH-CENTURY CRITIC. *Speaker*, 6 January 1906, 352. Review of *Lectures and Essays*, by Canon Ainger. Unsigned.

C3.2 REVIEW OF *After His Kind*, by M. Sturge Henderson. *Guardian*, 10 January 1906, 89. Unsigned.

C3.3 THE SISTER OF FREDERIC THE GREAT. *Academy*, 13 January 1906, 35-6. Review of *Wilhelmina Margravine of Baireuth*, by Edith E. Cuthell. Unsigned.

C3.4 REVIEW OF *The Scholar's Daughter*, by Beatrice Harraden. *TLS*, 16 February 1906, 52.

C3.5 REVIEW OF *A Supreme Moment*, by Mrs Hamilton Synge. *TLS*, 16 February 1906, 52.

C3.6 REVIEW OF *The House of Shadows*, by R. J. Farrer. *TLS*, 9 March 1906, 84.

C3.7 REVIEW OF *Blanche Esmead*, by Mrs Fuller Maitland. *TLS*, 23 March 1906, 104.

C3.8 REVIEW OF *The Face of Clay*, by H. A. Vachell. *TLS*, 13 April 1906, 133.

C3.9 THE POETIC DRAMA. *Guardian*, 18 April 1906, 651. Review of *King William I*, by Arthur Dillon; *Aurelian*, by Spencer Moore; *Sir Thomas More*, by Archibald Douglas Fox; *The Little Mermaid*, by Alexandra von Herder; *The City*, by Arthur Upson; *Plays and Poems*, by Paul Hookham; and *The Two Arcadias*, by Rosalind Travers. Unsigned.

C4 POETS' LETTERS. *Speaker*, 21 April 1906, 63-4. Review of *Elizabeth Barrett Browning in her Letters*, by Percy Lubbock and *Robert Browning and Alfred Domett*, edited by F. G. Kenyon. Signed A. V. Stephen.

C5 WORDSWORTH AND THE LAKES. *TLS*, 15 June 1906, 216. Review of *Wordsworth's Guide to the Lakes, with an Introduction . . .* by Ernest de Selincourt and *Months at the Lakes*, by the Rev. H. D. Rawnsley.

C5.1 REVIEW OF *The Compromise*, by Dorothea Gerard. *TLS*, 15 June 1906, 217.

C5.2 REVIEW OF *Mrs. Grundy's Crucifix*, by Vincent Brown. *TLS*, 22 June 1906, 226.

C5.3 THE BLUEST OF THE BLUE. *Guardian*, 11 July 1906, 1179. Review of *A Woman of Wit and Wisdom*, by Alice C. C. Gaussen. Unsigned.

C5.4 REVIEW OF *Coniston*, by Winston Churchill. *TLS*, 13 July 1906, 249.

C5.5 REVIEW OF The *Author's Progress*, by Adam Lorimer. *Guardian*, 25 July 1906, 1254. Unsigned.

C5.6 SWEETNESS – LONG DRAWN OUT. *Academy*, 28 July 1906, 81. Review of *A German Pompadour*, by Marie Hay. Unsigned.

C5.7 TRAFFICKS AND DISCOVERIES. *Speaker*, 11 August 1906, 440-1. Review of *English Voyages of the Sixteenth Century*, by Walter Raleigh. Unsigned.

## C. CONTRIBUTIONS TO PERIODICALS

### 1907

C5 .8 "THE PRIVATE PAPERS OF HENRY RYECROFT" by George Gissing. *Guardian*, 13 February 1907, 282–3. Unsigned.

C5 .9 REVIEW OF *Temptation*, by Richard Bagot. *TLS*, 22 February 1907, 62.

C5 .10 REVIEW OF *Fraulein Schmidt and Mr Anstruther*, by the author of *Elizabeth and Her German Garden, i.e.* Mary Annette, Countess von Arnim, later Countess Russell. *TLS*, 10 May 1907, 149.

C5 .11 REVIEW OF *The Glen o' Weeping*, by Marjorie Bowen. *TLS*, 24 May 1907, 166.

C5 .12 PHILIP SIDNEY. *TLS*, 31 May 1907, 173–4. Review of *Sir Fulke Greville's Life of Sir Philip Sidney*, with an introduction by Nowell Smith.

C6 LADY FANSHAWE'S MEMOIRS. *TLS*, 26 July 1907, 234. Review of *The Memoirs of Ann Lady Fanshawe, 1600–72.*

C6 .1 REVIEW OF The *New Religion*, by Maarten Maartens. *TLS*, 6 September 1907, 269.

C7 A SWAN AND HER FRIENDS. *TLS*, 14 November 1907, 348. Review of *A Swan and her Friends*, by E. V. Lucas.

C8 WILLIAM ALLINGHAM. *TLS*, 19 December 1907, 387. Review of *William Allingham: A Diary*, edited by H. Allingham.

### 1908

C9 THE SENTIMENTAL TRAVELLER. *TLS*, 9 January 1908, 14. Review of *The Sentimental Traveller*, by Vernon Lee.

Reprinted in: *Contemporary Writers*, 1965.

C10 THOMAS HOOD. *TLS*, 30 January 1908, 35. Review of *Thomas Hood: His Life and Times*, by Walter Jerrold.

Reprinted in: *Books and Portraits*, 1977.

C11 THE INWARD LIGHT. *TLS*, 27 February 1908, 68. Review of *The Inward Light*, by H. Fielding Hall.

Reprinted in: *Contemporary Writers*, 1965.

C12 SHELLEY AND ELIZABETH HITCHENER. *TLS*, 5 March 1908, 76–7. Review of *Letters from Percy Bysshe Shelley to Elizabeth Hitchener*, with introduction by Bertram Dobell.

Reprinted in: *Books and Portraits*, 1977.

C13 WORDSWORTH LETTERS. *TLS*, 2 April 1908, 108–9. Review of *Letters of the Wordsworth Family from 1787 to 1855 . . .* edited by William Knight.

C14 THE DIARY OF A LADY IN WAITING. *TLS*, 23 July 1908, 236–7. Review of *The Diary of a Lady in Waiting*, by Lady Charlotte Bury.

Reprinted in: *Books and Portraits*, 1977.

C15 THE STRANGER IN LONDON. *TLS*, 30 July 1908, 244. Review of *Londoner Skizzenbuch*, by Von A. Rutari and *Londres comme je l'ai vu, texte et dessins de Ch. Huard.*

C16 SCOTTISH WOMEN. *TLS*, 3 September 1908, 284. Review of *A Group of Scottish Women*, by Harry Graham.

C17 "A ROOM WITH A VIEW". *TLS*, 22 October 1908, 362. Review of *A Room with a View*, by E. M. Forster.

Reprinted in: *Contemporary Writers*, 1965.

C18 CHATEAU AND COUNTRY LIFE. *TLS*, 29 October 1908, 375. Review of *Chateau and Country Life in France*, by Mary King Waddington.

C19 LETTERS OF CHRISTINA ROSSETTI. *TLS*, 12 November 1908, 403. Review of *The Family Letters of Christina Rossetti*, edited by William Michael Rossetti.

C20 "BLACKSTICK PAPERS". *TLS*, 19 November 1908, 411. Review of *Blackstick Papers*, by Lady Ritchie.

C21 A VANISHED GENERATION. *TLS*, 3 December 1908, 445. Review of *Memoirs of a Vanished Generation 1813-1855*, edited by Mrs Warrenne Blake.

C22 THE MEMOIRS OF SARAH BERNHARDT. *Cornhill Magazine*, London, 1908, N.S. 24, 190-6.

Reprinted in: *Books and Portraits*, 1977.

C23 THE MEMOIRS OF LADY DOROTHY NEVILL. *Cornhill Magazine*, 1908, N.S. 24, 469-73.

C24 'JOHN DELANE'. *Cornhill Magazine*, 1908, N.S. 24, 765-70. Review of *The Life and Letters of John Thadeus Delane*, by Arthur Irwin Dasent.

Reprinted in: *Living Age*, Boston, 18 July 1908, 139-42;* *Books and Portraits*, 1977.

C25 REVIEW OF *A Week in the White House with Theodore Roosevelt*, by William Bayard Hale. *Cornhill Magazine*, 1908, N.S. 25, 217-22.

C26 REVIEW OF *Louise de la Vallière*, by J. Lair. *Cornhill Magazine*, 1908, N.S. 25, 523-7.

C27 REVIEW OF *The Journal of Elizabeth Lady Holland*, edited by the Earl of Ilchester and *The Holland House Circle*, by Lloyd Sanders. *Cornhill Magazine*, 1908, N.S. 25, 794-802.

Reprinted as: The Journal of Elizabeth Lady Holland. *Living Age*, 2 January 1909, 8-13;* Elizabeth Lady Holland, *Books and Portraits*, 1977.

## 1909

C28 VENICE. *TLS*, 7 January 1909, 5-6. Review of *Venice*, by Pompeo Molmenti, Parts 2 and 3; translated by Horatio F. Brown.

C29 THE GENIUS OF BOSWELL. *TLS*, 21 January 1909, 25. Review of *Letters of James Boswell to the Rev. W. J. Temple.*

Reprinted in: *Books and Portraits*, 1977.

C30 "ONE IMMORTALITY". *TLS*, 4 February 1909, 42. Review of *One Immortality*, by H. Fielding Hall.

Reprinted in: *Contemporary Writers*, 1965.

C31 MORE CARLYLE LETTERS. *TLS*, 1 April 1909, 126. Review of *The Love Letters of Thomas Carlyle and Jane Welsh*, edited by Alexander Carlyle.

C32 GENTLEMEN ERRANT. *TLS*, 15 April 1909, 144. Review of *Gentlemen Errant*, by Mrs Henry Cust.

C32.1 CAROLINE EMILIA STEPHEN. *Guardian*, 21 April 1909, 636–7. Obituary. Unsigned.

C32.2 "THE OPERA". *The Times*, London 24 April 1909, 15. Unsigned.

C33 A FRIEND OF JOHNSON. *TLS*, 29 July 1909, 276. Review of *Giuseppe Baretti and his Friends*, by Lacy Collison-Morley.

Reprinted in: *Granite and Rainbow*, 1958; *Collected Essays*, Vol. 3, 1967.

C34 ART AND LIFE. *TLS*, 5 August 1909, 284. Review of *Laurus Nobilis*, by Vernon Lee.

C35 STERNE. *TLS*, 12 August 1909, 289–90. Review of *The Life and Times of Laurence Sterne*, by Wilbur L. Cross.

Reprinted in: *Granite and Rainbow*, 1958; *Collected Essays*, Vol. 3, 1967.

C36 IMPRESSIONS AT BAYREUTH. *The Times*, London, 21 August 1909, 9. Unsigned.

Reprinted in: *Books and Portraits*, 1977.

C37 OLIVER WENDELL HOLMES. *TLS*, 26 August 1909, 305–6. Review of *Oliver Wendell Holmes*, by Lewis W. Townsend.

Reprinted in: *Granite and Rainbow*, 1958; *Collected Essays*, Vol. 4, 1967.

C38 A COOKERY BOOK. *TLS*, 25 November 1909, 457. Review of *The Cookery Book of Lady Clark of Tillypronie . . .* edited by Catherine Frances Frere.

C39 SHERIDAN. *TLS*, 2 December 1909, 461–3. Review of *The Life of Richard Brinsley Sheridan*, by Walter Sichel.

Reprinted in: *Books and Portraits*, 1977.

C40 MARIA EDGEWORTH AND HER CIRCLE. *TLS*, 9 December 1909, 482. Review of *Maria Edgeworth and her Circle in the Days of Buonaparte and Bourbon*, by Constance Hill.

Reprinted in: *Books and Portraits*, 1977.

C41 THE GIRLHOOD OF QUEEN ELIZABETH. *TLS*, 30 December 1909, 516. Review of *The Girlhood of Queen Elizabeth*, by Frank A. Mumby.

Reprinted in: *Books and Portraits*, 1977.

## 1910

C42 LADY HESTER STANHOPE. *TLS*, 20 January 1910, 20. Review of *Lady Hester Stanhope*, by Mrs Charles Roundell.

Reprinted in: *Books and Portraits*, 1977.

C43 MODES AND MANNERS OF THE NINETEENTH CENTURY. *TLS*, 24 February 1910, 64. Review of *Modes and Manners of the Nineteenth Century*; translated by M. Edwardes, introduction by Grace Rhys.

Reprinted in: *Books and Portraits*, 1977.

C44 EMERSON'S JOURNALS. *TLS*, 3 March 1910, 69–70. Review of *Journals of Ralph Waldo Emerson*, edited by E. W. Emerson and W. Emerson Forbes.

Reprinted in: *Books and Portraits*, 1977.

C45 MRS. GASKELL. *TLS*, 29 September 1910, 349. Review of *Mrs Gaskell: Haunts, Homes and Stories*, by Mrs Ellis H. Chadwick.

Reprinted in: *Books and Portraits*, 1977.

## 1911

C46 THE DUKE AND DUCHESS OF NEWCASTLE-UPON-TYNE. *TLS*, 2 February 1911, 40. Review of *The First Duke and Duchess of Newcastle-upon-Tyne*, by the author of *A Life of Sir Kenelm Digby* [*i.e.* Thomas Longueville].

C47 RACHEL. *TLS*, 20 April 1911, 155. Review of *Rachel: Her Stage Life and her Real Life*, by Francis Gribble.

## 1912

C48 THE NOVELS OF GEORGE GISSING. *TLS*, 11 January 1912, 9–10. Review of *The Odd Women; Eve's Ransom; The Whirlpool; The Unclassed; The Emancipated; In the Year of Jubilee; Denzil Quarrier; Human Odds and Ends*, by George Gissing.

C49 FRANCES WILLARD. *TLS*, 28 November 1912, 544. Review of *Frances Willard: Her Life and Work*, by Ray Strachey.

## 1913

C49.1 CHINESE STORIES. *TLS*, 1 May 1913, 184. Review of *Strange Stories from the Lodge of Leisures*, translated from the Chinese by George Soulié.

C49 .2 JANE AUSTEN. *TLS*, 8 May 1913, 189–90. Review of *Life and Letters of Jane Austen*, by W. and R. A. Austen-Leigh; and *Old Friends and New Faces*, by Sybil G. Brinton.

C49 .3 REVIEW OF *Les Copains*, by Jules Romains. *TLS*, 7 August 1913, 330.

## 1916

C50 QUEEN ADELAIDE. *TLS*, 13 January 1916, 19. Review of *The Life and Times of Queen Adelaide*, by Mary F. Sandars.

Reprinted in: *Books and Portraits*, 1977.

C51 "A SCRIBBLING DAME". *TLS*, 17 February 1916, 78. Review of *The Life and Romances of Mrs Eliza Haywood*, by George Frisbie Whicher.

Reprinted in: *Books and Portraits*, 1977.

C52 CHARLOTTE BRONTË. *TLS*, 13 April 1916, 169–70.

Partially incorporated in: "Jane Eyre" and "Wuthering Heights", *The Common Reader*, 1925; *Collected Essays*, Vol. 1, 1966.

C52 .1 PAST AND PRESENT AT THE ENGLISH LAKES. *TLS*, 29 June 1916, 307. Review of *Past and Present at the English Lakes*, by Canon Rawnsley.

C53 A MAN WITH A VIEW. *TLS*, 20 July 1916, 343. Review of *Samuel Butler: Author of Erewhon, the Man and his Work*, by John F. Harris.

Reprinted in: *Contemporary Writers*, 1965.

C54 HEARD ON THE DOWNS: THE GENESIS OF MYTH. *The Times*, London, 15 August 1916, 11. Unsigned.

C55 THE PARK WALL. *TLS*, 31 August 1916, 415. Review of *The Park Wall*, by Elinor Mordaunt.

Reprinted in: *Contemporary Writers*, 1965.

C55 .1 "THE FIGHTING NINETIES". *TLS*, 12 October 1916, 486. Review of *Nights*, by Elizabeth Robins Pennell.

C56 AMONG THE POETS. *TLS*, 2 November 1916, 523. Review of *An Evening in my Library Among English Poets*, by the Hon. Stephen Coleridge.

C57 LONDON REVISITED. *TLS*, 9 November 1916, 535. Review of *London Revisited*, by E. V. Lucas.

C58 IN A LIBRARY. *TLS*, 23 November 1916, 559. Review of *A Quiet Corner in a Library*, by William Henry Hudson.

Reprinted in: *Contemporary Writers*, 1965.

C59 HOURS IN A LIBRARY. *TLS*, 30 November 1916, 565–6.

Reprinted: New York, Harcourt, Brace, 1958. See A33. *Granite and Rainbow*, 1958; *Collected Essays*, Vol. 2, 1966.

C60 OLD AND YOUNG. *TLS*, 14 December 1916, 608. Review of *I Sometimes Think: Essays for the Young People*, by Stephen Paget.

C61 SOCIAL LIFE IN ENGLAND. *TLS*, 21 December 1916, 620. Review of *Social Life in England, 1750–1850*, by F. J. Foakes Jackson.

C62 MR. SYMONS'S ESSAYS. *TLS*, 21 December 1916, 623. Review of *Figures of Several Centuries*, by Arthur Symons.

## 1917

C63 ROMANCE. *TLS*, 18 January 1917, 31. Review of *Romance: Two Lectures*, by Sir Walter Raleigh.

C64 TOLSTOY'S "THE COSSACKS". *TLS*, 1 February 1917, 55. Review of *The Cossacks and Other Tales of the Caucasus*, by Leo Tolstoy; translated by Louise and Aylmer Maude.

C65 MELODIOUS MEDITATIONS. *TLS*, 8 February 1917, 67. Review of *An Apology for Old Maids*, by Henry Dwight Sedgwick.

C66 MORE DOSTOEVSKY. *TLS*, 22 February 1917, 91. Review of *The Eternal Husband and Other Stories*, by Fyodor Dostoevsky; translated by Constance Garnett.

Reprinted in: *Books and Portraits*, 1977.

C67 BEFORE MIDNIGHT. *TLS*, 1 March 1917, 104. Review of *Before Midnight*, by Elinor Mordaunt.

Reprinted in: *Contemporary Writers*, 1965.

C68 PARODIES. *TLS*, 8 March 1917, 112. Review of *Tricks of the Trade*, by J. C. Squire.

C69 SIR WALTER RALEIGH. *TLS*, 15 March 1917, 127. Review of *Sir Walter Raleigh: Selections from his "Historie of the World", his Letters &c.*, edited . . . by G. E. Hadow.

Reprinted in: *Granite and Rainbow*, 1958; *Collected Essays*, Vol. 3, 1967.

C70 THE HOUSE OF LYME. *TLS*, 29 March 1917, 150. Review of *The House of Lyme from its Foundation to the End of the Eighteenth Century*, by the Lady Newton.

C71 POE'S HELEN. *TLS*, 5 April 1917, 162. Review of *Poe's Helen*, by Caroline Ticknor.

Reprinted in: *Granite and Rainbow*, 1958; *Collected Essays*, Vol. 4, 1967.

C72 A TALKER. *TLS*, 12 April 1917, 173. Review of *The Great Valley*, by Edgar Lee Masters.

C73 IN GOOD COMPANY. *TLS*, 12 April 1917, 175. Review of *In Good Company*, by Coulson Kernahan.

C74 A CAMBRIDGE V.A.D. *TLS*, 10 May 1917, 223. Review of *From Cambridge to Camiers under the Red Cross*, by E. M. Spearing.

C75 THE PERFECT LANGUAGE. *TLS*, 24 May 1917, 247. Review of *The Greek Anthology*, with an English translation by W. R. Paton, Vol. 2.

C76 MR. SASSOON'S POEMS. *TLS*, 31 May 1917, 259. Review of *The Old Huntsman and Other Poems*, by Siegfried Sassoon.

Reprinted in: *Books and Portraits*, 1977.

C77 CREATIVE CRITICISM. *TLS*, 7 June 1917, 271. Review of *Creative Criticism: Essays on the Unity of Genius and Taste*, by J. E. Spingarn.

C78 SOUTH WIND. *TLS*, 14 June 1917, 283. Review of *South Wind*, by Norman Douglas.

Reprinted in: *TLS*, 18 January 1952, 55; *Contemporary Writers*, 1965.

C79 BOOKS AND PERSONS. *TLS*, 5 July 1917, 319. Review of *Books and Persons*, by Arnold Bennett.

Reprinted in: *Contemporary Writers*, 1965.

C80 THOREAU. *TLS*, 12 July 1917, 325-6.

Reprinted in: *Books and Portraits*, 1977.

C81 "LORD JIM". *TLS*, 26 July 1917, 355. Review of *Lord Jim: A Tale*, by Joseph Conrad.

C82 JOHN DAVIDSON. *TLS*, 16 August 1917, 390. Review of *John Davidson: A Study of the Relation of his Ideas to his Poetry*, by Hayim Fineman.

C83 A VICTORIAN ECHO. *TLS*, 23 August 1917, 403. Review of *Parables and Tales*, by Thomas Gordon Hake.

C84 MR. GALSWORTHY'S NOVEL. *TLS*, 30 August 1917, 415. Review of *Beyond*, by John Galsworthy.

Reprinted in: *Contemporary Writers*, 1965.

C85 TO READ OR NOT TO READ. *TLS*, 6 September 1917, 427. Review of *How to Lengthen our Ears*, by Viscount Harberton.

C86 MR. CONRAD'S "YOUTH". *TLS*, 20 September 1917, 451. Review of *Youth*, by Joseph Conrad.

C87 FLUMINA AMEM SILVASQUE. *TLS*, 11 October 1917, 489. Review of *A Literary Pilgrim in England*, by Edward Thomas. See also letters entitled 'Arnold as a Poet of Nature' from C.L.D., and W. G. Waters in the issues of 18 October, p. 506 and 1 November, p. 529.

Reprinted in: *Books and Portraits*, 1977.

C88 A MINOR DOSTOEVSKY. *TLS*, 11 October 1917, 489. Review of *The Gambler and Other Stories*, by Fyodor Dostoevsky; translated by Constance Garnett.

C89 THE OLD ORDER. *TLS*, 18 October 1917, 497–8. Review of *The Middle Years*, by Henry James.

Reprinted in: *The Death of the Moth*, 1942; *TLS*, 18 January 1952, 54–5; *Collected Essays*, Vol. 1, 1966.

C90 HEARTS OF CONTROVERSY. *TLS*, 25 October 1917, 515. Review of *Hearts of Controversy*, by Alice Meynell.

C91 A RUSSIAN SCHOOLBOY. *TLS*, 8 November 1917, 539. Review of *A Russian Schoolboy*, by Serge Aksakoff.

Reprinted in: *Books and Portraits*, 1977.

C91.1 STOPFORD BROOKE. *TLS*, 29 November 1917, 581. Review of *Life and Letters of Stopford Brooke*, by L. P. Jacks.

C92 MR. GLADSTONE'S DAUGHTER. *TLS*, 6 December 1917, 595. Review of *Some Hawarden Letters, 1878–1913*, chosen . . . by L. March-Phillipps and Bertram Christian. On Mrs Drew.

C93 CHARLOTTE BRONTË. *TLS*, 13 December 1917, 615. Review of *Charlotte Brontë: A Centenary Memorial*, edited by Butler Wood.

C94 REBELS AND REFORMERS. *TLS*, 20 December 1917, 634. Review of *Rebels and Reformers*, by Arthur and Dorothea Ponsonby.

C95 SUNSET REFLECTIONS. *TLS*, 20 December 1917, 636. Review of *The Happy Fields*, by E. M. Martin.

C95.1 "THE NEW CRUSADE". *TLS*, 27 December 1917, 647. Review of *Prose Papers*, by John Drinkwater.

## 1918

C96 VISITS TO WALT WHITMAN. *TLS*, 3 January 1918, 7. Review of *Visits to Walt Whitman in 1890–91*, by J. Johnston and J. W. Wallace.

Reprinted in: *Granite and Rainbow*, 1958; *Collected Essays*, Vol. 4, 1967.

C97 PHILOSOPHY IN FICTION. *TLS*, 10 January 1918, 18. Review of *Writings by L. P. Jacks: Mad Shepherds; The Country Air; Philosophers in Trouble; All Men Are Ghosts; Among the Idolmakers; From the Human End.*

Reprinted in: *Contemporary Writers*, 1965.

C98 A BOOK OF ESSAYS. *TLS*, 17 January 1918, 31. Review of *If the Germans Conquered England and Other Essays*, by Robert Lynd.

C99 THE GREEN MIRROR. *TLS*, 24 January 1918, 43. Review of *The Green Mirror*, by Hugh Walpole.

Reprinted in: *Contemporary Writers*, 1965.

C100 ACROSS THE BORDER. *TLS*, 31 January 1918, 55. Review of *The Supernatural in Modern English Fiction*, by Dorothy Scarborough.

Reprinted as: The Supernatural in Fiction, *Granite and Rainbow*, 1958; *Collected Essays*, Vol. 1, 1966.

C101 COLERIDGE AS CRITIC. *TLS*, 7 February 1918, 67. Review of *The Table Talk and Omniana of Samuel Taylor Coleridge*, with a note on Coleridge by Coventry Patmore.

Reprinted in: *Books and Portraits*, 1977.

C102 MR. CONRAD'S CRISIS. *TLS*, 14 March 1918, 126. Review of *Nostromo: A Tale of the Seaboard*, by Joseph Conrad.

C103 SWINBURNE LETTERS. *TLS*, 21 March 1918, 139. Review of *The Letters of Algernon Charles Swinburne*, with some Personal Recollections by Thomas Hake and Arthur Compton Rickett.

C104 PAPERS ON PEPYS. *TLS*, 4 April 1918, 161. Review of *Occasional Papers Read by Members at Meetings of the Samuel Pepys Club*, edited by the late H. B. Wheatley, Vol. 1.

Reprinted in: *Books and Portraits*, 1977.

C105 SECOND MARRIAGE. *TLS*, 25 April 1918, 195. Review of *Second Marriage*, by Viola Meynell.

C106 TWO IRISH POETS. *TLS*, 2 May 1918, 206. Review of *Last Songs*, by Francis Ledwidge and *Reincarnations*, by James Stephens.

C107 TCHEHOV'S QUESTIONS. *TLS*, 16 May 1918, 231. Review of *The Wife and Other Stories* and *The Witch and Other Stories*, by Anton Tchehov; translated by Constance Garnett.

C108 IMITATIVE ESSAYS. *TLS*, 23 May 1918, 243. Review of *The Gold Tree*, by J. C. Squire.

C109 MOMENTS OF VISION. *TLS*, 23 May 1918, 243. Review of *Trivia*, by Logan Pearsall Smith.

Reprinted in: *TLS*, 18 January 1952, 56; *Contemporary Writers*, 1965.

C110 DREAMS AND REALITIES. *TLS*, 30 May 1918, 253. Review of *Motley and Other Poems*, by Walter de la Mare.

C111 THE CLAIM OF THE LIVING. *TLS*, 13 June 1918, 275. Review of *A Novelist on Novels*, by W. L. George.

Reprinted in: *Contemporary Writers*, 1965.

C112 LOUD LAUGHTER. *TLS*, 20 June 1918, 287. Review of *Frenzied Fiction*, by Stephen Leacock.

C113 A VICTORIAN SOCIALIST. *TLS*, 27 June 1918, 299. Review of *Reminiscences and Reflections of a Mid and Late Victorian*, by Ernest Belfort Bax.

C114 MR. MERRICK'S NOVELS. *TLS*, 4 July 1918, 311. Review of *While Paris Laughed* and *Conrad in Quest of his Youth*, by Leonard Merrick, with introduction by Sir James Barrie.

Reprinted in: *Contemporary Writers*, 1965.

C115 TWO SOLDIER-POETS. *TLS*, 11 July 1918, 323. Review of *Counter-Attack and Other Poems*, by Siegfried Sassoon and *Poems*, by Geoffrey Dearmer.

Reprinted in: Mr Sassoon's Poems, *Books and Portraits*, 1977.

C116 ON RE-READING MEREDITH. *TLS*, 25 July 1918, 347. Review of *George Meredith: A Study of his Works and Personality*, by J. H. E. Crees.

Reprinted in: *Granite and Rainbow*, 1958; *Collected Essays*, Vol. 1, 1966.

C117 RUPERT BROOKE. *TLS*, 8 August 1918, 371. Review of *The Collected Poems of Rupert Brooke, with a Memoir.*

Reprinted in: *Books and Portraits*, 1977.

C118 A PRACTICAL UTOPIA. *TLS*, 15 August 1918, 380. Review of *The New Moon*, by Oliver Onions.

C119 THE SAD YEARS. *TLS*, 29 August 1918, 403. Review of *The Sad Years*, by Dora Sigerson.

C120 THE "MOVIE" NOVEL. *TLS*, 29 August 1918, 403. Review of *The Early Life and Adventures of Sylvia Scarlett*, by Compton Mackenzie.

Reprinted in: *Contemporary Writers*, 1965.

C121 WAR IN THE VILLAGE. *TLS*, 12 September 1918, 426. Review of *The Village Wife's Lament*, by Maurice Hewlett.

Reprinted in: *Contemporary Writers*, 1965.

C122 THE RIGHTS OF YOUTH. *TLS*, 19 September 1918, 439. Review of *Joan and Peter*, by H. G. Wells.

Reprinted in: *Contemporary Writers*, 1965.

C123 MR. HUDSON'S CHILDHOOD. *TLS*, 26 September 1918, 453. Review of *Far Away and Long Ago*, by W. H. Hudson.

Reprinted in: *Contemporary Writers*, 1965.

C124 CAUTION AND CRITICISM. *TLS*, 3 October 1918, 467. Review of *Modern English Writers*, by Harold Williams.

Reprinted in: *Contemporary Writers*, 1965.

C125 ADVENTURERS ALL. *TLS*, 10 October 1918, 477. Review of *The Cockpit of Idols*, by Muriel Stuart; *The Defeat of Youth and Other Poems*, by Aldous Huxley; *Clowns' Houses*, by Edith Sitwell; *Songs for Sale: An Anthology of Recent Poetry*, edited by E. B. C. Jones.

C126 HONEST FICTION. *TLS*, 10 October 1918, 481. Review of *Shops and Houses*, by Frank Swinnerton.

Reprinted in: *Contemporary Writers*, 1965.

C127 WOMEN NOVELISTS. *TLS*, 17 October 1918, 495. Review of *The Women Novelists*, by R. Brimley Johnson.

Reprinted in: *Contemporary Writers*, 1965.

C128 VALERY BRUSSOF. *TLS*, 24 October 1918, 509. Review of *The Republic of the Southern Cross and Other Stories*, by Valery Brussof.

C129 THE CANDLE OF VISION. *TLS*, 31 October 1918, 522. Review of *The Candle of Vision*, by A.E.

C130 ABRAHAM LINCOLN. *TLS*, 31 October 1918, 523. Review of *Abraham Lincoln: A Play*, by John Drinkwater.

C131 MR. HOWELLS ON FORM. *TLS*, 14 November 1918, 553. Review of *The Actor Manager*, by Leonard Merrick.

C132 BAD WRITERS. *TLS*, 21 November 1918, 566. Review of *Books in General*, by Solomon Eagle, [*pseud.* of J. C. Squire].

C133 TRAFFICKS AND DISCOVERIES. *TLS*, 12 December 1918, 618. Review of *English Seamen in the Sixteenth Century*, by J. A. Froude and *The Hakluyts' Voyages, Travels and Discoveries of the English Nation.*

C134 THE THREE BLACK PENNYS. *TLS*, 12 December 1918, 620. Review of *The Three Black Pennys*, by Joseph Hergesheimer.

Reprinted in: *Contemporary Writers*, 1965.

C135 A VIEW OF THE RUSSIAN REVOLUTION. *TLS*, 19 December 1918, 636. Review of *Petrograd: The City of Trouble, 1914–1918*, by Meriel Buchanan.

C136 THE RUSSIAN VIEW. *TLS*, 19 December 1918, 641. Review of *The Village Priest and Other Stories from the Russian of E. Militsina and M. Saltikov*; translated by Beatrix L. Tollemache.

C137 MUMMERY. *TLS*, 19 December 1918, 641. Review of *Mummery*, by G. Cannan.

Reprinted in: *Contemporary Writers*, 1965.

C138 THE METHOD OF HENRY JAMES. *TLS*, 26 December 1918, 655. Review of *The Method of Henry James*, by Joseph Warren Beach.

## 1919

C139 THE WAR FROM THE STREET. *TLS*, 9 January 1919, 14. Review of *Our Own History of the War from a South London View*, by D. Bridgman Metchim.

C140 SMALL TALK ABOUT MEREDITH. *TLS*, 13 February 1919, 81. Review of *George Meredith: His Life and Friends in Relation to his Work*, by S. M. Ellis.

C141 THE TUNNEL. *TLS*, 13 February 1919, 81. Review of *The Tunnel*, by Dorothy M. Richardson.

Reprinted in: *Contemporary Writers*, 1965.

C142 LADY RITCHIE. *TLS*, 6 March 1919, 123.

C143 SYLVIA AND MICHAEL. *TLS*, 20 March 1919, 150. Review of *Sylvia and Michael*, by Compton Mackenzie.

Reprinted in: *Contemporary Writers*, 1965.

C144 WITHIN THE RIM. *TLS*, 27 March 1919, 163. Review of *Within the Rim*, by Henry James.

Reprinted in: *The Death of the Moth*, 1942; *Collected Essays*, Vol. 1, 1966.

C145 DICKENS BY A DISCIPLE. *TLS*, 27 March 1919, 163. Review of *The Secret of Dickens*, by W. Walter Crotch.

C146 WASHINGTON IRVING. *TLS*, 3 April 1919, 179. Review of *Tales of Washington Irving*, selected and edited . . . by Carl van Doren.

C147 MODERN NOVELS. *TLS*, 10 April 1919, 189–90.

Reprinted (slightly revised) as: Modern Fiction, *The Common Reader*, 1925; *Selections from Her Essays*, [1966]; *Collected Essays*, Vol. 2, 1966.

C148 THE NOVELS OF DEFOE. *TLS*, 24 April 1919, 217–18.

Reprinted as: Defoe, *The Common Reader*, 1925; *Collected Essays*, Vol. 1, 1966.

C149 THE ECCENTRICS. *Athenaeum*, 25 April 1919, 230–1.

C150 THE OBSTINATE LADY. *TLS*, 1 May 1919, 236. Review of *The Obstinate Lady*, by W. E. Norris.

Reprinted in: *Contemporary Writers*, 1965.

C151 THE SOUL OF AN ARCHBISHOP. *Athenaeum*, 9 May 1919, 299–300. Review of *The Life and Letters of William Thomson, Archbishop of York*, by Ethel H. Thomson. Signed V.W.

Reprinted as: Archbishop Thomson, *The Common Reader*, 1925; *Collected Essays*, Vol. 4, 1967.

C152 THE ANATOMY OF FICTION. *Athenaeum*, 16 May 1919, 331. Review of *Materials and Methods of Fiction*, by Clayton Hamilton. Signed V.W.

Reprinted in: *Granite and Rainbow*, 1958; *Collected Essays*, Vol. 2, 1966.

C153 JAVA HEAD. *TLS*, 29 May 1919, 293. Review of *Java Head*, by Joseph Hergesheimer.

Reprinted in: *Contemporary Writers*, 1965.

C154 ON SOME OF THE OLD ACTORS. *Athenaeum*, 6 June 1919, 427–8. Review of *The Life of Augustin Daly*, by Joseph Francis Daly. Unsigned.

C155 JOSEPH ADDISON. *TLS*, 19 June 1919, 329-30.

Reprinted (slightly revised) as: Addison, *The Common Reader*, 1925; *Collected Essays*, Vol. 1, 1966.

C155 .1 IS THIS POETRY? *Athenaeum*, 20 June 1919, 491. Review of *The Critic in Judgment*, by J. M. Murry and *Poems*, by T. S. Eliot. Unsigned. This appears to have been a joint review of Virginia and Leonard Woolf with the former reviewing Murry's *The Critic in Judgment* and the latter Eliot's *Poems*. See *The Question of Things Happening* (A47*a*), pp. 373, 437.

C156 THE WAY OF ALL FLESH. *TLS*, 26 June 1919, 347. Review of *The Way of All Flesh*, by Samuel Butler.

Reprinted in: *Contemporary Writers*, 1965.

C157 FORGOTTEN BENEFACTORS. *Athenaeum*, 4 July 1919, 555-6. Review of *Edward Jerningham and his Friends*, edited by Lewis Bettany. Signed V.W.

C158 A POSITIVIST. *TLS*, 17 July 1919, 386. Review of *Obiter Scripta, 1918*, by Frederic Harrison.

C159 HORACE WALPOLE. *TLS*, 31 July 1919, 411. Review of *Supplement to the Letters of Horace Walpole, Fourth Earl of Orford* . . . edited . . . by Paget Toynbee.

Reprinted in: *Granite and Rainbow*, 1958; *Collected Essays*, Vol. 3, 1967.

C160 "THESE ARE THE PLANS". *Athenaeum*, 1 August 1919, 682-3. Review of *Poems*, by Donald F. Goold Johnson and *Marlborough and Other Poems*, by Charles Hamilton Sorley, 4th Edition. Signed V.W.

Reprinted in: *Books and Portraits*, 1977.

C161 HERMAN MELVILLE. *TLS*, 7 August 1919, 423. Essay to mark the Centenary of Melville's Birth.

Reprinted in: *Books and Portraits*, 1977.

C162 THE RUSSIAN BACKGROUND. *TLS*, 14 August 1919, 435. Review of *The Bishop and Other Stories*, by Anton Tchehov; translated by Constance Garnett.

Reprinted in: *Books and Portraits*, 1977.

C163 A REAL AMERICAN. *TLS*, 21 August 1919, 446. Review of *Free and Other Stories* and *Twelve Men*, by Theodore Dreiser.

Reprinted in: *Contemporary Writers*, 1965.

C164 THE ROYAL ACADEMY. *Athenaeum*, 22 August 1919, 774-6. Description of a visit to the Royal Academy's exhibition.

Reprinted in: *Granite and Rainbow*, 1958; *Collected Essays*, Vol. 4, 1967.

C165 SONIA MARRIED. *TLS*, 28 August 1919, 460. Review of *Sonia Married*, by Stephen McKenna.

Reprinted in: *Contemporary Writers*, 1965.

C166 WILCOXIANA. *Athenaeum*, 19 September 1919, 913–14. Review of *The Worlds and I*, by Ella Wheeler Wilcox. Signed V.W.

Reprinted in: *Books and Portraits*, 1977.

C167 SEPTEMBER. *TLS*, 25 September 1919, 513. Review of *September*, by Frank Swinnerton.

Reprinted in: *Contemporary Writers*, 1965.

C168 MR. GOSSE AND HIS FRIENDS. *TLS*, 2 October 1919, 529. Review of *Some Diversions of a Man of Letters*, by Edmund Gosse.

C169 MADELEINE. *TLS*, 9 October 1919, 547. Review of *Madeleine, One of Love's Jansenists*, by Hope Mirrlees.

C170 LANDOR IN LITTLE. *TLS*, 16 October 1919, 564. Review of *A Day-Book of Landor*, chosen by John Bailey.

C171 DOSTOEVSKY IN CRANFORD. *TLS*, 23 October 1919, 586. Review of *An Honest Thief and Other Stories*, by Fyodor Dostoevsky.

Reprinted in: *Books and Portraits*, 1977.

C172 WINGED PHRASES. *TLS*, 30 October 1919, 606. Review of *Avowals*, by George Moore.

Reprinted in: *Contemporary Writers*, 1965.

C173 REAL LETTERS. *TLS*, 6 November 1919, 627. Review of *Miss Eden's Letters*, edited by Violet Dickinson.

C174 THE LIMITS OF PERFECTION. *TLS*, 6 November 1919, 627. Review of *Seven Men*, by Max Beerbohm.

C175 GEORGE ELIOT. *TLS*, 20 November 1919, 657–8.

Reprinted in: *The Common Reader*, 1925; *Collected Essays*, Vol. 1, 1966.

C176 MATURITY AND IMMATURITY. *Athenaeum*, 21 November 1919, 1220–1. Review of *Edward Wyndham Tennant: A Memoir*, by Pamela Glenconner and *Joyce Kilmer*, edited with a memoir, by Robert Cortes Holliday. Signed V.W.

C177 WATTS-DUNTON'S DILEMMA. *TLS*, 11 December 1919, 730. Review of *Swinburne as I Knew Him*, by Coulson Kernahan.

C178 THE INTELLECTUAL IMAGINATION. *TLS*, 11 December 1919, 739. Review of *Rupert Brooke and the Intellectual Imagination: A Lecture*, by Walter de la Mare.

Reprinted in: *Books and Portraits*, 1977.

C179 BEHIND THE BARS. *Athenaeum*, 12 December 1919, 1331–2. Review of *The Life and Letters of Lady Dorothy Nevill*, by her son Ralph Nevill. Signed V.W.

Reprinted as: Lady Dorothy Nevill, *The Common Reader*, 1925; *Selections from Her Essays*, [1966]; *Collected Essays*, Vol. 4, 1967.

C180 MEMORIES OF MEREDITH. *TLS*, 18 December 1919, 765. Review of *Memories of George Meredith, O.M.*, by Lady Butcher.

C181 GOLD AND IRON. *TLS*, 25 December 1919, 780. Review of *Gold and Iron*, by Joseph Hergesheimer.

Reprinted in: *Contemporary Writers*, 1965.

## 1920

C182 PICTURES AND PORTRAITS. *Athenaeum*, 9 January 1920, 46–7. Review of *Personalities: 24 Drawings*, by Edmond X. Kapp. Signed V.W.

C182 .1 AN AMERICAN POET. *TLS*, 29 January 1920, 64. Review of *General William Booth Enters into Heaven and Other Poems*, by Nicholas Vachel Lindsay.

C183 ENGLISH PROSE. *Athenaeum*, 30 January 1920, 134–5. Review of *A Treasury of English Prose*, edited by Logan Pearsall Smith.

Reprinted in: *Books and Portraits*, 1977.

C184 CLEVERNESS AND YOUTH. *TLS*, 5 February 1920, 83. Review of *Limbo*, by Aldous Huxley.

Reprinted in: *Contemporary Writers*, 1965.

C185 MR. NORRIS'S METHOD. *TLS*, 4 March 1920, 153. Review of *The Triumphs of Sara*, by W. E. Norris.

Reprinted in: *Contemporary Writers*, 1965.

C186 A TALK ABOUT MEMOIRS. *New Statesman*, 6 March 1920, 642–3. Review of *Recollections of Lady Peel*, compiled by her daughter Ethel Peel; *Victorian Recollections*, by John A. Bridges; *The Manners of my Time*, by C. L. H. Dempster; *Sporting Reminiscences*, by Dorothea Conyers; *John Porter of Kingsclere: An Autobiography*, written in collaboration with Edward Moorhouse.

Reprinted in: *Granite and Rainbow*, 1958; *Collected Essays*, Vol. 4, 1967.

C187 MONEY AND LOVE. *Athenaeum*, 12 March 1920, 332–4. Review of *The Life of Thomas Coutts, Banker*, by Ernest Hartley Coleridge. Signed V.W.

Reprinted in: *Granite and Rainbow*, 1958; *Collected Essays*, Vol. 3, 1967.

C188 MEN AND WOMEN. *TLS*, 18 March 1920, 182. Review of *La Femme anglaise au XIXe Siècle et son Evolution d'après le Roman anglais contemporain*, by Léonie Villard.

Reprinted in: *Books and Portraits*, 1977.

C189 FREUDIAN FICTION. *TLS*, 25 March 1920, 199. Review of *An Imperfect Mother*, by J. D. Beresford.

Reprinted in: *Contemporary Writers*, 1965.

C190 THE LETTERS OF HENRY JAMES. *TLS*, 8 April 1920, 217–18. Review of *The Letters of Henry James*, edited by Percy Lubbock.

Reprinted in: *The Death of the Moth*, 1942; *Collected Essays*, Vol. 1, 1966.

C191 THE HIGHER COURT. *New Statesman*, 17 April 1920, 44. Dramatic review of *The Higher Court*, by M. E. M. Young, performed at a Sunday subscription theatre.

C192 AN IMPERFECT LADY. *TLS*, 6 May 1920, 283. Review of *Mary Russell Mitford and her Surroundings*, by Constance Hill. See also C192.1, 194.

Incorporated in: Miss Mitford, *The Common Reader*, 1925; *Collected Essays*, Vol. 4, 1967.

C192 A GOOD DAUGHTER. *Daily Herald*, 26 May 1920, 7. Re-
.1 view of *Mary Russell Mitford and her Surroundings*, by Constance Hill. See also C192, 194.

C193 AN OLD NOVEL. *TLS*, 27 May 1920, 333. Review of *A Lost Love*, by Ashford Owen, *pseud.* of Charlotte Ogle.

C194 THE WRONG WAY OF READING. *Athenaeum*, 28 May 1920, 695–7. Review of *Mary Russell Mitford and her Surroundings*, by Constance Hill. Signed V.W. See also C192, 192.1.

Partially incorporated in: Miss Mitford, *The Common Reader*, 1925.

C195 BODY AND BRAIN. *New Statesman*, 5 June 1920, 254, 256. Review of *Theodore Roosevelt: An Intimate Biography*, by William Roscoe Thayer. Unsigned.

Reprinted in: *Books and Portraits*, 1977.

C196 THE MILLS OF THE GODS. *TLS*, 17 June 1920, 383. Review of *The Mills of the Gods*, by Elizabeth Robins.

C197 A DISILLUSIONED ROMANTIC. *TLS*, 1 July 1920, 419. Review of *The Rescue*, by Joseph Conrad.

C198 THE PURSUIT OF BEAUTY. *TLS*, 8 July 1920, 437. Review of *Linda Condon*, by Joseph Hergesheimer.

Reprinted in: *Contemporary Writers*, 1965.

C199 PURE ENGLISH. *TLS*, 15 July 1920, 453. Review of *Gammer Gurton's Nedle*, by Mr. S. . . . edited by H. F. B. Brett-Smith.

C200 MR. KIPLING'S NOTEBOOK. *Athenaeum*, 16 July 1920, 75. Review of *Letters of Travel, 1892–1913*, by Rudyard Kipling.

Reprinted in: *Books and Portraits*, 1977.

C200.1 THE PLUMAGE BILL. *Woman's Leader*, 23 July 1920, 559–60.

Reprinted in: *The Diary of Virginia Woolf*, Vol. II, 1978.

C201 THE CHERRY ORCHARD. *New Statesman*, 24 July 1920, 446–7. Dramatic review of *The Cherry Orchard*, by Anton Tchekhov, performed at the Arts Theatre.

C202 A BORN WRITER. *TLS*, 29 July 1920, 485. Review of *Esther Waters*, by George Moore.

Reprinted in: *Contemporary Writers*, 1965.

C203 AN UNWRITTEN NOVEL. *London Mercury*, July 1920, 273–80.

Reprinted in: *Monday or Tuesday*, 1921; *A Haunted House*, 1944.

C204 GORKY ON TOLSTOI. *New Statesman*, 7 August 1920, 505–6. Review of *Reminiscences of Leo Nicolayevitch Tolstoi*, by Maxim Gorky. Unsigned.

C205 A CHARACTER SKETCH. *Athenaeum*, 13 August 1920, 201–2. Review of *Frederick Locker-Lampson: A Character Sketch*, edited by Augustinc Birrell. Signed V.W.

C206 THE INTELLECTUAL STATUS OF WOMEN. *New Statesman*, 9 October 1920, 15, 16 October 1920, 45–6. Letters to the Editor; correspondence conducted with 'Affable Hawk' (Desmond MacCarthy).

Reprinted in: *The Diary of Virginia Woolf*, Vol. II, 1978.

C207 SOLID OBJECTS. *Athenaeum*, 22 October 1920, 543–5.

Reprinted in: *A Haunted House*, 1944.

C208 JOHN EVELYN. *TLS*, 28 October 1920, 689–90. Review of *The Early Life and Education of John Evelyn, 1620–1641*, with a commentary by H. Maynard Smith. See also C209.1.

Reprinted in part as: Rambling Round Evelyn, *The Common Reader*, 1925; *Collected Essays*, Vol. 3, 1967.

C209 JANE AUSTEN AND THE GEESE. *TLS*, 28 October 1920, 699. Review of *Personal Aspects of Jane Austen*, by Mary Augusta Austen-Leigh.

Reprinted in: *Books and Portraits*, 1977.

C209.1 JOHN EVELYN. *TLS*, 11 November 1920, 739. Letter to the Editor signed Your Reviewer, in reply to H. Maynard Smith's criticism in the issue for 4 November, p. 720. See also C208.

C210 POSTSCRIPT OR PRELUDE? *TLS*, 2 December 1920, 795. Review of *The Lost Girl*, by D. H. Lawrence.

Reprinted in: *Contemporary Writers*, 1965.

C211 PLEASANT STORIES. *TLS*, 16 December 1920, 854. Review of *The Happy End*, by Joseph Hergesheimer.

Reprinted in: *Contemporary Writers*, 1965.

C212 A FLYING LESSON. *TLS*, 23 December 1920, 873. Review of *And Even Now*, by Max Beerbohm.

## 1921

C213 REVOLUTION. *TLS*, 27 January 1921, 58. Review of *Revolution*, by J. D. Beresford.

Reprinted in: *Contemporary Writers*, 1965.

C214 MR. NORRIS'S STANDARD. *TLS*, 10 February 1921, 89. Review of *Tony the Exceptional*, by W. E. Norris.

Reprinted in: *Contemporary Writers*, 1965.

C215 HENLEY'S CRITICISM. *TLS*, 24 February 1921, 123. Review of *Essays by William Ernest Henley.*

C216 A PRINCE OF PROSE. *TLS*, 3 March 1921, 141. Review of *Notes on Life and Letters*, by Joseph Conrad.

C216.1 GEORGE ELIOT (1819–1880). *Daily Herald*, 9 March 1921, 7. One of a series entitled 'Great Names'.

C217 CONGREVE. *New Statesman*, 2 April 1921, 756. Dramatic review of *Love for Love*, by William Congreve, performed at the Lyric Theatre, Hammersmith.

C218 ETHEL SMYTH. *New Statesman*, 23 April 1921, 80, 82. Review of *Streaks of Life*, by Ethel Smyth. Unsigned.

C219 SCOTT'S CHARACTER. *TLS*, 28 April 1921, 273. Review of *The Intimate Life of Sir Walter Scott*, by Archibald Stalker.

C220 GOTHIC ROMANCE. *TLS*, 5 May 1921, 288. Review of *The Tale of Terror: A Study of the Gothic Romance*, by Edith Birkhead.

Reprinted in: *Granite and Rainbow*, 1958; *Collected Essays*, Vol. 1, 1966.

C221 PATMORE'S CRITICISM. *TLS*, 26 May 1921, 331. Review of *Courage in Politics and Other Essays*, by Coventry Patmore.

Reprinted in: *Books and Portraits*, 1977.

C222 TROUSERS. *New Statesman*, 4 June 1921, 252, 254. Review of *The Things Which Are Seen*, by A. Trystan Edwards. Unsigned.

C223 A GLANCE AT TURGENEV. *TLS*, 8 December 1921, 813. Review of *The Two Friends and Other Stories*, by Ivan Turgenev; translated by Constance Garnett.

Reprinted in: *Books and Portraits*, 1977.

C224 FANTASY. *TLS*, 15 December 1921, 840. Review of *Legends of Smokeover*, by L. P. Jacks.

C225 HENRY JAMES' GHOST STORIES. *TLS*, 22 December 1921, 849–50.

Reprinted as: Henry James's Ghost Stories, *Granite and Rainbow*, 1958; *Collected Essays*, Vol. 1, 1966.

## 1922

C226 DOSTOYEVSKY THE FATHER. *TLS*, 12 January 1922, 25. Review of *Fyodor Dostoyevsky: A Study*, by Aimée Dostoyevsky.

Reprinted in: *Books and Portraits*, 1977.

C227 JANE AUSTEN PRACTISING. *New Statesman*, 15 July 1922, 419–20. Review of *Love and Friendship*, by Jane Austen, with a preface by G. K. Chesterton. Signed V.W.

C228 ON RE-READING NOVELS. *TLS*, 20 July 1922, 465–6. Review of *The Novels of Jane Austen*, with illustrations by G. E. Brock; *The Novels of Charlotte, Emily and Anne Brontë*; *The Works of George Meredith* and *The Craft of Fiction*, by Percy Lubbock.

Reprinted (considerably revised) in: *The Moment*, 1947. Reprinted in: *TLS*, 18 January 1952, 62–3. (With sub-title, Second Thoughts on the Craft of Fiction.) *Collected Essays*, Vol. 2, 1966.

C229 MODERN ESSAYS. *TLS*, 30 November 1922, 769–70. Review of *Modern English Essays*, edited by Ernest Rhys.

Reprinted (slightly revised) as: The Modern Essay, *The Common Reader*, 1925; *Selections from Her Essays*, [1966]; *Collected Essays*, Vol. 2, 1966.

C230 ELIZA AND STERNE. *TLS*, 14 December 1922, 839. Review of *Sterne's Eliza*, by Arnold Wright and William Lutley Sclater.

Reprinted in: *Granite and Rainbow*, 1958; *Collected Essays*, Vol. 3, 1967.

## 1923

C231 HOW IT STRIKES A CONTEMPORARY. *TLS*, 5 April 1923, 221–2.

Reprinted (revised) in: *The Common Reader*, 1925; *Collected Essays*, Vol. 2, 1966.

C232 IN THE ORCHARD. *Criterion*, April 1923, I:3, 243–5.

Reprinted in: *Broom*, New York, September 1923, 5:2, 70–2; *Books and Portraits*, 1977.

C232 TALKS WITH TOLSTOI: REVEALING DIARY ABOUT
.1 THE LIFE OF THE GREAT RUSSIAN. *Cassell's Weekly*, 18 and 25 April 1923, 5–6, 147–8, 187–8. See also B4.

C233 TO SPAIN. *Nation & Athenaeum*, 5 May 1923, 153-5.

Reprinted in: *New Republic*, New York, 6 June 1923, 39-40; *The Moment*, 1947; *Collected Essays*, Vol. 4, 1967.

C234 ROMANCE AND THE HEART. *Nation & Athenaeum*, 19 May 1923, 229. Review of *The Grand Tour*, by Romer Wilson and *Revolving Lights*, by Dorothy Richardson.

Reprinted in: *Contemporary Writers*, 1965.

C235 SIR THOMAS BROWNE. *TLS*, 28 June 1923, 436. Review of *Urn Burial; The Garden of Cyrus; Religio Medici.*

C236 AN IMPRESSION OF GISSING. *New Statesman*, 30 June 1923, 371-2. Review of *George Gissing: An Impression*, by May Yates and *The Private Life of Henry Maitland*, edited by Morley Roberts. Signed V.

C237 LAETITIA PILKINGTON. *Nation & Athenaeum*, 30 June 1923, 424-5.

Reprinted in: *The Common Reader*, 1925; *Collected Essays*, Vol. 4, 1967.

C238 MRS DALLOWAY IN BOND STREET. *Dail*, New York, July 1923, 75:1, 20-7.

Reprinted in: *Mrs Dalloway's Party*, 1973.

C239 MR. CONRAD: A CONVERSATION. *Nation & Athenaeum*, 1 September 1923, 681-2. Review of *Almayer's Folly and Tales of Unrest; An Outcast of the Islands; The Nigger of the Narcissus and Typhoon; Lord Jim; Youth; Romance*, by Joseph Conrad.

Reprinted in: *The Captain's Death Bed*, 1950; *Collected Essays*, Vol. 1, 1966.

C240 MR. BENNETT AND MRS. BROWN. *Literary Review* of the *New York Evening Post*, 17 November 1923, 4, 253-4.*

Reprinted in: *Nation & Athenaeum*, 1 December 1923, 342-3; *Living Age*, 2 February 1924, 229-32.*

C240.1 THE CHINESE SHOE. *Nation & Athenaeum*, 17 November 1923, 277-8. Review of *Lady Henry Somerset*, by Kathleen Fitzpatrick. Unsigned.

C241 JANE AUSTEN AT SIXTY. *Nation & Athenaeum*, 15 December 1923, 433-4. Review of *The Works of Jane Austen.*

Reprinted in: *New Republic*, N.Y., 30 January 1924, 261. Incorporated in: Jane Austen, *The Common Reader*, 1925; *Collected Essays*, Vol. 1, 1966.

## 1924

C242 THE COMPROMISE. *New Republic*, N.Y., 9 January 1924, 180-1. Review of *The Life of Mrs Humphry Ward*, by her daughter Janet Penrose Trevelyan.

First published in: *Nation & Athenaeum*, 29 September 1923, 810-11. Reprinted in: *Books and Portraits*, 1977.

C242 .1 REVIEW OF *The Poems, English and Latin of Edward, Lord Herbert of Cherburg*, edited by G. C. Moore Smith. *Nation & Athenaeum*, 19 January 1924, 584. Unsigned.

C243 MONTAIGNE. *TLS*, 31 January 1924, 57. Review of *Essays of Montaigne*, translated by Charles Cotton.

Reprinted in: *The Common Reader*, 1925; *Collected Essays*, Vol. 3, 1967.

C244 THE LIVES OF THE OBSCURE. *London Mercury*, January 1924, 261–8.

Reprinted (slightly revised) as: Taylors and Edgeworths, *The Common Reader*, 1925; The Lives of the Obscure, *Dial*, N.Y., May 1925, 78:5, 381–90; Taylors and Edgeworths, *Collected Essays*, Vol. 4, 1967.

C244 .1 REVIEW OF *Glimpses of Authors*, by Caroline Ticknor. *Nation & Athenaeum*, 9 February 1924, 678. Unsigned.

C244 .2 REVIEW OF *Unpublished Letters of Matthew Arnold*, edited by Arnold Whitridge. *Nation & Athenaeum*, 16 February 1924, 712. Unsigned.

C244 .3 REVIEW OF *Arthur Yates: An Autobiography*, written in collaboration with Bruce Blunt. *Nation & Athenaeum*, 16 February 1924, 712. Unsigned.

C244 .4 REVIEW OF *Letters and Journals of Anne Chalmers*, edited by her daughter. *Nation & Athenaeum*, 23 February 1924, 746. Unsigned.

C245 THE ENCHANTED ORGAN. *Nation & Athenaeum*, 15 March 1924, 836. Review of *The Letters of Anne Thackeray Ritchie* . . . edited by her daughter Hester Ritchie.

Reprinted in: *New Republic*, N.Y., 6 August 1924, 304–5; *The Moment*, 1947; *Collected Essays*, Vol. 4, 1967.

C245 .1 PARAGRAPH COMMENCING I was given the opportunity to see a demonstration of a new colour film process . . . *Nation & Athenaeum*, 5 April 1924, 16. Unsigned.

C246 THE PATRON AND THE CROCUS. *Nation & Athenaeum*, 12 April 1924, 46–7.

Reprinted in: *New Republic*, N.Y., 7 May 1924, 280–1; *The Common Reader*, 1925; *Selections from Her Essays*, [1966]; *Collected Essays*, Vol. 2, 1966.

C246 .1 PARAGRAPH COMMENCING Aesthetically speaking . . . *Nation & Athenaeum*, 19 April 1924, 85. Unsigned.

C246 .11 REVIEW OF *Anatole France, the Man and his Work*, by James Lewis May. *Nation & Athenaeum*, 3 May 1924, 154. Unsigned.

C246 .2 PARAGRAPH COMMENCING The private view of the Royal Academy . . . *Nation & Athenaeum*, 10 May 1924, 176. Unsigned.

C246 .3 MR. BENSON'S MEMORIES. *Nation &Athenaeum*, 10 May 1924, 182. Review of *Memories and Friends*, by A. C. Benson. Unsigned.

C246 .31 REVIEW OF *Marie Elizabeth Towneley: A Memoir*, preface by the Bishop of Southwark. *Nation & Athenaeum*, 7 June 1924, 332. Unsigned.

C246 .4 REVIEW OF *Unwritten History*, by Cosmo Hamilton. *Nation & Athenaeum*, 21 June 1924, 392. Unsigned.

C246 .5 REVIEW OF *The Life and Last Words of Wilfrid Ewart*, by Stephen Graham. *Nation & Athenaeum*, 21 June 1924, 392. Unsigned.

C246 .6 REVIEW OF *Robert Smith Surtees (Creator of "Jorrocks") 1803–1864*, by himself and E. D. Cuming. *Nation & Athenaeum*, 21 June 1924, 392. Unsigned.

C247 THUNDER AT WEMBLEY. *Nation & Athenaeum*, 28 June 1924, 409–10.

Reprinted in: *The Captain's Death Bed*, 1950; *Collected Essays*, Vol. 4, 1967.

C248 THE WEEKEND. *TLS*, 3 July 1924, 416. Review of *The Week End Book*, edited by V. Mendel and Francis Meynell.

C249 STENDHAL. *Nation & Athenaeum*, 5 July 1924, 452. Review of *Stendhal: Journal*, texte établi et annoté par Henry Debraye et Louis Royer, tome 1; *Le Rouge et le Noir; Vie de Rossini*, texte établi et annoté par Jules Marsan. Unsigned.

C249 .1 REVIEW OF *Days that are Gone*, by B. de Sales La Terrière. *Nation & Athenaeum*, 5 July 1924, 454. Unsigned.

C250 REVIEW OF *Before the Mast – And After*, by Sir Walter Runciman. *Nation & Athenaeum*, 12 July 1924, 490. Unsigned.

C250 .1 REVIEW OF *The Truth at Last*, by Charles Hawtrey. *Nation & Athenaeum*, 19 July 1924, 518. Unsigned.

C251 CHARACTER IN FICTION. *Criterion*, July 1924, 2:8, 409–30. A paper read to the Heretics, Cambridge, 18 May 1924.

Reprinted as: *Mr Bennett and Mrs Brown*, London, Hogarth Press, 1924; *New York Herald Tribune*, 23 August 1925, Section 5 Books, 1–3 and 30 August 1925, Section 5 Books, 1–4; *The Hogarth Essays*, N.Y., Doubleday, Doran, 1928, 1–28;* *The Captain's Death Bed*, 1950; *Selections from Her Essays*, [1966]; *Collected Essays*, Vol. 1, 1966.

C252 JOSEPH CONRAD. *TLS*, 14 August 1924, 493–4.

Reprinted in: *The Common Reader*, 1925; *Collected Essays*, Vol. 1, 1966.

C253 EDITIONS-DE-LUXE. *Nation & Athenaeum*, 23 August 1924, 645–6. Review of *A Midsommer Night's Dreame*, by William Shakespeare and *Studio Plays*, by Clifford Bax. Unsigned.

C253.1 PARAGRAPH COMMENCING The cheapening of motor cars is another step towards the ruin of the country road . . . *Nation & Athenaeum*, 27 September 1924, 777. Unsigned.

C254 APPRECIATIONS. *Nation & Athenaeum*, 27 September 1924, 782–3. Review of *Figures in Modern Literature*, by J. B. Priestley. Unsigned.

C255 THE SCHOOLROOM FLOOR. *TLS*, 2 October 1924, 609. Review of *A Nineteenth Century Childhood*, by Mary MacCarthy.

C255.1 PARAGRAPH COMMENCING It is strange as one enters the Mansard Gallery to-day . . . *Nation & Athenaeum*, 18 October 1924, 111. Unsigned.

C255.2 PARAGRAPH COMMENCING Not the least pitiable victims of the deplorable summer . . . *Nation & Athenaeum*, 18 October 1924, 112. Unsigned.

C255.3 REVIEW OF *Richard Hakluyt*, by Foster Watson. *Nation & Athenaeum*, 25 October 1924, 164. Unsigned.

C255.4 REVIEW OF *Smoke Rings and Roundelays*, compiled by Wilfred Partington. *Nation & Athenaeum*, 25 October 1924, 164. Unsigned.

C256 "THE ANTIQUARY". *Nation & Athenaeum*, 22 November 1924, 293–4.

Reprinted in: *New Republic*, N.Y., 3 December 1924, 42–3. Reprinted (revised) in: *The Moment*, 1947; *Collected Essays*, Vol. 1, 1966.

C256.1 REVIEW OF *Memories of a Militant*, by Annie Kenney. *Nation & Athenaeum*, 8 November 1924, 226, 228. Unsigned.

C256.2 REVIEW OF *Peggy: The Story of One Score Years and Ten*, by Peggy Webling. *Nation & Athenaeum*, 8 November 1924, 228. Unsigned.

C256.21 FROM ALPHA TO OMEGA [Paragraph commencing:] "Can neither war nor peace teach the French . . . English?". *Nation & Athenaeum*, 22 November 1924, 297. Unsigned.

C256.3 REVIEW OF *These Were Muses*, by Mona Wilson. *Nation & Athenaeum*, 22 November 1924, 308. Unsigned.

C256.4 INDISCRETIONS. *Vogue*, late November 1924, 64:10, 47, 88.

Reprinted as: Indiscretions in Literature. *Vogue*, N.Y., 1 June 1925, 144, 146.

C257 MISS ORMEROD. *Dial*, N.Y., December 1924, 77:6, 466–74. Founded upon *Autobiography and Correspondence of Eleanor Ormerod*, edited by Robert Wallace, 1904.

Reprinted in: *The Common Reader*, N.Y., 1925;* *The Common Reader First and Second Series Combined in One Volume*, 1948.

## 1925

C258 RESTORATION COMEDY. *New Republic*, N.Y., 11 February 1925, 315–16. Review of *The Life of William Congreve*, revised edition, by Edmund Gosse and *Restoration Comedy*, by Bonamy Dobrée.

First published in: *Nation & Athenaeum*, 18 October 1924, 122. Unsigned.

C259 NOTES ON AN ELIZABETHAN PLAY. *TLS*, 5 March 1925, 145–6.

Reprinted (revised) in: *The Common Reader*, 1925; *Collected Essays*, Vol. 1, 1966.

C259 .1 FROM ALPHA TO OMEGA [Paragraph commencing:] Coming back to London . . . – a battered cottage . . . has replaced . . . Devonshire House. *Nation & Athenaeum*, 14 March 1925, 812–13. Unsigned.

C260 OLIVE SCHREINER. *New Republic*, N.Y., 18 March 1925, 103. Review of *The Letters of Olive Schreiner*, edited by Cronwright Schreiner.

C260 .01 REVIEW OF *This for Remembrance*, by Bernard, Lord Coleridge. *Nation & Athenaeum*, 28 March 1925, 896. Unsigned.

C260 .1 THE TWO SAMUEL BUTLERS. *Nation & Athenaeum*, 11 April 1925, 53–4. Review of *The Life and Letters of Dr Samuel Butler*, by Samuel Butler. Unsigned.

C260 .2 REVIEW OF *Guests and Memories: Annals of a Seaside Villa*, by Una Taylor. *Nation & Athenaeum*, 11 April 1925, 54. Unsigned.

C260 .3 REVIEW OF *Mainly Victorian*, by Stewart M. Ellis. *Nation & Athenaeum*, 11 April 1925, 54. Unsigned.

C261 JOHN ADDINGTON SYMONDS. *Nation & Athenaeum*, 18 April 1925, 79. Review of *Out of the Past*, by Margaret Symonds. Unsigned.

Reprinted in: *New Republic*, N.Y., 3 June 1925, 51–2.

C261 .1 REVIEW OF *Further Reminiscences, 1864–1894*, by S. Baring-Gould. *Nation & Athenaeum*, 18 April 1925, 82. Unsigned.

C261 .2 REVIEW OF *The Letters of Mary Russell Mitford*, selected with an introduction by R. Brimley Johnson. *Nation & Athenaeum*, 18 April 1925, 82. Unsigned.

C262 PICTURES. *Nation & Athenaeum*, 25 April 1925, 101–2.

Reprinted in: *New Republic*, N.Y., 13 May 1925, 315–16; *The Moment*, 1947.

C262 .1 PARAGRAPH COMMENCING What the bloods of the 'nineties used to say . . . *Nation & Athenaeum*, 25 April 1925, 105. Unsigned.

C262 .2 REVIEW OF *A Player under Three Reigns*, by Sir Johnston Forbes-Robertson. *Nation & Athenaeum*, 25 April 1925, 114. Unsigned.

C262 .3 REVIEW OF *The Tragic Life of Vincent Van Gogh*, by Louis Piérard, translated by Herbert Garland. *Nation & Athenaeum*, 9 May 1925, 182. Unsigned.

C262 .4 GIPSY OR GOVERNESS? *Nation & Athenaeum*, 16 May 1925, 209. Review of *Places and Persons*, by Margot Asquith. Unsigned.

C262 .5 REVIEW OF *Celebrities of Our Times*, by Herman Bernstein. *Nation & Athenaeum*, 16 May 1925, 214. Unsigned.

C263 HARRIETTE WILSON. *Nation & Athenaeum*, 13 June 1925, 320–2. Review of *The Memoirs of Harriette Wilson*, written by herself.

Reprinted as: On the Wrong Side of the Sword, *New Republic*, N.Y., 24 June 1925, 122–3; Harriette Wilson, *The Moment*, 1947; *Collected Essays*, Vol. 3, 1967.

C263 .1 GEORGE MOORE. *Vogue*, early June 1925, 65:11, 63, 84.

Reprinted in: *The Death of the Moth*, 1942; *Collected Essays*, Vol. 1, 1966.

C264 THE TALE OF GENJI. *Vogue*, late July 1925; 66:2, 53, 80. Review of *The Tale of Genji*, Vol. 1, by Lady Murasaki; translated from the Japanese by Arthur Waley.

C265 AMERICAN FICTION. *Saturday Review of Literature*, New York, 1 August 1925, 2:1, 1–3.

Reprinted in: *The Moment*, 1947; *Collected Essays*, Vol. 2, 1966.

C265 .1 "PATTLEDOM". *Nation & Athenaeum*, 1 August 1925, 547. Review of *Memories and Reflections*, by Lady Troubridge. Unsigned.

C265 .2 REVIEW OF *Unknown Essex*, by Donald Maxwell. *Nation & Athenaeum*, 8 August 1925, 575–6. Unsigned.

C265 .3 REVIEW OF *In My Anecdotage*, by W. G. Elliot. *Nation & Athenaeum*, 8 August 1925, 576. Unsigned.

C265 .4 REVIEW OF *Time, Taste and Furniture*, by John Gloag. *Nation & Athenaeum*, 15 August 1925, 604. Unsigned.

C266 "DAVID COPPERFIELD". *Nation & Athenaeum*, 22 August 1925, 620–1. Review of *The Uncommercial Traveller; Reprinted Pieces and Christmas Stories*, by Charles Dickens.

Reprinted in: *The Moment*, 1947; *Collected Essays*, Vol. 1, 1966.

C266 .1 PARAGRAPH COMMENCING A brillian Englishwoman writes to me . . . *Nation & Athenaeum*, 5 September 1925, 672. Unsigned.

C267 "DAVID COPPERFIELD". *Nation & Athenaeum*, 12 September 1925, 699. Letter to the Editor.

Reprinted in: *The Moment*, 1947; *Collected Essays*, Vol. 1, 1966.

C267 .1 PARAGRAPH COMMENCING In any family save the Darwins . . . *Nation & Athenaeum*, 26 September 1925, 758. Unsigned.

C268 SWIFT'S JOURNAL TO STELLA. *TLS*, 24 September 1925, 605–6.

Reprinted (revised) in: *The Common Reader: Second Series*, 1932; *Collected Essays*, Vol. 3, 1967.

C268 .1 CONGREVE. *Nation & Athenaeum*, 17 October 1925, 124. Review of *Comedies of William Congreve*, Oxford University Press. Unsigned.

C268 .2 REVIEW OF *Twenty Years of My Life*, by Louise Jopling-Rowe. *Nation & Athenaeum*, 17 October 1925, 126. Unsigned.

C269 STERNE'S GHOST. *Nation & Athenaeum*, 7 November 1925, 207–9.

Reprinted in: *The Moment*, 1947; *Collected Essays*, Vol. 3, 1967.

C269 .1 SAINT SAMUEL OF FLEET STREET. *Nation & Athenaeum*, 14 November 1925, 248. Review of *The Life of Samuel Johnson*, by James Boswell, edited with Notes by Arnold Glover, with an Introduction by Austin Dobson; *The Life of Samuel Johnson*, by James Boswell, edited by Roger Ingpen; *Boswell's Life of Johnson*, abridged and edited by F. H. Pritchard. Unsigned.

C269 .2 MELBA. *Nation & Athenaeum*, 5 December 1925, Christmas Book Supplement, 372. Review of *Memories and Melodies*, by Nellie Melba. Unsigned.

C269 .3 REVIEW OF *Some of the Smaller Manor Houses of Sussex*, by Viscountess Wolseley. *Nation & Athenaeum*, 5 December 1925, Christmas Book Supplement, 382. Unsigned.

C269 .4 REVIEW OF *From Hall-Boy to House-Steward*, by W. Lanceley. *Nation & Athenaeum*, 26 December 1925, 476. Unsigned.

## 1926

C270 ON BEING ILL. *New Criterion*, January 1926, 4:1, 32–45.

Reprinted as: Illness: An Unexplored Mine, *Forum*, New York, April 1926, 582–90. Reprinted (slightly revised) as: *On Being Ill*, London, Hogarth Press, 1930; *The Moment*, 1947; *Collected Essays*, Vol. 4, 1967.

C270 .1 REVIEW OF *Mary Elizabeth Haldane: A Record of a Hundred Years*, edited by her daughter. *Nation & Athenaeum*, 30 January 1926, 624. Unsigned.

C271 ROBINSON CRUSOE. *Nation & Athenaeum*, 6 February 1926, 642–3. Review of *The Life and Adventures of Robinson Crusoe; Further Adventures of Robinson Crusoe* and *Serious Reflections of Robinson Crusoe.*

Reprinted (considerably revised) in: *The Common Reader: Second Series*, 1932; *Collected Essays*, Vol. 1, 1966.

C271 .1 REVIEW OF *Queen Alexandra the Well-Beloved*, by Elizabeth Villiers. *Nation & Athenaeum*, 6 February 1926, 654. Unsigned.

C272 THE LIFE OF JOHN MYTTON. *Vogue*, early March 1926, 67:5, 61, 85. Review of *Memoirs of the Life of John Mytton Esq.*, by Nimrod, [*pseud.* of C. J. Apperley].

Reprinted (slightly revised) as: Jack Mytton, *The Common Reader: Second Series*, 1932; *Collected Essays*, Vol. 4, 1967.

C272 .1 REVIEW OF *Paradise in Piccadilly*, by Harry Furniss. *Nation & Athenaeum*, 6 March 1926, 786. Unsigned.

C272 .2 REVIEW OF *Reminiscences of Mrs Comys Carr*, edited by Eve Adam. *Nation & Athenaeum*, 20 March 1926, 870. Unsigned.

C272 .3 REVIEW OF *The Days of Dickens*, by Arthur L. Hayward. *Nation & Athenaeum*, 20 March 1926, 870. Unsigned.

C272 .4 REVIEW OF *The Flurried Years*, by Violet Hunt. *Nation & Athenaeum*, 20 March 1926, 870, 872. Unsigned.

C272 .5 REVIEW OF *Steeple-Jacks and Steeplejacking*, by William Larkins. *Nation & Athenaeum*, 27 March 1926, 906. Unsigned.

C273 A PROFESSOR OF LIFE. *Vogue*, early May 1926, 67:9, 69, 94. Review of *The Letters of Walter Raleigh*, edited by Lady Raleigh.

Reprinted as: Walter Raleigh, *The Captain's Death Bed*, 1950; *Selections from Her Essays*, [1966]; *Collected Essays*, Vol. 1, 1966.

C274 CINEMA. *Arts*, New York, June 1926, 9:6, 314–16.*

Reprinted as: Cinema, *Nation & Athenaeum*, 3 July 1926, 381–3; The Movies and Reality, *New Republic*, N.Y., 4 August 1926, 308–10; The Cinema, *The Captain's Death Bed*, 1950; *Selections from Her Essays*, [1966]; *Collected Essays*, Vol. 2, 1966.

C274 .1 JONES AND WILKINSON. *Bermondsey Book*, June 1926, 3:3, 48–53. Drawn from *Memoirs of His Own Life*, by Tate Wilkinson, 4 vols., 1790.

Reprinted in: *The Death of the Moth*, 1942; *Collected Essays*, Vol. 3, 1967.

C274 .2 ROMANCE AND THE 'NINETIES. *Nation & Athenaeum*, 3 July 1926, 392. Review of *The Romantic Nineties*, by Richard Le Gallienne. Unsigned.

C275 "IMPASSIONED PROSE". *TLS*, 16 September 1926, 601-2. On Thomas De Quincey.

Reprinted in: *Granite and Rainbow*, 1958; *Collected Essays*, Vol. 1, 1966.

C276 THE COSMOS. *Nation & Athenaeum*, 9 October 1926, 26. Review of *The Journals of Thomas James Cobden-Sanderson, 1879-1922.*

Reprinted in: *The Captain's Death Bed*, 1950; *Collected Essays*, Vol. 4, 1967.

C276 .1 LAUGHTER AND TEARS. *Nation & Athenaeum*, 16 October 1926, 89. Review of *My Life and Times*, by Jerome K. Jerome. Unsigned.

C276 .2 GEORGE ELIOT. *Nation & Athenaeum*, 30 October 1926, 149. Review of *The Letters of George Eliot*, selected, with an Introduction, by R. Brimley Johnson. Unsigned.

C277 HOW SHOULD ONE READ A BOOK? *Yale Review*, New Haven, Conn., October 1926, 16:1, 32-44.

Reprinted (considerably revised) in: *The Common Reader: Second Series*, 1932; *Collected Essays*, Vol. 2, 1966.

C278 LIFE AND THE NOVELIST. *New York Herald Tribune*, 7 November 1926, Section 7 Books, 1, 6. Review of *A Deputy Was King*, by G. B. Stern.

Reprinted in: *Granite and Rainbow*, 1958; *Collected Essays*, Vol. 2, 1966.

C279 GENIUS. *Nation & Athenaeum*, 18 December 1926, 419-21. Review of *The Autobiography and Memoirs of Benjamin Robert Haydon*, with an introduction by Aldous Huxley.

Reprinted in: *New Republic*, N.Y., 29 December 1926, 157-9; *The Moment*, 1947; *Collected Essays*, Vol. 4, 1967.

## 1927

C279 .1 REVIEW OF *Victorian Jottings*, by Sir James Crichton-Browne. *Nation & Athenaeum*, 12 February 1927, 672. Unsigned.

C280 GEORGE GISSING. *Nation & Athenaeum*, 26 February 1927, 722-3. Review of *The Letters of George Gissing to Members of his Family*, collected and arranged by Algernon and Ellen Gissing.

Reprinted as: George Gissing, *New Republic*, N.Y., 2 March 1927, 49-50. Introduction to *Selections Autobiographical and Imaginative*, by George Gissing, London, Cape, 1929, 9-16. Reprinted (revised) as: George Gissing, *The Common Reader: Second Series*, 1932; *Collected Essays*, Vol. 1, 1966.

C280 .1 REVIEW OF *The Immortal Isles*, by Seton Gordon. *Nation & Athenaeum*, 5 March 1927, 766, 768. Unsigned.

C280 WHAT IS A NOVEL? *Weekly Dispatch*, 27 March 1927, 2.

.2 Reprinted in: *Now & Then*, Summer 1927, No. 24, 16.

C281 A GIANT WITH VERY SMALL THUMBS. *Nation & Athenaeum*, 2 April 1927, 928, 930. Review of *Turgenev: The Man, his Art and his Age*, by Avrahm Yarmolinsky.

Reprinted in: *Books and Portraits*, 1977.

C282 TWO WOMEN. *Nation & Athenaeum*, 23 April 1927, 78-9. Review of *Emily Davies and Girton College*, by Lady Stephen and *Letters of Lady Augusta Stanley*, edited by the Dean of Windsor and Hector Bolitho.

Reprinted in: *New Republic*, N.Y., 18 May 1927, 358-9; *The Moment*, 1947; *Collected Essays*, Vol. 4, 1967.

C283 THE NEW DRESS. *Forum*, N.Y., May 1927, 77:5, 704-11.

Reprinted in: *A Haunted House*, 1944; *Mrs Dalloway's Party*, 1973.

C284 POETRY, FICTION AND THE FUTURE. *New York Herald Tribune*, 14 August 1927, Section 7 Books, 1, 6-7 and 21 August 1927, Section 6 Books, 1, 6.

Reprinted as: The Narrow Bridge of Art, *Granite and Rainbow*, 1958; *Collected Essays*, Vol. 2, 1966.

C285 LIFE ITSELF. *New Republic*, N.Y., 17 August 1927, 330-2. Review of *The Diary of a Country Parson*, Vol. 3, by James Woodforde, edited by John Beresford.

Reprinted in: *Nation & Athenaeum*, 20 August 1927, 661-3. Reprinted in part with additions in: James Woodforde, *The Common Reader: Second Series*, 1932. Reprinted: Life Itself, *The Captain's Death Bed*, 1950; James Woodforde, *Collected Essays*, Vol. 3, 1967.

C286 A TERRIBLY SENSITIVE MIND. *New York Herald Tribune*, 18 September 1927, Section 7 Books, 1-2. Review of *The Journal of Katherine Mansfield, 1914-1922*, edited by J. Middleton Murry.

Reprinted in: *Granite and Rainbow*, 1958; *Collected Essays*, Vol. 1, 1966.

C287 AN ESSAY IN CRITICISM. *New York Herald Tribune*, 9 October 1927, Section 7 Books, 1, 8. Review of *Men Without Women*, by Ernest Hemingway.

Reprinted in: *Granite and Rainbow*, 1958; *Collected Essays*, Vol. 2, 1966.

C288 IS FICTION AN ART? *New York Herald Tribune*, 16 October 1927, Section 7 Books, 1, 5-6. Review of *Aspects of the Novel*, by E. M. Forster.

Reprinted (revised) as: The Art of Fiction, *Nation & Athenaeum*, 12 November 1927, Literary Supplement, 247-8; *The Moment*, 1947; *Collected Essays*, Vol. 2, 1966.

C289 NOT ONE OF US. *New York Herald Tribune*, 23 October 1927, Section 7 Books, 1, 6. Review of *Shelley: His Life and Work*, by Walter Edwin Peck.

Reprinted in: *The Death of the Moth*, 1942; *Collected Essays*, Vol. 4, 1967.

C290 THE NEW BIOGRAPHY. *New York Herald Tribune*, 30 October 1927, Section 7 Books, 1, 6. Review of *Some People*, by Harold Nicolson.

Reprinted in: *Granite and Rainbow*, 1958; *Selections from Her Essays*, [1966]; *Collected Essays*, Vol. 4, 1967.

C291 STREET HAUNTING: A LONDON ADVENTURE. *Yale Review*, October 1927, N.S. 17, 49-62.

Reprinted: *Street Haunting*, San Francisco, Westgate Press, 1930; *The Death of the Moth*, 1942; *Collected Essays*, Vol. 4, 1967.

C292 THE NOVELS OF E. M. FORSTER. *Atlantic Monthly*, Boston, November 1927, 642-8.

Reprinted in: *The Death of the Moth*, 1942; *Collected Essays*, Vol. 1, 1966.

C293 RUSKIN LOOKS BACK ON LIFE, "PRAETERITA": SERENE THOUGHTS WITH THE ECHOES OF THUNDER. *T.P.'s Weekly*, 3 December 1927, 9, 235. Review of *Praeterita*, by John Ruskin.

Reprinted as: Praeterita, *New Republic*, N.Y., 28 December 1927, 165-6; *Books and Portraits*, 1977.

## 1928

C294 THOMAS HARDY'S NOVELS. *TLS*, 19 January 1928, 33-4.

Reprinted (revised) as: The Novels of Thomas Hardy, *The Common Reader: Second Series*, 1932; *Collected Essays*, Vol. 1, 1966.

C295 "SLATER'S PINS HAVE NO POINTS". *Forum*, N.Y., January 1928, 58-63.

Reprinted as: Moments of Being: "Slater's Pins Have No Points", *A Haunted House*, 1944.

C296 THE SUN AND THE FISH. *Time and Tide*, 3 February 1928, 99-100.

Reprinted in: *New Republic*, N.Y., 8 February 1928, 321-3; *The Captain's Death Bed*, 1950; *Collected Essays*, Vol. 4, 1967.

C297 THE NOVELS OF GEORGE MEREDITH. *TLS*, 9 February 1928, 85-6.

Reprinted as: George Meredith, *New York Herald Tribune*, 12 February 1928, Section 12 Books, 1, 5-6. Reprinted in part as: The Novels of George Meredith, *The Common Reader: Second Series*, 1932; *Collected Essays*, Vol. 1, 1966.

C297.1 REVIEW OF *Memories and Notes*, by Anthony Hope. *Nation & Athenaeum*, 11 February 1928, 728. Unsigned.

C297.2 REVIEW OF *The Cornish Miner*, by A. K. Hamilton Jenkin. *Nation & Athenaeum*, 25 February 1928, 792. Unsigned.

C298 AN ENGLISH ARISTOCRAT. *TLS*, 8 March 1928, 167. Review of *The Characters of Lord Chesterfield*, edited by Charles Whibley.

Reprinted as: Lord Chesterfield and the Graces, *New Republic*, N.Y., 21 March 1928, 160–1. Incorporated in: Lord Chesterfield's Letters to his Son, *The Common Reader: Second Series*, 1932; *Collected Essays*, Vol. 3, 1967.

C298.1 REVIEW OF *Stalky's Reminiscences*, by L. C. Dunsterville. *Nation & Athenaeum*, 7 April 1928, 22. Unsigned.

C299 WAXWORKS AT THE ABBEY. *New Republic*, N.Y., 11 April 1928, 245–6.

Reprinted as: *The* Waxworks *at the* Abbey, *Eve*, 23 May 1928, 33, 429; Waxworks at the Abbey, *Granite and Rainbow*, 1958; *Collected Essays*, Vol. 4, 1967.

C300 PREFERENCE OF FOUR CRITICS: VIRGINIA WOOLF. *New York Herald Tribune*, 15 April 1928, Section 12 Books, 1.

C301 MR. YEATS. *Nation & Athenaeum*, 21 April 1928, 81. Review of *The Tower*, by W. B. Yeats. Unsigned.

C301.1 REVIEW OF *Behind the Scenes with Cyril Maude*, by himself. *Nation & Athenaeum*, 28 April 1928, 120. Unsigned.

C301.2 REVIEW OF *Behind the Brass Plate*, by A. T. Schofield. *Nation & Athenaeum*, 5 May 1928, 152. Unsigned.

C301.3 REVIEW OF *The Book of Catherine Wells*, with an Introduction by her husband H. G. Wells. *Nation & Athenaeum*, 26 May 1928, 260. Unsigned.

C301.4 REVIEW OF *On the Stage: An Autobiography*, by George Arliss. *Nation & Athenaeum*, 30 June 1928, 436. Unsigned.

C301.5 REVIEW OF *Clara Butt: Her Life Story*, by Winifred Ponder. *Nation & Athenaeum*, 14 July 1928, 506. Unsigned.

C301.6 REVIEW OF *Day In, Day Out*, by Mrs Aubrey Le Blond. *Nation & Athenaeum*, 11 August 1928, 629. Unsigned.

C302 THE NEW CENSORSHIP. *Nation & Athenaeum*, 8 September 1928, 726. Letter to the Editor signed by E. M. Forster and Virginia Woolf; protest against the banning of *The Well of Loneliness*, by Radclyffe Hall.

C303 A SENTIMENTAL JOURNEY. *New York Herald Tribune*, 23 September 1928, Section 12 Books, 1, 6.

Reprinted as: Introduction to *A Sentimental Journey Through France and Italy*, by Laurence Sterne, World's Classics Edition, 1928, [v]–xvii. Reprinted (slightly revised) as: The "Sentimental Journey", *The Common Reader: Second Series*,

1932; *Selections from Her Essays*, [1966]; *Collected Essays*, Vol. 1, 1966.

C303 .1 REVIEW OF *The Diaries of Mary, Countess of Meath*, edited by her husband. *Nation & Athenaeum*, 29 September 1928, 832. Unsigned.

C304 DOROTHY OSBORNE'S LETTERS. *New Republic*, N.Y., 24 October 1928, 278–9. Review of *The Letters of Dorothy Osborne to William Temple*, edited by G. C. Moore Smith.

Reprinted as: Dorothy Osborne, *TLS*, 25 October 1928, 777. Partially incorporated in: Dorothy Osborne's "Letters", *The Common Reader: Second Series*, 1932; *Collected Essays*, Vol. 3, 1967.

C305 THE NIECE OF AN EARL. *Life and Letters*, October 1928, 1:5, 356–61.

Reprinted in: *The Common Reader: Second Series*, 1932; *Selections from Her Essays*, [1966]; *Collected Essays*, Vol. 1, 1966.

C305 .1 PARAGRAPH I, UNDER HEADING 'PLAYS AND PICTURES'. Review of *The Tale of a Soldier*, by Igor Stravinsky; *A Lover's Complaint*, by William Shakespeare and some dancing, by Hedley Briggs, three pieces at the A.D.C. Theatre, Cambridge. *Nation & Athenaeum*, 17 November 1928, 255. Unsigned.

C305 .2 MEMORIES. *Nation & Athenaeum*, 17 November 1928, 264. Review of *Shapes that Pass*, by Julian Hawthorne. Unsigned.

C306 HALF OF THOMAS HARDY. *Nation & Athenaeum*, 24 November 1928, 289–91. Review of *The Early Life of Thomas Hardy*, by Florence Emily Hardy.

Reprinted in: *New Republic*, N.Y., 5 December 1928, 70–2; *The Captain's Death Bed*, 1950.

C307 LADY STRACHEY. *Nation & Athenaeum*, 22 December 1928, 441–2. Signed V.W.

Reprinted in: *Books and Portraits*, 1977.

## 1929

C308 ON NOT KNOWING FRENCH. *New Republic*, N.Y., 13 February 1929, 348–9.

C309 GERALDINE AND JANE. *TLS*, 28 February 1929, 149–50. Review of *Zoe* and *The Half Sisters*, by Geraldine Jewsbury.

Reprinted (with additions) in: *Bookman*, New York, February 1929, 612–20. Reprinted (slightly revised) in: *The Common Reader: Second Series*, 1932; *Collected Essays*, Vol. 4, 1967.

C310 WOMEN AND FICTION. *Forum*, N.Y., March 1929, 179–83.

Reprinted in: *Granite and Rainbow*, 1958; *Collected Essays*, Vol. 2, 1966.

C310 .1 THE AMERICAN LANGUAGE. *New Republic*, N.Y., 24 April 1929, 281. Letter to the Editor in reply to one in the same issue by Harriot T. Cooke on 'On Not Knowing French'. See C308.

C311 THE "CENSORSHIP" OF BOOKS. *Nineteenth Century and After*, April 1929, 446–7.

C312 PHASES OF FICTION. *Bookman*, N.Y., April 1929, 123–32; May 1929, 269–79 and June 1929, 404–12.

Reprinted in: *Granite and Rainbow*, 1958; *Collected Essays*, Vol. 2, 1966.

C313 DR. BURNEY'S EVENING PARTY. *New York Herald Tribune*, 21 July 1929, Section 11 Books, 1, 6 and 28 July, Section 11 Books, 1, 5–6.

Reprinted in: *Life and Letters*, September 1929, 3:16, 243–63; *The Common Reader: Second Series*, 1932; *Collected Essays*, Vol. 3, 1967.

C314 COWPER AND LADY AUSTEN. *Nation & Athenaeum*, 21 September 1929, 793–5.

Reprinted in: *New York Herald Tribune*, 22 September 1929, Section 12 Books, 1, 6; *The Common Reader: Second Series*, 1932; *Collected Essays*, Vol. 3, 1967.

C315 BEAU BRUMMELL. *Nation & Athenaeum*, 28 September 1929, 824–6.

Reprinted in: *New York Herald Tribune*, 29 September 1929, Section 12 Books, 1, 6; New York, Rimington and Hooper, 1930; *The Common Reader: Second Series*, 1932; *Collected Essays*, Vol. 3, 1967.

C316 MARY WOLLSTONECRAFT. *Nation & Athenaeum*, 5 October 1929, 13–15.

Reprinted in: *New York Herald Tribune*, 20 October 1929, Section 12 Books, 1, 6; *The Common Reader: Second Series*, 1932; *Collected Essays*, Vol. 3, 1967.

C317 DOROTHY WORDSWORTH. *Nation & Athenaeum*, 12 October 1929, 46–8.

Reprinted: *New York Herald Tribune*, 29 September 1929, Section 12 Books, 1, 6; New York, Rimington and Hooper, 1930; *The Common Reader: Second Series*, 1932; *Collected Essays*, Vol. 3, 1967.

C318 CHARLES LAMB. *Nation & Athenaeum*, 19 October 1929, 102. Letter to the Editor.

C319 WOMEN AND LEISURE. *Nation & Athenaeum*, 16 November 1929, 248. Letter to the Editor; reply to the review by Lyn Ll. Irvine of *A Room of One's Own* in the *Nation & Athenaeum*, 9 November 1929, 201–3.

C320 AN EXCERPT FROM "A ROOM OF ONE'S OWN". *Time and Tide*, 22 November 1929, 1403–4 and 29 November 1929, 1434–6. See also A12.

C321 BEAU BRUMMELL. *Listener*, 27 November 1929, 720–1. A talk broadcast in the series 'Miniature Biographies' on 20 November 1929.

C322 THE LADY IN THE LOOKING CLASS: A REFLECTION. *Harpers Magazine*, December 1929, 46–9.

Reprinted as: In the Looking Glass, *Harper's Bazaar*, January 1930, 43, 98; The Lady in the Looking Glass: A Reflection, *A Haunted House*, 1944.

## 1930

C322 .1 "LURIANA LURILEE". *Sunday Times*, 18 May 1930, 14. Letter on the refrain in *To the Lighthouse* (A10). See also letter in the issue of 11 May, p. 12 by John Fenwick.

C323 AUGUSTINE BIRRELL. *Yale Review*, June 1930, N.S. 19, 754–61. Review of *The Collected Essays and Addresses of Augustine Birrell.*

Reprinted as: The Essays of Augustine Birrell, *Life and Letters*, July 1930, 5:26, 29–38.

C324 FANNY BURNEY'S HALF-SISTER. *TLS*, 28 August 1930, 673–4.

Reprinted as: "Evelina's" Step Sister, *New York Herald Tribune*, 14 September 1930, Section 11 Books, 1, 6 and 21 September 1930, Section 11 Books, 1, 6; Fanny Burney's Half-Sister, *Granite and Rainbow*, 1958; *Collected Essays*, Vol. 3, 1967.

C325 WM. HAZLITT THE MAN. *New York Herald Tribune*, 7 September 1930, Section 11 Books, 1, 4. Review of *The Complete Works of William Hazlitt*, edited by P. P. Howe, Vols. I, IV, V.

Reprinted (revised) as: William Hazlitt, *TLS*, 18 September 1930, 721–2; *The Common Reader: Second Series*, 1932; *Collected Essays*, Vol. 1, 1966.

C326 MEMORIES OF A WORKING WOMEN'S GUILD. *Yale Review*, September 1930, N.S. 20, 121–38.

Reprinted (revised) as: Introduction to *Life as We Have Known It*, edited by Margaret Llewelyn Davies, London, Hogarth Press, 1931, xv–xxxix. Reprinted as: Memories of a Working Women's Guild, *The Captain's Death Bed*, 1950; *Selections from Her Essays*, [1966]; *Collected Essays*, Vol. 4, 1967.

C327 "THE BOOK OF BEAUTY": A PROTEST. *Nation & Athenaeum*, 29 November 1930, 291 and 20 December 1930, 403. Letters to the Editor.

C328 "I AM CHRISTINA ROSSETTI". *Nation & Athenaeum*, 6 December 1930, 322–4. Review of *The Life of Christina Rossetti*, by Mary F. Sandars and *Christina Rossetti and her Poetry*, by Edith Birkhead.

Reprinted in: *New York Herald Tribune*, 14 December 1930, Section 11 Books, 1, 6; *The Common Reader: Second Series*, 1932; *Collected Essays*, Vol. 4, 1967.

## 1931

C329 ALL ABOUT BOOKS. *New Statesman & Nation*, 28 February 1931, 14–15.

Reprinted in: *New Republic*, N.Y., 15 April 1931, 226–8; *The Captain's Death Bed*, 1950; *Selections from Her Essays*, [1966]; *Collected Essays*, Vol. 2, 1966.

C330 LOCKHART'S CRITICISM. *TLS*, 23 April 1931, 323. Review of *Lockhart's Literary Criticism*, with introduction and bibliography by M. Clive Hildyard.

Reprinted as: The Pundits of the Quarterly, *New Republic*, N.Y., 15 July 1931, 227–9; Lockhart's Criticism, *The Moment*, 1947; *Collected Essays*, Vol. 1, 1966.

C331 EDMUND GOSSE. *Fortnightly Review*, 1 June 1931, 766–73. Review of *The Life and Letters of Sir Edmund Gosse*, by Evan Charteris.

Reprinted as: As a Light to Letters, *New York Herald Tribune*, 26 July 1931, Section 11 Books, 1, 4; Edmund Gosse, *The Moment*, 1947; *Collected Essays*, Vol. 4, 1967.

C332 "AURORA LEIGH". *Yale Review*, June 1931, N.S. 20, 677–90.

Reprinted (slightly revised) in: *TLS*, 2 July 1931, 517–18; *The Common Reader: Second Series*, 1932; *Collected Essays*, Vol. 1, 1966.

C332 .1 THE DOCKS OF LONDON. *Good Housekeeping*, December 1931, 20:4, 16–17, 114, 116–17. First essay in the series 'The London Scene'.

Reprinted in: *The London Scene*, [1975].

## 1932

C332 .2 OXFORD STREET TIDE. *Good Housekeeping*, January 1932, 20:5, 18–19, 120. Second essay in the series 'The London Scene'.

Reprinted in: *The London Scene*, [1975].

C333 THE REV. WILLIAM COLE: A LETTER. *New Statesman & Nation*, 6 February 1932, 164–5. Review of *The Blecheley Diary of the Rev. William Cole* . . . edited by Francis Griffin Stokes.

Reprinted in: *The Death of the Moth*, 1942; *Selections from Her Essays*, [1966]; *Collected Essays*, Vol. 3, 1967.

C333 .1 GREAT MEN'S HOUSES. *Good Housekeeping*, March 1932, 21:1, 10–11, 102–3. Third essay in the series 'The London Scene'.

Reprinted in: *The London Scene*, [1975].

C333 .2 ABBEYS AND CATHEDRALS. *Good Housekeeping*, May 1932, 21:3, 18–19, 102. Fourth essay in the series 'The London Scene'.

Reprinted in: *The London Scene*, [1975].

C334 LETTER TO A YOUNG POET. *Yale Review*, June 1932, N.S. 21, 696–710.

Reprinted: London, Hogarth Press, 1932; *The Death of the Moth*, 1942; *Collected Essays*, Vol. 2, 1966.

C334 .1 "THIS IS THE HOUSE OF COMMONS". *Good Housekeeping*, October 1932, 22:2, 18–19, 110–12. Fifth essay in the series 'The London Scene'.

Reprinted in: *The London Scene*, [1975].

C335 LESLIE STEPHEN, THE PHILOSOPHER AT HOME: A DAUGHTER'S MEMORIES. *The Times*, 28 November 1932, 15–16. Published on the centenary of Sir Leslie Stephen's birth.

Reprinted as: My Father: Leslie Stephen, *Atlantic Monthly*, March 1950, 39–41; Leslie Stephen, *The Captain's Death Bed*, 1950; *Collected Essays*, Vol. 4, 1967.

C335 .1 PORTRAIT OF A LONDONER. *Good Housekeeping*, December 1932, 22:4, 28–9, 132. On Mrs Crowe. Sixth in the series 'The London Scene'.

## 1933

C336 GISSING'S "BY THE IONIAN SEA". *TLS*, 20 April 1933, 276 and 4 May 1933, 312. Letters to the Editor. See letter from A. C. Gissing in the issue of 8 April, p. 417.

C337 LONDON SQUARES. *New Statesman & Nation*, 24 June 1933, 843. Letter to the Editor.

C338 FLUSH: AN AUTOBIOGRAPHY. *Atlantic Monthly*, Part 1, July 1933, 1–12; Part 2, Mr Browning in Wimpole Street, August 1933, 163–74; Part 3, Wimpole Street and Whitechapel, September 1933, 326–37; Part 4, A Cocker Recaptures his Youth, October 1933, 439–53. The complete work. See also A19.

C339 "TWELFTH NIGHT" AT THE OLD VIC. *New Statesman & Nation*, 30 September 1933, 385–6. Dramatic review of the Old Vic's production of *Twelfth Night.*

Reprinted in: *The Death of the Moth*, 1942; *Collected Essays*, Vol. 1, 1966.

C340 THE PROTECTION OF PRIVACY. *New Statesman & Nation*, 28 October 1933, 511. Letter to the Editor.

C341 THE NOVELS OF TURGENEV. *TLS*, 14 December 1933, 885–6.

Reprinted in: *Yale Review*, December 1933, N.S. 23, 276–83; *The Captain's Death Bed*, 1950; *Collected Essays*, Vol. 1, 1966.

## 1934

C342 OLIVER GOLDSMITH. *TLS*, 1 March 1934, 133–4. Review of *The Citizen of the World and The Bee*, by Oliver Goldsmith, introduction by Richard Church.

Reprinted in: *The Captain's Death Bed*, 1950; *Collected Essays*, Vol. 1, 1966.

C343 WHY? *Lysistrata*, Oxford, May 1934, I:2, 5–12.

Reprinted in: *The Death of the Moth*, 1942; *Selections from Her Essays*, [1966]; *Collected Essays*, Vol. 2, 1966.

C344 A CONVERSATION ABOUT ART. *Yale Review*, September 1934, N.S. 24, 52–65.

Reprinted (slightly revised): *Walter Sickert*, London, Hogarth Press, 1934; *The Captain's Death Bed*, 1950; *Collected Essays*, Vol. 2, 1966.

C345 ROYALTY. *Time and Tide*, 1 December 1934, 1533–4. Review of *The Story of my Life*, by Marie, Queen of Roumania.

Reprinted in: *The Moment*, 1947; *Collected Essays*, Vol. 4, 1967.

## 1935

C346 THE CAPTAIN'S DEATH BED. *TLS*, 26 September 1935, 585–6.

Reprinted in: *The Captain's Death Bed*, 1950; *Collected Essays*, Vol. 1, 1966.

## 1936

C347 WHY ART TO-DAY FOLLOWS POLITICS. *Daily Worker*, 14 December 1936, 4.

Reprinted as: The Artist and Politics, *The Moment*, 1947; *Collected Essays*, Vol. 2, 1966.

## C. CONTRIBUTIONS TO PERIODICALS

### 1937

C348 THE HISTORIAN AND "THE GIBBON". *TLS*, 24 April 1937, 297–8.

Reprinted in: *The Death of the Moth*, 1942; *Collected Essays*, Vol. 1, 1966.

C349 CRAFTSMANSHIP. *Listener*, 5 May 1937, 868–9. A talk broadcast in the series 'Words Fail Me' on 29 April 1937.

Reprinted in: *The Death of the Moth*, 1942; *Collected Essays*, Vol. 2, 1966.

C350 REFLECTIONS AT SHEFFIELD PLACE. *New Statesman & Nation*, 19 June 1937, 1001–3.

Reprinted in: *The Death of the Moth*, 1942; *Collected Essays*, Vol. 1, 1966.

C351 MISS JANET CASE: CLASSICAL SCHOLAR AND TEACHER, [by] An Old Pupil. *The Times*, 22 July 1937, 16. An obituary. Unsigned.

C352 CONGREVE'S COMEDIES: SPEED, STILLNESS AND MEANING. *TLS*, 25 September 1937, 681–2.

Reprinted in: *The Moment*, 1947; *Collected Essays*, Vol. 1, 1966.

### 1938

C353 THE SHOOTING PARTY. *Harper's Bazaar*, March 1938, 72, 100, 102.

Reprinted in: *Harper's Bazaar*, N.Y., March 1938, 76–7. Reprinted (slightly revised) in: *A Haunted House*, 1944.

C354 LADY OTTOLINE MORRELL. *The Times*, 28 April 1938, 16; in two early editions only. An obituary.

C355 AMERICA WHICH I HAVE NEVER SEEN INTERESTS ME MOST IN THIS COSMOPOLITAN WORLD OF TODAY . . . *Hearst's International Combined with Cosmopolitan*, New York, April 1938, 21, 144–5.

C356 THE DUCHESS AND THE JEWELLER. *Harper's Bazaar*, April 1938, 40–1, 116, 118.

Reprinted in: *Harper's Bazaar*, N.Y., May 1938, 74–5; *A Haunted House*, 1944.

C357 WOMEN MUST WEEP. *Atlantic Monthly*, May 1938, 585–94 and June 1938, 750–9 (sub-title added: – Or Unite Against War).

A summary of: *Three Guineas*, 1938.

## 1939

C358 TWO ANTIQUARIES: WALPOLE AND COLE. *Yale Review*, March 1939, N.S. 28, 530–9. Review of *Letters of Horace Walpole to the Rev. William Cole*, edited by W. S. Lewis and A. D. Wallace.

Reprinted in: *The Death of the Moth*, 1942; *Collected Essays*, Vol. 3, 1967.

C359 THE ART OF BIOGRAPHY. *Atlantic Monthly*, April 1939, 506–10.

Reprinted in: *The Death of the Moth*, 1942; *Collected Essays*, Vol. 4, 1967.

C360 LAPPIN AND LAPINOVA. *Harper's Bazaar*, April 1939, 36–7, 96, 98.

Reprinted in: *Harper's Bazaar*, N.Y., April 1939, 90–1, 146, 148. Reprinted (slighted revised): *A Haunted House*, 1944.

C361 WHITE'S SELBORNE. *New Statesman & Nation*, 30 September 1939, 460–1.

Reprinted in: *The Captain's Death Bed*, 1950; *Collected Essays*, Vol. 3, 1967.

C362 REVIEWERS. *New Statesman & Nation*, 11 November 1939, 678–9. Letter to the Editor.

C363 LEWIS CARROLL. *New Statesman & Nation*, 9 December 1939, Christmas Books Supplement, 829. Review of *The Complete Works of Lewis Carroll*.

Reprinted in: *The Moment*, 1947; *Collected Essays*, Vol. 1, 1966.

## 1940

C364 GAS AT ABBOTSFORD. *New Statesman & Nation*, 27 January 1940, 108–9. Review of *Sir Walter Scott's Journal*, Vol. 1, edited by J. G. Tait.

Reprinted in: *The Moment*, 1947; *Collected Essays*, Vol. 1, 1966.

C365 THE DREAM. *Listener*, 15 February 1940, 333. Review of *Marie Corelli: The Life and Death of a Best Seller*, by George Bullock.

Reprinted in: *Granite and Rainbow*, 1958; *Collected Essays*, Vol. 4, 1967.

C366 THE HUMANE ART. *New Statesman & Nation*, 8 June 1940, 726. Review of *Horace Walpole*, by R. W. Ketton-Cremer.

Reprinted in: *The Death of the Moth*, 1942; *Collected Essays*, Vol. 1, 1966.

C367 REVIEW under heading Books in General. *New Statesman & Nation*, 6 July 1940, 16. Review of *Hary-O: The Letters of Lady Harriet Cavendish*, edited by Sir George Leveson-Gower.

Reprinted as: Selina Trimmer, *Atlantic Monthly*, April 1950, 73–4; *The Captain's Death Bed*, 1950; *Collected Essays*, Vol. 3, 1967.

C368 THE MAN AT THE GATE. *New Statesman & Nation*, 19 October 1940, 382. Review of *Coleridge the Talker*, edited by Richard W. Armour and Raymond F. Howes.

Reprinted in: *The Death of the Moth*, 1942; *Collected Essays*, Vol. 3, 1967.

C369 THOUGHTS ON PEACE IN AN AIR RAID. *New Republic*, N.Y., 21 October 1940, 549–51.

Reprinted in: *The Death of the Moth*, 1942; *New Republic*, N.Y., 2 November 1954, 51–2; *Selections from Her Essays*, [1966]; *Collected Essays*, Vol. 4, 1967.

C370 SARA COLERIDGE. *New Statesman & Nation*, 26 October 1940, 418, 420. Review of *Coleridge Fille: A Biography of Sara Coleridge*, by Earl Leslie Griggs.

Reprinted in: *The Death of the Moth*, 1942; *Collected Essays*, Vol. 3, 1967.

C371 GEORGIANA AND FLORENCE. *Listener*, 31 October 1940, 639. Review of *Two Generations*, edited by Osbert Sitwell.

C372 THE LEANING TOWER. *Folios of New Writing*, Autumn 1940, 11–33. Edited by John Lehmann; published London, November 1940. A paper read to the Workers' Educational Association, Brighton, May 1940.

Reprinted in: *The Moment*, 1947; *Selections from Her Essays* (extract), [1966]; *Collected Essays*, Vol. 2, 1966.

## 1941

C373 ELLEN TERRY. *New Statesman & Nation*, 8 February 1941, 133–4.

Reprinted in: *The Moment*, 1947; *Collected Essays*, Vol. 4, 1967.

C374 MRS. THRALE. *New Statesman & Nation*, 8 March 1941, 250. Review of *Hester Lynch Piozzi*, by James L. Clifford.

Reprinted in: *The Moment*, 1947; *Collected Essays*, Vol. 3, 1967.

## 1950

C375 FLYING OVER LONDON. *Vogue*, New York, 1 March 1950, 132–3.

Reprinted in: *The Captain's Death Bed*, 1950; *Collected Essays*, Vol. 4, 1967.

## 1965

C376 THE . . . *TLS*, 17 June 1965, 495. A hitherto unpublished story illustrated by Duncan Grant and found in the manuscript of *Mrs Dalloway*, Vol. 2, leaves 104–6. See 'Virginia Woolf for Children?' by Wallace Hildick, *TLS*, 17 June 1965, 496, and 'In that Solitary Room', *Kenyon Review*, Spring 1965, 27:2, 302–17, by the same author.

Reprinted as: *Nurse Lugton's Golden Thimble*, 1966.

## 1972

C377 THREE CHARACTERS. *Adam International Review*, 1972, 364–366, Thirty-seventh Year, 24–6. Title in Contents: The Low Brow, The High Brow, The Broad Brow. See also F14 for letters.

C378 STENDHAL. *Adam International Review*, 1972, 364–366, Thirty-seventh Year, 26–8.

## 1973

C379 THE INTRODUCTION. *Sunday Times Magazine*, 18 March 1973, 68–9, 71. Illustrated by Duncan Grant.

Reprinted in: *Mrs Dalloway's Party*, 1973; *Ms.*, New York, July 1973, 11:1, 54–5, 93–4.

## 1979

C380 Byron and Mr. Briggs. *Yale Review*, March 1979, N.S. 68, 325–49. Introduction by Edward A. Hungerford, pp. 321–4.

## DOUBTFUL AND UNTRACED CONTRIBUTIONS

(the source of each reference follows the item)

a. The following may be by Virginia Woolf:

1. Review of *Social England: A Record of the People*, edited by H. D. Traill and J. S. Mann. *Guardian*, 7 December 1904, 2059 – *Diary*, Christmas 1904–31 May 1905.
2. Review of *The Feminine Note in Fiction*, by W. L. Courtney. *Guardian*, 25 January 1905, 168 – ibid.
3. The Story of the Mutiny. *Guardian*, 22 February 1905, 311–12. Review of *A History of the Indian Mutiny*, by G. W. Forrest – ibid.
4. Review of *By Beach and Bogland*, by Jane Barlow. *Guardian*, 22 March 1905, 507–8 – ibid.
5. Review of *Nancy Stair*, by Elinor MacCartney Lane. *Guardian*, 10 May 1905, 803 – ibid.
6. Review of *Arrows of Fortune*, by Algernon Gissing. *Guardian*, 17 May 1905, 856 – ibid.
7. The American Woman. *Guardian*, 31 May 1905, 939. Review

of *The Women of America*, by Elizabeth McCracken – ibid.

8. Review of *The Oxford History of Music*, Vol. V: *The Viennese Period*, by W. H. Hadow. *Guardian*, 14 June 1905, 1020 – ibid.
9. Review of *Fenwick's Career*, by Mrs Humphry Ward. *Guardian*, 16 May 1906, 844 – Monk's House Papers B.
10. Review of *The Last Days of Marie Antoinette*, by G. Lenotre, translated by Mrs Rodolph Stawell. *TLS*, 7 November 1907, 339 – *The Flight of the Mind*, 316.
11. Review of *The Post Impressionists*, by C. Lewis Hind. *Nation*, 14 October 1911, 108 – Berg Collection (letter from Vanessa Bell to VW, 20 October 1911).

b. The following have not been traced:

1. 30 October [1904]: 'Would Mrs Lyttleton like a description of a Q.[Quaker] Meeting from my gifted pen, d'you think.' – *The Flight of the Mind*, 148.
2. 1905: New Forest; possibly review of *The New Forest*, by Horace G. Hutchinson and *The New Forest*, by Mrs Willingham Rawnsley both published in April 1904 – *Diary*, Christmas 1904–31 May 1905.
3. [May 1905]: 'I have been pouring my life blood into the grim bones of early English history all morning [*Town Life in the Fifteenth Century*, by A. S. Green]: they wont care for it.' – *The Flight of the Mind*, 190; see also 170.
4. 5 May 1905: Protestant Cemetery at Lisbon – *Diary*, Christmas 1904–31 May 1905, 'possibly for *Academy*'.
5. [June 1905]: 'Mrs Lyttleton wants me to write her a 'literary article' so I shall sit in a corner and wrestle with some melancholy minor poet. Can you suggest anybody?' – *The Flight of the Mind*, 193.
6. [July 1905]: 'I am going to produce a real historical work this summer; for which I have solidly read and annotated 4 volumes of medieval English' – *The Flight of the Mind*, 202.
7. 1906: De Quincey's Autobiography; his *Autobiographical Sketches* was included in an edition published by Newnes in October 1906 entitled *Autobiography and Confessions* – Monk's House Papers B.
8. May 1906: Review of *A House of Letters*, edited by Ernest Betham; noted as contributed to *The Speaker* on 11 May – Monk's House Papers B.
9. [4 August 1906]: 'Read your Guardian carefully, and see if you find anything about Henry James' – *The Flight of the Mind*, 234.
10. 28 December 1906: 'I have 5 volumes of poetry to review for the Guardian – and one takes for hero the Almighty, and

Jesus Christ, and the villain is Satan' – ibid., 272-3.

11. [25 August 1907]: 'I have 7 volumes of poetic drama to review for the Guardian, and a novel for the Times [possibly C6.1]' – ibid., 307.
12. [April 1908]: 'I hope De Morgan is done to your liking [possibly review of *Somehow Good*, by William de Morgan]' – ibid., 324.
13. July 1908: 'entered into a long correspondence with Prothero [Sir George Prothero, Editor of the *Quarterly Review*], and we decide that I am probably to write about Ly. May Montagu [Lady Mary Wortley Montagu]' – ibid., 337.
14. [5 April 1916]: 'I've got to review a book on Ruskin. I wish you'd tell me something about Ruskin and Turner [possibly *A Sketch of John Ruskin*, by Peggy Webling published in February 1916] – *The Question of Things Happening*, 88.
15. [*c.* October 1917]: 'Virginia has written charmingly about our [Co-operative] Congress in the Suff. Mag.' – Monk's House Papers A (letter from Margaret Llewelyn Davies to Leonard Woolf).
16. 10 October 1917: 'And another article upon the country in Hardy & E. Brontë is suggested' – *The Diary*, Vol. I, 57.
17. 19 March 1919: 'I meant to write about the Barnetts . . . But I only scratch the surface of what I feel about these two stout volumes'; possibly review of *Canon Barnett: His Life and Work, and Friends*, by his wife, published in 1918 – ibid., 255-6.
18. 7 January 1920: '& now finish Ros[s]etti' – *The Diary*, Vol. II, 5.
19. 20 May 1920: 'rejected by the Times though not by the Womans Times [*The Times Woman's Supplement*]' – ibid., 40.
20. February 1921: payment of £1. 11s. 6d. received from CC probably for a review – Leonard Woolf's record of payments.
21. [2 November 1921]: '& Betsy Bibesco wishes me to review her book'; *i.e. I Have Only Myself to Blame*, by Princess Elizabeth Bibesco, published in February 1922 – *The Diary*, Vol. II, 141.
22. [26 April 1922]: 'Here come this moment some remarks upon Princess Bibesco, not very profound, but in payment of 17/6 which I owe Ray [Strachey] for her damnable sheet [*Woman's Leader*]'; possibly the same as Item 21 – *The Question of Things Happening*, 523.
23. [May 1922]: Review of the Royal Academy's 155th Exhibition, 1 May-7 August 1922 – Berg Collection (*Jacob's Room*, Notebook, No. 3).

24. August 1922: payment of £4. 10s. received from 'Times' probably for a review in the *TLS* – Leonard Woolf's record of payments.

25. [November 1922]: Review of *Maud-Evelyn and Other Stories* and *The Sacred Fount*, by Henry James, both published in May 1923 in Macmillan's edition of his *Complete Works* which was announced in the *TLS*, 16 November 1922 – Berg Collection (*Jacob's Room*, Notebook, No. 3).

26. [June 1923]: Review of *The Art of Thomas Hardy*, by Lionel Johnson, John Lane – Berg Collection (ibid.).

27. [September 1924]: Review of *The Passing Years*, by Richard Greville Verney, Lord Willoughby de Broke; the review in the *TLS*, 4 September 1924, 535 is not by VW – British Library Reference Division (*Mrs Dalloway* manuscript, Vol. 3, f. 137b).

28. [1925]: Review of *The Rape of the Lock*, by Alexander Pope, Haslewood Press – Berg Collection (Articles, Essays, Fiction and Reviews, Vol. 1).

29. [May 1925]: Review of *Elizabethan Home in Two Dialogues*, Haslewood Press – Berg Collection (ibid.).

30. [September 1925]: Review of *Letters of Thomas Manning to Charles Lamb*, edited by G. A. Anderson, Secker – Berg Collection (ibid.).

31. [October 1925]: Review of *Later Days*, by W. H. Davies, Cape – Berg Collection (ibid.).

32. [February 1926]: Review of *Miniature Portraits*, by Gédéon Tallemant, Guy Chapmen – Berg Collection (ibid.).

33. [5 August 1927]: 'When's your book out? [*Aphra Behn*, by V. Sackville-West] Not in September so that I could review it for America?'; it is unlikely that VW reviewed the book as there is no review by her among the author's clippings of reviews – *A Change of Perspective*, 408.

34. [8 October 1930]: 'would you . . . send me, on loan the Ladies of Llangollen – if that is their name? [*The Hamwood Papers of the Ladies of Llangollen and Caroline Hamilton*, edited by John Travers (Mrs G. H. Bell)] I cant find anything to do for Mrs Van Doren [Editor, *New York Herald Tribune, Weekly Book Section*], and this might suit' – *A Reflection of the Other Person*, 227.

35. [December 1930]: Review of *Christina Rossetti*, by Dorothy Margaret Stuart, English Men of Letters Series – Berg Collection (Articles, Essays, Fiction and Reviews, Vol. 4).

36. October 1937: payment of £7. 10s. received from 'Times' probably for a review in the *TLS* – Leonard Woolf's record of payments.

# D.
# TRANSLATIONS INTO FOREIGN LANGUAGES

Arranged alphabetically by language
and chronologically within each group

## CATALAN

### *Books*

D1 *a.* MRS. DALLOWAY | PER | VIRGINIA WOOLF | TRADUCCIÓ DE L'ANGLÉS | PER C. A. JORDANA | 1930 | EDICIONS PROA-BADALONA

Small crown 8vo. 260 pp. $7\frac{1}{2} \times 4\frac{3}{4}$ in. (Collecció Els d'Ara).

A translation by C. A. Jordana of *Mrs Dalloway.*

*b.* VIRGINIA WOOLF | MRS. DALLOWAY | TRADUCCIÓ DE C. A. JORDANA | [*device*] | 1970 | EDICIONS PROA. BARCELONA

Foolscap 8vo. 194 pp. $6\frac{5}{8} \times 4\frac{3}{8}$ in. (Biblioteca A tot vent, 150).

Translation by C. A. Jordana.

D2 ELS ANYS | [*rule*] | VIRGINIA WOOLF | AMB UNA NOTA EPÍLEG SOBRE "VIRGINIA | WOOLF O LA NOVA REALITAT" PER MARIA | AURÈLIA CAPMANY. | EDITORIAL NOVA TERRA | CANALEJAS, 65 | BARCELONA – 14

Crown 8vo. 400 pp. $7\frac{3}{8} \times 5$ in.

A translation by Maria Antónia Oliver of *The Years*; published 1973.

## CHINESE

### *Book*

D3 [SINO-BRITISH CULTURAL ASSOCIATION LITERARY SERIES] | TAO TÊNG T'A CH'Ü | VIRGINIA WOOLF | [TRANSLATION AND INTRODUCTION BY] HSIEH CH'ING-YAO | [PUBLISHED BY COMMERCIAL PRESS]

Crown 8vo. [ii], x, 64 pp. $7\frac{1}{4} \times 5$ in.

A translation by Hsieh Ch'ing-yao of *To the Lighthouse*; published Shanghai, 1946. First published in Chungking, 1945.

## CZECH

### *Books*

D4 [*in black:*] VIRGINIA | WOOLFOVÁ | [*in red: rule*] | O [*in black:*] RLANDO | IMAGINÁRNÍ ŽIVOTOPIS | V PRAZE 1929 | [*in red: rule*] | S [*in black:*] YMPOSION

Crown 8vo. 264 pp. 5 illus. $7\frac{1}{8} \times 5\frac{1}{8}$ in.

A translation by Staša Jílovská of *Orlando.*

D5 VIRGINIA WOOLF | FLUSH | ŽIVOTOPIS PEJSKA ALŽBĚTY BARRETTOVÉ-BROWNINGOVÉ | Z ANGLIČTINY PŘELOŽILA | BOŽENA ŠIMKOVÁ | [*device*] | JAN LAICHTER V PRAZE 1938

Small crown 8vo. 180 pp. 3 plates. $7\frac{1}{8} \times 4\frac{3}{4}$ in. (Laichterova Sbírka Krásného Písemnictví, 43).

A translation by Božena Šimková of *Flush*.

D6 [*rule*] | VIRGINIA WOOLFOVÁ | K MAJÁKU | [*rule*] | ČESKOSLOVENSKÝ SPISOVATEL/PRAHA 1965

Large crown 8vo. 196 pp. 4 coloured plates. $8 \times 5\frac{1}{8}$ in. (Edice ilustrovaných Novel, 105).

A translation by Jarmila Fastrová, with illustrations by Ludmila Jiřincová, of *To the Lighthouse*.

D7 VIRGINIA WOOLFOVÁ | MEZI AKTY | [*rule*] | ODEON | PRAHA | 1968

Foolscap 8vo. 184 pp. $6\frac{1}{2} \times 4\frac{1}{2}$ in. (Světová Četba, Svazek 393).

A translation by Hana Skoumalová, with an introduction by Radoslav Nenadál, of *Between the Acts*.

D8 [*rule*] | VIRGINIA WOOLFOVÁ | [*rule*] | [*in dull pink:*] PANÍ DALLOWAYOVA | [*in black: rule*] | ODEON

Foolscap 8vo. 272 pp. $6\frac{1}{2} \times 4\frac{1}{4}$ in.

A translation by Vlasta Dvořáčková, with a postscript by Martin Hilský, of *Mrs Dalloway*; published Prague, 1975.

## DANISH

*Books*

D9 VIRGINIA WOOLF | AARENE GAAR | [*device and monogram*] | [*double rule*] | H. HAGERUP – KØBENHAVN | 1941

Demy 8vo. 324 pp. $8\frac{7}{8} \times 5\frac{7}{8}$ in.

A translation by Paula Biehe of *The Years*.

D10 VIRGINIA WOOLF | MRS. DALLOWAY | PAA DANSK VED | OVE BRUSENDORFF | GYLDENDAL | KØBENHAVN 1945

Large crown 8vo. 252 pp. $8\frac{1}{2} \times 5\frac{3}{8}$ in.

A translation by Ove Brusendorff of *Mrs Dalloway*.

D11 VIRGINIA WOOLF | BREV | TIL EN UNG | DIGTER | BORGENS FORLAG | JARL BORGEN | [*rule*] | KØBENHAVN 1949

Crown 8vo. 28 pp. $7\frac{1}{2} \times 5\frac{1}{8}$ in.

A translation by Martin Melsted of *A Letter to a Young Poet*.

D12 VIRGINIA WOOLF | ET LONDON-EVENTYR | OG ANDRE ESSAYS | UDVALGT OG OVERSAT AF | NIELS LYHNE

JENSEN | [*device*] | KØBENHAVN | STEEN HASSELBALCHS FORLAG | MCMLIII

Small crown 8vo. 56 pp. 7 × $4\frac{3}{4}$ in. (Hasselbalchs Kultur-Bibliotek, 120).

A translation by Niels Lyhne Jensen of 'Robinson Crusoe', 'Modern Novels', an extract from *A Room of One's Own*, 'On Being Ill', and *Street Haunting: A London Adventure.*

D13 VIRGINIA WOOLF | FLUSH | [*rule*] | HISTORIEN OM EN COCKER SPANIEL | OVERSAT AF | MOGENS BOISEN | [*monogram*] | ASCHEHOUG DANSK FORLAG | KØBENHAVN 1953

Crown 8vo. 136 pp. $7\frac{5}{8}$ × $4\frac{3}{4}$ in. (Levende Litteratur, 27).

A translation by Mogens Boisen of *Flush.*

D14 VIRGINIA WOOLF | ORLANDO | EN BIOGRAFI | PÅ DANSK VED | JØRGEN ÅRUP HANSEN | GYLDENDALS | BEKKASINBØGER | 1962

Small crown 8vo. 228 pp. $7\frac{3}{8}$ × $4\frac{5}{8}$ in.

A translation by Jørgen Årup Hansen of *Orlando*; published Copenhagen.

D15 VIRGINIA WOOLF | EGET | VÆRELSE | [*device*] | SAMLERENS PICCOLOBØGER

Crown 8vo. 144 pp. $7\frac{3}{4}$ × $4\frac{3}{4}$ in.

A translation by Elsa Gress and David Gress-Wright, with a foreword by Elsa Gress, of *A Room of One's Own*; published Copenhagen, 1973. Reprinted in 1978 by Samlerens Billigbøger.

## DUTCH

### *Books*

D16 VIRGINIA WOOLF | MRS. DALLOWAY | [*monogram*] | 1948 | G. A. VAN OORSCHOT-UITGEVER | AMSTERDAM

Crown 8vo. 224 pp. $7\frac{1}{2}$ × $5\frac{1}{8}$ in.

A translation by N. Brunt of *Mrs Dalloway.*

D17 *a.* VIRGINIA WOOLF | EEN KAMER VOOR | JEZELF | [*monogram*] | G. A. VAN OORSCHOT/UITGEVER | AMSTERDAM | 1958

Crown 8vo. 148 pp. $7\frac{3}{4}$ × $4\frac{3}{4}$ in.

A translation by C. E. van der Waals-Nachenius of *A Room of One's Own.*

*b.* VIRGINIA WOOLF | EEN KAMER VOOR JEZELF | 1977 | UITGEVERIJ DE BEZIGE BIJ | AMSTERDAM

Narrow large crown 8vo. 124 pp. $7\frac{3}{4}$ × $4\frac{7}{8}$ in.

Translation by C. E. van der Waals-Nachenius.

D18 VIRGINIA WOOLF | ORLANDO | BIOGRAFIE | VERTALING GERARDINE FRANKEN | NAWOORD JAMES NAREMORE | 1976 | UITGEVERIJ DE BEZIGE BIJ | AMSTERDAM

Crown 8vo. 328 pp. $7\frac{3}{4} \times 4\frac{3}{4}$ in.

A translation by Gerardine Franken, with a foreword by James Naremore, of *Orlando*.

D19 VIRGINIA WOOLF | SCHRIJVERSDAGBOEK I | 1918–1932 [II | 1933–1941] | EEN KEUZE UIT HET DAGBOEK | VAN VIRGINIA WOOLF | SAMENGESTELD DOOR LEONARD WOOLF | VERTALING, NAWOORD EN AANTEKENINGEN | VAN JOOP VAN HELMOND | [*monogram*] | AMSTERDAM · UITGEVERIJ DE ARBEIDERSPERS

Small crown 8vo. 2 vols. Vol. 1: 248 pp. Vol. 2: 224 pp. $7\frac{5}{8} \times 4\frac{5}{8}$ in. (Privé-Domein, 37).

A translation, with a foreword and postscript by Joop van Helmond, of *A Writer's Diary*; published 1977.

D19 .1 VIRGINIA WOOLF | FLUSH | BIOGRAFIE | VPRTALING GERARDINE FRANKEN | NAWOORD THOMAS F. STALEY | [*publisher's device*] | 1978 DE BEZIGE BIJ AMSTERDAM

Crown 8vo. 160 pp. $7\frac{7}{8} \times 5$ in.

A translation by Gerardine Franken, with a postscript by Thomas F. Staley, of *Flush*.

## FINNISH

*Books*

D20 VIRGINIA WOOLF | MRS. DALLOWAY | ROMAANI | SUOMENTANUT | KYLLIKKI HÄMÄLÄINEN | JOHDANNON KIRJOITTANUT | IRMA RANTAVAARA | [*publisher's device*] | HELSINGISSÄ | KUSTANNUSOSAKEYHTIÖ OTAVA

Crown 8vo. 296 pp. $7\frac{5}{8} \times 5$ in.

A translation by Kyllikki Hämäläinen, with an introduction by Irma Rantavaara, of *Mrs Dalloway*; published 1956.

D21 VIRGINIA WOOLF | MAJAKKA | KIRJAYHTYMÄ · HELSINKI

Large crown 8vo. 262 pp. $7\frac{7}{8} \times 5$ in.

A translation by Kai Kaila of *To the Lighthouse*; published 1977.

D21 .1 VIRGINIA WOOLF | AALLOT | KIRJAYHTYMÄ · HELSINKI

Large crown 8vo. 216 pp. $7\frac{7}{8} \times 5\frac{1}{8}$ in.

A translation by Kai Kaila of *The Waves*; published 1979.

# D. TRANSLATIONS

## FRENCH

### *Books*

D22 *a.* VIRGINIA WOOLF | MRS. DALLOWAY | ROMAN TRADUIT DE L'ANGLAIS PAR | S. DAVID | PRÉFACE DE | ANDRÉ MAUROIS | [*device*] | 1929 | TOUS DROITS RÉSERVÉS POUR TOUS PAYS. | [*double rule*] | LIBRAIRIE STOCK | DELAMAIN ET BOUTELLEAU – PARIS | 7, RUE DU VIEUX-COLOMBIER

Crown 8vo. xii, 240 pp. $7\frac{3}{8} \times 5$ in. (Le Cabinet Cosmopolite, 31).

A translation by S. David of *Mrs Dalloway*. Reprinted in 1948 in the series *Bibliothèque anglaise*.

*b.* VIRGINIA WOOLF | MRS. DALLOWAY | ROMAN TRADUIT DE L'ANGLAIS PAR S. DAVID | PRÉFACE DE ANDRÉ MAUROIS | STOCK

Foolscap 8vo. 256 pp. $6\frac{1}{2} \times 4\frac{3}{8}$ in. (Le Livre de Poche).

Translation by S. David; published Paris, 1956.

*c.* MRS DALLOWAY, PARIS, LAUSANNE, ÉDITIONS RENCONTRE, 1969*

295 pp.

Translation by S. David.

*d.* [*rule:*] VIRGINIA | WOOLF | MRS | DALLOWAY | PRÉFACE D'ANDRÉ MAUROIS | DE L'ACADÉMIE FRANÇAISE | FRONTISPICE DE | FRANÇOISE MULLER | ÉDITIONS FAMOT | [*rule*]

Crown 8vo. 280 pp. front. (col.) $7\frac{1}{2} \times 5$ in.

Translation by S. David; published Geneva, 1978.

D23 *a.* VIRGINIA WOOLF | LA PROMENADE | AU PHARE | TRADUIT DE L'ANGLAIS PAR | M. LANOIRE | 1929 | [*double rule*] | LIBRAIRIE STOCK | DELAMAIN & BOUTELLEAU – PARIS | 7, RUE DU VIEUX-COLOMBIER

Crown 8vo. 248 pp. $7\frac{3}{8} \times 5$ in. (Le Cabinet Cosmopolite).

A translation by M. Lanoire of *To the Lighthouse.*

*b.* [*across two pages:*] [*signature in facsimile:*] VIRGINIA WOOLF | TO THE LIGHTHOUSE | "A NEW . . . " LA | PROMENADE AU PHARE | PRIX FEMINA-VIE HEUREUSE | 1927 | LIBRAIRIE STOCK

Crown 8vo. 256 pp. illus. $7\frac{1}{2} \times 5\frac{1}{4}$ in.

Translation by M. Lanoire, with a preface by Monique Nathan; published Paris, 1957.

*c.* VIRGINIA WOOLF | LA PROMENADE AU PHARE | TRADUIT DE L'ANGLAIS PAR M. LANOIRE | PRÉFACE DE MONIQUE NATHAN | STOCK

Foolscap 8vo. 288 pp. $6\frac{1}{2} \times 4\frac{1}{4}$ in. (Le Livre de Poche).

Translation by M. Lanoire, with a preface by Monique Nathan; published Paris, 1968.

D24 VIRGINIA WOOLF | ORLANDO | TRADUCTION ET PRÉFACE DE | CHARLES MAURON | [*device*] | 1931 | [*double rule*] | LIBRAIRIE STOCK | DELAMAIN ET BOUTELLEAU | 7, RUE DU VIEUX-COLOMBIER | PARIS

Crown 8vo. 266 pp. $7\frac{3}{8} \times 5$ in. (Le Cabinet Cosmopolite, 57).

A translation by Charles Mauron of *Orlando.*

D25 LES MAÎTRES ÉTRANGERS | [*rule*] | VIRGINIA WOOLF | [*rule*] | NUIT ET JOUR | ROMAN | TRADUIT DE L'ANGLAIS PAR MAURICE BEC | INTRODUCTION DE RENÉ LALOU | PARIS | ÉDITIONS DU SIÈCLE | CATALOGNE & CIE | 7, RUE SERVANDONI, 7

Small crown 8vo. xvi, 372 pp. $7\frac{1}{8} \times 4\frac{1}{2}$ in. (Les Maîtres Étrangers).

A translation by Maurice Bec of *Night and Day*; published 1933.

D26 VIRGINIA WOOLF | FLUSH | BIOGRAPHIE | TRADUITE DE L'ANGLAIS PAR CHARLES MAURON | PRÉFACE DE | LOUIS GILLET | [*device*] | 1935 | [*double rule*] | LIBRAIRIE STOCK | DELAMAIN ET BOUTELLEAU | 7, RUE DU VIEUX-COLOMBIER, 7 | PARIS

Crown 8vo. xvi, 208 pp. $7\frac{1}{2} \times 5$ in. (Le Cabinet Cosmopolite, 75).

A translation by Charles Mauron of *Flush.*

D27 VIRGINIA WOOLF | LES VAGUES | TRADUIT DE L'ANG-
*a.* LAIS, AVEC UNE PRÉFACE, PAR | MARGUERITE YOURCENAR | 1937 | [*double rule*] | LIBRAIRIE STOCK | DELAMAIN ET BOUTELLEAU | 7, RUE DU VIEUX-COLOMBIER, 7 | PARIS

Crown 8vo. 272 pp. $7\frac{3}{8} \times 5$ in. (Le Cabinet Cosmopolite).

A translation by Marguerite Yourcenar of *The Waves.*

*b.* LES | VAGUES | PAR | VIRGINIA | WOOLF | TRADUCTION | DE | L'ANGLAIS | PAR | MARGUERITE | YOURCENAR | C. 53

Large crown 8vo. [vi], 284 pp. $8\frac{1}{8} \times 5\frac{3}{8}$ in. (Romans, 135).

Translation by Marguerite Yourcenar; published Paris, 1953 by Le Club français du Livre. 'Virginia Woolf et son Oeuvre', by Marguerite Yourcenar, pp. 276–82.

*c.* FEUX CROISÉS | AMES ET TERRES ÉTRANGÈRES | [*rule*] | VIRGINIA WOOLF | LES VAGUES | PRÉFACÉ ET TRADUIT DE L'ANGLAIS PAR | MARGUERITE YOURCENAR | [*device*] | LIBRAIRIE PLON | 8, RUE GARANCIÈRE – PARIS-6e

Small crown 8vo. [6], viii, 306 pp. $7\frac{3}{8} \times 4\frac{5}{8}$ in.

Translation by Marguerite Yourcenar; published July 1957. Stock surrendered the publication rights to Plon in June 1956.

D28 VIRGINIA WOOLF | ANNÉES | TRADUIT DE L'ANGLAIS PAR GERMAINE DELAMAIN | PRÉFACE | DE | RENÉ LALOU | [*device*] | 1938 | [*double rule*] | ÉDITIONS STOCK | DELAMAIN ET BOUTELLEAU | 6, RUE CASIMIR-DELAVIGNE, 6 | PARIS

Crown 8vo. viii, 408 pp. $7\frac{3}{8} \times 5\frac{1}{8}$ in. (Le Cabinet Cosmopolite, 88).

A translation by Germaine Delamain of *The Years*.

D29 *a.* VIRGINIA WOOLF | LA CHAMBRE | DE JACOB | TRADUCTION DE JEAN TALVA | 1942 | [*double rule*] | LIBRAIRIE STOCK | DELAMAIN ET BOUTELLEAU | 6, RUE CASIMIR DELAVIGNE, 6 | PARIS

Small crown 8vo. 256 pp. $7\frac{1}{4} \times 4\frac{1}{2}$ in.

A translation by Jean Talva of *Jacob's Room*.

*b.* FEUX CROISÉS | AMES ET TERRES ÉTRANGÈRES | [*rule*] | VIRGINIA WOOLF | LA CHAMBRE | DE JACOB | ROMAN | TRADUIT DE L'ANGLAIS PAR | JEAN TALVA | [*device*] | LIBRAIRIE PLON | 8, RUE GARANCIÈRE – PARIS-6e

Small crown 8vo. [vi], 250 pp. $7\frac{3}{8} \times 4\frac{5}{8}$ in.

Translation by Jean Talva; published February 1958. Stock surrendered the publication rights to Plon in June 1956.

D30 *a.* VIRGINIA WOOLF | ENTRE LES ACTES | TRADUCTION D'YVONNE GENOVA | COLLECTION | LES CINQ CONTINENTS | DIRIGÉE PAR | PHILIPPE SOUPAULT | EDITIONS | [*rule*] | CHARLOT

Crown 8vo. 224 pp. $7\frac{5}{8} \times 4\frac{3}{4}$ in. (Collection Les Cinq Continents).

A translation by Yvonne Genova of *Between the Acts*; printed in Algiers in 1944 and published in 1945. This edition was not for sale in France.

*b.* VIRGINIA WOOLF | ENTRE | LES ACTES | TRADUIT PAR CHARLES CESTRE | PRÉFACE DE | MAX-POL FOUCHET | 1947 | [*double rule*] | ÉDITIONS STOCK | DELAMAIN ET BOUTELLEAU | 6, RUE CASIMIR DELAVIGNE | PARIS

Small crown 8vo. 240 pp. $7\frac{1}{4} \times 4\frac{1}{2}$ in.

Translation by Charles Cestre. Both translations of *Between the Acts* were authorised. This edition was not for sale in North Africa.

D31 VIRGINIA | WOOLF | LA MAISON | HANTÉE | TRADUIT | DE L'ANGLAIS | PAR HÉLÈNE | BOKANOWSKI | CHARLOT

Small crown 8vo. 272 pp. $7\frac{1}{8} \times 4\frac{1}{2}$ in. (Collection Les Cinq Continents).

A translation by Hélène Bokanowski of *A Haunted House and Other Short Stories*; published Paris, 1946. *La Mort de l'Ephémère*, translated by Madeleine Brémont was advertised on the wrapper but does not appear to have been published.

D32 *a.* VIRGINIA WOOLF | LA | TRAVERSÉE | DES | APPARENCES | ROMAN TRADUIT DE L'ANGLAIS | PAR LUDMILLA SAVITZKY | PRÉFACÉ PAR | MAX-POL | FOUCHET | LE CAHIER GRIS

Small crown 8vo. 544 pp. $7\frac{1}{4} \times 4\frac{3}{4}$ in.

A translation by Ludmila Savitzky of *The Voyage Out*; published Paris, 1948. Owing to a misunderstanding two translations of *The Voyage Out* were published in France, neither was technically speaking unauthorised.

*b.* VIRGINIA WOOLF | CROISIERE | ROMAN | TRADUIT DE L'ANGLAIS PAR ARMEL GUERNE | FRONTISPICE D'HÉLÈNE NEVEUR | CHEZ ROBERT MARIN

Large crown 8vo. 440 pp. front. $7\frac{5}{8} \times 5\frac{1}{2}$ in.

Translation by Armel Guerne; published Paris, 1952.

*c.* [*within a rule:*] [*within a rule:*] VIRGINIA WOOLF | [*below rule: vertical rule, short thick column, vertical rule*] CONNECTIONS [*vertical rule, short thick column, vertical rule*] | [*thick rule across page*] | LA | TRAVERSÉE | DES | APPARENCES | TRADUIT DE L'ANGLAIS PAR LUDMILA SAVITZKY | PRÉFACE DE JULIE PAVESI | [*double rule, thin, thick, across page*] | [*illustration*] | [*within a rule:*] FLAMMARION*

Large crown 8vo. 470 pp. $7\frac{3}{4} \times 5\frac{1}{4}$ in.

Translation by Ludmila Savitsky, with a preface by Julie Pavesi; published Paris, 1977.

D33 *a.* VIRGINIA WOOLF | UNE CHAMBRE | A SOI | TRADUIT DE L'ANGLAIS PAR | CLARA MALRAUX | ROBERT MARIN

Small crown 8vo. 224 pp. $7\frac{3}{8} \times 4\frac{5}{8}$ in.

A translation by Clara Malraux of *A Room of One's Own*; published Paris, 1951.

*b.* VIRGINIA WOOLF | UNE CHAMBRE | À SOI | TRADUIT DE L'ANGLAIS PAR CLARA MALRAUX | [*publisher's initial*] | DENOËL/GONTHIER

Small demy 8vo. 158 pp. $8\frac{3}{8} \times 5\frac{3}{8}$ in. (Collection Femme).

Translation by Clara Malraux; published 1977.

D34 MONIQUE NATHAN | VIRGINIA WOOLF | PAR ELLE-MÊME | "ÉCRIVAINS DE TOUJOURS" | AUX ÉDITIONS DU SEUIL

Small crown 8vo. 192 pp. illus. 7 × $4\frac{3}{4}$ in.

Pp. 145–89 translations of chapters from *Orlando, To the Lighthouse, The Waves* and of 'The Duchess and the Jeweller' and 'Professions for Women'; published Paris, 1956.

D35 *a.* VIRGINIA | WOOLF | JOURNAL | D'UN ÉCRIVAIN | TRADUIT DE L'ANGLAIS | PAR GERMAINE BEAUMONT | ÉDITIONS DU ROCHER | 28, RUE COMTE FÉLIX GASTALDI | MONACO

Crown 8vo. 592 pp. $7\frac{5}{8}$ × $5\frac{1}{2}$ in.

A translation by Germaine Beaumont of *A Writer's Diary*; published April 1958.

*b.* VIRGINIA WOOLF | JOURNAL | D'UN ECRIVAIN I [II] | PRÉFACE DE LÉONARD WOOLF | TRADUIT DE L'ANGLAIS PAR GERMAINE BEAUMONT | EDITIONS DU ROCHER

Foolscap 8vo. 2 vols. Vol. 1: 288 pp. Vol. 2: 304 pp. 7 × $4\frac{1}{4}$ in.

Translation by Germaine Beaumont; published Paris, 1977. Line 4 omitted in Vol. II.

D36 VIRGINIA WOOLF | L'ART DU ROMAN | TRADUIT ET PRÉFACÉ PAR | ROSE CELLI | ÉDITIONS DU SEUIL | 27, RUE JACOB, PARIS VIe

Demy 8vo. 206 pp. $8\frac{1}{2}$ × $5\frac{5}{8}$ in.

Translations by Rose Celli of 'Modern Novels', 'The Russian Point of View', 'How It Strikes a Contemporary', 'Character in Fiction', 'Poetry, Fiction and the Future', 'Women and Fiction', 'Phases of Fiction', 'How Should One Read a Book?', 'A Letter to a Young Poet' and 'The Leaning Tower'; published 1963.

D37 BIBLIOTHÈQUE DE STYLISTIQUE COMPARÉE | SOUS LA DIRECTION DE A. MALBLANC | [*rule*] IV [*rule*] | L. BONNEROT | [*one line*] | CHEMINS DE LA TRADUCTION | DOMAINE ANGLAIS | DU FRANÇAIS À L'ANGLAIS [*vertical rule*] DE L'ANGLAIS AU FRANÇAIS | NOTES ET COMMENTAIRES DE | L. LECOCQ ET J. RUER [*vertical rule*] H. APPIA ET H. KERST | [*two lines*] | AVEC LA COLLABORATION DE | J. DARBELNET | [*one line*] | [*rule*] | DIDIER | 4 ET 6, RUE DE LA SORBONNE | PARIS

Small royal 8vo. viii, 306 pp. $9\frac{1}{4}$ × $5\frac{7}{8}$ in.

Pp. 160–3 Flying Over London – En Avion au dessus de Londres; in English and French; published 1963.

D38 VIRGINIA WOOLF | LA MORT | DE LA PHALÈNE | NOUVELLES | TRADUITES DE L'ANGLAIS PAR | HÉLÈNE BOKANOWSKI | PRÉFACE DE SYLVÈRE LOTRINGER | ÉDITIONS DU SEUIL | 27, RUE JACOB, PARIS VIe

Large crown 8vo. 256 pp. 8 × $5\frac{1}{2}$ in.

Translations, with a preface by Sylvère Lotringer, by Hélène Bokanowski of 'A Haunted House', 'Heard on the Downs: The Genesis of Myth', 'Monday or Tuesday', 'The String Quartet', 'Blue and Green', 'Kew Gardens', 'In the Orchard', 'The Moment: Summer's Night', 'The Mark on the Wall', 'Solid Objects', 'The Death of the Moth', 'Old Mrs Grey', 'An Unwritten Novel', 'Thunder at Wembley', 'Flying over London', 'The Sun and the Fish', 'Street Haunting: A London Adventure', 'To Spain', 'Together and Apart', 'The Man Who Loved his Kind', 'The New Dress', 'A Summing Up', 'A Woman's College from Outside', 'Moments of Being: Slater's Pins Have No Points', 'The Lady in the Looking Glass', 'The Legacy', 'Lappin and Lapinova', 'The Shooting Party', 'The Duchess and the Jeweller', 'The Searchlight'; published 1968.

A translation by Madeleine Brémont entitled *La Mort de l'Ephémère* was advertised on the wrapper of *La Maison hantée*, Paris, Charlot, 1946 but does not appear to have been published.

D39 VIRGINIA WOOLF | L'OEUVRE | ROMANESQUE | [*ornament*] | LA CHAMBRE DE JACOB | MRS DALLOWAY | LA PROMENADE AU PHARE | STOCK

Medium 8vo. xii, 516 pp. $8\frac{1}{2}$ × $5\frac{3}{4}$ in.

Translations of *Jacob's Room*, by Jean Talva – *Mrs Dalloway*, by S. David, with a preface by André Maurois – *To the Lighthouse*, by M. Lanoire, with a preface by Monique Nathan; published 1973.

D40 VIRGINIA WOOLF | L'OEUVRE | ROMANESQUE | [*ornaments*] | ORLANDO | LES VAGUES | ENTRE LES ACTES | STOCK

Medium 8vo. 560 pp. $8\frac{1}{2}$ × $5\frac{3}{4}$ in.

Translations of *Orlando*, by Charles Mauron, with a preface by Diane de Margerie – *The Waves*, by Marguerite Yourcenar – *Between the Acts*, by Charles Cestre, with a preface by Max-Pol Fouchet; published 1974.

D41 VIRGINIA WOOLF | ESSAIS | TRADUIT DE L'ANGLAIS PAR | CLAUDINE JARDIN | ET FLORENCE HERBULOT | PRÉFACE DE CLAUDINE JARDIN | SEGHERS

Large crown 8vo. 316 pp. 8 × $5\frac{1}{4}$ in.

Translations, with a preface by Claudine Jardin, by Claudine Jardin and Florence Herbulot of 'Jane Austin', '*Jane Eyre* and *Wuthering Heights*', 'George Eliot', 'The Novels of George Meredith', 'The Novels of Thomas Hardy', 'Henry James: I, *Within the Rim*; II, 'The Old Order'; III. 'The Letters of Henry James', 'Joseph Conrad', 'Notes on D. H. Lawrence', 'A Terribly Sensitive Mind', 'The Modern Essay', 'Life and the Novelist', 'The Anatomy of Fiction', 'The Patron and the

Crocus', 'Middlebrow', 'Professions for Women', 'Montaigne', 'Madame de Sévigné', 'De Quincey's Autobiography', 'Poe's Helen', 'Visits to Walt Whitman', 'A Talk About Memoirs', 'The Art of Biography', 'The New Biography'; published Paris, 1976.

D42 *a.* VIRGINIA WOOLF | TROIS GUINÉES | TRADUIT DE L'ANGLAIS | PAR | VIVIANE FORRESTER | DES FEMMES

Crown 8vo. 336 pp. 7 × $5\frac{3}{8}$ in.

A translation by Viviane Forrester of *Three Guineas*, with an introduction by the translator entitled 'L'Autre Corps'; published Paris, 1977.

*b.* VIRGINIA WOOLF | TROIS GUINÉES | SUIVI DE | L'AUTRE CORPS | PAR | VIVIANE FORRESTER | DES FEMMES

Foolscap 8vo. 320 pp. 7 × $4\frac{1}{4}$ in. (Pour Chacune, 19). Translation by Viviane Forrester; published Paris, 1978.

D43 VIRGINIA WOOLF | INSTANTS DE VIE | TRADUIT DE L'ANGLAIS | PAR | COLETTE-MARIE HUET | PRÉFACE DE VIVIANE FORRESTER | LE CABINET COSMOPOLITE | STOCK*

Narrow large crown 8vo. 364 pp. $7\frac{3}{4}$ × $4\frac{3}{4}$ in.

A translation by Colette-Marie Huet, with a preface by Viviane Forrester, of *Moments of Being*; published Paris, 1977. The Introduction, Appendix and Index are omitted.

D43 .1 VIRGINIA WOOLF | L'OEUVRE | ROMANESQUE | [*ornaments*] | FLUSH | ANNÉES | INSTANTS DE VIE | PRÉFACE DE VIVIANE FORRESTER | STOCK

Medium 8vo. [ii], 698 pp. $8\frac{1}{2}$ × $5\frac{3}{4}$ in.

Translations of *Flush*, by Charles Mauron, with a preface by Louis Gillet, *The Years*, by Germaine Delamain, with a preface by René Lalou, *Moments of Being*, by Colette-Marie Huet, with a preface by Viviane Forrester; published 1979.

## *Periodicals*

D44 LE TEMPS PASSE. *Commerce*, Paris, hiver 1926, Cahier 10, 91-133.

A translation by Charles Mauron of 'Time Passes' from *To the Lighthouse*. See also D23.

D45 LA CHAMBRE DE JACOB – FRAGMENTS. *Bibliothèque universelle et Revue de Genève*, décembre 1926, 119, 682-702 (with preliminary note, 681-682 by Marie Kieffer, and Remarques, 805 by Claude Dravaine), janvier et février 1927, 120, 28-50, 198-220.

D46 LA CHAMBRE DE JACOB. *La Revue nouvelle*, Paris, 3e Année, No. 28, mars 1927, 27-37.

A translation by Claude Dravaine and Marie Kieffer of *Jacob's Room*, Chapter 8. See also D29.

D47 LA CHAMBRE DE JACOB. *Revue politique et littéraire: Revue bleue*, Paris, 6 aout 1927, 462–5.

A translation by Claude Dravaine and Marie Kieffer of an extract from *Jacob's Room*, Chapter 1. See also D29.

D48 JARDINS DE KEW. *Nouvelles littéraires*, Paris, 13 aout 1927, 4.

A translation by Georgette Camille of *Kew Gardens*. See also D31.

D49 LE QUATUOR À CORDES. *La Revue nouvelle*, Paris, octobre 1928, 41–5.

A translation by Georgette Camille of 'The String Quartet'. See also D31.

D50 QUAND ON NE SAIT PAS LE FRANÇAIS . . . *Figaro*, Paris, 10 février 1929, 1–2.

A translation of 'On Not Knowing French'.

D51 LA SOIRÉE DU DOCTEUR BURNEY. *Figaro*, Paris, 19 aout 1929, 4; 20 aout, 4; 22 aout, 4; and 23 aout, 4.

A translation by J. Fournier-Pargoire of 'Dr Burney's Evening Party'.

D52 COWPER ET LADY AUSTEN. *Figaro*, Paris, 22 septembre 1929, 4; and 23 septembre, 4.

A translation by J. Fournier-Pargoire of 'Cowper and Lady Austen'.

D53 LE BEAU BRUMMELL. *Figaro*, Paris, 14 octobre 1929, 4; and 15 octobre, 4.

A translation by J. Fournier-Pargoire of *Beau Brummell.*

D54 LE SIGNE SUR LE MUR. *Revue européenne*, Paris, 1 décembre 1929, 505–14.

A translation by Yves de Longevialle of *The Mark on the Wall.* See also D31.

D55 LES EPINGLES DE CHEZ SLATER NE PIQUENT PAS. *Échanges*, Paris, No. 1, décembre 1929, 38–44.

A translation by Georgette Camille of 'Slater's Pins have No Points'. See also D31.

D56 DOROTHY WORDSWORTH. *Figaro*, Paris, 5 mai 1930, 6; and 6 mai, 10.

A translation by J. Fournier-Pargoire of 'Dorothy Wordsworth'.

D57 LES ESSAIS D'AUGUSTIN BIRRELL. *Figaro*, Paris, 28 aout 1930, 5; and 29 aout, 5.

A translation by J. Fournier-Pargoire of 'Augustine Birrell'.

D58 LA DEMI-SOEUR DE FANNY BURNEY. *Figaro*, Paris, 16 fevrier 1931, 6; 17 fevrier, 10; and 18 fevrier, 7.

A translation by J. Fournier-Pargoire of 'Fanny Burney's Half-Sister'.

D59 EDMOND GOSSE. *Figaro*, Paris, 5 aout 1931, 5.

A translation by J. Fournier-Pargoire of 'Edmund Gosse'.

D60 LA FIN DU GRAND GEL. *Échanges*, Paris, No. 4, 1931, 11–18.

A translation by Charles Mauron of an extract from *Orlando*. See also D24.

D61 UN ROMAN-POEME "AURORA LEIGH". *Figaro*, Paris, 5 janvier 1932, 7; 6 janvier, 8; and 7 janvier, 4.

A translation by J. Fournier-Pargoire of 'Aurora Leigh'.

D62 LA DAME DANS LE MIROIR. *Les Nouvelles littéraires*, Paris, 8 octobre 1932, 4.

A translation by Simone David of 'The Lady in the Looking Glass'. See also D31.

D63 VIE DE FLUSH. *Revue des Deux Mondes*, Paris, 15 novembre 1934, 24, 342–69; 1 décembre, 24, 603–31; and 15 décembre, 24, 871–900.

A translation by Charles Mauron of *Flush*. See also D26.

D64 UNE OPINION: LES ROMANS DE TOURGUÉNIEFF. *Le Mois*, Paris, 1 mars–1 avril 1935, 153–62.*

A translation of 'The Novels of Turgenev'.

D65 VAGABONDAGE: UNE AVENTURE LONDONIENNE. *Fontaine*, Algiers, Nos. 37–40, 1944, 234–46.

A translation by J.-M. Rivet and M.-P. Fouchet of *Street Haunting*.

D66 LA ROBE NEUVE. *L'Arche*, Paris, No. 9, septembre 1945, 44–53.

A translation by Hélène Bokanowski of 'The New Dress'. See also D31.

D67 JOURNAL [1925–1926–1927]. *Roman*, Saint Paul, No. 1, 1951, 9–13.

A translation by Rose Celli of extracts from *A Writer's Diary*. See also D35.

D68 MADAME DE SÉVIGNÉ. *La Nouvelle Nouvelle Revue française*, Paris, Iième Année, No. 11, 1 novembre 1953, 945–9.

A translation by Madeleine Brémont of 'Madame de Sévigné'.

## GERMAN

*Books*

D69 *a.* VIRGINIA WOOLF | [*rule*] | EINE FRAU VON FÜNFZIG JAHREN | ~ MRS. DALLOWAY ~ | EIN ROMAN | ÜBER-

TRAGEN VON TH. MUTZENBECHER | [*rule*] | IM INSEL // VERLAG ZU LEIPZIG | 1928

Small crown 8vo. 280 pp. $7\frac{5}{8} \times 4\frac{3}{4}$ in.

A translation by Therese Mutzenbecher of *Mrs Dalloway*.

*b.* VIRGINIA WOOLF | MRS. DALLOWAY | ROMAN | 1955 | [*rule*] | S. FISCHER VERLAG

Small crown 8vo. 244 pp. $7\frac{1}{2} \times 4\frac{5}{8}$ in.

Translation by Herberth E. and Marlys Herlitschka. Both translations of *Mrs Dalloway* were authorised. Reprinted in 1977 by Fischer Taschenbuch Verlag.

*c.* VIRGINIA WOOLF | MRS. DALLOWAY | ROMAN | FISCHER BÜCHEREI

Small crown 8vo. 160 pp. (Fischer Bücherei, 632).

Translation by Herberth E. and Marlys Herlitschka; published Frankfurt-am-Main, 1964.

*d.* VIRGINIA WOOLF | MRS. DALLOWAY | ROMAN | 1977 | INSEL-VERLAG · LEIPZIG

Crown 8vo. 258 pp. $7\frac{1}{2} \times 4\frac{5}{8}$ in.

Translation by Therese Mutzenbecher, with conclusion and notes by Wolfgang Wicht.

D70 ORLANDO | DIE GESCHICHTE EINES LEBENS | VON
*a.* | VIRGINIA WOOLF | ÜBERTRAGEN VON KARL LERBS | [*rule*] | IM INSEL-VERLAG ZU LEIPZIG

Small crown 8vo. 340 pp. $7\frac{5}{8} \times 4\frac{3}{4}$ in.

A translation by Karl Lerbs of *Orlando*; published 1929.

*b.* VIRGINIA WOOLF | ORLANDO | EINE BIOGRAPHIE | 1961 | S. FISCHER VERLAG

Small crown 8vo. 292 pp. $7\frac{1}{2} \times 4$ in.

Translation by Herberth E. and Marlys Herlitschka. Both translations of *Orlando* were authorised. Reprinted in 1961 by Moderner Buchklub and in 1964 by Fischer Verlag as *Die Bücher der Neunzehn*, Vol. 119.

*c.* VIRGINIA WOOLF | ORLANDO | EINE BIOGRAPHIE | FISCHER TASCHENBUCH VERLAG

Foolscap 8vo. 234 pp. $7\frac{1}{8} \times 4\frac{1}{8}$ in.

Translation by Herberth E. and Marlys Herlitschka; published Frankfurt-am-Main, 1977.

D71 VIRGINIA WOOLF | DIE FAHRT ZUM LEUCHTTURM |
*a.* EIN ROMAN | ÜBERTRAGEN VON KARL LERBS | [*rule*] | IM INSEL-VERLAG ZU LEIPZIG

Crown 8vo. 292 pp. $8 \times 4\frac{3}{4}$ in.

A translation by Karl Lerbs of *To the Lighthouse*; published 1931.

*b.* VIRGINIA WOOLF | DIE FAHRT | ZUM LEUCHTTURM | ROMAN | 1956 | [*rule*] | S. FISCHER VERLAG

Small crown 8vo. 256 pp. $7\frac{1}{2} \times 4\frac{1}{2}$ in.

Translation by Herberth E. and Marlys Herlitschka. Both translations of *To the Lighthouse* were authorised.

D72 VIRGINIA WOOLF | FLUSH | DIE GESCHICHTE EINES
*a.* BERÜHMTEN HUNDES | MIT 6 ZEICHNUNGEN VON RENÉE SINTENIS | S. FISCHER VERLAG | BERLIN*

Small crown 8vo. 184 pp. $7\frac{3}{4} \times 4\frac{3}{8}$ in.

A translation by Herberth E. and Marlys Herlitschka of *Flush*; published 1934.

*b.* VIRGINIA WOOLF | FLUSH | DIE GESCHICHTE | EINES BERÜHMTEN HUNDES | FISCHER BÜCHEREI

Foolscap 8vo. 160 pp. 4 plates. $7\frac{1}{8} \times 4\frac{1}{4}$ in. (Fischer Bücherei, 166).

Translation by Herberth E. and Marlys Herlitschka; published Frankfurt-am-Main and Hamburg, 1957.

*c.* VIRGINIA WOOLF | FLUSH | DIE GESCHICHTE | EINES BERÜHMTEN HUNDES | MIT EINEM NACHWORT VON | GÜNTER BLÖCKER | S. FISCHER VERLAG

Small crown 8vo. 176 pp. $7\frac{1}{2} \times 4\frac{1}{2}$ in.

Translation by Herberth E. and Marlys Herlitschka, with a postscript by Günter Blöcker; published Frankfurt-am-Main, 1977.

D73 VIRGINIA WOOLF | DIE JAHRE | ROMAN | 1954 | [*rule*]
*a.* | S. FISCHER VERLAG

Small crown 8vo. 452 pp. $7\frac{1}{2} \times 4\frac{5}{8}$ in.

A translation by Herberth E. and Marlys Herlitschka of *The Years.*

*b.* VIRGINIA WOOLF | DIE JAHRE | ROMAN | FISCHER TASCHENBUCH VERLAG

Foolscap 8vo. 376 pp. $7 \times 4\frac{1}{8}$ in.

Translation by Herberth E. and Marlys Herlitschka; published Frankfurt-am-Main, 1979.

D74 DER SCHIEFE TURM. MÜNCHEN, LANGEN/MÜLLER, 1957*

Small crown 8vo. 68 pp. $7\frac{1}{4} \times 4\frac{3}{8}$ in. (Kleine Geschenkbücher, 65).

Translations by Herberth E. and Marlys Herlitschka of 'The Death of the Moth', 'The Moment: Summer's Night', 'Old Mrs Grey', 'Middlebrow: A Letter Written but Not Sent' and 'The Leaning Tower'.

D75 VIRGINIA WOOLF | DIE WELLEN | ROMAN | 1959 | [*rule*] | S. FISCHER VERLAG

Small crown 8vo. 296 pp. $7\frac{1}{2} \times 4\frac{1}{2}$ in.

A translation by Herberth E. and Marlys Herlitschka of *The Waves*; published Frankfurt-am-Main. Reprinted in 1962 by Moderner Buchklub and in 1964 by Suhrkamp.

D76 MODERNE ENGLISCHE KURZGESCHICHTEN | EDITION LANGEWIESCHE-BRANDT

Small crown 8vo. 152 pp. $7\frac{1}{4} \times 4\frac{1}{2}$ in.

Pp. 22–43 translation by Friedrich Bralitz of 'The Duchess and the Jeweller'; in German and English; published Munich, 1960. See also D77.

D77 DIE DAME IM SPIEGEL, ÜBERTRAGEN VON HERBERTH UND MARLYS HERLITSCHKA. FRANKFURT-AM-MAIN, INSEL-VERLAG, 1960*

Small crown 8vo. 59 pp. $7\frac{1}{4} \times 4\frac{1}{2}$ in. (Insel-Bücherei).

Translations by Herberth E. and Marlys Herlitschka of 'The Lady in the Looking Glass', 'The Duchess and the Jeweller', 'The Searchlight', 'The Legacy' and 'The Shooting Party'.

D78 VIRGINIA WOOLF | GRANIT UND REGENBOGEN | ESSAYS | SUHRKAMP VERLAG | BERLIN UND FRANKFURT AM MAIN

Small crown 8vo. 192 pp. $7\frac{1}{8} \times 4\frac{1}{2}$ in.

Translations by Herberth E. Herlitschka of 'How Should One Read a Book?', 'Reviewing', 'Poetry, Fiction and the Future', 'Is Fiction an Art?', 'Phases of Fiction', 'On Re-Reading Novels' and 'Character in Fiction'; published 1960.

D79 VIRGINIA WOOLF | ZWISCHEN DEN | AKTEN | 1963 | S. FISCHER VERLAG

Small crown 8vo. 204 pp. $7\frac{1}{2} \times 4\frac{1}{2}$ in.

A translation by Herberth E. and Marlys Herlitschka of *Between the Acts*, with forewords by Leonard Woolf and the translators; published Frankfurt-am-Main. Reprinted in 1978 by Fischer Taschenbuch Verlag.

D80 VIRGINIA WOOLF | DIE ERZÄHLUNGEN | UND | FLUSH | 1965 | S. FISCHER VERLAG

Small crown 8vo. 292 pp. 4 plates. $7\frac{1}{2} \times 4\frac{1}{2}$ in.

Translations by Herberth E. and Marlys Herlitschka, with a foreword by Leonard Woolf, of *A Haunted House and Other Short Stories* and *Flush*; published Frankfurt-am-Main.

D81 VIRGINIA WOOLF | DIE DAME IM SPIEGEL | UND ANDERE ERZÄHLUNGEN | FISHER TASCHENBUCH VERLAG

Foolscap 8vo. [ii], 174 pp. $7 \times 4\frac{1}{4}$ in.

A translation by Herberth E. and Marlys Herlitschka of *A Haunted House and Other Short Stories*; published Frankfurt-am-Main, 1978.

D82 VIRGINIA WOOLF | EIN ZIMMER FÜR SICH ALLEIN | GERHARDT VERLAG

Foolscap 4to. 118 pp. illus. 8 × $6\frac{1}{2}$ in.

A translation by Renate Gerhardt of *A Room of One's Own*, with the poems translated by Wulf Teichmann; translation of Louie Mayer's reminiscences from *Recollections of Virginia Woolf*, edited by Joan Russell Noble added as a postscript; published Berlin, 1978.

D82 .1 VIRGINIA WOOLF | DREI GUINEEN

Small crown 8vo. 216 pp. $7\frac{3}{8}$ × $4\frac{3}{4}$ in.

A translation by Anita Eichholz of *Three Guineas*; published by Verlag Frauenoffensive, Munich, 1978.

*Periodicals*

D83 EINE UNGESCHRIEBENE GESCHICHTE. *Die neue Rundschau*, Berlin, Leipzig, Bd. 1, 1929, 628–41.

A translation by Hans B. Wagenseil of 'An Unwritten Novel'.

D84 DER MODERNE ENGLISCHE ROMAN. *Die neue Rundschau*, Berlin, Leipzig, Juli 1930, 112–20.

A translation by Hans B. Wagenseil of 'Modern Novels'.

D85 JOSEPH CONRAD. *Almanach*, Berlin, S. Fischer Verlag, 48. J. 1934, 94–102.*

A translation by Kathe Rosenberg of 'Joseph Conrad'. See also D93.

D86 DER BEAU. *Karussel*, Kassel, 1. J. Folge 5, November 1946, 26–32.*

A translation by Hans B. Wagenseil of *Beau Brummell.*

D87 EINE UNGESCHRIEBENE GESCHICHTE. *Erzähler von Drüben*, Wiesbaden, Bd. 2, 1947, 84–100.*

A translation by Hans B. Wagenseil of 'An Unwritten Novel'.

D88 DER GENEIGTE LESER UND DER KROKUS. *Aufbau*, Berlin, 3. J. Heft 10, Oktober 1947, 261–3.*

A translation by Kurt Wagenseil of 'The Patron and the Crocus'.

D89 LEBEN EINES BEAU. *Erzähler von Drüben*, Wiesbaden, 3. Bd., 1948, 112–16.*

A translation by Hans B. Wagenseil of *Beau Brummell.*

D90 DER RUSSISCHE STANDPUNKT. *Literarische Revue*, Munich, 3. J. Heft 9, 1948, 541–8.*

A translation by Kurt Wagenseil of 'The Russian Point of View'.

D91 DAS STREICHQUARTETT. *Prisma*, Munich, Heft 17, 1948, 7–8.*

A translation by Hans B. Wagenseil of 'The String Quartet'.

D92 ANREGUNG DURCH BILDER, *Sonntag*, Berlin, 4. J. Nr. 2, 9 Januar 1949, 2.*

A translation by Theodor Rocholt of 'Pictures'.

D93 JOSEPH CONRAD. *Berliner Hefte für geistiges Leben*, N.F. 4. J. Heft 7, 1949, 70–5.*

A translation by Hans B. Wagenseil of 'Joseph Conrad'. See also D85.

D94 ARNOLD BENNETT UND FRAU BROWN. *Die neue Rundschau*, Amsterdam, Frankfurt a. M. 61. J. Heft 2, 1950, 215–35.

A translation by Friedrich Burschell of 'Character in Fiction'. See also D78.

D95 ZWEI ERZÄHLUNGEN. *Die neue Rundschau*, Frankfurt a. M. 63. J. 1952, 396–407.

A translation by Herberth E. and Marlys Herlitschka of 'The Searchlight' and 'The Legacy'. See also D77.

D96 VERFRÜHTER BESUCH. *Almanach*, Berlin, S. Fischer Verlag, 67. J. 1953, 110–15.*

A translation by Herberth E. and Marlys Herlitschka of an extract from *The Years*, published by Fischer. See also D73.

D97 SO STAND SIE DA UND SANN. *Die Welt*, Hamburg, 21 November 1953, 20.*

A translation by Herberth E. and Marlys Herlitschka of 'The Lady in the Looking Glass'. See also D77.

D98 DER TOD DES NACHTFALTERS. *Almanach*, Frankfurt a. M., S. Fischer Verlag, 68. J. 1954, 133–6.*

A translation by Herberth E. and Marlys Herlitschka of 'The Death of the Moth'.

D99 AUS DEN TAGEBÜCHERN. *Die neue Rundschau*, Frankfurt a. M. 66. J. 1955, 136–56, 316–48.

A translation by Herberth E. and Marlys Herlitschka of extracts from *A Writer's Diary*.

D100 DIE JAGDGESELLSCHAFT. *Die neue Rundschau*, Frankfurt a. M., 1960, Heft 2, 214–22.

A translation by Herberth E. and Marlys Herlitschka of 'The Shooting Party'.

## GREEK

### *Periodicals*

D101 TO STOIHEIŌMENO SPITI. *Nea Hestia*, Athens, Vol. 39, No. 444, 1946, 22–3.

A translation by Sofia Papasunesiou of 'A Haunted House'.

D102 TA KUMATA. *Nea Hestia*, Athens, Vol. 43, No. 495, 1948, 224–32.

A translation by Dēmētrēs Staurou of extracts from *The Waves.*

D103 LA MAISON DE L'OMBRE – LUNDI OU MARDI. *Prosperos*, Corfu, Vol. 1, 1949, 11–18.*

Translations by Marie Aspioti and Michael Desyllas of 'A Haunted House' and 'Monday or Tuesday'; in Greek.

D104 EIKONES TREIS. *Nea Hestia*, Athens, Vol. 45, No. 516, 1949, 80–2.

A translation by Geōrgos Delios of 'Three Pictures'.

D105 Ē KURIA KI O KATHREFTĒS. *Nea Hestia*, Athens, Vol. 47, No. 544, 310–12.

A translation by Sofia Papasunesiou and Errikos Hatzēanestēs of 'The Lady in the Looking Glass'.

D106 OI KARFITSES TĒS SLATER DEN TRUPOUN. *Nea Hestia*, Athens, Vol. 54, No. 635, 1953, 87–91.

A translation by Geōrgos Delios of 'Slater's Pins Have No Points'.

D107 APO TO ĒMEROLOGIO TĒS [1940–1941]. *Nea Hestia*, Athens, Vol. 57, No. 661, 1955, 117–18; and No. 662, 179–81.

A translation by Geōrgos Delios of extracts from *A Writer's Diary.*

D108 FRAGMENT TRADUIT DE LA PROMENADE AU PHARE. *Prosperos*, Corfu, Vol. 7, 1957, 231–5.*

A translation by Marie Aspioti and Michael Desyllas of an extract from *To the Lighthouse*; in Greek.

## HEBREW

### *Books*

D109 VIRGINIAH WOOLF | ORLANDO | BIYOGRAPHIYAH | [*device*] | HOSA'ATH MAḤBAROTH LE-SIPHRUTH

Small demy 8vo. 244 pp. $8\frac{1}{2} \times 5\frac{3}{8}$ in.

A translation by Ṣviy Arad of *Orlando*; published Tel-Aviv, 1964. Reprinted in 1974 by Machbarot Lesifrut Ltd.

D110 VIRGINIA WOOLF | FLUSH | KOROT CHAYAV | HOTZAAT DVIR

Foolscap 8vo. [viii], 124 pp. $7 \times 4\frac{1}{4}$ in.

A translation by Ch. Kalai of *Flush*; published by Hotzaat Dvir, Tel-Aviv, 1973.

D111 VIRGINIA WOOLF | MARAT DALLOWAY | TARGUM ME'ANGLIT VE'ACHARIT DAVAR | RINA LITVIN | ZMURAH, BEITAN, MUDAN – HOTZAAH LE'OR | [*long rule*] | TEL AVIV

Large crown 8vo. 180 pp. $8\frac{1}{8} \times 5\frac{1}{4}$ in.

A translation by Rina Litvin of *Mrs Dalloway*; published by Machbarot Lesifrut Publishing House, 1974.

D112 VIRGINIA WOOLF | EL HA'MIGDALOR | ME'ANGLIT: MEIR WIESELTIER | SIFREI SIMAN KRIAH | MIFALIM UNIVERSITAIIM LE'HOTZAAH LE'OR | HAMIFAL LETARGUM SIFREI MOFET | HA'MOATZA HA'TZIBURIT LE'TARBUT UL'OMANUT | [*at left of last three lines:*] M

Large crown 8vo. [ii], 218 pp. $8\frac{1}{2} \times 5\frac{3}{8}$ in.

A translation by Meir Wieseltier of *To the Lighthouse*; published by Mifalim Universitaiim Le'Hotzaah Le'Or, Tel-Aviv, 1975.

## HUNGARIAN

### *Books*

D113 VIRGINIA WOOLF | ÉVEK | ELSŐ KÖTET | [*Vol.* 1; *Vol.* 2 MÁSODIK KÖTET] FRANKLIN-TÁRSULAT KIADÁSA

Small crown 8vo. 2 vols. Vol. 1: 240 pp. Vol. 2: 228 pp. $7\frac{3}{8} \times 4\frac{5}{8}$ in.

A translation by András Hevesi, with an introduction by Aladár Schöpflin, of *The Years*; published Budapest, 1940.

D114 VIRGINIA WOOLF | ORLANDO | REGÉNY | RÉVAI

*a.* Crown 8vo. 340 pp. $7\frac{1}{4} \times 5$ in.

A translation by Nándor Szávai, with postscript by Albert Gyergyai, of *Orlando*; published Budapest, 1945.

*b.* VIRGINIA WOOLF | ORLANDO | [*monogram*] | EURÓPA KÖNYVIADÓ | BUDAPEST 1966

Foolscap 8vo. 264 pp. 16 plates. $6\frac{1}{8} \times 4\frac{3}{4}$ in. (Világrész Könyvei, 5).

Translation by Nándor Szávai, with postscript by Albert Gyergyai. Reprinted in 1977 in the series *Olcsó Könyvtár.*

D115 [*in black:*] VIRGINIA WOOLF | [*in red:*] FLUSH | [*in*
*a.* *black:*] REGÉNY | RÉVAI

Foolscap 8vo. 160 pp. $6\frac{7}{8} \times 4\frac{1}{8}$ in.

A translation by György Rónay of *Flush*; published Budapest, 1947.

*b.* VIRGINIA WOOLF | FLUSH | II. KIADÁS | MAGVETÖ KÖNYVKIADÓ | BUDAPEST 1957

Foolscap 8vo. 192 pp. 4 illus. $6\frac{1}{2} \times 4\frac{3}{4}$ in.

Translation by György Rónay.

*c.* VIRGINIA | WOOLF | [*in pale orange:*] FLUSH | [*in black:*] FORDÍTOTTA | RÓNAY GYÖRGY | ILLUSZTRÁLTA | KOVÁCS TAMAS | [*device in pale orange*] | MAGYAR HELIKON | 1976

Small crown 8vo. 120 pp. 4 plates (col.). $7\frac{1}{4} \times 4\frac{3}{4}$ in.

Translation by György Rónay; published Budapest.

D116 *a.* VIRGINIA WOOLF | CLARISSA | FRANKLIN-TÁRSULAT KIADÁSA

Small crown 8vo. 240 pp. $7\frac{3}{8} \times 4\frac{3}{4}$ in. (Külföldi Regények).

A translation by István Nagypál of *Mrs Dalloway*; published Budapest, 1948.

*b.* VIRGINIA | WOOLF | MRS. DALLOWAY | FORDÍTOTTA | TANDORI DEZSÖ | MAGYAR HELIKON | 1971

Foolscap 8vo. 404 pp. $5\frac{1}{4} \times 3$ in.

Translation by Dezsö Tandori; published Budapest.

D116 .1 ÍRÓK ÍRÓKRÓL | [*rule*] | [*list of essays translated in sixteen lines*] | EURÓPA*

756 pp.

An anthology entitled *Authors from Authors.* Pp. 302–15 'Jane Austen' translated by Adam Réz; published Budapest, 1970.

D117 VIRGINIA WOOLF | [*in red:*] A VILÁGÍTÓTORONY | [*in black:*] MAGVETŐ KIADÓ, BUDAPEST

Small crown 8vo. 264 pp. front. (port.). $7\frac{1}{8} \times 4\frac{3}{4}$ in.

A translation by Sándor Mátyás of *To the Lighthouse*; published 1971.

D117 .1 VIRGINIA WOOLF | HULLÁMOK | EURÓPA KÖNYV-KIADÓ | BUDAPEST 1978

Small crown 8vo. 292 pp. $7 \times 4\frac{3}{4}$ in.

A translation by Sándor Mátyás of *The Waves.*

## ITALIAN

### *Books*

D118 *a.* [*within a quadruple rule in green: in black:*] ORLANDO | ROMANZO | DI | VIRGINIA WOOLF | [*ornament*] | A. MONDADORI · EDITORE | [*irregular rule*] | 1 · 9 · 3 · 3

Small crown 8vo. 304 pp. 8 plates. $7\frac{5}{8} \times 4\frac{5}{8}$ in. (Medusa, 15).

A translation by Alessandra Scalero of *Orlando.* Reprinted in 1974 by Mondadori in *I Capolavori della Medusa*, Seconda Serie.

*b.* VIRGINIA WOOLF | ORLANDO | GARZANTI

Foolscap 8vo. xvi, 236 pp. port. $7 \times 4\frac{1}{4}$ in. (I Grandi Libri, 220).

Translation by Alessandra Scalero, with a preface by Attilio Bertolucci; published Milan, 1978.

D119 *a.* VIRGINIA WOOLF | GITA AL FARO | ROMANZO | TRADUZIONE DALL'INGLESE DI GIULIA CELENZA |

PREFAZIONE DI EMILIO CECCHI | [*device*] | MILANO | FRATELLI TREVES EDITORI | 1934 – XII

Small crown 8vo. xii, 292 pp. $7\frac{1}{8} \times 4\frac{3}{8}$ in.

A translation by Giulia Celenza of *To the Lighthouse*.

*b.* VIRGINIA WOOLF | GITA AL FARO | ROMANZO | GARZANTI

Crown 8vo. [iv], 264 pp. $7\frac{5}{8} \times 5$ in. (Romanzi moderni Garzanti).

Translation by Giulia Celenza; published Milan, 1954.

*c.* VIRGINIA WOOLF | GITA AL FARO | ROMANZO | GARZANTI

Small crown 8vo. 232 pp. $7\frac{1}{2} \times 4\frac{3}{4}$ in.

Translation by Giulia Celenza; published Milan, 1965. Reprinted in 1971 in the series *I Garzanti*, with an introduction.

D120 [*within a quadruple rule in green: in black:*] FLUSH | VITA DI UN CANE | DI | VIRGINIA WOOLF | [*ornament*] | A. MONDADORI · MILANO | [*irregular rule*] | 1 · 9 · 3 · 4

Small crown 8vo. 224 pp. front. 9 plates. $7\frac{3}{4} \times 4\frac{5}{8}$ in. (Medusa, 41).

A translation by Alessandra Scalero of *Flush.*

D121 *a.* [*within a compartment: in black:*] VIRGINIA WOOLF | [*in pink:*] LA SIGNORA | DALLOWAY | [*in black:*] CON | OTTO ILLUSTRAZIONI | DI | LUIGI BROGGINI | [*device in pink*] | [*in black:*] ARNOLDO MONDADORI | EDITORE

Large crown 8vo. 288 pp. 8 plates (included in the pagination). $8 \times 5\frac{1}{2}$ in. (Il ponte i grandi narratori italiani e stranieri).

A translation by Alessandro Scalero of *Mrs Dalloway*; published 1946.

*b.* VIRGINIA WOOLF | LA SIGNORA DALLOWAY | A CURA DI SERGIO PEROSA | TRADUZIONE DI ALESSANDRA SCALERO | ARNOLDO MONDADORI EDITORE

Foolscap 8vo. xlviii, 224pp. illus. $7\frac{1}{4} \times 4\frac{1}{4}$ in. (Oscar Biblioteca).

Translation by Alessandra Scalero; published 1979.

D122 [*within a compartment: in black:*] VIRGINIA WOOLF | [*in pink:*] LA CAMERA | DI GIACOBBE | [*in black:*] CON OTTO ILLUSTRAZIONI | DI | CARLO DE ROBERTO | [*device in pink*] | [*in black:*] ARNOLDO MONDADORI | EDITORE

Large crown 8vo. 256 pp. 8 coloured plates, 14 illus. $8 \times 5\frac{1}{2}$ in. (Il ponte i grandi narratori italiani e stranieri, 24).

A translation by Anna Banti of *Jacob's Room*; published 1950.

D123 [*within a triple rule in green: in black:*] LA CASA | DEGLI SPIRITI | DI | VIRGINIA WOOLF | [*ornament*] | ARNOLDO MONDADORI EDITORE | [*irregular rule*] | 1 · 9 · 5 · 0

Small crown 8vo. 224 pp. $7\frac{5}{8} \times 4\frac{5}{8}$ in. (Medusa, 252).

A translation by Desideria Pasolini of *A Haunted House and Other Short Stories.*

D124 [*within a triple rule in green: in black:*] GLI ANNI | ROMANZO | DI | VIRGINIA WOOLF | [*ornament*] | ARNOLDO MONDADORI EDITORE | [*irregular rule*] | 1 · 9 · 5 · 5

Small crown 8vo. 412 pp. $7\frac{1}{2} \times 4\frac{1}{2}$ in. (Medusa, 345).

A translation by Giulio de Angelis of *The Years.*

D125 [*within a triple rule in green: in black:*] LE ONDE | ROMAN-
*a.* ZO | DI | VIRGINIA WOOLF | [*ornament*] | ARNOLDO MONDADORI EDITORE | [*irregular rule*] | 1 · 9 · 5 · 6

Small crown 8vo. 254 pp. $7\frac{1}{2} \times 4\frac{1}{2}$ in. (Medusa, 375).

A translation by Giulio de Angelis of *The Waves.*

*b.* VIRGINIA WOOLF | LE ONDE | INTRODUZIONE DI STEPHEN SPENDER | TRADUZIONE DI GIULIO DE ANGELIS | CRONOLOGIA, GIUDIZI CRITICI E BIBLIOGRAFIA | A CURA DI FRANCO MARUCCI | BIBLIOTECA UNIVERSALE RIZZOLI

Foolscap 8vo. [vi], 246 pp. port. $7 \times 4\frac{1}{4}$ in.

Translation by Giulio de Angelis, with an introduction by Stephen Spender and a chronology, critical guide and bibliography edited by Franco Marucci; published Milan, 1979.

D126 VIRGINIA WOOLF | LA CROCIERA | RIZZOLI-EDITORE

Foolscap 8vo. 400 pp. $6\frac{1}{4} \times 4\frac{1}{8}$ in. (Biblioteca universale Rizzoli, 995–8).

A translation by Oriana Previtali of *The Voyage Out*; published Milan, 1956.

D127 VIRGINIA WOOLF | NOTTE E GIORNO | ROMANZO | [*monogram*] | MILANO*

Large crown 8vo. 292 pp. $8 \times 5\frac{1}{4}$ in.

A translation by Luisa Quintavalle Theodoli of *Night and Day*; published by Edizioni Librarie Italiane, 1957.

D128 [*within a double rule, within a frame in orange:*] VIRGINIA WOOLF | DIARIO | DI UNA SCRITTRICE | CON UNA PREFAZIONE DI LEONARD WOOLF | E 16 ILLUSTRAZIONI FUORI TESTO | ARNOLDO MONDADORI EDITORE | [*double rule*] | 1.9.5.9

Small crown 8vo. 482 pp. 8 plates. $7\frac{1}{2} \times 4\frac{1}{2}$ in. (I "Quaderni" della Medusa, 44).

A translation by Giuliana de Carlo and Vittoria Guerrini of *A Writer's Diary.*

D129 VIRGINIA WOOLF | PER LE STRADE | DI LONDRA |
*a.* TRADUZIONE DI LIVIO BACCHI WILCOCK | E. J. RODOLFO WILCOCK | [*device*] CASA EDITRICE IL SAGGIATORE

Demy 8vo. 320 pp. $8\frac{3}{8} \times 6\frac{1}{8}$ in.

Translations by Livio Bacchi and J. Rodolfo Wilcock of 'On Not Knowing Greek', 'Joseph Addison', 'Jane Austen', 'The Russian Point of View', 'The Novels of George Meredith', ' "I Am Christina Rossetti" ', 'The Novels of Thomas Hardy', 'How Should One Read a Book?' *Street Haunting: A London Adventure*, 'Madame de Sévigné', 'The Man at the Gate', 'Sara Coleridge', 'The Letters of Henry James', 'A Letter to a Young Poet', 'Thoughts on Peace in an Air Raid', 'On Being Ill', '*David Copperfield*', 'American Fiction', 'The Leaning Tower', 'Pictures', *A Room of One's Own*; published Milan, 1963. The Club degli Editori, Milan issued a reprint in 1964.

*b.* VIRGINIA WOOLF | PER LE STRADE DI LONDRA | GARZANTI*

Crown 8vo. 304 pp. $7\frac{1}{2} \times 5$ in.

Translation by Livio Bacchi Wilcock and J. Rodolfo Wilcock; published Milan, 1974.

D130 VIRGINIA WOOLF | [*in grey:*] LE TRE | GHINEE | [*in black:*] EDIZIONI LA TARTARUGA

Small crown 8vo. [ii], 230 pp. $7\frac{5}{8} \times 4\frac{5}{8}$ in.

A translation by Adriana Bottini of *Three Guineas*; published Milan, 1975.

D131 VIRGINIA WOOLF | IL DITALE D'ORO | DISEGNI DI FLAMINIA SICILIANO | [*illus.*] | EMME EDIZIONI

Crown 4to. [24] pp. illus. $9\frac{1}{2} \times 7\frac{1}{4}$ in.

A translation by Enzo Siciliano of *Nurse Lugton's Golden Thimble*; published Milan, 1976.

D132 VIRGINIA WOOLF | MOMENTI DI | ESSERE | SCRITTI AUTOBIOGRAFICI INEDITI | INTRODUZIONE E NOTE DI JEANNE SCHULKIND | LA TARTARUGA

Small crown 8vo. 260 pp. $7\frac{5}{8} \times 4\frac{3}{4}$ in.

A translation by Adriana Bottini of *Moments of Being*; published Milan, 1977.

D133 VIRGINIA WOOLF | ROMANZI E ALTRO | A CURA DI SERGIO PEROSA | [*device*] | ARNOLDO MONDADORI | EDITORE

Foolscap 8vo. xlviii, 1056 pp. $6\frac{3}{4} \times 4$ in.

Translations of *Mrs Dalloway*, by Alessandra Scalero, *To the Lighthouse*, by Giulia Celenza, *Orlando*, by Alessandra Scalero, *A Room of One's Own*, 'Pictures', 'The Leaning Tower', and 'Thoughts on Peace in an Air Raid', by Livio

Bacchi Wilcock and J. Rodolfo Wilcock, *The Letters of Virginia Woolf*, by A. Cagidemetrio and *A Writer's Diary*, by Giuliana de Carlo; published Milan, 1978.

D133 .1 [*device*] | VIRGINIA WOOLF | TRA UN ATTO E L'ALTRO | A CURA DI FRANCO CORDELLI | TRADUZIONE DI FRANCESCA WAGNER E FRANCO CORDELLI | GUANDA

Demy 8vo. 182 pp. $8\frac{5}{8} \times 5\frac{3}{8}$ in.

A translation by Francesca Wagner and Franco Cordelli of *Between the Acts*; published Milan, 1979.

D133 .2 VIRGINIA WOOLF | LA SIGNORA DELL'ANGOLO | DI FRONTE | INTRODUZIONE DI GINEVRA BOMPIANI | TRADUZIONE DI MASOLINO D'AMICO | IL SAGGIATORE

8vo. 304 pp. $8\frac{1}{4} \times 6\frac{1}{8}$ in. (Saggi di Arte e di Letteratura, 51).

Translations by Masolino d'Amico, with an introduction by Ginevra Bompiani, of 'Montaigne', 'Defoe', 'The Modern Essay', 'How It Strikes a Contemporary', 'The Pastons and Chaucer', 'Notes on an Elizabethan Play', 'George Eliot', 'Joseph Conrad', 'The Patron and the Crocus', 'The Strange Elizabethans', 'Donne after Three Centuries', 'Dorothy Osborne's Letters', 'Swift's "Journal to Stella" ', 'The "Sentimental Journey" ', 'De Quincey's Autobiography', 'Dorothy Wordsworth', 'Dr Burney's Evening Party', 'The Moment: Summer's Night', 'Personalities', 'Evening over Sussex', ' "Not One of Us" ', 'The Art of Biography', 'Phases of Fiction', 'An Essay in Criticism', 'A Friend of Johnson', 'Leslie Stephen', 'The Sun and the Fish', 'The Death of the Moth', 'The Novels of E. M. Forster', 'Lewis Carroll', 'Mr Bennett and Mrs Brown'; published Milan, 1979.

## JAPANESE

### *Books*

D134 [*within a rule:*] ORLANDO | VĀJINIA WURUFU CHO | ODA MASANOBU YAKU | [*ornament*] | SHUNYODO BAN*

Crown 8vo. 370 pp. $7\frac{3}{8} \times 5$ in.

A translation by Masanobu Oda of *Orlando*; published Tokyo, 1932.

D135 WURUFU TANPENSHU | VĀJINIA WURUFU KUZUKAWA ATSUSHI YAKU | RESSATSU SHINBUNGAKU KENKYU | KINSEIDO EDITION | IMAGAWAKIJI KANDA TŌKYŌ JAPAN*

Crown 8vo. 100 pp. $7\frac{5}{8} \times 5\frac{1}{2}$ in.

Translations by Atsushi Kuzukawa of 'The String Quartet', 'A Haunted House', *Kew Gardens*, 'Monday or Tuesday',

'The Mark on the Wall', 'Blue and Green', ' "Slater's Pins Have No Points" ', and 'Time Passes' from *To the Lighthouse*: published 1932. See also D138, 143.

D136 WURUFU BUNGAKURON | VĀJINIA WURUFU | MURAOKA TATSUJI YAKU | RESSATSU SHINBUNGAKU KENKYU HYORON BU. DAI 9 HEN | KINSEIDO EDITION | IMAGAWAKOJI KANDA TŌKYŌ JAPAN*

Crown 8vo. 98 pp. $7\frac{5}{8} \times 5\frac{1}{2}$ in.

Translations by Tatsuji Muraoka of 'Modern Novels', 'How It Strikes a Contemporary', 'The Russian Point of View', 'Joseph Conrad', ' "Jane Eyre" and "Wuthering Heights" ', and 'Modern Essays'; published 1933.

D137 SUZUKI YUKIO YAKU | VĀJINIA WURUFU YAKU |
*a.* NAMI | SHŌNAN SHOBO TŌKYŌ*

Crown 8vo. 392 pp. $7\frac{3}{8} \times 5\frac{1}{2}$ in.

A translation by Yukio Suzuki of *The Waves*; published 1943. See also D140.

*b.* [*within a rule:*] NAMI | VĀJINIA WURUFU | SUZUKI YUKIO YAKU | [*ornament*] | KADOKAWA BUNKO | 756*

Foolscap 8vo. 328 pp. $6\frac{1}{8} \times 4\frac{1}{8}$ in.

Translation by Yukio Suzuki; published Tokyo, 1954.

D138 VĀJINIA WURUFU | TŌDAI E | [TRANSLATED BY]
*a.* ŌSAWA MINORU | [*ornament*] | ONDORISHA

Crown 8vo. [vi], 302 pp. front. (port.). $7\frac{1}{4} \times 5$ in.

A translation by Minoru Ōsawa of *To the Lighthouse*, with an appreciation by Edmund Blunden; published Tokyo, 1949. See also D135, 143.

*b.* [*within a rule:*] SHINCHO BUNKO | TODAI E | VĀJINIA WURUFU | NAKAMURA SAKIKO YAKU | [*ornament*] | [*rule*] | SHINCHOSHA HAN | 974*

Foolscap 8vo. 296 pp. $6\frac{1}{8} \times 4\frac{1}{8}$ in.

Translation by Sakiko Nakamura; published Tokyo, 1956.

D139 [*within a rule:*] SHINCHŌ BUNKO | WATAKUSHI DAKE NO HEYA | JOSEI TO BUNGAKU | VĀJINIA WURUFU | NISHIKAWA MASAMI · ANDŌ ICHIRŌ YAKU | [*ornament*] | [*rule*] | SHINCHŌSHA HAN | 366

Demy 16mo. 192 pp. $6 \times 4$ in. (Josei to Bungaku).

A translation by Masami Nishikawa and Ichirō Andō of *A Room of One's Own*; published Tokyo, 1952. This translation was first published in Japan in 1942 and revised for the 1952 edition.

D140 DALLOWAY FUJIN · NAMI · TŌKYŌ, MIKASA SHOBO, 1954*

414 pp.

Translations by Minoru Ōsawa of *Mrs Dalloway* and *The Waves*. See also D137, 141, 143.

D141 *a.* [*within a rule:*] DALLOWAY FUJIN | TOMITA AKIRA YAKU | [*ornament*] | KADOKAWA BUNKO | 1073*

Foolscap 8vo. 304 pp. $6\frac{1}{8} \times 4\frac{1}{8}$ in.

A translation by Akira Tomita of *Mrs Dalloway*; published Tokyo, 1955. See also D143.

*b.* [*within a rule:*] DALLOWAY FUJIN | VĀJINIA WURUFU | ANDŌ ICHIRŌ YAKU | [*ornament*] | [*rule*] | SHINCHOSHA HAN | L*

Foolscap 8vo. 304 pp. $6\frac{1}{8} \times 4\frac{1}{8}$ in.

Translation by Ichirō Andō; published Tokyo, 1958.

D142 VĀJINIA WURUFU | GETSUYOBI KA KAYOBI · FLUSH | EIBEI MEISAKU | [*rule*] | ŌSAWA MINORU · SHIBATA TETSUO · YOSHIDA YASUO YAKU | EIHŌSHA*

Small crown 8vo. 332 pp. $6\frac{7}{8} \times 4\frac{7}{8}$ in.

Translations by Minoru Ōsawa of 'A Haunted House', 'Monday or Tuesday', 'Blue and Green', 'The String Quartet', 'The Mark on the Wall', *Kew Gardens*, 'An Unwritten Novel', 'A Conversation about Art', and by Tetsuo Shibata and Yasuo Yoshida of *Flush*; published Tokyo, 1956.

D143 TODAI E · DALLOWAY FUJIN · WAKAKI HI NO GEIZITSUKA NO SHŌZŌ · TŌKYŌ, KAWADE SHOBO SHINSHA, 1956*

399 pp. (Sekai Bungaku Zenshū, 15).

Translations by Minoru Ōsawa of *To the Lighthouse*, by Ichirō Andō of *Mrs Dalloway*, and by Kazuo Nakahashi of *A Portrait of the Artist as a Young Man*, by James Joyce.

D144 VĀJINIA WURUFU | WAKAKI SHIJIN E NO TEGAMI | ŌSAWA MINORU YAKU | [*rule*] | SŌSHO FUAN NO JIDAI | TŌKYŌ NAN'UN-DŌ KANDA

Small crown 8vo. [ii], 174 pp. plate. $7\frac{1}{4} \times 4\frac{3}{4}$ in.

Translations by Minoru Ōsawa of 'A Letter to a Young Poet', 'The Leaning Tower', 'The Artist and Politics', 'Professions for Women', 'Thoughts on Peace in an Air Raid', 'The Death of the Moth', 'How It Strikes a Contemporary', 'The Letters of Henry James', 'On Re-Reading Novels', 'Joseph Conrad', 'Notes on D. H. Lawrence', 'The Novels of E. M. Forster', and 'Is Fiction an Art?'; published 1958.

D145 VĀJINIA WURUFU | SAIGETSU | ŌSAWA MINORU YAKU | MIKASA SHOBŌ

Crown 8vo. [ii], 352 pp. front. (port.). $7\frac{1}{2} \times 5\frac{1}{4}$ in.

A translation by Minoru Ōsawa of *The Years*; published Tokyo, 1958.

D146 [*within a rule in mauve:*] 20 B NIJUSSEIKI EIBEIBUNGAKU ANNAI 10 | [*rule*] | VIRGINIA WOOLF | VĀJINIA WURUFU | ŌSAWA MINORU HEN | [*rule*] | KENKYUSHA

Small crown 8vo. [2], [ii], 278 pp. 2 plates. $6\frac{3}{4} \times 4\frac{3}{4}$ in. (Introduction to 20th Century English and American Literature, 10).

Translations of selections from *The Voyage Out*, and *Night and Day*, by Shigeru Kurozawa – *Jacob's Room*, by Tetsuo Shibata – *Mrs Dalloway*, by Ichirō Andō – *To the Lighthouse*, by Ryo Nonaka – *The Waves*, by Yukio Suzuki – *The Years*, by Misako Himuro – *Between the Acts*, by Tatsuo Matsumura – 'Kew Gardens', 'The Mark on the Wall', 'The String Quartet', 'Monday or Tuesday', 'A Haunted House', 'An Unwritten Novel', 'The Shooting Party', 'The Legacy', 'The Duchess and the Jeweller', and 'Lappin and Lapinova', translated by Tetsuo Shibata; with essays on the author by Minoru Ozawa and Hideo Kashiwagi; published Tokyo, 1966.

D147 HENSHU KAISETSŪ | SASAKI MOTOICHI | BUNGAGKU NO SŌZŌ | 5 GENDAIJIN NO SHISŌ | HEIBONSHA

Crown 8vo. [ii], 424 pp. $7\frac{1}{8} \times 5$ in. (Thought of Modern People, 5: Creation of Literature).

Pp. 122–44 a translation of 'The Leaning Tower' in the *Creation of Literature*, compiled with explanatory notes by Motoichi Sasaki; published Tokyo, 1968.

*Periodical*

D148 NIKKI-SHŌ. *Bungakukai*, Tokyo, October 1954, Vol. 8, No. 10, 102–13.

A translation, with introduction and notes, by Yūji Tanaka of extracts from *A Writer's Diary*.

## KOREAN

*Book*

D149 DALLOWAY BU'IN · SEOUL, DONG'A'CHUL'PAN'SA*

120 pp.

A translation by Ra Yeong-gyun of *Mrs Dalloway*; published 195–.

## MACEDONIAN

*Book*

D150 VIRDŽINIJA | VULF | GOSPOĐA | DELOVEJ | KULTURA | SKOPJE | 1967

Small crown 8vo. 228 pp. $7\frac{3}{8} \times 4\frac{3}{4}$ in. (Biblioteka Sovremena Proza).

A translation by Sveto Serafimov of *Mrs Dalloway*.

## D. TRANSLATIONS

### NORWEGIAN

*Books*

D151 VIRGINIA WOOLF | DE DRO TIL | FYRET | OVERSATT
*a.* AV | PETER MAGNUS | OSLO 1948 | [*rule*] | ERNST G. MORTENSENS FORLAG

Large crown 8vo. 264 pp. 8 × $5\frac{3}{8}$ in. (Serien Moderne Mestere).

A translation by Peter Magnus of *To the Lighthouse.*

*b.* DE DRO TIL FYRET, OSLO, MORTENSENS FORLAG 1967*

219 pp.

Translation by Peter Magnus.

D152 VIRGINIA WOOLF | [*rule*] | ROMANKUNSTENS | FASER | TIL NORSK VED | LOUISE BOHR NILSEN | [*device*] | [*rule*] | J. W. CAPPELENS FORLAG | OSLO 1959

Large crown 8vo. 68 pp. $7\frac{3}{4}$ × $5\frac{1}{4}$ in.

A translation by Louise Bohr Nilsen of 'Phases of Fiction'.

D153 [*device*] | VIRGINIA WOOLF | ET EGET ROM | INNLEDNING VED KARI SKJØNSBERG | OVERSATT AV DAISY SCHJELDERUP | GYLDENDAL NORSK FORLAG · OSLO

Small crown 8vo. [ii], 134 pp. $7\frac{1}{4}$ × $4\frac{1}{2}$ in. (Fakkel-Bøkene, 345).

A translation by Daisy Schjelderup, with an introduction by Kari Skjønsberg, of *A Room of One's Own*; published 1976.

### POLISH

*Books*

D154 [*within a border in brown: in black:*] VIRGINIA WOOLF | [*in brown:*] LATA | [*in black:*] TLUMACŽYLA | MALGORZATA SZERCHA | [*ornament in brown; in black:*] CZYTELNIK 1958

Crown 8vo. 496 pp. $7\frac{3}{4}$ × $4\frac{7}{8}$ in.

A translation by Malgorzata Szercha of *The Years*; published Warsaw.

D155 VIRGINIA WOOLF | PANI DALLOWAY | PRZELOZYLA | KRYSTYNA TARNOWSKA | PAŃSTWOWY INSTYTUT WYDAWNICZY

Crown 8vo. 236 pp. $7\frac{3}{4}$ × 5 in. (Powieści XX Wieku).

A translation by Krystyna Tarnowska of *Mrs Dalloway*; published Warsaw, 1961.

D156 DO LATARNI MORSKIEJ · WARSAW, CZYTELNIK, 1962*

317 pp.

A translation by Krzysztof Klinger of *To the Lighthouse.*

# D. TRANSLATIONS

## PORTUGUESE

*Books*

D157 *a.* [*within a triple rule with an ornament in each angle:*] VIRGINIA WOOLF | [*double rule*] | MRS. | DALLOWAY | TRADUÇÃO DE | MARIO QUINTANA | [*device*] | EDIÇÃO DE LIVRARIA DO GLOBO | RIO DE JANEIRO–PÔRTO ALEGRE–SÃO PAULO

Crown 8vo. [ii], 260 pp. front. (port.). $7\frac{5}{8} \times 5\frac{3}{8}$ in.

A translation by Mário Quintana of *Mrs Dalloway*; published 1946.

*b.* MRS DALLOWAY · EDICÃO LIVROS DO BRASIL, LISBOA, 1954*

Foolscap 8vo. 182 pp. $6\frac{3}{8} \times 4\frac{1}{4}$ in. (Coleção Miniatura, 38).

Translation by Mário Quintana.

*c.* VIRGINIA WOOLF | MRS. DALLOWAY | TRADUÇÃO DE MÁRIO QUINTANA | INTRODUÇÃO DE TEREZINHA FONSECA | BRUGUERA

Foolscap 8vo. 240 pp. $6\frac{3}{4} \times 4\frac{1}{4}$ in.

Translation by Mário Quintana, with an introduction by Terezinha Fonseca; published Rio de Janeiro, 1970.

D158 *a.* [*within a double rule at head and foot: device*] | VIRGINIA WOOLF | ORLANDO | BIOGRAFIA | TRADUÇÃO DE | CECILIA MEIRELES | [*device*] | EDITÔRA GLOBO | RIO DE JANEIRO–PÔRTO ALEGRE–SÃO PAULO

Crown 8vo. 268 pp. front. (port.). $7\frac{1}{2} \times 5\frac{3}{8}$ in. (Coleçao Nobel, 74).

A translation by Cecília Meireles of *Orlando*; published 1948.

*b.* [*within a triple rule in mauve: in black:*] COLEÇÃO MINIATURA | VIRGINIA WOOLF | [*in mauve:*] ORLANDO | [*in black:*] TRADUÇÃO DE | CECÍLIA MEIRELES | [*device*] | EDIÇÃO "LIVROS DO BRASIL" LISBOA

Foolscap 8vo. 224 pp. $6\frac{3}{8} \times 4\frac{1}{4}$ in. (Coleção Miniatura, 136). 136).

Translation by Cecília Meireles; published 1962.

*c.* VIRGINIA WOOLF | ORLANDO | UMA BIOGRAFIA | TRADUÇÃO | E INTRODUÇÃO DE | CECILIA MEIRELES | [*in script:*] EDITORIAL [*monogram*] BRUGUERA

Foolscap 8vo. [ii], 334 pp. $6\frac{3}{4} \times 4$ in.

Translation by Cecília Meireles; published Rio de Janeiro, 1969.

*d.* VIRGINIA WOOLF | ORLANDO | TRADUÇÃO DE | CECÍLIA MEIRELES | [*device*] | EDITORA | NOVA | FRONTEIRA

Large crown 8vo. 186 pp. $8\frac{1}{8} \times 5\frac{3}{8}$ in.

Translation by Cecília Meireles; published Rio de Janeiro, 1978.

D159 VIRGINIA WOOLF | [*wavy line*] | AS ONDAS | TRADUÇÃO DE | SYLVIA VALLADÃO AZEVEDO | SÃO PAULO | 1946

Crown 8vo. 264 pp. $7\frac{1}{4} \times 4\frac{7}{8}$ in.

A translation by Sylvia Valladão Azevedo of *The Waves*; published by Livraria do Globo.

D160 VIRGINIA WOOLF | PASSEIO AO FAROL | TRADUÇÃO DE | OSCAR MENDES | EDITORIAL LABOR DO BRASIL S.A.

Small crown 8vo. 218 pp. $7 \times 4\frac{1}{2}$ in.

A translation by Oscar Mendes of *To the Lighthouse*; published Rio de Janeiro, 1976.

## ROMANIAN

*Books*

D161 VIRGINIA WOOLF | [*rule*] | DOAMNA DALLOWAY | ÎN ROMÂNEŞTE DE PETRU CREŢIA | PREFAŢĂ DE VERA CĂLIN | EDITURA PENTRU LITERATURĂ UNIVERSALĂ | [*rule*] | BUCUREŞTI – 1968

Foolscap 8vo. 296 pp. $6\frac{1}{2} \times 4\frac{1}{4}$ in. (Colecţia Meridiane).

A translation by Petru Creţia, with a preface by Vera Călin, of *Mrs Dalloway*.

D162 VIRGINIA WOOLF | [*rule*] | ORLANDO | O BIOGRAFIE | ÎN ROMÂNEŞTE DE VERA CĂLIN | EDITURA PENTRU LITERATURĂ UNIVERSALĂ | [*rule*] | BUCUREŞTI – 1968

Foolscap 8vo. 328 pp. $6\frac{1}{2} \times 4\frac{1}{8}$ in. (Colecţia Meridiane).

A translation by Vera Călin of *Orlando*.

D163 SPRE FAR | ANTOANETA RALIAN | BUCUREŞTI | MINERVA*

xx, 320 pp.

A translation by Antoaneta Ralian of *To the Lighthouse*; published 1972.

D164 VALURILE | PETRU CREŢIA | BUCUREŞTI | UNIVERS*

243 pp.

A translation by Petru Creţia of *The Waves*; published 1973.

## SERBO-CROAT

*Books*

D165 [*in black:*] VIRGINIA WOOLF | [*in red:*] GODINE | [*in black:*] PREVEO S ENGLESKOGA | JOSIP TORBARINA | ZAGREB 1946 | MATICA HRVATSKA

Crown 8vo. 368 pp. $7\frac{3}{4} \times 5\frac{1}{2}$ in.

A translation by Josip Torbarina of *The Years.*

D166 [*in brown:*] VIRJINIYA VULF | [*in black: rule*] | IZLET |
*a.* NA SVETIONIK | [*in brown:*] PROSVETA · BEOGRAD | [*in black: rule*] | [*in brown:*] 1955

Foolscap 8vo. 208 pp. $7 \times 4\frac{3}{8}$ in. (Biblioteka Putevi, 15).

A translation by Zora Minderovič of *To the Lighthouse.*

*b.* VIRGINIA WOOLF | SVJETIONIK | [*device*] | STVARNOST | ZAGREB

Small crown 8vo. 228 pp. $7\frac{1}{8} \times 4\frac{3}{8}$ in.

Translation, and epilogue, by Tomislav Ladan; published 1974.

D167 GOSPODJA DALOVEJ · PREVELA (I PREDGOVOR),
*a.* VIRDŹINIJA VULF I GOSPODJA DELOVEJ (NAPISALA) MILICA MIHAJLOVIĆ · BEOGRAD, NOLIT, 1955*

Small crown 8vo. 215 pp. $7\frac{1}{2} \times 4\frac{1}{2}$ in. (Biblioteka Neolit).

A translation by Milica B. Mihajlović of *Mrs Dalloway.*

*b.* GOSPODJA DALOVEJ · PREVELA (I POGOVOR NAPISALA) MILICA MIHAJLOVIĆ · BEOGRAD, RAD, 1964*

Foolscap 8vo. 176 pp. $7 \times 4\frac{1}{2}$ in. (Biblioteka 'Reč i Misao', 122).

Translation by Milica B. Mihajlović.

*c.* VIRDŽINIJA VULF | GOSPOĐA DALOVEJ | SARAJEVO | 1966.

Foolscap 8vo. 200 pp. $6\frac{1}{4} \times 4\frac{1}{4}$ in. (Džepna Biblioteka, Izabranih Djela).

Translation by Milica B. Mihajlović; published by Svjetlost Izdavačko Preduzeće.

D168 ESEJI · IZBOR · PREVELA SA ENGLESKOG (I POGOVOR); O VIRDŽINIJI VULF I NJENIM ESEJIMA (NAPISALA), MILICA B. MIHAJLOVIĆ · BEOGRAD, NOLIT, 1956*

Foolscap 8vo. 309 pp. $7 \times 4\frac{1}{2}$ in. (Mala Knjiga, 36).

A translation by Milica B. Mihajlović of *The Common Reader* and *The Common Reader: Second Series.*

D169 TALASI · ROMAN · PREVELA, MILICA MIHAJLOVIĆ, (PREDGOVOR) VIRDŽINIJA VULF (NAPISALA) MARIJA STANSFILD-POPOVIĆ · BEOGRAD, SRPSKA KNJIŽEVNA ZADRUGA, 1959*

Small crown 8vo. 287 pp. $7\frac{1}{2} \times 4\frac{1}{2}$ in.

A translation by Milica B. Mihajlović, with a foreword by Marija Stansfild-Popović, of *The Waves.*

## SLOVAK

*Book*

D170 VIRGINIA | WOOLFOVÁ | PANI | DALLOWAYOVÁ | SMENA | BRATISLAVA | 1976

Crown 8vo. [viii], 152 pp. illus. $7\frac{7}{8} \times 5$ in.

A translation by Michal Breznický, with illustrations by Jana Želibská of *Mrs Dalloway*.

## SLOVENE

*Book*

D171 GOSPA | DALLOWAY | VIRGINIA WOOLF | CANKARJEVA ZALOŽBA V LJUBLJANI 1965

Small crown 8vo. 220 pp. $6\frac{7}{8} \times 4\frac{5}{8}$ in.

A translation by Jože Udovič, with introduction by Rapa Šuklje, of *Mrs Dalloway*.

D172 VIRGINIA WOOLF | ORLANDO | MLADINSKA KNJIGA | 1974

Large crown 8vo. 224 pp. $7\frac{3}{4} \times 5\frac{1}{4}$ in.

A translation by Maila Golob of *Orlando*; published Ljubljana.

## SPANISH

*Books*

D173 *a.* VIRGINIA WOOLF | ORLANDO | UNA BIOGRAFÍA | SUR | BUENOS AIRES

Crown 8vo. 324 pp. $7\frac{3}{8} \times 5\frac{1}{2}$ in.

A translation by Jorge Luis Borges of *Orlando*; published 1937.

*b.* VIRGINIA WOOLF | ORLANDO | UNA BIOGRAFÍA | TRADUCCIÓN DE | JORGE LUIS BORGES | EDITORIAL SUDAMERICANA | BUENOS AIRES

Crown 8vo. 348 pp. $7\frac{1}{4} \times 5$ in. (Colección Horizonte).

Translation by Jorge Luis Borges; published 1943. Reprinted in 1945.

*c.* VIRGINIA WOOLF | ORLANDO | UNA BIOGRAFÍA | TRADUCCIÓN DE | JORGE LUIS BORGES | EDITORIAL SUDAMERICANA | BUENOS AIRES

Crown 8vo. 328 pp. $7\frac{1}{4} \times 5$ in. (Colección Horizonte).

Translation by Jorge Luis Borges; published 1951.

*d.* VIRGINIA WOOLF | ORLANDO | UNA BIOGRAFÍA | PRÓLOGO DE ELISEO DIEGO | EDITORA DEL CONSEJO NACIONAL DE CULTURA | EDITORIAL NACIONAL DE CUBA / LA HABANA, 1966

Crown 8vo. xx, 228 pp. illus. (port.). $7\frac{1}{2} \times 5\frac{1}{2}$ in.

Translation by Jorge Luis Borges, with an introduction by Eliseo Diego.

*e.* VIRGINIA WOOLF | ORLANDO | TRADUCCIÓN DE JORGE LUIS BORGES | EDITORIAL SUDAMERICANA | BUENOS AIRES

Foolscap 8vo. 196 pp. $6\frac{7}{8} \times 4\frac{1}{4}$ in. (Colección Índice Ficcion).

Translation by Jorge Luis Borges; published 1968.

D174 VIRGINIA WOOLF | AL FARO | EDITORIAL SUR |
*a.* BUENOS AIRES 1938*

Crown 8vo. 267 pp. $7\frac{3}{8} \times 5\frac{1}{2}$ in.

A translation by Antonio Marichalar of *To the Lighthouse.*

*b.* VIRGINIA WOOLF | AL FARO | TRADUCCIÓN DE | ANTONIO MARICHALAR | EDITORIAL SUDAMERICANA | BUENOS AIRES

Crown 8vo. 320 pp. $7\frac{3}{8} \times 5$ in. (Colección Horizonte).

Translation by Antonio Marichalar; published October 1946. Reprinted in 1976.

*c.* AL FARO · BUENOS AIRES, EDITORIAL SUDAMERICANA, 1958*

242 pp. (Collección Piragua).

Translation by Antonio Marichalar.

*d.* [*in sky-blue:*] MAESTROS INGLESES | [*in black:*] V | RUDYARD KIPLING | JOHN GALSWORTHY | WILLIAM SOMERSET MAUGHAM | MAURICE BARING | VIRGINIA WOOLF | SELECCIÓN Y ESTUDIOS DE | SEBASTIÁN JUAN ARBÓ | Y | RICARDO FERNÁNDEZ DE LA REGUERA | EDITORIAL PLANETA Y PLAZA & JANÉS, S.A. | BARCELONA

Crown 8vo. 1896 pp. port. $7\frac{1}{4} \times 5\frac{1}{8}$ in.

Pp. 1699–1890 Translation by Antonio Marichalar of *To the Lighthouse*; published 1962.

D175 VIRGINIA WOOLF | LA SEÑORA DALLOWAY | EDI-
*a.* TORIAL SUDAMERICANA | BUENOS AIRES 1939*

304 pp. (Collección Sur).

A translation by Ernesto Palacio of *Mrs Dalloway*. Reprinted in the series *Colección Horizonte.*

*b.* VIRGINIA WOOLF | LA SEÑORA | DALLOWAY | TRADUCCIÓN DE ANDRÉS BOSCH | EDITORIAL LUMEN

Crown 8vo. 224 pp. $7\frac{1}{4} \times 5$ in. (Palabra en el Tiempo, 115).

Translation by Andrés Bosch; published Barcelona, 1975. Reprinted in 1979 bv Editorial Lumen in *Ediciońes de Bolsillo.*

D176 VIRGINIA WOOLF | LAS OLAS | (THE WAVES) | TRADU-
*a.* CIDO DEL INGLÉS, CON UN PRÓLOGO, | POR | LENKA

FRANULIC | [*device*] | EDICIONES ERCILLA | SANTIAGO DE CHILE | 1940

Demy 8vo. xii, 214 pp. $8\frac{3}{4} \times 5\frac{1}{2}$ in. (Colección Condor).

A translation by Lenka Franulic of *The Waves*.

*b.* VIRGINIA WOOLF | LAS OLAS | TRADUCCIÓN DE ANDRÉS BOSCH | EDITORIAL LUMEN

Crown 8vo. 272 pp. $7\frac{1}{8} \times 5$ in. (Palabra en el Tiempo, 89).

Translation by Andrés Bosch; published Barcelona, 1972.

*c.* LAS OLAS | VIRGINIA WOOLF | EDITORIAL | BRUGUERA, S.A.

Foolscap 8vo. 288 pp. $6\frac{7}{8} \times 4\frac{1}{4}$ in. (Libro Amigo, 575).

Translation by Andrés Bosch; published Barcelona, Buenos Aires, Bogotá, Caracas, México, 1978.

D177 VIRGINIA WOOLF | TRES GUINEAS | EDITORIAL SUR |
*a.* BUENOS AIRES 1941*

Crown 8vo. 242 pp. $7\frac{3}{8} \times 5\frac{1}{2}$ in.

A translation by J. Jiménez of *Three Guineas*.

*b.* VIRGINIA WOOLF | TRES GUINEAS | TRADUCCIÓN DE ANDRÉS BOSCH | EDITORIAL LUMEN

Crown 8vo. 240 pp. $7\frac{1}{8} \times 5$ in. (Palabra en el Tiempo, 133).

Translation by Andrés Bosch; published Barcelona, 1977.

*c.* VIRGINIA WOOLF | TRES GUINEAS | TRADUCCIÓN DE | ROMÁN J. JIMÉNEZ | EDITORIAL SUDAMERICANA | BUENOS AIRES

Small crown 8vo. 244 pp. $7\frac{1}{8} \times 4\frac{7}{8}$ in.

Translation by Román J. Jiménez; published 1979.

D178 VIRGINIA WOOLF | ENTREACTO | (BETWEEN THE
*a.* ACTS) | VERSIÓN CASTELLANA DE | LENKA FRANULIC | EDICIONES ERCILLA | SANTIAGO DE CHILE | 1943

Demy 8vo. 280 pp. $8\frac{3}{4} \times 5\frac{5}{8}$ in. (Colección Condor).

A translation by Lenka Franulic of *Between the Acts*.

*b.* VIRGINIA WOOLF | ENTRE ACTOS | TRADUCCIÓN DE ANDRÉS BOSCH | EDITORIAL LUMEN

Crown 8vo. 184 pp. $7\frac{1}{8} \times 5\frac{1}{8}$ in. (Palabra en el Tiempo, 121).

Translation by Andrés Bosch; published Barcelona, 1976.

D179 VIRGINIA WOOLF | FLUSH | [*device*] | EDICIONES DESTINO S. L. | PELAYO, 28, – BARCELONA

Small Crown 8vo. 176 pp. $7\frac{1}{4} \times 4\frac{1}{2}$ in. (Áncora y Delfín, 18).

A translation by Rafael Vázquez-Zamora of *Flush*; published 1944.

D180 [*in black:*] VIRGINIA WOOLF | [*in green:*] LOS AÑOS | [*device*] | [*in black:*] EDICIONES LAURO | 1946

Crown 8vo. 320 pp. $7\frac{1}{2} \times 5\frac{1}{2}$ in. (Los Escritores de Ahora).

A translation by Pedro Fraga de Porto of *The Years*; published Barcelona, January 1946.

D181 *a.* [*in black:*] VIRGINIA WOOLF | [*in green:*] EL CUARTO DE JACOB | [*device*] | [*in black:*] EDICIONES LAURO | 1946

Crown 8vo. 192 pp. $7\frac{1}{2} \times 5\frac{1}{2}$ in.

A translation by Simón Santainés of *Jacob's Room*; published Barcelona, April 1946.

*b.* EL CUARTO DE JACOB | POR | VIRGINIA WOOLF | [*device*] | EDICIONES G. P. – BARCELONA

Foolscap 8vo. 160 pp. $7 \times 4$ in. (Libros Plaza, 127).

Translation by Simón Santainés; published, 1958.

*c.* EL CUARTO DE JACOB · MADRID, DÉDALO, 1960*

64 pp. $9\frac{1}{4}$ in.

Translation by Simón Santainés.

*d.* VIRGINIA WOOLF | EL CUARTO | DE JACOB | TRADUCCIÓN DE ANDRÉS BOSCH | EDITORIAL LUMEN

Crown 8vo. 232 pp. $7\frac{1}{8} \times 5$ in. (Palabra en el Tiempo, 124).

Translation by Andrés Bosch; published Barcelona, 1977.

D182 *a.* VIRGINIA WOOLF | [*rule*] | FIN DE VIAJE | (THE VOYAGE OUT) | VERSION ESPAÑOLA | DE | GUILLERMO GOSSÉ | LUIS DE CARALT | EDITOR | BARCELONA

Crown 8vo. 288 pp. $7 \times 5\frac{1}{8}$ in. (Grandes Novelistas).

A translation by Guillermo Gossé of *The Voyage Out*; published November, 1946.

*b.* VIRGINIA WOOLF | FIN DE VIAJE | [*rule*] | PRÓLOGO DE | MARTA PESSARRODONA

Small crown 8vo. 324 pp. $7 \times 4\frac{1}{2}$ in. (Biblioteca Universal Caralt, 68).

Translation by Guillermo Gossé, with an introduction by Marta Pessarrodona; published Barcelona, Luis de Caralt, 1976.

D183 *a.* [*in black:*] VIRGINIA WOOLF | [*in green:*] NOCHE Y DÍA | [*device*] | [*in black:*] LAURO | JOSÉ JANÉS, EDITOR | 1947

Crown 8vo. 330 pp. $7\frac{1}{2} \times 5\frac{3}{8}$ in. (Los Escritores de Ahora).

A translation by Eduardo de Guzmán of *Night and Day*; published Barcelona.

*b.* [*across two pages:*] VIRGINIA WOOLF | NOCHE | Y DIA | EDICIONES G. P. BARCELONA [*device*]

Foolscap 8vo. 496 pp. 7 × $3\frac{7}{8}$ in. (Libros Reno).

Translation by Eduardo de Guzmán; published 1963.

D184 DIARIO DE UNA ESCRITORA · BUENOS AIRES, EDITORIAL SUR. 1954*

Crown 8vo. 325 pp. $7\frac{3}{8}$ × $5\frac{1}{2}$ in.

A translation by José M. Coco Ferraris of *A Writer's Diary.*

D185 UN CUARTO PROPIO · BUENOS AIRES, EDITORIAL

*a.* SUR, 1956*

Crown 8vo. 110 pp. $7\frac{3}{8}$ × $5\frac{1}{2}$ in.

A translation by Jorge Luis Borges of *A Room of One's Own.*

*b.* VIRGINIA WOOLF | UNA HABITACION | PROPIA | [*device*] | BIBLIOTECA BREVE | EDITORIAL SEIX BARRAL, S.A. | BARCELONA, 1967

Foolscap 8vo. 164 pp. $6\frac{7}{8}$ × $4\frac{1}{4}$ in. (Biblioteca Breve, 264).

Translation by Laura Pujol.

D186 [*within a quadruple rule in blue: in black:*] VIRGINIA WOOLF | OBRAS | COMPLETAS | [*ornament in blue*] | JOSÉ JANES EDITOR BARCELONA | 1956

Foolscap 8vo. xxiv, 1370 pp. front. (port.). $6\frac{7}{8}$ × $4\frac{1}{8}$ in. (Los Clasicos del Siglo, 20).

Volume 1 containing translations of *The Years*, by Pedro Fraga de Porto, *Jacob's Room*, by Simón Santainés, *To the Lighthouse*, by Antonio Marichalar, *Mrs Dalloway*, by Ernesto Palacio, and *Night and Day*, by Eduardo de Guzmán, with an introduction by Fernando Gutierrez.

D187 UNA CASA ENCANTADA POR VIRGINIA WOOLF. EDICIONES G. P. BARCELONA*

Foolscap 8vo. 160 pp. 7 × 4 in. (Libros Plaza, 194).

A translation by Alfredo Crespo of *A Haunted House and Other Short Stories*; published 1959.

D188 LA SEÑORA DALLOWAY RECIBE | VIRGINIA WOOLF | EDITADO POR STELLA McNICHOL | TRADUCCIÓN DE RAMÓN GIL NOVALES

Small crown 8vo. 80 pp. $7\frac{1}{4}$ × $4\frac{3}{4}$ in. (Palabra Menor).

A translation by Ramón Gil Novales of *Mrs Dalloway's Party*; published Barcelona, Editorial Lumen, 1974.

D189 VIRGINIA WOOLF | LA TORRE INCLINADA | Y OTROS ENSAYOS | TRADUCCIÓN DE ANDRÉS BOSCH | EDITORIAL LUMEN

Crown 8vo. 230 pp. $7\frac{1}{8}$ × 5 in. (Palabra en el Tiempo, 129).

A translation by Andrés Bosch of a selection from the *Collected Essays*; published Barcelona, 1977.

Contents: 'The Russian Point of View' — 'Mr Bennett and Mrs Brown' — 'How Should One Read a Book?' — 'Phases of

Fiction' – 'Modern Fiction' – 'On Re-Reading Novels' – 'Life and the Novelist' – 'Women and Fiction' – 'How It Strikes a Contemporary' – 'The Narrow Bridge of Art' – 'The Leaning Tower'.

*Periodical*

D190 UN CUARTO PROPIO. *Sur*, Buenos Aires, Nos. 15–18, December 1935–March 1936.*

A translation by Jorge Luis Borges of *A Room of One's Own.*

## SWEDISH

*Books*

D191 DEN NYA ROMANEN | [*double rule*] | VIRGINIA WOOLF | JACOBS RUM | BEMYNDIGAD ÖVERSÄTTNING | | FRÅN ENGELSKAN AV | SIRI THORNGREN-OLIN | [*monogram*] | STOCKHOLM | HUGO GEBERS FÖRLAG

Crown 8vo. 252 pp. $7\frac{5}{8} \times 5$ in.

A translation by Siri Thorngren-Olin of *Jacob's Room*; published 1927.

D192 ÅREN | AV VIRGINIA WOOLF | [*rule*] | FRÅN ENGELSKAN AV | INGALISA MUNCK | ALBERT BONNIERS FÖRLAG | STOCKHOLM

Medium 8vo. 432 pp. $8\frac{7}{8} \times 6$ in.

A translation by Ingalisa Munck of *The Years*; published 1941.

D193 DE LUTANDE TORNET: TRE ESSAYER · STOCKHOLM, WÄHLSTRÖM & WIDSTRAND, 1952*

Small crown 8vo. 62 pp. $7 \times 4\frac{3}{4}$ in. (Wählström & Widstrands Kulturbibliotek, 3).

Translations by Erik Wahlund of 'Montaigne', 'Jane Austen' and 'The Leaning Tower'.

D194 VIRGINIA WOOLF | MOT FYREN | STOCKHOLM |
*a.* ALBERT BONNIERS FÖRLAG | 1953

Large crown 8vo. 232 pp. $8 \times 5\frac{1}{4}$ in. (Gula Serien).

A translation by Ingalisa Munck and Sonja Bergvall, with an introduction by Anders Österling, of *To the Lighthouse.*

*b.* VIRGINIA WOOLF | [*rule*] | MOT FYREN | [*ornament, within a rule:*] FORUM [*ornament*]

Foolscap 8vo. 208 pp. $7\frac{3}{8} \times 4$ in.

Translation by Ingalisa Munck and Sonja Bergvall, with an introduction by Heidi von Born; published by Hos Bohusläningens AB, Uddevalla, 1975.

D195 ETT EGET RUM | OCH ANDRA ESSÄER | VIRGINIA WOOLF | [*device*] | ENGELSKA KLASSIKER | TIDENS FÖRLAG STOCKHOLM

Small crown 8vo. 168 pp. $7\frac{1}{8} \times 4\frac{1}{2}$ in. (Tidens Engelska Klassiker, 8).

Translations by Jane Lundblad of *A Room of One's Own*, 'On Not Knowing Greek', and 'How Should One Read a Book?'; published 1958. Reprinted in 1977 in the series *Tidens Klassiker.*

D196 VIRGINIA WOOLF | ÖGONBLICK AV LIV | ÖVERSÄTTNING AV | HARRIET ALFONS | ALBA

Large crown 8vo. 208 pp. $7\frac{7}{8} \times 4\frac{7}{8}$ in.

A translation by Harriet Alfons of *Moments of Being*; published Stockholm, 1977. 'Reminiscences', the Index and most of the Editor's Note are omitted.

D197 VIRGINIA WOOLF | MRS DALLOWAY | ÖVERSÄTTNING ELSE LUNDGREN | FORUM

Small demy 8vo. 210 pp. $8\frac{3}{8} \times 5\frac{1}{4}$ in.

A translation by Else Lundgren of *Mrs Dalloway*; published Stockholm, 1977.

## TURKISH

*Books*

D198 VIRGINIA WOOLF | DENİZ FENERİ | (TO THE LIGHTHOUSE) | NACIYE AKSEKİ TARAFINDAN DILIMIZE ÇEVRILMIŞTIR. | İSTANBUL 1945 – ÜLKÜ BASIMEVİ

Small crown 8vo. [x], xii, 316 pp. $7\frac{3}{8} \times 4\frac{1}{2}$ in. (Dünya Edebiyatindan Tercümeller).

A translation by Naciye Akseki, with a foreword to the series by President İsmet İnönü and a preface by Hasan-Âli Yücel, of *To the Lighthouse.*

D199 VIRGINIA WOOLF | MRS DALLOWAY | TÜRKÇESI: | TOMRİS UYAR | YENİ ANKARA YAYINEVİ

Crown 8vo. 240 pp. $7\frac{3}{4} \times 5$ in.

A translation by Tomris Uyar of *Mrs Dalloway*; published Istanbul, 1976.

# E.

# FOREIGN EDITIONS

# PARODY

# ANNOUNCED BUT NOT PUBLISHED

# LARGE PRINT EDITIONS FOR THE BLIND

# COMMUNICATIONS TO THE PRESS

## FOREIGN EDITIONS

E1 MRS. DALLOWAY | BY | VIRGINIA WOOLF | COPYRIGHT EDITION | LEIPZIG | BERNHARD TAUCHNITZ

Foolscap 8vo. 272 pp. $6\frac{3}{8} \times 4\frac{1}{2}$ in. (Collection of British and American Authors, 4867).

Published in 1929.

E2 ORLANDO | A BIOGRAPHY | BY | VIRGINIA WOOLF | COPYRIGHT EDITION | LEIPZIG | BERNHARD TAUCHNITZ | 1929

Foolscap 8vo. 280 pp. $6\frac{1}{2} \times 4\frac{3}{4}$ in. (Collection of British and American Authors, 4866).

E3 TO | THE LIGHTHOUSE | BY | VIRGINIA WOOLF | THE ALBATROSS | HAMBURG · PARIS · MILANO | MCMXXXII

Small crown 8vo. 248 pp. $7\frac{1}{8} \times 4\frac{3}{8}$ in. (The Albatross Modern Continental Library, 7).

E4 THE WAVES | BY | VIRGINIA WOOLF | THE ALBATROSS | HAMBURG · PARIS · BOLOGNA

Small crown 8vo. 272 pp. $7\frac{1}{8} \times 4\frac{3}{8}$ in. (The Albatross Modern Continental Library, 65).

Published in 1933. Twelve copies specially bound, not for sale, were issued in the same year in marbled paper boards, yellow leather spine and corners with raised bands on spine; lettered in gold on spine; top edges gilt, others partially trimmed.

E4.1 KENKYUSHA GENDAIEIBUNGAKU SOSHO | [*rule*] | TO THE LIGHTHOUSE | BY | VIRGINIA WOOLF | WITH INTRODUCTION AND NOTES | BY | T. SAWAMURA | ASSISTANT PROFESSOR OF ENGLISH LITERATURE IN THE | IMPERIAL UNIVERSITY OF TOKYO | TOKYO | KENKYUSHA*

Small crown 8vo. 318 pp. $7\frac{1}{8} \times 4\frac{3}{4}$ in.

Published in 1934. See also E12.1.

E5 [*within a frame, within a compartment, within a frame:*] MRS. DALLOWAY | BY | VIRGINIA WOOLF | [*irregular rule*] | PUBLISHED BY | THE ALBATROSS | MCMXLVII

Small crown 8vo. 288 pp. $7\frac{1}{8} \times 4\frac{3}{8}$ in. (The Albatross Modern Continental Library, 4867).

E6 [*within a compartment:*] THE YEARS | BY | VIRGINIA WOOLF | PUBLISHED BY | THE ALBATROSS | MCMXLVII

Small crown 8vo. 336 pp. $7\frac{1}{8} \times 4\frac{3}{8}$ in. (The Albatross Modern Continental Library, 566).

E7 THE WAVES | BY | VIRGINIA WOOLF | PUBLISHED BY | THE ALBATROSS | MCMXLIX

Small crown 8vo. 272 pp. $7\frac{1}{8} \times 4\frac{3}{8}$ in. (The Albatross Modern Continental Library, 65).

E8 [*within a quadruple rule with an ornament in each angle:*] BETWEEN | THE ACTS | BY | VIRGINIA WOOLF | PUBLISHED BY | THE ALBATROSS | MDCCCCL

Small crown 8vo. 256 pp. $7\frac{1}{8} \times 4\frac{3}{8}$ in. (The Albatross Modern Continental Library, 578).

E9 VIRGINIA WOOLF | FLUSH | ABRIDGED EDITION | WITH ANNOTATIONS | 1950 | CORNELSEN VERLAG | BERLIN // BIELEFELD

Medium 16mo. 96 pp. $6 \times 4\frac{1}{8}$ in. and insert [2], 95–124 pp. $6 \times 4$ in. (Cornelsen Fremdsprachenreihe, 74).

E10 V. WOOLF | A HAUNTED HOUSE | AND | OTHER SHORT STORIES | EDITED WITH NOTES | BY | I. MIYAZAKI | H. TAKAHASHI | [*device*] | TOKYO | NAN'UN-DO

Small crown 8vo. [vi], 92 pp. front. (port.). $7\frac{1}{4} \times 5$ in.

A selection of eight stories from *A Hunted House and Other Short Stories*; published 1953.

E11 MRS. DALLOWAY | BY | VIRGINIA WOOLF | WITH INTRODUCTION AND NOTES | BY | TETSUO SHIBATA | YASUO YOSHIDA | TOKYO | KENKYUSHA

Small crown 8vo. xlvi, 454 pp. front. (port.), map. $6\frac{7}{8} \times 4\frac{3}{4}$ in. (Kenkyusha British & American Classics, 202).

Published in 1953.

E12 A ROOM OF ONE'S OWN | BY | VIRGINIA WOOLF | ANNOTATED | BY | YASUO YOSHIDA | PROFESSOR OF ENGLISH IN THE | UNIVERSITY OF OSAKA | [*rule*] | KINSEIDO LTD | TOKYO

Small crown 8vo. [iv], 108 pp. $7\frac{1}{4} \times 5$ in. (Modern English Series).

Published in 1954.

E12.1 NAN'UN-DO'S CONTEMPORARY LIBRARY | [*rule*] | VIRGINIA WOOLF | TO THE LIGHTHOUSE | EDITED WITH NOTES | BY | HIDEO KANŌ | [*device*] | TOKYO | NAN'UN-DO

Small crown 8vo. [2], xii, 170 pp. front. (port.). $7 \times 4\frac{7}{8}$ in. (Nan'un-do's Contemporary Library).

Abridged edition; published 1954. See also E4.1.

E12.2 VIRGINIA WOOLF | MRS. DALLOWAY | A SELECTION | EDITED WITH NOTES BY | AAGE SALLING | GYLDENDAL | 1956

Small crown 8vo. 92 pp. $7\frac{3}{4} \times 4\frac{3}{4}$ in.

Abridged edition; published Copenhagen.

E12 .3 NAN'UN-DO'S CONTEMPORARY LIBRARY | [*rule*] | VIRGINIA WOOLF | THE DEATH OF THE MOTH | AND OTHER ESSAYS | EDITED WITH NOTES | BY | KIYOSHI IKEJIMA | [*device*] | TOKYO | NAN'UN-DO

Small crown 8vo. [2], vi, 72 pp. front. (port.). $7\frac{1}{4} \times 5$ in. (Nan'un-do's Contemporary Library).

Contents: 'The Death of the Moth' – 'Professions for Women' – 'Thoughts of Peace in an Air Raid' – 'The Leaning Tower'; published 1958.

E12 .4 NAN'UN-DO'S CONTEMPORARY LIBRARY | [*rule*] | VIRGINIA WOOLF | KEW GARDENS | AND OTHER STORIES | EDITED WITH NOTES | BY | ISAO MIYAZAKI | GEN'ICHI MURAOKA | [*device*] | TOKYO | NAN'UN-DO

Small crown 8vo. [2], viii, 80 pp. front. (port.). (Nan'un-do's Contemporary Library).

Contents: 'The Legacy' – 'The Duchess and the Jeweller' – 'The Searchlight' – 'The Lady in the Looking Glass' – 'Kew Gardens'.

E12 .5 A LETTER TO A YOUNG POET | AND OTHER ESSAYS | BY | VIRGINIA WOOLF | EDITED WITH INTRODUCTION AND NOTES | BY | MINORU OSAWA | [*device*] | TAISHUKAN

Crown 8vo. xxii, 122 pp. front. (port.). $7\frac{1}{4} \times 5\frac{1}{8}$ in. (Cosmos Library, 7).

Contents: 'Modern Novels' – 'Character in Fiction' – 'A Letter to a Young Poet' – 'A Conversation About Art'; published 1960.

E12 .6 THREE | SHORT | STORIES | BY THREE | WOMEN | WRITERS | SELECTED AND EDITED BY | NILS FISCHERSTRÖM AND | BERTIL JOHANSSON | GLEERUPS

Crown 8vo. 64 pp. $7\frac{5}{8} \times 5\frac{1}{8}$ in.

Pp. 11–20 'The Legacy'; published Stockholm, 1965.

E12 .7 HOW SHOULD ONE READ A BOOK? | FROM THE COMMON READER SECOND SERIES | BY | VIRGINIA WOOLF | [*illustration*] | EDITED WITH NOTES | BY | SHIGERU | KUROSAWA | [*monogram*] | CENTURY BOOKS | [*rule*] | SHIMIZU SHOIN | TOKYO

Crown 8vo. 96 pp. illus. $7\frac{1}{2} \times 4\frac{1}{2}$ in. (Century Books).

Contents: 'Robinson Crusoe' – 'Lord Chesterfield's Letters to his Son' – 'James Woodforde' – 'Mary Wollstonecraft' – 'Dorothy Wordsworth' – 'How Should One Read a Book?'; published 1966.

E12 .8 FLUSH | A BIOGRAPHY | VIRGINIA WOOLF | [*in Japanese:*] AKIBA MINORU | MASUDA HIDEO | [*one line*] | YASHIO SHUPPANSHA

Small crown 8vo. vi, 110 pp. $7\frac{1}{8} \times 5$ in.

Abridged edition edited and annotated by Minoru Akiba and Hideo Masuda; published Tokyo, 1978.

## PARODY

E13 [*title on upper cover:*] PAPER NO. 5 JUNE 1930 | THE BROADSHEET PRESS | MRS WOOLF ATTENDS THE PROCEEDINGS | OF THE BRITISH PSYCHO-ANALYTICAL SOCIETY | THE SNOBBERY OF MODERNISM

Crown 8vo. 8 pp. $7\frac{1}{2} \times 5$ in.

Pp. 1–4 text of Mrs Woolf's address; pp. 5–[7] text of: The Snobbery in Modernism; p. [8] blank.

Cinnamon paper wrappers $7\frac{1}{2} \times 5\frac{1}{4}$ in.; printed on upper cover as above and on lower cover: Printed by B. Brown and M. Stewart, 27 Cheyne Walk S.W. | Subscription, 4s. a year post free. Single copies 3d. each.

Published during June 1930; *c.* 250 copies printed on a hand-press.

'The Snobbery in Modernism' is incorrectly printed on the upper cover.

It is evident that this essay is a parody of Virginia Woolf's style. The author is believed to be Yvonne Cloud author of *Nobody Asked You.*

## ANNOUNCED BUT NOT PUBLISHED

E14 POETRY, FICTION & THE FUTURE. Announced as having appeared in the *Hogarth Essays* series at 2s. 6d. on the dust-jacket of *I Speak of Africa*, by William Plomer, published by the Hogarth Press in September 1927; this information also appeared on the dust-jacket to the 'cheap edition' issued in 1938. The essay first appeared in the *New York Herald Tribune*, 14 and 21 August 1927. See C284.

E15 PHASES OF FICTION. Announced as 'In Preparation' in the *Hogarth Lectures on Literature Series*, Vol. 1, *A Lecture on Lectures*, by Sir Arthur Quiller-Couch, published by the Hogarth Press in February 1928 (dated 1927). This note remained until Vol. 14, *Some Religious Elements in English Literature*, by Rose Macaulay, published in May 1931, when the list of volumes in preparation was omitted. The essay first appeared in the *Bookman*, April, May and June 1929. See C312.

## LARGE PRINT EDITIONS FOR THE BLIND

E16 TO | THE LIGHTHOUSE | VIRGINIA WOOLF | [*monogram*] | LYTHWAY PRESS | BATH

Small demy 8vo. [iv], 332 pp. $8\frac{3}{8} \times 5\frac{3}{8}$ in.

Published 1974.

## COMMUNICATIONS TO THE PRESS SIGNED BY VIRGINIA WOOLF

Apart from her own Letters to the Press, listed in Section C, Virginia Woolf signed the following communications to the Press:

E17 Hommage d'un groupe d'écrivains anglais. *La Nouvelle Revue française*, 1923, 20, 248-9. Signed Lascelles Abercrombie, Harley Granville Barker, Clive Bell and others including Virginia Woolf. Tribute on the death of Marcel Proust.

E18 Britain and the Spanish War. *New Statesman & Nation*, 22 August 1936, 250-1. Signed Lascelles Abercrombie, Norman Angell and others including Virginia Woolf. Letter in support of the Spanish Government.

# F.

## BOOKS AND ARTICLES CONTAINING SINGLE LETTERS OR EXTRACTS FROM LETTERS

F01 Newbolt, Sir Henry. *My World as in My Time: Memoirs . . . 1862–1932.* London, Faber and Faber, [1932], 250.

F02 Rhys, Ernest. ed. *Letters from Limbo.* London, J. M. Dent, [1936], 242–4. (two letters to Ernest Rhys with a facsimile of one).

F1 Trevelyan, R. C. 'Virginia Woolf'. *Abinger Chronicle*, April–May 1941, 23–4.

F1 Smith, Logan Pearsall. 'Tavistock Square'. *Orion*, 1945, 2,
.1 75–8, 80–6.

F1 Delattre, Floris. *Feux d'Autumne: Essais choisis.* Paris, Marcel
.2 Didier, 1950, 237, 239.

F1 Spender, Stephen. *World Within World.* London, Hamish
.3 Hamilton, 1951, 153. (quotation from a letter to V. Sackville-West).

F2 Hart-Davis, Rupert. *Hugh Walpole: A Biography.* London, Macmillan, 1952, 309, 327, 338.

F3 Su Hua. *Ancient Melodies.* London, Hogarth Press, 1953, 7–8.

F4 Lehmann, John. 'Working with Virginia Woolf'. *Listener*, 13 January 1955, 60–2.

F5 Sackville-West, V. 'Virginia Woolf and Orlando'. *Listener*, 27 January 1955, 157–8.

F6 Pippett, Aileen. *The Moth and the Star: A Biography of Virginia Woolf.* Boston, Toronto, Little, Brown, 1955, *passim.* (letters to V. Sackville-West).

F7 Lehmann, John. *The Whispering Gallery: Autobiography, I.* London, [etc.], Longmans, Green, 1955, 171–2, 183, 201–2, 310.

F8 Garnett, David. *The Flowers of the Forest.* London, Chatto & Windus, 1955, 248.

F9 Bell, Clive. *Old Friends: Personal Recollections.* London, Chatto & Windus, 1956, 103–7 (letter to Barbara Bagenal).

F10 St John, Christopher. *Ethel Smyth: A Biography.* London, [etc.], Longmans, Green, 1959, 48, 134, 226–37, and 219 (quotation from a letter to Lytton Strachey).

F11 Hassall, Christopher. *Rupert Brooke: A Biography.* London, Faber and Faber, [1964], 529 (letter to Gwen Raverat), and 154, 272, 280 (brief quotations).

F12 Cunard, Nancy. 'The Hours Press: A Retrospect – Catalogue – Commentary'. *Book Collector*, 1964, 13:4, 488. The author also refers to this incident in *Grand Man: Memories of Norman Douglas*, London, Secker & Warburg, 1954, 78.

F13 Lehmann, John. 'Leonard Woolf'. *TLS*, 30 October 1969, 1258. (quotation from letter to the author's mother).

F14 [Issue on Virginia Woolf]. *Adam International Review*, 1972, 364-366, Thirty-seventh Year, 11 (letter to the Editor of *Impressions*), 12 (quotation from a letter to Roger Fry), 14 (quotation from a letter to Mark Gertler), 28-30 (letters to Angus Davidson; one a holograph facsimile).

F15 Noble, Joan Russell. ed. *Recollections of Virginia Woolf*. London, Peter Owen, [1972], 32-9, 42, 44-5 (letters to John Lehmann), 41 (quotation from letter to John Lehmann's mother), 57-9 (quotations from letters to Angus Davidson), plate (holograph facsimile) facing p. 128 (letter to Barbara Bagenal).

F16 Stevens, Michael. *V. Sackville-West: A Critical Biography*. London, Michael Joseph, [1973]. 38, 41.

F17 Szladits, Lola L. *Other People's Mail: Letters of Men and Women of Letters selected from the Henry W. and Albert A. Berg Collection of English and American Literature*. [New York], The New York Public Library & Readex Books, [1973], 71-4 (letter to Barbara Bagenal, including holograph facsimile).

F17.1 Christie, Manson & Woods Ltd. *Modern Printed Books and Manuscripts . . . sold at Auction . . . April 4, 1973*. London, 1973, 66-7, 71 (quotations from letters to Saxon Sydney-Turner, including holograph facsimile, and to Tom Driberg).

F18 Lehmann, John. *Virginia Woolf and Her World*. London, Thames and Hudson, [1975], 82-3, 112.

F19 Sotheby Parke Bernet & Co., London. *Catalogue of Nineteenth Century and Modern First Editions, Presentation Copies, Autograph Letters and Literary Manuscripts*. No. 7 of 1976/77. London, 1976, 27 (letter to [Henry, known as Bogey], Harris).

F20 Passages excluded from Volume II of the *Letters of Virginia Woolf* – Letters 905, 1020, 1126, 1127, 1179, 1261. *Virginia Woolf Miscellany*, Special Summer Issue 1977, 8, [2]; with note by Nigel Nicolson, p. [1]. See also A47.

F21 Lehmann, John. *Thrown to the Woolfs*. London, Weidenfeld and Nicolson, [1978], 27-32, 45, 60, 97 (to the author's mother), 98, 100, 102.

F22 Dunbar, M. J. Virginia Woolf to T. S. Eliot: Two Letters. *Virginia Woolf Miscellany*, Spring 1979, 12, 2 (letter to T. S. Eliot dated 15 January 1933; see A53 for letter dated 2 November [1930]).

F23 Christie, Manson & Woods Ltd. *Modern Literature, Art and Art Reference Books . . . sold at Auction . . . July 11, 1979.* London, 1979, 10 (letter to Lady Robert Cecil, holograph facsimile).

# G.
# MANUSCRIPTS

See *Virginia Woolf: A Biography*, Vol. 1, pp. xi–xiii by Quentin Bell (B14) for a general description of the three major collections: The Henry W. and Albert A. Berg Collection of English and American Literature (Astor, Lenox and Tilden Foundations), New York Public Library; The Charleston Papers, King's College, Cambridge; and The Monk's House Papers, University of Sussex Library. See also 'Proposed Policy on Virginia Woolf's Unpublished Material' by Quentin Bell, *Virginia Woolf Miscellany*, Spring/Summer 1978, No. 10, p. [3]; the forthcoming special issue (due 1980) on Virginia Woolf of *Twentieth Century Literature*, Fall/Winter 1979, Vol. 25, No. 3/4 edited by Lucio P. Ruotolo which will include unpublished material in the Berg Collection and the Knole manuscript of *Orlando*; and the *Bulletin of Research in the Humanities*, Autumn 1979, Vol. 82, No. 3 due for publication in December 1979.

Locations for letters have been omitted since these are recorded in *The Letters of Virginia Woolf*, edited by Nigel Nicolson and assistant editor Joanne Trautmann of which the following have been published to date: *The Flight of the Mind*, Volume I: 1888–1912; *The Question of Things Happening*, Volume II: 1912–1922; *A Change of Perspective*, Volume III: 1923–1928; *A Reflection of the Other Person*, Volume IV: 1929–1931; and *The Sickle Side of the Moon*, Volume V: 1932–1935 (see A44, 47, 51, 53–4). *Leave the Letters Till We're Dead*, Volume VI: 1936–1941 is due for publication in September 1980.

G1 HENRY W. AND ALBERT A. BERG COLLECTION OF ENGLISH AND AMERICAN LITERATURE, NEW YORK PUBLIC LIBRARY (ASTOR, LENOX AND TILDEN FOUNDATIONS)

*The Voyage Out.* 2 notebooks, 2 typescripts.

*Jacob's Room* (including preliminary notes for *Mrs Dalloway*). 3 notebooks.

*Night and Day*, Chapters 11–17. 121 pp.

*Mrs Dalloway.* 4 notebooks (see also G2).

*To the Lighthouse.* 2 notebooks, 1 loose-leaf folder.

*The Waves.* 7 notebooks, 1 loose-leaf folder (see A16*g–h*).

*Flush.* 4 notebooks, one containing reading notes.

*The Years.* 8 notebooks. See 'Virginia Woolf's Manuscript Revisions of *The Years*' by Charles G. Hoffmann, *PMLA*,

January 1969, 84:1, 79-89; ' "I Am Not a Hero": Virginia Woolf and the First Version of *The Years*' by Grace Radin, *Massachusetts Review*, Winter 1975, 16:1, 195-208; her ' "Two enormous chunks": Episodes Excluded during the Final Revisions of *The Years*', *Bulletin of the New York Public Library*, Winter 1977, 80:2, 221-51; and Jane Marcus's 'Notes on the "Two Enormous Chunks" ', pp. 427-31 of her 'Pargeting "The Pargiters": Notes on an Apprentice Plasterer', ibid., Spring 1977, 80:3, 416-35.

*Three Guineas.* [230] pp.

*Roger Fry: A Biography.* holograph notes etc. including later typescript, 512 pp.

*Between the Acts.* 3 notebooks, corrected typescript, 36 pp.

Articles, Essays, Fiction and Reviews. 10 notebooks, 1925-40. See 'The Drafts of Virginia Woolf's "The Searchlight" ' by J. W. Graham, *Twentieth Century Literature*, December 1976, 22:4, 379-93.

Diary. 1 notebook, 3 January 1897-1 January 1898.

Diaries. 7 notebooks, 4 August-23 September 1899; 30 June-1 October 1903?; Christmas 1904-31 May 1905; 11 August-14 September 1905; April 1906-1/14 August 1908; 3 August 1917-6 October 1918; 7 September-1 October 1919.

Diaries. 27 vols. 1915-41 (see A48, 52).

Reading Notes. 26 vols.

For further details see John D. Gordan's 'New in the Berg Collection: 1959-1961', *Bulletin of the New York Public Library*, 1964, 68:2, 77-80; and 'Novels in Manuscript: An Exhibition from the Berg Collection', ibid., 1965, 69:3, 405-6; and Lola L. Szladits's 'New in the Berg Collection: 1962-1964', ibid., 1969, 73:4, 237-9, plate facing p. 247; and 'New in the Berg Collection: 1965-1969', ibid., 1971, 75:1, 14-15.

G2 BRITISH LIBRARY REFERENCE DIVISION, DEPARTMENT OF MANUSCRIPTS

*Mrs Dalloway.* 3 vols. [Add. MS 51044-51046]. See 'From 'The Hours' to Mrs Dalloway' by A. J. Lewis, *British Museum Quarterly*, Summer 1964, 28:1/2, 15-18; 'In that Solitary Room' by Wallace Hildick, *Kenyon Review*, Spring 1965, 27:2, 302-17; 'Virginia Woolf: *Mrs Dalloway*', *Word for Word: A Study of Author's Alterations with Exercises*, by Wallace Hildick, London, Faber and Faber, [1965], pp. 176-87; 'The Origin of "Mrs Dalloway" ' by Jacqueline E. M. Latham, *Notes and Queries*, March 1966, 211, 98-9; 'From Short Story to Novel: The Manuscript Revisions of Virginia Woolf's *Mrs. Dalloway*' by Charles G. Hoffmann, *Modern Fiction Studies*, Summer 1968, 14:2, 171-86; and 'The Manuscript Revisions of Virginia Woolf's *Mrs. Dalloway*: A Postscript' by Jacqueline E. M. Latham, *Modern Fiction Studies*, Autumn 1972, 18:3, 475-6.

G3 CHARLESTON PAPERS, KING'S COLLEGE, CAMBRIDGE
Papers of Clive Bell, Vanessa Bell and Duncan Grant.

G4 INDIANA UNIVERSITY, LILLY LIBRARY
*Mrs Dalloway*. Proofs of first edition extensively revised.

G5 SIR GEOFFREY KEYNES
*On Being Ill*. 19 leaves. See *Bibliotheca Bibliographici*, by Sir Geoffrey Keynes, London, Trianon Press, 1964, p. 426.

G6 KNOLE, SEVENOAKS, KENT
*Orlando*. 291 leaves. Reproduced on microfilm by Micro Methods Ltd, East Ardsley, Wakefield, Yorkshire in 1970. See 'Fact and Fantasy in *Orlando*: Virginia Woolf's Manuscript Revisions' by Charles G. Hoffmann, *Texas Studies in Literature and Language*, Fall 1968, 10, 435-44.

G7 MR G. L. LAZARUS
*A Letter to a Young Poet*. 52 pp.

G8 MONK'S HOUSE PAPERS, UNIVERSITY OF SUSSEX LIBRARY
See *Catalogue: July 1972*, [28] 1. and [1] 1., 1976 issued by the Library.

G9 UNIVERSITY OF TEXAS AT AUSTIN, HUMANITIES RESEARCH CENTER
*Kew Gardens*. 12 leaves (typescript) with holograph corrections.
'Thoughts on Peace in an Air Raid'. 8 pp. (typescript) with holograph corrections.

G10 YALE UNIVERSITY LIBRARY, BEINECKE RARE BOOK AND MANUSCRIPT COLLECTION

General Collection:
'Notes on Oliver Goldsmith'. 22 pp. (manuscript).

*Yale Review* papers, Collection of American Literature:
'The Art of Walter Sickert'. 27 leaves (typescript), with holograph corrections; and revised draft, 20 leaves (typescript), with holograph corrections.
'Augustine Birrell'. 13 pp. (typescript), with holograph correction; and corrected galley proofs, 3 leaves, with holograph corrections.
'Aurora Leigh'. 18 leaves (typescript), with holograph corrections.
'How Should One Read a Book?'. 31 pp. (typescript), with holograph corrections.
*A Letter to a Young Poet*. 22 leaves (typescript), with holograph corrections.
'The Novels of Turgenev'. 11 leaves (typescript), with holo-

graph corrections; and corrected galley proofs, 3 leaves, with holograph corrections.

*Street Haunting: A London Adventure.* 20 leaves (typescript), with holograph corrections; and later draft, 17 pp. (typescript).

# INDEX

# INDEX